1988

WESTERN INTERESTS AND U.S. POLICY OPTIONS IN THE CARIBBEAN BASIN

WESTERN INTERESTS AND U.S. POLICY OPTIONS IN THE CARIBBEAN BASIN

Report of The Atlantic Council's Working Group on the Caribbean Basin

James R. Greene and Brent Scowcroft

Cochairmen

Richard E. Feinberg

Rapporteur

Robert Kennedy

Corapporteur

Foreword by Kenneth Rush

OG &H **Oelgeschlager, Gunn & Hain, Publishers, Inc.**
Boston, Massachusetts

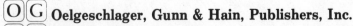

Published in 1984 by Oelgeschlager, Gunn & Hain, Publishers, Inc., for
The Atlantic Council of the United States.

International Standard Book Number: 0-89946-181-6 (cloth)
0-89946-183-2 (paper)

Library of Congress Catalog Card Number: 84-3571

Printed in the U.S.A.

Library of Congress Cataloging in Publication Data
Main entry under title:

Western interests and U.S. policy options in the Caribbean Basin.

Includes index.
1. Caribbean Area—Foreign relations—United States.
2. United States—Foreign relations—Caribbean Area.
I. Greene, James R.   II. Scowcroft, Brent.   III. Atlantic Council's Working Group
on the Caribbean Basin.
F2178.U6W47   1984   327.730729   84-3571
ISBN 0-89946-181-6
ISBN 0-89946-183-2 (pbk.)

Contents

Foreword   *Kenneth Rush*   vii

Preface   xi

Map of Caribbean Basin   xiv

**Members of The Atlantic Council's Working Group
on the Caribbean Basin**   xv

About the Cochairmen   xix

Chapter 1   Western Interests and U.S. Policy Options in the
            Caribbean Basin: The Policy Paper   1

Chapter 2   Changing Realities and U.S. Policy in the
            Caribbean Basin: An Overview
            Howard J. Wiarda   55

v

Chapter 3 U.S. Policy Issues in the Caribbean Basin in the
1980s: Economic, Social, and Political Aspects
David Scott Palmer   99

Chapter 4 Issues for U.S. Policy in the Caribbean Basin in
the 1980s: Security *Jack Child*   139

Chapter 5 U.S. Security on the Southern Flank: Interests,
Challenges, Responses *Robert Kennedy and
Gabriel Marcella*   187

Chapter 6 Issues for U.S. Policy in the Caribbean Basin
in the 1980s: Migration *Robert H. McBride,
Harry E. Jones, and David Gregory*   243

Chapter 7 Caribbean Energy Issues and U.S. Policy
Edward F. Wonder and J. Mark Elliott   269

Chapter 8 Options for U.S. Policy in the Caribbean Basin in
the 1980s *Sidney Weintraub*   305

Index   327

Foreword

The Caribbean Basin is on a bumpy road full of detours leading away from achievement of the goals of social, economic, and political development and friendly and mutually beneficial relations with its neighbors in the whole area, including the United States.

The unpleasant facts of life in the Caribbean Basin include overpopulation and, in most countries, inadequate material resources and skilled manpower combined with, in some countries, a tradition of one-man government, changed ordinarily by force. These problems have, in recent years, been compounded by the revolution of rising expectations, increasing unrest, adverse terms of trade, a stagnant global economy, overoptimistic borrowing and lending, and Soviet-Cuban overt and covert efforts to extend Soviet strategic, political, and psychological influence in the area.

Our desire to help our neighbors help themselves is frustrated by the polarization in many countries between rich and poor, right and left, as well as the lack of a middle class and of enlightened middle-of-the-road governments. The ability of the United States to cope with these problems has been handicapped by general ignorance of the area on the part of the public, the media, the Congress, and the higher echelons of successive presidential administrations.

United States policy has suffered from chronic conflict between soft-headedness and bullheadedness, between those who believe that sweetness and light can somehow prevail against Soviet weapons and those who believe that military force and assistance can solve deep-seated economic and social problems and win the people's hearts and minds. It is the ebb and flow of this conflict in the public, the Executive Branch, and, above all, in the Congress that constantly vitiates the possibility of success for either a hard- or a soft-line policy.

A basic problem for the U.S. government is to find policies that combine enlightenment and realism, not as uneasy and unstable partners but as a firmly forged single element. To the extent that such policies can be found, they may be expected to receive wide public support, in this country and elsewhere in the Caribbean area, to constitute a counterforce to Soviet influence and to lead the way toward stability, progress, and a good-neighbor relationship.

Those members of the Atlantic Council's Working Group who have had to deal in practice with the problems involved know well the difficulty of finding such policies and securing official and congressional acceptance of them. Nevertheless, this book is a modest attempt to contribute toward that end. I strongly recommend it to all those interested in the urgent and complex problems of the Caribbean Basin.

* * *

I want to take this opportunity also, on behalf of the Atlantic Council, to extend my profound thanks to the Tinker Foundation, the Xerox Foundation, the George Olmsted Foundation, the U.S. Agency for International Development, and the U.S. Department of Defense, whose partial financial support made this project possible. The views expressed in the individual chapters are those of their authors. The opinions, findings, and recommendations contained in the first chapter (the "Policy Paper") are those of the Atlantic Council's Caribbean Basin Working Group. They should not be construed as an official AID or Department of Defense position, policy, or decision unless so designated by other official documentation.

My warm thanks also go to the two cochairmen, James R. Greene and Brent Scowcroft, who conducted the meetings with their usual insight and skill; the rapporteur, Richard E. Feinberg, and co-rapporteur, Robert Kennedy, who faced the difficult task of finding a consensus in a large group of individuals with differing perspectives and experiences; the project director, Joseph W. Harned; the authors of all eight individual chapters; and all the distinguished members of the Working Group (listed in page 000), who have contributed freely of their time and their talents in order to complete this excellent report.

As in other publications of the Atlantic Council, each individual member of the Working Group does not necessarily subscribe to every argument expressed or every position taken. We believe, however, that this book, and in particular its first chapter, does seek to reflect the bipartisan consensus that emerged from the discussions and correspondence.

I would also like to express the Council's appreciation of the many individuals who, in a personal capacity, provided constructive critiques in the course of the project. They bear no responsibility whatever for the final product, but their participation in the process at one stage or another was most helpful: Misael Pastrana Borrero, Harry Carr, William G. Demas, Thomas H. Etzold, Robert Fenton, Maurice A. Ferré, Francis X. Gannon, W. H. Krome George, James A. Gravette, James Holway, Peter B. Johnson, Jorge Ruiz Lara, Val T. McComie, John P. Merrill, Rick Moran, Felipe Pazos, Marco Pollner, Gert Rosenthal, Charles Skeete, Jorge Sol, Harry E. B. Sullivan, Herbert B. Thompson, Gustavo J. Vollmer, and John Weltman. Finally, my special thanks go to Jose Luis Restrepo, who encouraged the Council to undertake the two-year project at its inception.

Only by free and informed discussion of our problems and opportunities can we hope to find the solutions that history demands of us. It is in that spirit that I commend this book to the U.S. Executive Branch and the Congress for action and to the interested public for study and debate.

Kenneth Rush
Chairman
The Atlantic Council
of the United States

Preface

The fall of the Somoza government in Nicaragua and the rise to power of the Marxist-Leninist Sandinistas, guerrilla movements in Guatemala and El Salvador, the revolutionary upheaval in Suriname, and recent and past events in Grenada have marked a half decade of increasing turmoil in Central America and the Caribbean. Advances in transportation and communication have brought a view of the modern world to the most remote villages of the region, sparking desires for social and economic improvement. Yet poverty, high inflation, unemployment, inequalities of opportunity, and inequities in the distribution of income and wealth remain, fueling instabilities and revolution in a number of countries of the region. Inadequate domestic infrastructure, insufficient capital formation, errors in domestic economic management, underdeveloped markets, lack of economic diversification, and the general economic turndown resulting from the international economic recession of the past few years have complicated developmental efforts and added to the internal political pressures within the region. In some countries the less privileged are now challenging what they perceive as unresponsive governments and political structures and are seeking the political means to alter their status.

Lack of social and economic development, however, is not the only cause of increasing instabilities in the region. The Soviet Union, Cuba, Sandinista Nicaragua, and other Soviet bloc countries have been actively exploiting the situation. Moscow has attempted to conceal its involvement in the region. It has preferred to channel arms through Cuba, allowing the Cubans to take the lead. Nevertheless, the Soviet Union has been persistent in its support of insurgency, terrorism, and radical, antidemocratic forces and regimes in the Caribbean Basin. The Kremlin's interest in the region was underscored recently by documents recovered from Grenada which indicated that the Soviet Union was willing to *donate* (an action almost unprecedented in Soviet approaches to foreign assistance) over $37 million in military equipment to the Marxist-Leninist regime in that country and to train Grenadian military personnel in the USSR at Soviet expense.

Cuba, on the other hand, has been more visible in its support for guerrilla and terrorist movements in Central America and the Caribbean. Despite its own economic failures, Cuba's willingness to project itself into the region and worldwide has not diminished. Cuba has over 35,000 military personnel serving in combat and assistance roles in Africa alone. In the Caribbean it has trained revolutionaries in urban and rural warfare; supplied or arranged for the supply of weapons to support guerrilla efforts; and encouraged terrorism to provoke indiscriminate violence and repression in order to weaken governments and attract converts to armed struggle. Cuba has also played a key role in uniting the traditionally splintered radical groups in El Salvador and Guatemala. In Costa Rica a special legislative commission has documented Cuba's role in establishing a supply network during the Nicaraguan war. The network has since been used to supply Salvadoran insurgents. Cuba has been implicated in the training of M19 guerrillas in Colombia and is active in nurturing an insurgency in Honduras. In some countries Cuban and Soviet support for revolutionaries has led to a crippling political polarization which has seriously complicated efforts designed to achieve social and economic progress.

The resulting dilemma for American leadership has been a serious one. On the one hand, the United States is sympathetic to demands for socioeconomic and political reform. Such demands are consonant with our own ideals as a nation. On the other hand, the radicalization of many of the reform movements within the region with Soviet and Cuban assistance suggests a high probability that should an immediate collapse of the existing order occur, it will simply be replaced by Marxist-Leninist structures likely to be even less capable of fulfilling the social and economic aspirations of the people and inclined, as in Nicaragua and previously in Grenada, to impose an even more narrowly based political system along totalitarian lines that will be fundamentally and sharply anti-American.

It is within this context that strategies must be fashioned which assist the peoples and countries of the region in their attempts at socioeconomic and political reform. The task is not an easy one. No quick fixes are likely to solve the region's problems. The growing economic and strategic importance of the Caribbean Basin makes it impossible to ignore the region. What is required is patience, persistence, consistency, and an understanding that Washington alone cannot bring stability to the region. The United States, however, remains a powerful influence. If stability and progress are to be achieved, the United States must underscore its support for social and economic reform and be prepared to increase its economic assistance to the region to support needed reforms. The United States also must continue to encourage movement toward democratic government and emphasize its commitment to human dignity. It must reject violence and terrorism as a solution to the problems that beset the region, and be prepared to assist its neighbors in countering Cuban- and Soviet-supported subversion as each situation dictates. In this regard, it must clearly signal the Soviet Union and its Cuban surrogate that it will not tolerate any extension of Soviet military facilities or bases in the region, and that it is prepared to assist the region in rejecting the establishment of Soviet-style totalitarian governments and Soviet, Cuban, or Nicaraguan efforts to undermine progress toward democracy.

James R. Greene
Cochairman
Working Group on
the Caribbean Basin

Brent Scowcroft
Cochairman
Working Group on
the Caribbean Basin

November 1983

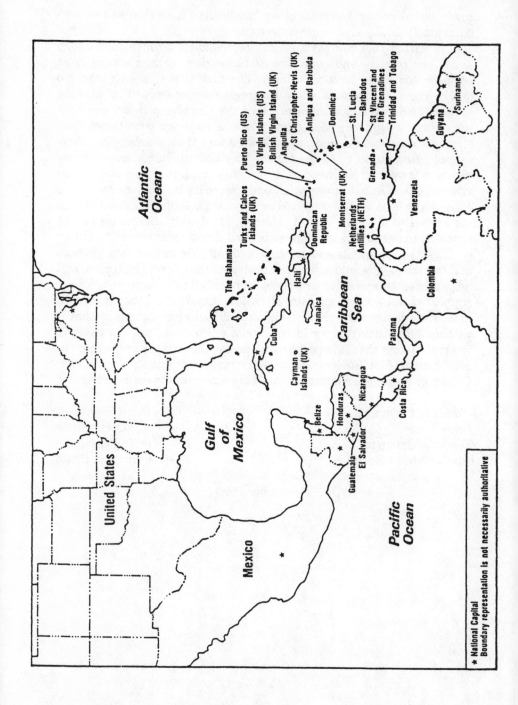

Members of the Atlantic Council's Working Group on the Caribbean Basin

COCHAIRMEN

James R. Greene, Dean, School of Business, Monmouth College; Adjunct Professor, Graduate School of Business, Columbia University; former President, American Express International Banking Corp.

Brent Scowcroft*, former Assistant for National Security Affairs to the President of the United States.

RAPPORTEUR

Richard E. Feinberg, Vice President, Overseas Development Council; Adjunct Professor, School of Foreign Service, Georgetown University.

CORAPPORTEUR

Robert Kennedy, Professor of Military Strategy, Army War College.

PROJECT DIRECTOR

Joseph W.Harned, Deputy Director General, Atlantic Council.

MEMBERS

Nicolas Ardito Barletta†, Vice President, Latin America and the Caribbean Region, The World Bank.

*Names of Directors of the Atlantic Council are in italics.

†While a full Member of the Working Group, Sr. Barletta did not participate in the formulation of sections *re* U.S. political and security interests.

Maurice M. Bernbaum, former U.S. Ambassador to Venezuela.

Robert D. Bond, Assistant Vice President, First National Bank of Chicago.

Jack Child, Associate Professor of Spanish and Latin American Studies, The American University.

Emilio G. Collado, former President, ADELA, S.A.; first U.S. Executive Director, The World Bank; and Executive Vice President, Exxon.

Henry N. Conway, Jr., Senior Vice President, International Bank.

William C. Doherty, Jr., Executive Director, American Institute for Free Labor Development (AFL-CIO).

J. Mark Elliott, Vice President and Principal Consultant, International Energy Associates Limited.

Robert P. Foster, Chairman, Foreign Relations Commission, The American Legion.

Dale E. Good, Special Assistant to the AFL-CIO President for International Affairs.

Andrew J. Goodpaster, former Supreme Allied Commander, Europe.

Samuel L. Hayden, former President, Council of the Americas.

Margaret Daly Hayes, Professional Staff, Senate Foreign Relations Committee.

Sylvia Ann Hewlett, Executive Director, United Nations Association Economic Policy Council.

Pat M. Holt, consultant and writer on Latin American affairs; former Chief of Staff, Senate Foreign Relations Committee.

John J. Jova, former U.S. Ambassador to the OAS, Mexico, and Honduras.

Isaac C. Kidd, Jr., former Supreme Allied Commander, Atlantic.

Robert S. Leiken, Senior Associate, Carnegie Endowment for International Peace.

Abraham F. Lowenthal, Director, Latin American Programs, Woodrow Wilson Center, Smithsonian Institution.

Gabriel Marcella, Professor of Third World Studies, Department of National Security, U.S. Army War College.

Russell E. Marks, Jr., President, Americas Society.

Edwin M.. Martin, former U.S. Ambassador to Argentina and Assistant Secretary of State for Latin American Affairs.

Francis L. Mason, Senior Vice President, Chase Manhattan Corporation.

Robert H. McBride, former U.S. Ambassador to Mexico.

Martha T. Muse, Chairman and President, The Tinker Foundation.

Gary J. Pagliano, Specialist in Energy, Congressional Research Service.

David Scott Palmer, Chairman, Latin American Program, Foreign Service Institute.

David H. Popper, former U.S. Ambassador to Chile and Special Representative for Panama Canal Treaties Affairs.

Alejandro Portes, Professor of Social Relations, Johns Hopkins University.

Susan Kaufman Purcell, Senior Fellow and Director, Latin American Studies Program, Council on Foreign Relations (New York).

Riordan Roett, Professor and Director of Latin American Studies Program, SAIS, Johns Hopkins University.

William D. Rogers, attorney; former Assistant Secretary of State for Latin American Affairs and Under Secretary of State.

Robert M. Sayre, Director, Office for Combatting Terrorism, Department of State; former U.S. Ambassador to Uruguay, Panama, and Brazil.

Sam F. Segnar, Chairman, Caribbean/Central American Action; President, Internorth.

Richard R. Sexton*, former Senior Fellow, Atlantic Council

Daniel A. Sharp, Director of International Relations, Xerox Corporation.

Sally A. Shelton, former U.S. Ambassador to Barbados and Deputy Assistant Secretary of State.

Rufus Z. Smith, Executive Director, Visitor Program Service of Meridian House International; Secretary-Treasurer, Association for Canadian Studies in the U.S.

Helmut Sonnenfeldt, Guest Scholar, Brookings Institution; former Counselor, Department of State.

Viron Peter Vaky, Research Professor of Diplomacy in North-South Relations, School of Foreign Service, Georgetown University; former U.S. Ambassador to Costa Rica, Colombia, and Venezuela.

Sidney Weintraub, Professor of Government, LBJ School of Public Affairs, University of Texas; former Assistant Secretary of State for Economic Affairs.

Howard J. Wiarda, Resident Scholar and Director, Center for Hemispheric Studies, American Enterprise Institute.

Curtin Winsor, Jr.†, former Chairman, Eastern Sewell Coal Co.

Edward J. Wonder, Senior Consultant, International Energy Associates Limited.

EX OFFICIO MEMBERS

Theodore C. Achilles, Vice Chairman, The Atlantic Council.

Kenneth Rush, Chairman, The Atlantic Council.

Francis O. Wilcox, Director General, The Atlantic Council.

---

*Served as a Member of the Working Group until his appointment as Deputy Director, Plans and Policy, SHAPE.

†Served as a Member of the Working Group until his appointment as U.S. Ambassador to Costa Rica.

SENIOR FELLOWS

Christopher H. Brown, Office of the Secretary of Defense.
Drue L. DeBerry, U.S. Air Force.
Harry L. Jones, Department of State.
Alfred D. Wilhelm, Office of the Secretary of Defense.

PROJECT ASSISTANTS

Eliane Lomax, Atlantic Council.
Robert Means, Atlantic Council.

About the Cochairmen

James R. Greene is Dean of the School of Business at Monmouth College. Until 1982, he was president of the American Express International Banking Corporation, and prior to that, senior vice president and deputy general manager of the Manufacturers Hanover Trust Company. Mr. Greene also served as president of the Bankers' Association for Foreign Trade.

Lt. Gen. Brent Scowcroft is vice chairman of Kissinger Associates, an international business consulting firm. He served as national security adviser to President Ford and, most recently, as chairman of the President's Commission on Strategic Forces.

Chapter 1

Western Interests and U.S. Policy Options in the Caribbean Basin: The Policy Paper

Atlantic Council's Working Group on the Caribbean Basin

Revolutionary upheavals in Nicaragua, Grenada, and Suriname, Cuban-backed guerrilla movements in El Salvador and Guatemala, the sudden exodus of 125,000 Cubans to Florida, the intervention in Grenada by six Caribbean states and the United States, and the financial crisis of Mexico—these are among the events in the Caribbean Basin* that captured the headlines in the late 1970s and early 1980s. Other events contributed to a growing awareness among Americans of the importance of the region to the United States. The continual flow of migrants from the Caribbean Basin to the United States; the emergence of Mexico, Colombia, and Venezuela as significant actors competing for influence in the region; the debt crises of Mexico, Venezuela, and other countries; the recently acquired independence of the Eastern Caribbean mini-states; and the Soviet-supplied military buildup in Cuba—all affect our view of the region, its people, and their future.

*For the purpose of this study, in addition to the United States, the Caribbean Basin is defined as the Caribbean Islands and Central America, Colombia, Guyana, Mexico, Panama, Suriname, and Venezuela.

Interest in the Caribbean Basin is not confined to the media, the Executive Branch, and Congress. A growing list of cities, from Los Angeles to New York, have significant communities of immigrants from Mexico, Central America, and the Caribbean islands. The societies and economies of the United States and the rest of the Basin have become increasingly interdependent. Although many Americans know little about the region, a growing number of religious and citizens' groups are actively seeking to influence U.S. policy toward the Basin.

This increased interest in the Caribbean Basin comes at a difficult historical juncture for the region. Many countries are experiencing rapid economic change and some are undergoing wrenching political transformations. Tensions both within and between states are rising. At the same time, the larger countries of the region—Mexico, Venezuela, Colombia, and Cuba—as well as Canada and the extra-hemispheric nations of Western Europe, Japan, and the Soviet Union—are displaying greater interest in the Basin. Several South American countries are also seeking to play a more important role in Basin politics.

The countries of the region confront serious problems. Poverty, population pressures, inflation, inequalities of opportunity, and inequities in the distribution of income and wealth frequently have resulted in pressures for social and economic change. Today, average per capita income is only a fraction of that of the United States, significantly below the official U.S. poverty level. In a number of countries, traditional political, economic, and social structures have been unable to accommodate needed reform. Regional cooperation in seeking solutions to common problems has been hindered by historic, racial, ethnic, and cultural divisions, and, more recently, by growing ideological cleavages. The combined international factors of debt, fluctuating commodity prices, trade protectionism, and the uncertain recovery in the industrial countries will shape the region's social and political environment in the coming years. The resulting environment presents opportunities for Cuban and Soviet penetration and the emergence of governments antithetical to U.S. interests, thus adding an East-West dimension to an already complex North-South problem.

This chapter examines the changing nature and problems of the Caribbean Basin, U.S. and other Western interests in the region, and the implications of recent trends for U.S. policy. It also considers the constraints which confront U.S. policymakers as they seek to protect U.S. interests and to assist the countries in the region to meet today's challenges. Finally, it analyzes the major issues and options facing the United States and suggests specific courses of action.

THE DYNAMICS OF A CHANGING CARIBBEAN BASIN

A major challenge to the United States is to find the proper mix between regionwide, subregional, and country-specific policies.

Diversity and Commonalities in the Basin

The twenty-six independent states and sixteen dependent territories of the Caribbean Basin are characterized by considerable racial, linguistic and ethnic diversity, differences in size, resource endowments, and levels of economic development, and by types of governments that range across the political spectrum. (For further discussion, see Chapter 2.)

But these states share traits beyond their geographical proximity to each other. They are mostly open economies with increasingly "Western" cultures; they are also facing serious economic problems which in some cases have translated into political unrest.

Common bonds are stronger at the subregional level. Five Central American nations (Guatemala, El Salvador, Honduras, Nicaragua, and Costa Rica) and Panama share a common language and culture, somewhat similar economic problems, and intertwined histories. Today, businessmen, labor leaders, politicians, churchmen, generals, and guerrillas are in contact with each other across borders, in formal organizations, and in informal support networks. News of events in any one country travels quickly and affects the mood and political calculations of people throughout the region.

In Central America, with the exception of Costa Rica, democracy does not have strong historical roots. Wealth often has been concentrated in the hands of a small, land-owning elite. In general, living standards and literacy rates are relatively low. The development of a middle class center has been slow. In contrast, the English-speaking states of the Caribbean inherited a different societal structure. Most are still functioning democracies based on a Westminster parliamentary model.

Certainly, U.S. policy toward one portion of the region must be cognizant of its impact on the rest of the Basin. For some issues, a regionwide approach will be necessary. Other issues, however, will require a subregional or bilateral approach if the problems confronting particular countries are to be addressed effectively.

Causes of the Current Crises

Cyclical and Secular Economic Problems. For most countries of the Caribbean Basin, per capita economic growth rates were stagnant or negative in 1981–1983. While errors in domestic management contributed to this poor economic performance, the overriding causes stemmed from the international economic recession. High oil prices, devastatingly low prices for other commodities, sluggish markets for imports in the industrial countries, and the record-high real interest rates have shaken the Caribbean economies as they have the developing world in general. Countries with access to private financial markets borrowed to finance widening current-account deficits, but by 1982 commercial banks were hesitant to increase their exposure in countries of lessening creditworthiness. In fact, many banks have been and are now actively reducing their outstanding loans to these countries. As a result, one country after another has been forced to announce drastic cutbacks in government spending programs while real income has fallen. Deteriorating social services and rising unemployment characterized most of the region. Despite their possession of oil, Mexico and Venezuela did not escape this global downturn. Mexico maintained high growth rates until the middle of 1982. After the real price of oil began to slide, the Mexican government ran out of cash reserves, and many foreign banks halted new loans. To improve its balance of payments, Mexico was compelled to devalue the peso and to curtail sharply government spending and imports. Soaring inflation cut into living standards. Partly because of a reduction in oil production, Venezuela has been in a recession since 1979, and like Mexico has had to reschedule its international debt burden.

These problems are consequences of recent global disturbances exacerbated in many cases by national policies. During periods when the international economy provided a healthier environment, some of the Basin countries managed a reasonably good economic record. From 1960 to 1978, Central American economies grew at annual rates of 5 to 6 percent, and the Dominican Republic and Panama enjoyed respectable GNP growth rates. Mexico performed well throughout most of the period since World War II. This would suggest that, at least for some countries, economic growth is possible if they enjoy the felicitous combination of a dynamic international economy and sound domestic management.

The region does, however, face serious impediments to growth. Many of the nations are not rich in natural resources, although countries in other parts of the world have demonstrated that impressive levels of development are attainable without favorable natural endowments. Good agricultural land is in short supply on many Caribbean islands, and population/land ratios are especially high in El Salvador and Haiti. Development is further hindered by the small size of the markets of the Central American "city-states" and the Caribbean "mini-states." Other impediments include deficiencies in public administration and low levels of education and occupational skills. For some of these countries, development possibilities may be limited. Some may do modestly well on the basis of tourism, primary goods exports, and light manufacturing. However, as Howard J. Wiarda points out in Chapter 2, there are likely to be no developmental "miracles" and only a few modest success stories, at least in the absence of greater regional economic integration.

Throughout the region, potential entrants into the labor market have exceeded the creation of new jobs. The causes include high population growth, mechanization and neglect of agriculture, capital-intensive industrialization, and low savings rates. The result has been chronic and rising pressures to emigrate.

Specific national policies have hindered economic development in some countries. A number of governments have overborrowed to maintain consumption rather than investment. Short-term money has been borrowed to fund long-term development projects. In order to subsidize and protect industries, governments have disrupted market mechanisms and distorted prices, and have seriously neglected agriculture. Many countries are dependent upon one or a few commodity exports and have failed to diversify into nontraditional exports. University training has remained oriented toward the liberal arts professions, despite the need for business managers, technicians, and skilled workers. In some countries the social structure prevents the rational development of a work force with the skills and attitudes toward work necessary for efficient public administration and economic growth. In one or two cases powerful segments of the ruling elite view extensive or participatory economic development as a potential threat to their power. At the same time, investments in the basic needs of the people often have been deficient. In some countries, widespread corruption seriously distorts the allocation of resources. Nevertheless, in the Caribbean Basin as elsewhere in the developing world, determined efforts can gradually overcome these obstacles.

Political Change and Breakdown. Recent economic disruptions have exacerbated the already severe political crises in many Caribbean Basin countries. In some countries—especially in Central America—political conflicts are the result of systemic problems, resulting from the failure of existing political institutions to adjust to new conditions and to incorporate widening sectors of an increasingly politicized and mobilized population.

In Central America, economic growth has often been disruptive of traditional social and political systems. The very process of modernization created new social groups not content with the political status quo. In the rural areas, the mechanization of export-oriented agriculture replaced peasant laborers. Similarly, new industries in the cities gave birth to an incipient urban proletariat. Their political leadership emerged from the increasing numbers of secondary schools and universities and the expanding middle class. During the 1970s, political systems in some countries did not adapt adequately to these newly emerging social forces.

Inefficient government intervention in market mechanisms has slowed economic growth and contributed to instability. Highly skewed income distribution is another factor contributing to actual or potential unrest (see Chapter 3). The gap between rich and poor, while relatively narrow in some English-speaking nations, is wide enough in most Spanish-speaking countries to generate feelings of antagonism and resentment. In Mexico, the bottom 20 percent of the households receive less than 3 percent of national income, while the richest 20 percent enjoy 58 percent. The steep inflation and rising unemployment that have accompanied the current recession have worsened income distribution in many countries. The result is an increase in social tensions and, in some cases, open violence, both spontaneous and organized.

At the same time, these elements of instability and conflict are sometimes balanced by elements of continuity and resiliency. In most English-speaking countries, parliamentary systems retain a high degree of legitimacy. The disparaging tone in which the Grenadian government under Maurice Bishop spoke of elections was widely rejected in the Eastern Caribbean by groups across the political spectrum. In Jamaica and Barbados, parliamentary systems have provided the avenues for periodic political rejuvenation. In the Dominican Republic, democratic rule has been strengthened and Costa Rica continues to serve as a model democracy. In the English-speaking Caribbean (as in the Dominican Republic and Costa Rica), labor unions have been an important force in sustaining or creating democratic institutions and in providing the means for employees and workers to redress economic grievances.

In Central America, the old ruling triad of landowners/church/military has broken apart. In some countries, the church has become an outspoken proponent of political and economic reforms. In Nicaragua, business organizations launched waves of strikes against the

Somoza regime. In Honduras, elements of the armed forces supported agrarian reform in the 1970s and then returned at least a portion of power to civilians through elections. In El Salvador, elements of the armed forces promoted, and the church supported, agrarian reform. In Guatemala, however, business and senior military officers have remained more conservative. It remains to be seen whether these centers of power will be capable of forging a new consensus around rejuvenated institutions.

Where open political institutions or enlightened elites are capable of absorbing or accommodating forces for change, gradual change is probable. But in several countries of the region institutions are so rigid or the leadership so resistant to change that abrupt and possibly even revolutionary change is a distinct possibility. U.S. policy can make gradual change more likely, but the United States must also be prepared to deal with discontinuity.

External Causes of Crises. Uneven social, economic, and political development, however, is not the only cause of the disorder and political disintegration that is currently plaguing some countries of the region. Cuba and the Soviet Union have been active in exploiting demands for social and economic improvement and political participation. This has added a significant East-West dimension to what were essentially internal and North-South problems.

Most of the revolutionary groups in the region are of indigenous origin. However, Cuba has trained and armed cadres in urban and rural guerrilla warfare. In Colombia, Cuban-trained guerrillas attempted to establish a "people's army." Some 3000 to 5500 Cuban civilians are serving in Nicaragua, many of them reportedly as key advisors to the government. These civilians are joined by an estimated 2000 Cuban as well as Eastern European security advisors. In El Salvador, Cuba has played an important role in arming the guerrillas, although the guerrillas undoubtedly obtain arms from a variety of sources. Castro has admitted that Cuba has been actively engaged in supplying arms to guerrilla groups in El Salvador at least prior to January 1981. Likewise in Guatemala, Cuba has been active in training and arming guerrilla cadres. Cuba has also worked to unite the traditionally splintered guerrilla groups operating within each country, sometimes apparently as a prior condition to providing increased assistance.

The Aspirations and Capabilities of the Developing Countries

In the 1950s, the governments of Central America were generally willing to follow the U.S. lead in international affairs, and most island states had still not obtained their independence from colonial rule. Today, many Caribbean Basin nations have been caught up in the movement toward "Third Worldism". Third Worldism includes not just a political agenda (nonaligment and greater participation in international decisionmaking) and an economic agenda (redistribution of the world's resources or at least a more equitable and stable economic system), but also incorporates initiatives to fashion indigenous political and economic systems attuned to local history and traditions. This movement is only beginning in the Caribbean and is likely to gain force in the future.

Most of the region's leaders have developed a stronger sense of their national interests. They seek a diversity of international ties in order to increase their room for maneuver. The interest of extra-hemispheric powers is considered by some a welcome development that allows countries to diversify their international relations. As mass participation in politics increases, nationalism becomes a stronger force, and the opposition to foreign intervention in their domestic affairs becomes a major theme. Economic development has become an overriding preoccupation in the region and control over natural resources a central security concern.

Extra-Hemispheric Powers

The governments and political parties of West Germany, France, Spain, and other Western European nations have become increasingly involved in the region, although their involvement is still modest compared to that of the United States. During the last ten years, Central America has become a battleground where social and Christian democratic activists, supported by political foundations and parties, have been providing their local counterparts with ideological training and financing. To promote nonalignment and domestic pluralism, some Western European governments have extended economic and small amounts of military assistance to the Nicaraguan government. Several Western European governments have urged the United States to seek a peaceful political solution to the civil war in El Salvador, partly out of concern that Central America might become an irritant in the Atlantic community.

The Soviet Union traditionally considered the Caribbean Basin to be a U.S. sphere of influence—until the Cuban revolution. In 1982, Cuba was the largest recipient of Soviet economic assistance in the Third World, acquiring aid worth $4 billion (mostly in price subsidies for sugar and petroleum). This was equivalent to over 25 percent of Cuba's GNP. During 1981–1982, Soviet bloc military aid to Cuba exceeded $7 billion. These Soviet aid levels to one country vastly exceeded U.S. bilateral economic and security assistance to the entire region.

The Soviets have made heavy economic and diplomatic commitments in Cuba, but have not made comparable investments elsewhere in the region. The Soviets rejected appeals during the 1970s for economic aid from then Jamaican Prime Minister Michael Manley and, even taking into account Cuban economic aid, have provided the current Nicaraguan regime with only a fraction of what it has requested. Moscow has been cautious about *direct* involvement, preferring to allow the Cubans to take the lead in the region. The Soviets may fear a strong U.S. reaction; consider that Cuba already provides them with a sufficient asset in the area; not want to incur the costs of financing a "second Cuba"; or may simply be waiting for better opportunities.

In sum, the Caribbean Basin has become a complex, dynamic, turbulent region. The United States will have to adjust to the region's growing nationalism and assertiveness. U.S. policy will have to take into account the presence of other powers, some relatively friendly, others hostile, but all pursuing their own interests. These new realities will affect the nature of U.S. interests and the threats we face, as well as the choices of policies open to us.

THE CHANGING NATURE OF U.S. AND WESTERN INTERESTS

U.S. national interests in the Caribbean Basin—their importance and relative priority—are not self-evident. Different groups within the United States would define the national interest differently. Moreover, U.S. interests and the threats they face have been changing over time.

During the early days of the republic, the Monroe Doctrine was designed to prevent the European colonial powers from further intruding into the hemisphere. By the late nineteenth century, a chief preoccupation of the United States was to prevent the Europeans from further extending their influence in the region and to keep Caribbean coaling stations out of potentially hostile control. As the United States expanded its international trade and its naval power, the security of the sea lanes and the Panama Canal became increasingly important.

During World War II, even though the United States committed substantial naval forces to reduce German interference with allied shipping, losses were high. The Panama Canal was a heavily used waterway for commercial shipping and for transferring naval vessels from one ocean to the other. Today, with the growth of world trade and the need to support allies around the world, freedom of movement in the Carribbean Basin is an important consideration in security planning.

While the United States has an interest in militarily securing its southern flank, other interests have also assumed increasing importance. Access to the region's trading and financial markets; the production of oil in Mexico and Venezuela; the vulnerability of Caribbean refineries; the influx of large numbers of migrants from a growing list of Basin states; and the accumulation of risky debts owed to commercial banks—each of these issues has captured the attention of policymakers and the U.S. public.

As a great power, the United States is concerned with its global credibility. To the extent that the United States seems unable to protect its interests in the Caribbean Basin, the credibility of its commitments elsewhere may erode.

U.S. Security Interests

Cuba and the Soviet Union in the Region. The geographic proximity of the Caribbean Basin to major sea lines of communication (SLOCs) and to the continental United States marks the region as strategically critical. In peacetime, 44 percent of all foreign cargo tonnage and 45 percent of the crude oil imported into the United States pass through the Caribbean. In a protracted conventional conflict, reinforcements destined for U.S. forces in Europe would also sail from Gulf ports.

In peacetime, as long as the United States adheres to the rules of international law, it cannot deny hostile powers access to the region's waterways. Even without facilities in Cuba, Soviet submarines and surface vessels can ply the Caribbean and Atlantic. However, Soviet or Cuban interference with U.S. shipping is unlikely except in the context of a wider Soviet-American crisis or conflict. Cuba in particular is unlikely to attack U.S. assets for fear of retaliation. Nevertheless, during crises and in conventional war, Soviet military bases in the region would threaten Caribbean and Atlantic SLOCs.

Given their physical proximity to the United States, hostile nations allied with the USSR could provide the Soviets with cost-effective options for direct attack on the United States during times of crisis or conflict. Such engagement in a great power conflict would entail tremendous risks for the Caribbean Basin nation, exposing it to immediate devastation. Nevertheless, the mere threat of such a possibility is likely to affect U.S. decisionmaking processes during times of crisis. In a conventional conflict with the Soviet Union in

Europe or elsewhere, the United States would have to divert significant military resources to neutralize Cuban and possibly deployed Soviet capabilities.

The combat radius of Cuba's MiG-23s would permit Havana to strike targets throughout much of the Gulf, to threaten approaches to the Panama Canal, and to attack installations in the United States as far north as Savannah. The radius of potential air and sea interdiction would expand to include almost the entire Caribbean Basin if Cuban and/or Soviet aircraft were permitted to operate from bases in Grenada and Nicaragua. Moreover, if the Cubans were provided more advanced aircraft such as the Fencer (Su-19), they would be able to strike targets deeper in the United States.

Cuba also could be used as a logistics base, recovery point, and turnaround facility for Soviet aircraft, ships, and submarines operating in the Gulf of Mexico, the Caribbean Basin, and the Atlantic. Backfire (Tu-26) bombers launched from the Kola Peninsula and recovered and relaunched from Cuba would permit strategic surveillance and attack throughout much of the North and South Atlantic. Similarly, Soviet submarines already at sea could use Cuba for refueling and ammunition resupply and thus avoid interdiction by U.S./NATO antisubmarine warfare forces operating in the Greenland–Iceland–United Kingdom gap. (For a further discussion of U.S. security interests, see Chapter 5.)

For its part, the U.S. has many bases and facilities in the Caribbean, including:

The substantial port and logistic facilities at Guantanamo Bay, Roosevelt Roads for fleet training and support operations, and the logistics and administration facility at Fort Buchanan.

In Panama a range of bases and facilities including Howard Air Base with its jet-capable runway and Fort Clayton, headquarters of the 193rd Infantry Brigade for canal defense. U.S. Southern Command headquarters at Quarry Heights in Panama City, and the U.S. Army School of the Americas in Fort Gulick.

Elsewhere, such facilities as the Eastern Test Range missile and space support facilities on the Grand Bahamas Island, at Grand Turk, and in Antigua; the oceanographic research facilities in Eleuthera, Grand Turk, and Antigua; the long-range navigation (LORAN) facilities on San Salvador Island and South Caicos; and the U.S. Atlantic Underseas Test and Evaluation Center in the Bahamas.

Other installations, such as the Ramey Air Force Base in Puerto Rico, which could be activated if necessary.

At present, the Soviet role in Cuba makes it impossible to speak of "denying" the Soviets any presence in the Caribbean Basin. The

United States has, however, succeeded in limiting the ability of the Soviet Union to use Cuba as a military base that could directly threaten the U.S. In 1962, the Soviet Union agreed to withdraw strategic weapons from Cuba (in exchange for the expectation that the U.S. would not invade Cuba). In 1970, the Soviets agreed that their navy would not use Cuban ports as a base for strategic operations. In 1979, the Soviets agreed not to introduce combat troops into Cuba in the future and asserted that their present military personnel in Cuba had principally a training purpose. However, during times of severe crisis or limited conflict, these accords may not hold.

Grenada. Since the March 1979 coup led by Maurice Bishop of the New Jewel Movement, Grenada has in large measure followed the foreign policy lines of Cuba and the Soviet Union. (For current views on Grenada, see preface by James R. Greene and Brent Scowcroft.) Cuba has provided military, technical, security, and propaganda assistance to the Bishop government. Cuba also is aiding in the construction of a 75-kilowatt transmitter for Radio Free Grenada that may be used to beam Cuban and Soviet propaganda into the Caribbean and South America.

The greatest security concern is the construction of the Point Salines Airport, whose runway clearly will have a military potential. Such a runway could accommodate every aircraft in the Cuban and Soviet inventory. If allowed to use the Grenadian airfields, Cuba's MiG aircraft would enjoy a greater radius of operation including the potential for operations into the northern portions of South America. The Grenadian government, however, contends that the airport will be solely for civilian use, is necessary for tourism, and notes that other commercial airports in the region have runways of approximately equal length.

Nicaragua. The Sandinista National Liberation Front (FSLN), which controls Nicaragua's government, faces the twin tasks of economic reconstruction and political consolidation. Contrary to their initial promises of democratic pluralism, the Marxist-dominated FSLN has established itself as the dominant political force. While elections are scheduled for 1985, it is doubtful that the FSLN is prepared to relinquish power. It has gained control over key government positions and the security apparatus and is subordinating opposition political forces by limiting the freedom of the media, controlling public dissent, and reducing the role of the private sector.

For the time being, the Sandinistas bear the mantle of legitimacy based on their role in the overthrow of Somoza. They are using this legitimacy to promote a new revolutionary mystique that justifies their sociopolitical programs and foreign policies and undermines the opposition. Opposition is considered "counterrevolutionary."

Cuban influence is pervasive in Nicaragua. With Cuban assistance as well as advisers from East Germany, Bulgaria, North Korea, and the Soviet Union, the Sandinistas are improving internal security and enlarging their standing army.

Moreover, between October 1980 and February 1981, Nicaragua was the staging site for a Cuban-directed flow of arms to Salvadoran guerrillas. Periodic reports indicate that arms destined for Salvadoran and Guatemalan guerillas continue to pass through Nicaragua (presumably with the authorization of the Sandinista National directorate).

The Sandinistas have been lengthening landing strips, which will be able to accommodate sophisticated jet aircraft. Nicaraguans have been trained as jet pilots and mechanics in Bulgaria. While there is no evidence of MiG aircraft in Nicaragua, any future emplacement of MiGs in Nicaragua would greatly increase the potential for total coverage of the region by hostile combat aircraft. Furthermore, such improvements coupled with the growth of the Sandinista Army; the extraordinary size of the reserve, police, and milita forces; and current Sandinista support for radical groups are perceived as a threat by Nicaragua's neighbors. As a result, other Central American countries are feeling the need to pump additional money into their armed forces to counter the Nicaraguan threat, thus reducing the funds that might otherwise be available for internal socioeconomic programs.

The emergence in Nicaragua of a full-fledged Communist state with formal security ties to Cuba and indirectly to the Soviet Union—while not inevitable—is a genuine possibility. In a worst-case scenario, the installation of Cuban or Soviet air and naval power in Nicaragua in peacetime or during a crisis would complicate U.S. defense planning on the southern flank and contribute largely to the elimination of the "economy-of-force" approach the United States has taken with respect to Caribbean security, already upset by Cuban ties to the Soviet Union.

Despite disturbing trends, several obstacles remain to the communization of Nicaragua. First, while Castro is highly regarded by the Sandinista leadership and his magnetic personality clearly captivates many of those who supported the revolution, it is far from certain that the majority of the Sandinistas want to become totally dependent on the Eastern bloc for support. Further, to date the Soviet Union apparently has been unwilling to provide the sort of economic support to Nicaragua that it did to Cuba. Without a clear indication that such support would be forthcoming, it is unlikely that Nicaragua would willingly and totally break its economic ties with the West. Second, movement toward more authoritarian government controls is meeting some vigorous opposition from within the FSLN and from the private sector, the church, and other groups within Nicaragua. Elements within the Sandinista government have publicly declared their intention to maintain pluralism and elections in Nicaragua. Third, if the Sandinista leadership wishes to avoid further economic disruption, it must reactivate the private sector, which is closely linked to the Western economic system. Today Nicaragua depends greatly upon Western sources of capital and assistance for its post-revolution reconstruction.[1]

Among other reasons, the long association of the United States with the deposed Somoza regime has made it difficult for the United States to develop close relations with the new Nicaraguan government.[2] For many years, the United States provided military assistance and considerable political support to the Somozas. The United States is resented by some Nicaraguans for its past role and is feared for its anti-Sandinista policy. A policy of confrontation is unlikely to move the Sandinistas in a moderate direction in the long run; they appear too strongly entrenched to be ousted, except perhaps at considerable cost. To moderate Sandinista behavior, the United States will need not only to obtain and maintain the confidence of the democratic sectors in Nicaraguan society, but also to offer the Sandinista leadership alternatives which permit them to adopt more pragmatic, less ideological approaches to the solution of Nicaragua's current difficulties. Even then, a favorable result is by no means assured. The United States cannot expect to "buy" the Sandinistas, in the sense of transforming them into close friends, but the U.S. can have some hope to steer them toward genuine nonalignment. Their historic suspicion of the United States need not be transformed into pro-Sovietism.[3]

The extreme difficulties of this approach cannot be exaggerated. The pervasive influence of Cuban and Soviet bloc advisors can impose great pressure to prevent such an outcome. Cuban and Soviet propaganda will continue to work to impede improved U.S.-Nicaraguan relations. In addition, "anti-imperalist" rhetoric sometimes serves Sandinista political objectives. The effectiveness of Cuban and Soviet propaganda might well be reduced should the U.S. avoid a policy of confrontation. Ultimately, however, Nicaraguan leaders will have to convince themselves of the advantages of not following the Cuban path.[4]

El Salvador. The seeds of political disintegration were sown in El Salvador throughout the 1970s, and polarization was further heightened by the fall of Somoza in Nicaragua. The left was encouraged, while a siege mentality gripped traditional conservative elements.

The younger officers and moderate civilians who seized power on October 15, 1979, hoped to halt this process of polarization. They committed themselves to reforming the country's antiquated economic, social, and political structures. The government promised to end repression, create a democratic political system, and implement agrarian reform. The so-called October Junta, however, could not muster sufficient support from within the military and security forces to carry out its program. A new junta, formed in January 1980, included more Christian Democrats and announced sweeping banking and agrarian reforms. Its reform package was attacked from the left as insufficient and from the right as threatening. Moreover, the polarization and subsequent militarization of society left the government in a position where it could neither effectively control right-wing terrorism nor put an end to the terrorism and guerrilla activities of the left. Nevertheless, the fragile government coalition survived and the reforms proceeded. A major military offensive by the insurgents was blunted by government forces in January 1981, and rightist coup efforts were thwarted. In elections held in March 1982, Salvadorans elected a new constituent assembly to write a constitution and set up full presidential elections.[5]

The violence of the right and left, however, remains an immediate threat not only to the existence of the current government, but also to the prospects of democratic socioeconomic and political reform. Right-wing "death squads" and the repressive acts of some elements within the National Guard, the Treasury and National Police, and the Civil Defense forces, although perhaps diminishing, continue to alienate *campesinos,* workers, teachers, and student groups and lend credibility to the revolutionary left's contention that real reform requires a significant reordering of the political and security apparatus. Killings by right-wing forces also represent the greatest immediate threat to continued U.S. support for the government of El Salvador. On the other hand, leftist violence not only begets rightist reaction but also constrains the ability of the government to pursue economic reform as it is forced to devote increasing resources to containing the insurgency.

Today, the revolutionary left is able to mount strikes against government security forces and highly visible infrastructure targets, to disrupt harvests, and to deprive the government of a decisive victory. Nevertheless, the revolutionary left confronts some formidable obstacles. First, the government is not as discredited as was the Somoza regime. It has the conditional support of some elements in the church and apparently has the support of many citizens as demonstrated by the March 1982 elections. Second, even though the principal guerrilla groups united in 1980, the left is far from monolithic, as evidenced by violent internal struggles among guerrilla leaders. Third, elections have given the current government of El Salvador an edge in the "legitimacy" test and a boost in the continuing battle for international recognition and support. Fourth, through aid and training, the U.S. is attempting to improve the capability of the Salvadoran armed forces.

Guatemala. On the heels of the Sandinista victory in Nicaragua and the insurgency in El Salvador, the intensification of insurgency in Guatemala in 1979–1981 refocused attention on the long-standing problems of one of the most important countries in Central America. Guatemala is a country of approximately 7.5 million, endowed with a comparatively strong and diversified economy.

Today, the proponents of change—including many students, intellectuals, professionals, and other members of the new urban middle and working classes—want social and economic reform, a more open and competitive political system, and better treatment for the large Indian population. In the past, the aspirations of such groups were stifled by a governing alliance of some businessmen and military officers primarily concerned with maintaining the *status quo*. The tendency to label reformists as "subversive" led to increasing polarization and violence from both the right and left during the later days of the regime of President Romeo Lucas Garcia (1978–1982). The targets of violence involved members of student and labor groups, the clergy, educators, lawyers, doctors, journalists, community workers, as well as the urban poor and peasantry.

At the end of 1981, the Guatemalan government put the insurgents' armed strength at 2000 to 4000. By February 1982 the four major guerrilla forces had formed a coalition called the National Patriotic United Front and were reported to be increasingly effective in securing converts among the Indian population. In the past insurgents had received little support from the traditionally passive Indians, who comprise over 40 percent of Guatemala's population.

More recently, the governments of General Efrain Rios-Montt and his successor, General Oscar Mejia, have been attempting to pacify the countryside through draconian security operations combined with civic action programs. Guerrilla activities have been set back, but renewed violence is likely unless the government can bring about a substantial improvement in social and economic conditions and in political participation.

Political Interests

Defining U.S. political interests in the Caribbean Basin is a challenging task. Traditionally, the United States has sought governments that were positively friendly and reliable. This did not necessarily imply that governments be democratic, however. The United States found that a one-party state in Mexico or authoritarian systems in Central America were compatible with U.S. economic and security interests as then defined.

The Caribbean Basin today displays an increasing diversity of political systems, ranging from Marxist-Leninist (Cuba), to various forms of liberal democratic and nationalist populist, to traditional dynastic (Haiti). How can the United States decide which are compatible with U.S. interests?

Americans differ on the range of tolerable choices and where the lines ought to be drawn (see Chapter 8). Western Europeans also differ among themselves, although they tend to be willing to deal with a wider range of ideologies, especially on the left, in the Third World, as, indeed, does Canada. These differing political perceptions have hindered the formulation of a concerted and effective Western policy toward the Caribbean Basin.

The Working Group suggests that the United States apply four rough guidelines to all countries in the region. First, a government should not grant access to military facilities to hostile powers nor follow a policy of automatic alignment with the Soviet Union. Second, it should not interfere in the internal affairs of other states. Third, the government's legitimacy should derive not from force but from its responsiveness to the will of the people, optimally as expressed through free elections. Fourth, as required by amendments to U.S. foreign assistance legislation, the government should not engage in "gross and consistent" violations of the basic human rights of its population. These guidelines should be applied flexibly and in ways that are most likely to achieve U.S. objectives.

Economic Interests

The nature of U.S. economic interests in the region has changed significantly. In early years, U.S. interests were concentrated in mining, agriculture, and shipping (including the Panama Canal). Today, they are more diverse and complex. Mexico, Venezuela, and Colombia are important markets for U.S. exports. The tightening interdependence between the U.S. and other Caribbean Basin economies revolves around finance, oil, other basic commodities, and migration flows.

U.S. interests in the small economies of Central America and the Caribbean islands are relatively less significant than they once were. Major U.S. firms are less dependent upon single holdings than, say, United Fruit was in the 1950s. These economies account for a small percentage of global U.S. trade and foreign investment. On the other hand, U.S. economic and financial interests are substantial in Mexico and Venezuela.

The Caribbean Basin as a whole is the fourth largest market in the world for U.S. products (following the European Economic Community, Canada, and Japan) and currently accounts for about 14 and 11 percent of total U.S. exports and imports, respectively. Basin countries supply two strategically important resources: the United States gets 85 percent of its imported bauxite and 70 percent of its imported refined petroleum products from the region. While the growth of U.S. direct investment in the Caribbean has not kept pace with the growth of U.S. investments elsewhere, approximately 8 percent of U.S. worldwide investment and 32 percent of U.S. investments in developing countries are located in the region—mostly in Mexico and Venezuela (see Chapter 3).

The nature of the threat to U.S. economic interests has changed. Some of the largest direct U.S. investments—oil in Venezuela, bauxite in Jamaica—have been nationalized. U.S. firms, by and large, have divested themselves of large agricultural holdings in Central America, preferring to operate in the more secure downstream activities of commercialization and marketing. Moreover, when nationalization does occur where U.S. firms still hold direct equity in natural resource-based enterprises, the principle of fair and timely compensation is generally observed. A rising percentage of U.S. investment is taking place in manufacturing and services, where the requirements of technology, management, and marketing generally give the U.S. parent company sufficient leverage to protect its interests.

Still, some governments have or might adopt trade and investment restrictions. The impact of these restrictions, however, is often overshadowed by the "income effect" of growth; where economies are healthy, expanding opportunities exist for U.S. traders and investors. Moreover, nearly all political leaders now accept the inevitability of economic interdependence with the United States; few still imagine that the "New International Economic Order" or "self-reliance" offers realistic alternatives. Nor is a government's rhetoric necessarily a good guide to its actions; despite his free-market rhetoric, Prime Minister Edward Seaga of Jamaica purchased Exxon's oil refinery (paying adequate compensation), whereas the radical nationalist Sandinista government has not nationalized Exxon's holdings in Nicaragua.

U.S. commercial banks have substantial outstanding loans in Mexico and Venezuela and lesser amounts in several other Caribbean basin countries. Many countries are having difficulty remaining current on interest payments, causing commercial banks to hesitate to extend new credits. Because the health of the U.S. economy depends importantly on the stability of its financial system, it is in the U.S. national interest that developing countries not default on their debts. At the same time, governments will have great difficulty implementing austerity measures that may be economically necessary but are politically destabilizing. In the long run, the ability of countries to service debt will depend upon their own economic growth; and this, in turn, will depend significantly upon the performance of the U.S. and the world economies.

Economic growth in the Caribbean Basin is important to the United States. First, over the long run, the "push" factors behind migration would be gradually alleviated by rising standards of living in the sending states. Second, while the relationship between political stability and economic growth is complex, political stability can be threatened when economies stagnate.[6] Third, U.S. prestige in the world will be enhanced if its smaller neighbors flourish.

U.S. Influence: Diminished but Still Significant

U.S. influence in the Caribbean Basin has declined in recent decades, but the United States remains by far the most powerful single country in the region. The United States should not overestimate its strength, but neither should it feel incapable of dealing with the potential challenges in the region.

Several factors account for the decline of U.S. influence. Governments are better able to interpret and assert their own self-interests. The emergence of regional actors (Mexico, Venezuela, Cuba) has created centers of power independent of the United States. This permits governments to reach out to Third World economic and political groupings, which in turn provide different viewpoints and, to a degree, alternative support mechanisms. The increased activities of external actors (Western Europe, Canada, the Soviet Union) add further sources of power that make it difficult for the U.S. to shape events in the region unilaterally. Despite continuing influence, the United States' ability to assure the survival of friendly governments, or otherwise to shape the internal politics of states, is increasingly limited. Moreover, the presence of the Soviet Union in Cuba and diplomatic constraints on the use of force make it impossible for the U.S. to guarantee a southern flank devoid of potentially hostile elements.

Nevertheless, the asymmetry of power between the United States and all the other states in the Basin remains great. The United States has overwhelming conventional and strategic military superiority. It is still the largest market, most important trading partner, and major source of investment and capital for most Caribbean countries. It has the means to protect its economic interests, narrowly defined in the Basin. The very attraction of the international economy generally assures the U.S. access to materials and markets. U.S. military and economic strength is clearly predominant, but U.S. political interests are more difficult to define and defend.

The Interests of Other Western Powers

The commercial and political interests of Western Europe, Canada, and Japan have been expanding in the Caribbean Basin. The flow of commodities and credits has expanded significantly, as has interest in the region's political evolution. There are differences in interests and degrees of involvement between the United States and its principal world partners. However, there are important Western European, Canadian, and Japanese interests that are compatible with those of the United States including: containment of Soviet influence, access to markets and goods in growing economies, and the promotion of basic human rights and participatory political systems. European social democratic and Christian democratic movements and governments have differed among themselves with regard to which tactics are most likely to produce these results in the Caribbean Basin. Nevertheless, many Western Europeans (and Canadians) seem willing to accept that significant social change, perhaps even passing through a revolutionary period, is compatible with their interests. Social democrats in particular have argued that greater tolerance toward political change is more likely to protect fundamental Western interests in the Caribbean Basin, and in the Third World generally. To date, other Western powers have left much of the responsibility for the region's security to the United States. There has been a lag between the growing economic, commercial and financial interests of Canada, Western Europe, and Japan in the area, and a concomitant interest on their part in Caribbean political and military security.

ISSUES AND OPTIONS

The Framework for U.S. Policy

Constraints on U.S. Policy. U.S. influence in the Caribbean Basin has been diminished by a series of developments in the international system. U.S. policy is further constrained by several domestic factors. Failure to take these factors into account can lead to overambitious policies, and the inevitable policy corrections often leave the appearance of inconsistency and incompetence.

The intensity and extent of U.S. interest in the region have tended to swing sharply, from periods of crisis management and deep involvement to periods of benign neglect. Because the region—relative to others in the world—has lacked power and resources, it has not generally been considered important, except when threats suddenly arise. The inability to maintain a consistent level of sustained interest becomes in itself a constraint on U.S. influence.

Budgetary and other domestic considerations have impinged upon U.S. policy. Although U.S. economic and security assistance to the region has risen appreciably in recent years, it remains insufficient to protect American interests in the region. U.S. economic policy must also take into account the interests of sometimes conflicting domestic groups. For example, some agriculture and business groups oppose sharp restrictions on immigration, while labor favors them. Both small business and labor have opposed eliminating duties on imports from the region under President Reagan's Caribbean Basin Initiative.

As is the case with other regions of the world, the U.S. policy process itself has hampered the pursuit of U.S. interests. It has been slowed and sometimes paralyzed by the absence of a consensus within the bureaucracy or in the public at large. Moreover, a multilayered and polycentric bureaucracy, which has difficulty in rapidly processing information, and even greater difficulty in making timely decisions, has often found itself "behind the power curve" as it has tried to influence political events in the Basin.

Policymakers should strive to break free from some of these constraints. Budgets can increase, and policy can be based on more accurate and timely assessments of local situations. Nevertheless, some of these constraints are inherent in the American political system. Moreover, the United States should not expect that its ability to fine-tune the domestic politics of Basin states will substantially improve.

The Need for Consistency. Given the depth of U.S. involvement in the Caribbean Basin, events there inevitably have an effect on us. It is therefore important that the United States have a clear, consistent, long-term policy toward the region. This policy should be supported with an adequate level of resources and continuing attention at the middle and higher reaches of the foreign policy bureaucracy.

U.S. policy should, however, be realistic in its objectives. A policy that fails to take into account different local realities or constraints that are either inevitable or too costly to remove will falsely raise expectations. The result will be a cycle of disillusionment and retreat. A policy that sets modest, incremental goals can both be effective and sustain interest and support over the long run.[7]

U.S. policy must also be built around a new domestic consensus. Because of geographic proximity, the presence of a growing immigrant population, and the region's instability, the U.S. public is increasingly aware of and concerned about events in the region. A policy that does not retain broad popular support at home and congressional approval will not obtain the material resources needed to sustain that policy over time. If it combines enlightenment, realism, and consistency, U.S. policy may elicit that support.

Multilateralism. The emergence of regional powers (Mexico, Venezuela) and the increased activities of Western Europe, Canada, and Japan have created new opportunities and problems for U.S. diplomacy. Where U.S. resources are limited, cooperation with friendly states in the pursuit of common objectives can augment leverage. If orchestrated unwisely, however, multilateral approaches can diminish U.S. leverage. At times, objectives will differ, reflecting differing national interests, and cooperation may not be possible. On other occasions, cooperation may require that the United States or its allies modify policies in order to obtain more broadly acceptable goals.

Multilateral cooperation can occur at various levels. The United States can work with one or several regional powers, perhaps in concert with additional groupings of smaller states, such as the Contadora Group (Colombia, Mexico, Venezuela, and Panama). The United States can also attempt to work through the Organization of American States, and, more selectively, in the United Nations. Finally, it can collaborate with Western Europe, Canada, and Japan either in a bilateral or a multilateral framework. The United States should work to strengthen its diplomacy at each of these levels.

The United States in recent years has had considerable difficulty in working with Mexico on Central American issues. It has been distrustful of Mexican perceptions and capabilities, and sometimes even of Mexican intentions. While the United States cannot simply follow Mexico's lead, greater cooperation should be possible because objectives are broadly consonant. Mexico has, for example, been attempting to play a constructive role in Nicaragua in defending the private sector against Sandinista encroachment. It is well placed to help negotiate or reduce differences among warring factions and nations within the region.

The United States has been more successful in working with Venezuela, although swings in Venezuela's internal politics and international objectives have affected the bilateral relationship and Venezuela's willingness to work with the United States. More recently, Venezuela has been coordinating its policy more closely with Mexico. The United States should react sympathetically to such joint efforts. While the United States may not fully agree with some of the immediate policies of the two countries, their objectives are generally compatible with fundamental U.S. economic and security interests.

The United States has either not sought or been unable to gain the support of the Organization of American States for some of its Caribbean Basin policies. For example, the OAS rejected a U.S. proposal for an inter-American peacekeeping force meant to help ease the post-Somoza transition in Nicaragua. The OAS could, however, play a constructive role in reducing tensions in the Basin and, potentially, in providing or policing guarantees that were part of any treaties or settlements. For example, the OAS can send observers to validate elections, as was done in El Salvador in March 1982. Potentially, the OAS could provide the framework for a multilateral observer system to discourage the infiltration of men and arms across national frontiers.

U.S. policy cannot be captive to the OAS. The United States should, however, make a greater effort to build broader support in the hemisphere for its policies. This may at times require modifications in policies and greater sensitivity to the perspectives of other hemispheric nations. Only then might the OAS be able to fulfill its potential role as mediator and keeper of the peace.

The greater participation of Western Europe, Canada, and Japan in the affairs of the Caribbean Basin brings increased economic resources to the region. These nations provide private investment and economic aid through the multilateral agencies as well as through active bilateral programs. Western European political parties and foundations have trained many cadres and influenced the intellectual climate in the Basin. More generally, Western European countries can, to some degree, compensate for the decline in U.S. influence. Clearly, it is much better for Western European countries to do so than for the Soviet Union or Cuba. Moreover, the Western Europeans can absorb some of the blame inevitably placed on "outside powers." Providing that the Western Europeans and the United States are not working at cross-purposes, this political advantage for the United States may well outweigh whatever we might lose in direct influence.

The Role of Nongovernmental Organizations. The U.S. government is only one conduit through which American society interacts with the Caribbean Basin. American business, labor, religious, professional, and educational organizations have firmly established ties throughout the region. When they succeed in strengthening their local counterparts, they fortify the institutional infrastructures for political pluralism.

To increase the activities of U.S. business in the Basin and to foster the indigenous private sector, President Carter encouraged U.S. firms to form Caribbean/Central American Action. This non-governmental, non-profit organization seeks to interest U.S. corporations in the economies of the Caribbean Basin and to strengthen the indigenous private sector by introducing it to export markets in the United States, assisting local business organizations, and tightening relationships between U.S. and Caribbean Basin business chambers and other institutions.

While the U.S. government played a role in stimulating its initial activities, Caribbean/Central American Action is dependent upon U.S. business for its success. Because of the diversity and decentralization of the U.S. business community and its autonomy from (and historic wariness of) the government, the ability of the U.S. government to influence business decisions is limited.[8] It is therefore important for leadership and organization to come from the private sector itself. The formation by David Rockefeller of the U.S. Business Committee on Jamaica is a worthy example of such an initiative.

The AFL-CIO, through the American Institute for Free Labor Development (AIFLD), has long been active in support of the trade union movement throughout the Caribbean Basin. During 1983 alone, AIFLD will allocate around $2 million for education and leadership training and other programs intended to strengthen local union organization.[9] These ties are especially important in the English-speaking Caribbean, where unions play a significant role in their nation's political life. The role of labor unions in Central America has been limited by the difficulty of organizing rural workers and by government intimidation, but their strength may increase in the future.

Catholic and Protestant churches in the United States have close ties with their counterparts in many Basin countries. They provide financial and moral support to their colleagues abroad, just as they serve as a conduit through which their Caribbean Basin associates can make their views known in the United States. Similarly, U.S. and international human rights organizations are playing an increasingly active role in monitoring the human rights situation in Basin countries and in supporting indignenous, like-minded organizations.

Finally, U.S. universities and educational foundations are also active throughout the Basin. They assist citizens from the Basin to visit and study in the United States, while also helping to strengthen indigenous research and educational institutions.

The activities of these diverse, non-governmental organizations will not always be in harmony with U.S. government policy. Moreover, if they involve themselves too visibly in internal partisan affairs, they can become an irritant in bilateral relations. In general, however, they serve to increase mutual understanding between peoples in the United States and the Caribbean Basin, and may help strengthen democratic sentiments and institutions in the Basin.

Security and Military Issues

U.S. security interests in the Caribbean Basin need to be conceived broadly, to include not only military issues but also political and economic interests. (For a more complete discussion, see Chapter 4.) A narrower definition of security—such as the maintenance of the *status quo*—would ignore the economic and social foundations of stability. It would also place the United States at odds with many leaders in the Caribbean Basin who perceive their security as intimately tied to economic and social development. At the same time, traditional security concerns—the containment of Soviet influence and the protection of sea lanes and the southern flank—do demand attention. This section will deal with related military issues, while following sections will discuss political and economic issues, recognizing that they are at least as important to long-term security as are military interests.

Protecting the Southern Flank. The Soviet Union is the only power today that poses a military threat to the survival of the United States. Optimally, there would be no countries in the Basin that would provide military facilities to the Soviets. However, the Soviets have a bridgehead in Cuba. Nevertheless, the agreements between the United States and the Soviet Union constrain somewhat the ability of the Soviets to use Cuba as a forward, offensive base. The United States must monitor Soviet military activities closely to be certain that these accords are not violated. In addition, the United States should make clear to the Soviet Union that it strongly opposes the establishment of bases elsewhere in the Caribbean Basin.[10]

Containing Soviet Influence. Where political and social processes fail to accommodate change or gross inequities accumulate, unrest is likely to occur. While the Soviet Union is not the original cause of regional instability, it habitually fishes in troubled waters. The best long-term strategy for containing Soviet influence is to go to the source of the unrest, i.e., to treat its underlying social and economic causes.

127637

A U.S. policy that accepts the new assertiveness and nationalism in the Basin can help to reduce the dangers of Soviet inroads. Similarly, a policy that encourages the settlement of disputes between nations, as well as internecine national strife, and which helps nations feel secure will reduce Soviet opportunities. The U.S. should avoid creating, or being drawn into, a situation in which an established government, such as Nicaragua, invites Soviet and/or Cuban troops, and by appealing to international legal norms is able to gain the diplomatic support of a significant number of other hemispheric states.

Cuba. U.S.-Cuban competition for influence in third countries will remain a fixture in the Caribbean Basin for the foreseeable future, even if U.S.-Cuban bilateral relations should improve. A strategy for containing Cuban influence should concentrate on reducing the attractiveness of the Cuban connection to regional politicians and discouraging Cuban adventurism. A policy of preventive measures is preferable to a policy that reacts after the Cubans have already advanced. Preventive measures can include policies to foster trade and economic development, as well as the provision for selective increases in security assistance to threatened governments. A U.S. diplomacy that accepts genuine non-alignment and self-determination and seeks to offer leftists an alternative to a pro-Cuban, pro-Soviet alignment would be another fundamental element in a positive strategy to contain Cuban influence.

Cuba itself is likely to remain closely tied to the Soviet Union, at least for the foreseeable future. The Cuban economy and security forces are heavily dependent upon Soviet assistance, and Cuba requires Soviet support to implement its policy of "international solidarity" with revolutionary movements and governments. Thus, even a more friendly U.S. posture would not produce a sudden rupture between Moscow and Havana. At the same time, the Cuban government is interested in Western trade, capital, and technology, and would like to diversify its economic relations. It may be willing to reduce its activities in the Basin in exchange for improved relations with the West.[11]

Even today there may be elements in the Cuban government tired of the strain of expensive and risky foreign adventures which may be willing to consider compromise solutions to the conflicts in Central America and southern Africa. Despite the absence of clear signs at present, this is a development that may be increasingly likely in the future. Accordingly, the United States should continue periodically to talk to the Cubans, to clarify U.S. interests and intentions, and to probe whether the Cubans might be seriously willing to accept solutions to these conflicts that protect fundamental U.S. and Western interests.

Political Issues

Dealing with Diversity. The earlier section of this Policy Paper dealing with political interests suggested criteria for judging whether political regimes are compatible with U.S. interests. A policy that tolerates a diversity of political views from the right and the left makes it more difficult for the Soviet Union to pose as the defender of Third World nationalism. It also makes it much harder for pro-Soviet elements to convince their population that their nation's security requires a Soviet umbrella.

Coping with Revolutionary Change. Many Caribbean Basin countries are unlikely to experience revolutionary upheaval, but the odds are good that some will during the 1980s.[12] If the revolutionary or other leadership is clearly aligned with the Soviet Union, persists in massive interference in the internal affairs of neighboring states, or engages in consistent and massive violations of basic human rights, a U.S. policy of hostility may well be warranted. In such cases, however, it is preferable for regional powers and neighboring states to take the lead in criticizing and isolating the pariah regime.

More often, however, the postrevolutionary situation will be fluid and uncertain. In such cases it may be possible to overcome historic hostilities and mutual distrust and to nudge the regime toward a non-aligned foreign policy and a degree of domestic pluralism. Again, it may be preferable for regional powers and organizations to take the lead in working with the revolutionary regime. In cooperating with other countries, the United States can try to moderate the regime's policies through a combination of penalties and incentives. The peaceful settlement or at least management of border disputes can also help alleviate tensions and moderate regime behavior.

The Sandinistas have not fulfilled their earlier pledges to be non-aligned and to develop fully pluralistic political and economic systems. Nevertheless, it may be too early to abandon relations with the Nicaraguan government. While a policy of hostility may force the regime to moderate its policies over the short term, it is likely that a hostile policy serves primarily to strengthen the hardline elements within the regime, possibly driving them even closer to the Soviet Union, while allowing them to appeal to popular support under the banner of nationalism.[13] A flexible U.S. diplomatic posture open to negotiating major differences but prepared to respond sharply to aggressive moves would have the advantage of possibly influencing Sandinista behavior in a favorable direction and, failing that, of at least not helping the Sandinistas to solidify their domestic hold. It would also improve the U.S. image elsewhere in the Caribbean Basin.

When confronted with revolutionary change, the United States should avoid prejudging regimes or overreacting to regime rhetoric. In some cases, a wait-and-see posture may be most appropriate. As the Atlantic Council's Policy Paper, *After Afghanistan—The Long Haul,* concluded:

> [In dealing with difficult Third World governments] there will be cases where international inaction on the part of the West may be the wisest policy at a certain time. If, for example, internal factional divisions in a particular country are numerous, deep and conflicting with Western goals, it may be best to stand back and let the dust settle. If short-term advantages are not attainable, and short-term risks are not forbidding, it would certainly seem wiser in such circumstances to rely on the longer-term probabilities that policies of moderation will in due course emerge.[14]

Supporting Democratic Governments. It is essential that the United States support existing democratic governments. U.S. support for democratic governments is consistent with our own ideals. (For an expanded discussion, see Chapter 5.) Moreover, failure to do so will gradually corrode our own democratic values. However, the United States should not anticipate that democratic governments will necessarily support U.S. diplomatic objectives or international economic policies, although they are more likely to do so.

The United States can express its support for democratic systems in several ways. A global human rights policy lends moral support to those who are fighting for democratic ideas. In the allocation of U.S. economic assistance, preferential treatment should normally be given to democratic countries. Similarly, the U.S. can help democratic governments meet their genuine defense needs and protect them by working to reduce tensions in the region.

The United States should not engage in a missionary campaign to reproduce its own political institutions in the Caribbean Basin. A policy which tolerates diversity is more likely to protect basic U.S. interests. But where democratic institutions do exist, the United States—both public and private sectors—should lend them wholehearted support.[15]

Economic Issues

U.S. global and domestic economic policies have a profound effect on Caribbean welfare. The United States can also devise policies at the regional and bilateral levels that improve the prospects for growth and employment in Basin nations.

For reasons noted in the earlier section on U.S. economic interests, it is in the U.S. interest for Caribbean Basin economies to enjoy sustained growth. The rekindling of global economic growth is essential if the deterioration in the region's economies is to be reversed. The United States and other industrial nations must pursue fiscal and monetary policies that stimulate noninflationary growth. Only then will export markets revive, commodity prices rise, real interest rates fall, and commercial banks regain the confidence they need to resume lending.

Finance. Many Caribbean Basin countries expanded their foreign debt substantially in the 1970s and early 1980s. Even excluding Mexico, Venezuela, and Colombia, the region's commercial debt had surpassed $5.6 billion by 1981.[16] In some cases, this debt accumulation proceeded at an evidently unsustainable rate. In all cases, lenders and borrowers were anticipating a healthy global international environment that would enable countries to meet their rising debt service burdens. These predictions were overly optimistic.

As throughout the developing world, many Caribbean Basin nations will have to reduce their borrowing rates and adjust their immediate growth prospects to take into account the adverse international environment. At the same time, public and private lenders should provide sufficient resources to facilitate this adjustment process, to make feasible the servicing of existing debt, and to set the stage for renewed growth. Steps also need to be taken now that will assure that adequate capital is available to finance development over the long run.

The Atlantic Council Working Group on International Monetary Affairs, in its February 1983 Policy Paper, *The International Monetary System: Exchange Rates and International Indebtedness,* advocated the following solutions to the balance of payments and debt crises of the developing countries: (1) agreement by such countries with the International Monetary Fund (IMF) on programs to tighten domestic economic management and accommodate their payments positions to the prospectively lower levels of foreign borrowing; (2) renegotiation of existing external debt in a constructive manner, so as to bring service charges within current capacity to pay; (3) an adequate amount of new funds from private financial institutions as well as from public loans and grants sufficient to permit developing countries both to spread their balance of payments adjustment over a reasonable period of time and to continue economic development; (4) an early increase in IMF quotas of at least 50 percent, supplemented by an increase in the borrowing facilities available to the Fund. These recommendations are also applicable to the Caribbean Basin. A rapid and substantial increase in IMF resources, a continual, if lower, flow of new loans from commercial banks, and sufficiently orderly and flexible debt rescheduling mechanisms are all relevant responses to the region's economic problems.

These policies can help the Caribbean Basin states through their immediate liquidity crises. The longer-term capital needs of most countries, however, can best be met by the multilateral development institutions that provide loans at maturities and terms more appropriate for investment projects. Substantial real increases in the activity levels of the World Bank and the Inter-American Development Bank are required if they are to realize their potential for stimulating growth in the Caribbean Basin. Regional aid institutions, including the Caribbean Development Bank and the Central American Bank for Economic Integration, also deserve support.

U.S. bilateral assistance to the Caribbean Basin has increased substantially since the mid-1970s. This growth should be sustained and expanded. For reasons of burden-sharing, efficiency, and political impact, bilateral aid programs should be coordinated with those of other bilateral and multilateral donors.

Trade. Without access to industrial-country markets, Caribbean Basin countries cannot earn the foreign exchange they need to generate growth and service their debts. In recognition of this nexus, President Reagan's Caribbean Basin Initiative (CBI) promises Central America and the Caribbean islands duty-free access to the huge U.S. market.

Different estimates exist regarding the likely impact of the CBI on Caribbean trade. Since 85 percent of U.S. imports from the CBI-eligible countries already enter duty-free and sugar and textiles are excluded, the added stimulus to trade may not be great. There is a danger that the CBI could be oversold. Nevertheless, it is an important demonstration of U.S. interest in the economic welfare of nearby developing countries.

As a preferential trading scheme, the CBI contradicts the principle of most-favored-nation treatment that guides U.S. and General Agreement on Trade and Tariffs (GATT) trade policy. Moreover, many members of the Working Group believe that preferential treatment can appear to be a paternalistic or even hegemonic device. Nevertheless, the majority of the members of the Working Group believe that these objections should not be overriding. The CBI is consistent with the U.S. trade principle of moving in the direction of freer trade, and a GATT waiver can most probably be obtained. Appearances of paternalism can be avoided if the President determines that the CBI is open to all potentially eligible countries (i.e., excluding Cuba) without political discrimination.

A reduction in trade barriers may result in the loss of jobs in the United States, at least in the short run. Primarily for this reason, some members of the Working Group oppose this aspect of the CBI. In any case, the U.S. government ought to assist workers displaced by imports to train for and to find new jobs and should provide unemployment compensation in the interim. Otherwise, one sector of American society will pay disproportionately for a foreign policy initiative taken in the broader national interest.

Migration. The Caribbean Basin is the largest source of immigrants coming, legally and illegally, into the United States. (See Chapter 6 for a more complete discussion of migration.) In the 1940s and 1950s, approximately 500,000 Puerto Ricans moved to the U.S. mainland. For political and economic reasons, some 500,000 Cubans migrated to the U.S. between 1959 and 1960. Since then, immigrants have been coming from throughout the Basin and settling in a growing number of American cities. Most recently, many Central Americans have been traveling through Mexico to enter the United States. But Mexico itself is the most important sending country, and Mexicans account for the majority of the roughly three to seven million illegal aliens in the U.S. Given population growth, economic problems, and political strife, as well as the large wage differentials between the sending countries and the U.S., immigration pressures will increase and remain strong at least throughout this century.

Economic development in the sending countries can, over the long run, reduce the incentives to emigrate. In the meantime, the United States needs to exercise greater control over the flow of illegal migrants, who have become an underclass living hidden within American society. The Simpson–Mazzoli Bill includes several significant proposals for reducing illegal migration, including sanctions against employers who knowingly hire illegal aliens and an expanded temporary worker program to aid U.S. employers unable to find needed workers domestically. Simpson–Mazzoli would also grant legal status to those persons who can demonstrate they have been residing in the United States since a certain date.

Emigration confers some benefits on the sending country. It relieves labor-market pressures, and emigrants working abroad normally remit a portion of their earnings. Emigration does, however, deprive sending nations of some of their best educated and entrepreneurial talents.

In seeking to restrict the flow of illegal immigrants, the United States needs to be sensitive to the impact on sending countries. The United States especially needs to consult closely with Mexico on both the substance and implementation of new immigration regulations, including the impact that sudden drastic changes might have on Mexico's economic and political stability. However, an open U.S. border should not be the means by which Mexico and other countries further postpone needed reforms. Moreover, the U.S. absorptive capacity is limited, and some people believe it has already been exceeded.

Energy. The United States has an interest in the continual development of secure sources of energy in the Caribbean Basin. (Energy is discussed more fully in Chapter 7.) While Venezuelan production has steadily declined in recent years, Mexico has become the single most important supplier of the U.S. market and a major source for purchases for the Strategic Petroleum Reserve.

The overriding U.S. interest in Mexico is political stability. Therefore, U.S. policy toward Mexican oil production should be framed in terms of the impact of oil on Mexico's broader economic and political development. The U.S. correctly has not been pressuring Mexico to raise production beyond a level where revenues can be usefully absorbed. Given the recent drop in the price of oil and Mexico's tremendous foreign exchange needs, Mexico possesses sufficient incentives of its own to increase petroleum production.

Venezuela's petroleum-rich Orinoco Tar Belt has attracted considerable attention as a means of enhancing a relatively secure source of supply. However, Orinoco development will be expensive and involve long lead times and difficult technological problems. The current softness in the oil market raises serious questions about the economic feasibility of developing the Orinoco deposits at this time.

Energy production in the smaller Caribbean Basin states, while having little influence on global or even U.S. supply, is important to the economies of the countries in question. The United States can take a number of steps to assist their development of energy resources, including: (1) AID can assist countries to develop energy projects that utilize the subsidies provided by the joint Mexico-Venezuela oil financing facility; (2) AID and other more specialized U.S. agencies can assist in the development of alternative energy sources, including solar, wind, biomass, alcohol, nuclear, and coal, as well as improving conservation measures; (3) the U.S. can encourage the World Bank to provide, possibly through the creation of an energy affiliate, increased financing for energy projects. The U.S. private sector can and should remain a major source of technology and capital for energy development in the Caribbean Basin.

GENERAL FINDINGS

1. The United States, Canada, Western Europe, and Japan need to focus concerted and sustained attention on the Caribbean Basin.

The problems facing the region, however, are complex, and simple solutions will not suffice. If the United States and Western Europe are to defend their interests and make a positive contribution to the region, policies must be developed that are consistent, enjoy broad domestic support, and can be sustained over the long term.

2. While it is useful to address the Caribbean Basin as a geopolitical entity, a major challenge to the United States will be to find the proper mix between regionwide, subregional, and country-specific policies. The circumstances of particular countries and subregions must be taken into account.

3. The political change and breakdown experienced by several countries in the region—notably in Central America—are the result of long-term systemic problems, aggravated by Cuban and Soviet support for revolutionary forces. Existing political institutions have failed to adjust to new economic and social conditions and refused to incorporate newly emerging sectors of the population that were increasingly mobilized and politically aware.

4. Faulty economic policies, inefficient government, and highly skewed income distribution also have contributed to political instability in some countries. While Soviet and Cuban propaganda, influence, subversion, and arms transfers certainly exist in the area, they are seriously aggravating factors rather than the fundamental cause of the problems of the region.

5. Recently, the economic disruptions emanating from the global recession have exacerbated underlying political problems. While domestic economic management clearly could have been better in some countries, the force with which the international recession hit the Caribbean Basin would have had a severe impact on the best-organized of governments. Per capita income levels are in serious decline throughout much of the region.

6. Despite the pressures for change and the gravity of the economic crisis, revolutionary upheaval will most probably be avoided in the majority of Basin nations. Open political institutions or enlightened elites, where they exist, should be capable of absorbing or accommodating forces for change. But in some countries in the region, institutions may be too rigid, the leadership too short-sighted, or the pressures too overwhelming to avoid more abrupt change.

7. Economic and political modernization have altered the self-perception of the inhabitants of the region. Most of the region's leaders have developed a greater sense of their own national interests.[17] They seek a diversity of international ties in order to increase their own room for maneuver. Used effectively, this emergent nationalism can be an asset in a Western strategy aimed at helping

the developing countries of the Basin defend their sovereignty against Soviet domination.

8. The Soviet Union has made a heavy economic and diplomatic investment in Cuba but has been unwilling to make similar commitments elsewhere in the region. The Soviets have been cautious, finding it more effective to act through the Cubans. For their part, the Cubans have stepped up their support to some guerrilla movements and are playing an active role in Nicaragua.

9. U.S. interests in the Caribbean Basin have increased and broadened. The United States will always want to secure its southern flank against military threats, but other interests have also assumed increasing weight. Economic interests—oil, debt, trade, migration—are more salient. The U.S. political interest is tied to economic development and basic human rights. Therefore, U.S. national security interests must be defined broadly to include their economic, political, and social concerns.

10. The Caribbean Basin today displays a widening diversity of types of political systems, ranging from Marxist-Leninist (Cuba), to various forms of liberal democratic and nationalist populist, to traditional dynastic (Haiti). In deciding a government's compatibility with U.S. interests, four rough guidelines can be applied. First, a government should not grant access to military facilities to hostile powers nor follow a policy of automatic alignment with the Soviet Union. Second, it should not interfere in the internal affairs of other states. Third, the government's legitimacy should derive not from force but from its responsiveness to the will of the people, optimally as expressed through free elections. Fourth, as required by U.S. foreign assistance legislation, the government should not engage in the "gross and consistent" violations of the basic human rights of its population.

11. U.S. intervention in the internal affairs of any nation in the area will arouse general antagonism, but U.S. opposition to intervention by others is in the interest of every country in Latin America, even though this may provoke the resentment of groups that might benefit from such intervention. The U.S. should make crystal clear its position that each nation has a right to determine its own political institutions; it should, however, oppose external intervention by others, particularly if such intervention involves or gives rise to the use of force, in the affairs of any country in the area.

12. U.S. influence in the Caribbean Basin has been diminished by a series of developments in the international system, including the emergence of regional "influentials" and the generalized diffusion of power. U.S. policy has been further constrained by several domestic realities, including political, budgetary, and bureaucratic ones. Policymakers

should strive to break free from some of these constraints. Budgets can be increased. Policy can be based on more accurate and timely assessments of local situations. Nevertheless, failure to take international and domestic constraints into account can lead to overambitious policies, and the inevitable policy corrections leave the appearance of inconsistency and incompetence.

13. Given these constraints on U.S. influence, it makes sense to seek to work closely with other countries who share our fundamental interests, including Mexico, Venezuela, Canada, Western Europe, and Japan. Such cooperation may require that the U.S., these, and other friendly states modify some of their policies in order to pursue fundamental goals.

CONCLUSIONS AND POLICY RECOMMENDATIONS

Immediate Security Interest and Political and Economic Cooperation

Security Through Development

Conclusion. Solid support for socioeconomic development must be a major component of long-term U.S. security policy in the Caribbean Basin.

Recommendations. The United States should embark on a comprehensive and imaginative program for Caribbean Basin economic development. Using all the instruments outlined below, this program can be realistically tailored to the present capabilities and future needs of this region. Such a plan should take into consideration the development experiences of the past and build upon the more successful efforts at regional integration, especially the Central American Common Market and the Caribbean Community (Caricom). It should be based on the strong desire of the countries in the area to participate actively and cooperatively in the design and implementation stages. The plan should focus on the development of infrastructure, agriculture, and exports; promote institution building and technical training; foster both private- and public-sector development; and be supported by multilateral as well as bilateral assistance.[18]

To be successful, U.S. economic policies should be based on regional cooperation. To this end, the U.S. should enter into an agreement with the Caribbean Basin countries and Canada for regular discussions at working levels and an annual review at the ministerial level. In addition, the United States should continue to support the world Bank-led Caribbean Group for Cooperation in Economic Development.

Enhanced Political Participation

Conclusions. In conjunction with an increased emphasis on socio-economic development, the United States should encourage the countries and peoples of the region in their efforts to further develop broadly based representative political institutions and democratic processes. In many of the countries of the English-speaking Caribbean, such an approach would contribute to a strengthening of existing democratic institutions. Most members of the Working Group believe that in some Spanish-speaking countries, despite historical and cultural tendencies toward more authoritarian models, trends suggest an increasing demand by the populace for political participation. Continued development of democratic institutions and processes would serve to develop mechanisms for interest articulation and to promote socio-political integration, thus enhancing the legitimacy of governments in the region.

Recommendation. The President and Congress should support the development of broadly based representative forms of government with local institutions building upon the history and culture of individual countries.

Military Basing

Conclusion. The United States should join with other Caribbean Basin countries to oppose the establishment in the region of additional Soviet or Cuban military bases, the major expansion of existing ones, or increased Soviet and Cuban access to existing facilities.

Recommendation. The United States should insist that the Soviet Union honor the three accords that limit its military capabilities in Cuba. The United States should also make clear to the Soviet Union and Cuba that it strongly opposes their establishing military bases elsewhere in the Caribbean Basin.[19]

Bilateral Security Assistance

Conclusions. The military forces of the Spanish-speaking Caribbean frequently play a central role in their respective countries. In the past the military elites have generally been conservative and allied with traditional power structures. In recent years, however, there have been indications of an awakening of social and political conscience within some sectors of the military. This awakening creates opportunities for bringing about changes that are essential if political disorder and disintegration are to be avoided. If democratically oriented, the military can be a powerful and constructive force. As a result, security assistance remains an important instrument of U.S. foreign policy in the region.

Recommendations. Consistent with the four guidelines set out above, and mindful of the budgetary constraints of recipient nations, the United States should selectively extend its security assistance efforts where warranted in the region. U.S. security assistance progams have not always been administered in a way that would be consistent with these guidelines. Training programs must highlight these goals. Most importantly, however, the impact of U.S. security assistance programs will depend heavily upon the broader political context in which they are implemented.

The U.S. should be disposed to increase military education and training programs for the states in the region that request it. These programs should include intensive discussions of the principles and practices of democratic government. In the Caribbean, the U.S. should provide assistance for maritime security and navigation safety as well as disaster relief. The role of the U.S. Coast Guard should be expanded in the Eastern Caribbean as part of the security assistance effort. The present restrictive legislation should be modified to permit police-type security assistance to those nations in the English-speaking Caribbean which rely exclusively on police and constabulary forces for security.[20]

Strategic Security

Conclusions. It is unrealistic and unwise for the United States to consider the Caribbean Basin a *mare nostrum.* Moreover, several of our European allies can play constructive roles with the U.S. through "coalitions of the willing" in promoting the common interest in the security of the area. Clearly, NATO cannot be expected to extend its jurisdiction to the Caribbean Basin, but some governments with substantial economic and security interests in the area can coordinate policy and take coordinated action in particular cases.

Various European governments have been reluctant to undertake any functions south of the Tropic of Cancer. Nevertheless, all NATO nations have an interest in the ability of the United States to resupply Europe in the event of hostilities, and the exchange of intelligence on developments in any part of the world is routine in NATO.

Recommendations. A clearinghouse should be established for the continuous sharing of intelligence on Soviet and Cuban activity in the region. The United States and its allies should consult regularly, share intelligence and, where practical, coordinate action in regard to Soviet and Cuban military and subversive penetration in the area. A coordinating mechanism should be established to facilitate doing so. Some members of NATO, together with appropriate regional powers, should be encouraged to extend military assistance in the area.[21]

The United States and other member states should reassess the mission and functions of the institutions of inter-American military cooperation to explore whether they should enhance their roles as channels of communication and fora for reducing tension.[22]

Dealing with Radical Nationalist Regimes

Conclusions. While Americans prefer liberal democracies, radical regimes of the left or the right have become a fact of life in the Caribbean Basin, and more may arise in the future. U.S. policy should strive to keep them integrated into the Western economic system and separate from the Soviet strategic network. A policy of confrontation will often fail to modify regime behavior in the desired direction, instead driving the regime further into a shell of distrust and hostility. There are times when a "wait-and-see" attitude will be preferable to sudden reaction to an immediate crisis.

Paramilitary covert action in Latin America tends to become public and thus be counterproductive—dividing Americans, discouraging enhanced U.S. participation in the region, and perhaps even escalating the involvement of outside interests. It also violates several international conventions, including the OAS Charter. In the Caribbean Basin, paramilitary covert action is especially likely to arouse nationalist sentiments against the United States and around the target regime and to cause other nations to distance themselves from the U.S.

Recommendations. There should be a presumption against paramilitary covert action, especially where vital interests are not at stake, but its appropriateness can only be decided upon a case-by-case basis.[23] Most of the members of the Working Group believe that, in general in the Caribbean Basin, a full assessment of the likely costs and ramifications will more often tilt against such a policy. Instead, the United States should concentrate on a "counter-interventionist" policy of preventing the Soviet Union, Cuba, and Nicaragua from arming and supporting guerrilla forces in the region.

U.S.-Nicaraguan relations are severely strained. The U.S. should continue to press vigorously for an end to Nicaraguan subversion in other countries. At the same time, the United States should maintain a flexible diplomatic posture that is open to negotiating the major bilateral and regional differences as a possible means of weaning Nicaragua away from Cuba and the Soviet Union.

The United States should make increasingly strong efforts to probe for possibilities of inducing the Cubans to cooperate seriously in the peaceful solutions of conflicts in Central America and southern Africa. If significant progress can be made on these issues, the U.S. should reconsider its policies toward Cuba. If progress is not forthcoming, the U.S. should explore appropriate sanctions with its Western European allies while not excluding the possibility of other forms of pressure on Cuba.[24] In any case, the U.S. should continue to conduct intelligence overflights to verify compliance with U.S.-Soviet accords limiting Soviet military presence in Cuba.

Regional Cooperation and Peacekeeping

Conclusions. The greater nationalism and assertiveness of the nations of the region and the entrance of other powers make it difficult and more costly for the United States to gain the outcomes it seeks by working alone. Multilateral diplomacy, to the extent that it can be effective, may frequently be preferable to a unilateral approach to the region's security problems. The United States needs to work closely with other friendly nations and with multilateral institutions.

Violence in Central America threatens the interests of many states in the region, as well as our own. Our national experience in various parts of the world suggests that a go-it-alone policy in dealing with local violence, despite its advantages, can expose us unduly to adverse political consequences and even to national disaster. These potential hazards are underscored by the strong prohibitions against intervention in the Charter of the Organization of American States and other multilateral treaties.

The United States should therefore continue to hold open its options for multilateral action in support of agreed objectives in Central American countries wracked by violence. We should not automatically exclude proposals for negotiations between political adversaries that go beyond a simple preparation for national elections.

Recommendations. The United States should be responsive to efforts of regional countries to coordinate approaches to the Caribbean Basin that are consistent with fundamental U.S. objectives. The U.S.

should encourage the Contadora Group (Colombia, Mexico, Panama, and Venezuela) to continue its efforts to find political solutions to the conflicts in Central America.

The U.S., as a member country, should encourage and assist the OAS in playing a constructive role in reducing tensions in the Basin and in providing or policing guarantees that are part of any treaties or settlements.

The U.S. should seek the establishment of international observer groups to monitor arms traffic and military movement across Central American frontiers. In appropriate circumstances and as elements of broader peaceful settlements, the U.S. should support multinational peacekeeping forces that serve as buffers and to maintain order.

The U.S. should continue to seek multilateral and bilateral political cooperation to counter such security-related problems as terrorism, gun-running, massive migration flows, and narcotics traffic.

The United States should try to work more closely with Canada, especially in the insular Caribbean. More particularly, the United States should encourage Canada to join the OAS; while Canada will sometimes differ with the U.S. on specific issues, its deeper involvement in the hemisphere's economic and security affairs is to be welcomed.

Cultural Exchange and Training

Conclusions. The countries of the region lack sufficient adequately trained leadership and middle-level cadres for the task of building more prosperous and stable societies. The Soviet Union and their Eastern European and Cuban allies sponsor thousands of scholarships to bring less privileged students from the area to study in their countries. While many students from the region study in the United States, most are privately or personally funded. U.S. government-funded programs are generally at the more advanced educational levels and frequently favor upper income groups whose families already have strong American connections. The United States should significantly increase its efforts to train middle-level technicians, managers, and future leaders and to familiarize them with the U.S.

Recommendations. The United States should expand its government-sponsored scholar programs and ensure that a higher proportion of funds are made available to the less-privileged for study in the United States in technical and vocational programs. The United States Information Agency (USIA) and other involved agencies should expand their leadership training programs in the region. They should reach across the social and professional spectrum to include business and labor leaders, public administrators, academics, journalists, military officers and clerics. The President and Congress should broaden the "Institute for Democracy" concept, as outlined in currently proposed legislation, to an "Institute for Democracy and Economic Development" approach.

U.S. and Western European labor unions (including the AIFLD), human rights, and other humanitarian organizations and foundations should maintain and expand their activities in the region. While government encouragement may be warranted at an initial stage, relations are best maintained on an informal basis. U.S. embassies, however, should provide appropriate assistance to these private organizations.

Human Rights

Conclusions. Many of the Caribbean countries have creditable human rights records. Under the stress of economic and social maladjustments, however, some have grossly violated their constitutional and international commitments to protect the civil and political rights of their people. The most glaring abuse is the practice of politically motivated murder by certain rightist Central American governments and by rightist and leftist terrorist groups. Similarly repugnant is the curtailment of civil and political rights by leftist regimes in the area.[25]

While the degree of emphasis has changed from time to time, human rights considerations have been a permanent element of United States foreign policy. In certain cases involving important national security interests, they must sometimes be subordinated to other factors. However, they should never be ignored. While avoiding interference in domestic politics, the United States ought to encourage improvement in human rights practices in the region through persuasion and, on occasion, through judicious modulation of political and economic instruments.

Recommendations. The United States should, on appropriate occasions, make known its concern for the improvement of human rights practices by offending Caribbean governments. Its attitude toward indiscriminate slaughter of civilians from whatever quarter should be unequivocally clear. If geopolitical interests require cooperation with regimes in countries where rights are being systematically violated, the U.S. should nevertheless exert such leverage as it can to ameliorate abuses of personal, political, and trade union rights.

The United States should encourage international observation of human rights practices in Caribbean countries charged with abuses.

For this purpose the U.S. should support investigation through OAS machinery, in particular through action by the Inter-American Commission on Human Rights. The public discussions engendered by the reports of this commission can have an appreciable influence on governments.

In conflict-ridden Central America, the United States should be generous in its support for Costa Rica, the democratic showcase of the area. It must not be said that Costa Rican democracy fell because of U.S. neglect, or because the U.S. concentrated its economic assistance too narrowly on countries where democratic solutions are at best doubtful.

Broadcasting

Conclusions. The Soviet Union spends approximately $3.3 billion annually on building its worldwide image through information programs. In contrast, the U.S. government spends about $550 million on cultural exchanges, Voice of America, films, speakers, exhibits, and other aspects of "public diplomacy." However, most American culture and news are disseminated through private channels.

The Soviet Union and Cuba broadcast 486 hours a week to the Caribbean and South America in ten languages. The United States government broadcasts 81 hours a week in three languages. While the Voice of America enjoys a high reputation as a timely and dependable source of information, Soviet and Cuban information programming is becoming more sophisticated and subtle. The United States needs to counter this propaganda by bringing objective information to listeners in the region.

Recommendation. The United States should substantially increase the hours of programming and the number of broadcast languages to the region so as to increase understanding of events and of U.S. policies.[26]

Financial Management and Economic Development

The Debt Crisis

Conclusions. The Caribbean Basin nations can recover from their deep economic recession only if the industrial countries resume sustained growth. Only then can their export markets expand, their terms of trade improve, and their attractiveness to investors be rekindled.

A most pressing problem facing the region is the management of the balance of payments. The immediate symptom of the financial imbalances in external accounts is the debt crisis. Alleviation of the debt crisis is a *sine qua non* for the reestablishment of an environment where investment and growth can occur.

During the 1970s, the nature of financial transactions between many Caribbean Basin countries and the industrial world changed radically. The ratio of private to official capital flows to the developing world rose rapidly as commercial banks undertook to recycle capital from surplus to deficit countries. In retrospect, it is now clear that the failure of official institutions to keep pace has resulted in a less stable international system. In the 1980s, a more balanced mix between official and private lending is required, both to manage the immediate liquidity crises and to finance future growth. Governments and multilateral institutions will have to play a greater role in steering financial relations between the OECD countries and the developing nations of the region.

Recommendations. Many Caribbean Basin countries are working closely with the International Monetary Fund. Yet the IMF needs to be strengthened if it is to contribute an adequate level of resources to the region. The U.S. Congress should approve the substantial increase in IMF resources negotiated by the IMF member nations so that the quota increases can enter into effect in early 1984. To be able to manage the large current-account imbalances still facing some countries, the IMF should be permitted to provide standby funding in excess of current country-specific ceilings (450 percent of quota over three years); and member governments should support IMF borrowing from national governments and international capital markets if additional capital is required. IMF stabilization programs are more likely to be sustainable and effective if they do not require measures so severe as to be politically destabilizing.[27]

International capital markets need to be stabilized. The IMF, World Bank, commercial banks, central banks, and national regulatory agencies and governments of the OECD countries should embark upon a process of consultation to search for better ways to collect and disseminate information regarding external debt, and, more generally, to bring greater stability to international capital markets. National regulatory authorities should devise lending criteria that inhibit imprudent expansions of exposure or destabilizing, sudden retrenchments. More specifically, the International Institute for Finance can be a positive step in the direction of creating a clearing house mechanism for data on debtor economies.

The rescheduling of public and private debt should take place when it is necessary to bring service charges into line with a country's capacity to pay. Debt rescheduling should cover a sufficient number of years so that economic management can proceed in an environment of relative predictability.

While commercial banks will inevitably reduce net lending to risky markets, they should not become agents of instability by suddenly and drastically reducing net lending, leaving countries unable to meet minimal import needs and service their external debt simultaneously. While such actions may appear rational to the individual bank, if taken by many banks they risk deepening liquidity crises and possibly even precipitating *de facto* defaults.[28]

The developing countries must balance their expenditures with available financing. The developing nations of the Caribbean Basin should, as necessary and in agreement with the IMF, the World Bank, and the Inter-American Development Bank, implement policies to stabilize their external and internal accounts and accommodate their payments positions to the prospectively lower level of foreign borrowing by restraining imports, promoting exports and increasing domestic savings.

Long Term Development

Conclusions. Future growth will require sustained inflows of long-term capital. Since substantial long-term flows from commercial banks cannot be expected by most countries in the region during the next several years, official institutions—multilateral and bilateral—will have to take the lead in making capital available. Most importantly, external lenders must adopt long-term strategies to promote development in the Caribbean Basin.

The current level of political conflict and uncertainty in Central America is a severe impediment to economic development. Private domestic and foreign investment will remain very low until the region's politics become more stable and predictable. Moreover, economic assistance to Central America cannot be fully effective in fostering productive investment and development until political and military conflicts are resolved.

Where suitable political conditions exist, the private sector can play an important role in fostering economic development. In particular, U.S. firms can provide capital, supply technology, create jobs, and locate export markets for the region's products.

Recommendations. To facilitate increased lending to the Caribbean Basin, the overall resources of the World Bank and the Inter-American

Development Bank should be increased in real terms. As first steps, the U.S. Congress should promptly approve the pending replenishments of the World Bank's International Development Association (IDA) and the Inter-American Development Bank (IADB). Regional aid institutions, including the Caribbean Development Bank and the Central American Bank for Economic Integration, should receive the support of AID and of the World Bank and the IADB. In addition, U.S. economic assistance to the Caribbean Basin should be expanded. Bilateral aid programs should be coordinated with other bilateral and multilateral donors.[29]

In order to stimulate foreign direct investment, the Overseas Private Investment Corporation (OPIC) and the Export-Import Bank should concentrate a rising percentage of their activities in the region to the extent that U.S. firms can be interested through the Caribbean/Central American Action program and other private-sector initiatives.

External donors and investors should give priority to training local manpower. At present, the ability of both the private and public sectors in some countries to absorb financial resources is hampered by the inadequate skills of labor and management. The Peace Corps and Executive Service Corps are among the mechanisms available for transferring skills on a people-to-people basis.

The United States should seek a reduction in tensions in Central America that meets its security objectives as an important contribution to enhancing the effectiveness of development assistance and to creating an environment conducive to private savings and investment.

Trade

Conclusions. Expanded trade opportunities for the Caribbean Basin countries are essential if balance-of-payments problems are to be resolved and growth sustained over the long run. The internal markets of Caribbean Basin countries are decidedly limited by population and income levels. Especially for the region's smaller economies, exports can be the main engine of growth. Access to external markets is essential if countries are to obtain the benefits of specialization of labor and economies of scale. The one-way free trade zone between the United States and the smaller countries of the region, which President Reagan proposed as part of the Caribbean Basin Initiative, is a promising start in this direction.

There is also a clear correlation in the long run between expanding trade and decreasing pressures for migration.

Recommendations. The Working Group applauds the adoption by the U.S. Congress of the Free Trade Area provision contained in the

CBI legislation. A majority of the members of the Working Group believe that all countries of the region (excluding Cuba) that wish to participate in the Free Trade Area should be permitted to do so on a non-political, nondiscriminatory basis.[30] The objective of the free trade areas is to increase economic integration and political understanding, not to drive countries further apart.

Foreign assistance should be oriented, among other objectives, toward supporting increased intraregional trade. Bilateral and multilateral aid programs should seek to promote export-oriented industries and agriculture. This can be accomplished by directly promoting private-sector firms, as well as by assisting the public sector to help create the necessary physical and human infrastructure, by financing transportation and communication projects, and by funding education and training for skilled laborers, management, and civil servants. To prevent increased financing of export-oriented efforts from reducing funding for basic needs projects that augment workers' productivity, total aid budgets must be increased.

Some U.S. workers will suffer from the rising level of imports from the region. Compensatory support should be provided to displaced American workers in the form of retraining and unemployment insurance.

Immigration

Conclusions. The United States wants to gain increased control over the flow of foreign immigrants across its borders. Additionally, Caribbean Basin efforts to reduce population pressures and attain sustained economic growth, combined with more open U.S. markets for Basin exports, can serve to alleviate migration pressures.

Recommendations. As a short-term measure, the Simpson-Mazzoli Bill should be approved. Over the long term, emigration pressures can be moderated only if Caribbean Basin countries achieve sustained economic expansion and reduced population growth.

The U.S. Immigration and Naturalization Service should be enlarged and the quality of its personnel upgraded through higher entry standards, increased salaries, and higher grade levels. Amnesty should be granted to immigrants living in the U.S. since a specified date.[31] Beyond that, the annual intake of immigrants and refugees should be adjusted yearly, based on projected labor needs in the United States and family reunification considerations.

Potential employers of nonresident aliens should be required to demonstrate both a need for foreign labor and evidence that they cannot fill this need by using U.S. citizens and legal resident aliens. Many members of the Working Group believe that the Department of State should concur in the choice of which countries are eligible for temporary worker programs, with the understanding that preferential treatment might be granted on an exceptional basis to certain nations for humanitarian, human rights and foreign policy considerations.

Technology Transfer

Conclusion. An effective and lasting way to expand technology transfer from developed nations to developing economies is through education and training.

Recommendation. The U.S. private sector and educational community should explore with Congress the utility of tax incentives targeted at U.S. firms active in the Caribbean Basin for the education and training of Caribbean Basin nationals.

Energy

Conclusion. The United States can take a number of steps to assist the smaller Caribbean Basin states as well as the major oil producers of the region to develop their energy resources. In particular, the United States should work closely with Mexico and Venezuela in addressing the region's energy problems.

Recommendations. The U.S. private sector should continue to be a major source of technology and capital for energy development in the Caribbean Basin. Moreover, the U.S. government, in cooperation with the World Bank and appropriate regional organizations, should:

Support increased World Bank financing for energy projects.

Encourage the formation of broadly owned private-sector Regional Energy Development Corporations to assess regional energy resources and requirements and to implement renewable and conventional energy supply and use programs.

Encourage the formation of public- and private-sector financed regional energy research and development centers to carry out educational and technical programs supportive of these energy supply and use programs.

Facilitate the transfer of technology for exploiting alternative energy resources: National laboratories should make available their technical resources on a low-cost or even cost-free basis to countries in the region. AID should step up its technical assistance, especially to enhance the region's institutional capabilities. AID should also work to develop energy projects that can utilize the funds generated by the joint oil-financing facility of Mexico and Venezuela. The Department of Energy should make judicious use of the contracts of the Strategic Petroleum Reserve to provide a market for Mexican and Venezuelan oil, as a means of enhancing future U.S. energy security and of strengthening bilateral ties.

APPENDIX
ADDITIONAL COMMENTS AND DISSENTS
BY MEMBERS OF THE WORKING GROUP

Comment *Robert Foster*

Although the Policy Paper represents a thorough analysis of U.S. interests and options in the Caribbean Basin, it places undue stress on limitations and constraints on U.S. policies. A bolder, more dynamic U.S. approach would better serve our long-term strategic interests.

The Caribbean Basin is important to the United States for its canal, sealanes, economic role, and petroleum. But overriding those tangible interests is the symbolic importance of the area. Although the United States does not and should not seek hegemony in the area, it must make a continuous, coordinated effort to influence area nations to cooperate in working toward common, mutually beneficial goals.

The establishment of a Communist regime in Cuba over two decades ago served to introduce a Soviet military presence in the Western Hemisphere and provided a base for subversion. Clearly, the United States must take prudent action, in cooperation with other nations, to prevent the emergence of more Cubas. Failure of the United States to exercise important influence in the Caribbean Basin would be another serious mark against America's world influence. Caribbean setbacks to U.S. foreign policy, added to those experienced recently in other areas, would be another substantiation of the Soviets' perception that the "correlation of forces" is moving in their direction.

Comment *Abraham F. Lowenthal*

I believe this report is timely, well informed, careful, measured, and balanced. It should contribute positively, therefore, to current discussions of U.S. policy options in which too many contributions lack these qualities. The report calls needed attention to the complexity of the policy conundrum for the United States in the Caribbean Basin, and thus effectively counters Washington's urge for simple answers.

But the report is ultimately disappointing, in part perhaps precisely because it strains so hard to be careful. The U.S. government, after all, is increasingly engaged in Central America's turmoil: undertaking major covert actions against Nicaragua, involving itself deeply in El Salvador's civil war, turning Honduras into a military base, staging massive naval and military maneuvers off the coasts of Central America, stepping up rhetorical and tangible pressures against Grenada and Cuba, and designing a long-term plan to assist the region's economic development. In this context of sharply escalating U.S. involvement, what is needed is a forthright statement of the nature and limits of U.S. interests in the Caribbean Basin and how best to protect them, a frank evaluation of current U.S. policy, and concrete suggestions for an alternative strategy. Instead, I fear, this report is somewhat unclear if not inconsistent in its analysis of U.S. interests, is excessively subtle—not to say muted—in its assessment of current U.S. policy, and is mainly lacking in specific suggestions for new policy options.

The report's analysis of underlying trends in the Caribbean Basin is sensible, nuanced, and up-to-date, but its discussion of U.S. interests and influence is considerably influenced by anachronistic notions, axioms of a bygone era.

The United States must decide, and soon, what kind of national involvement makes sense in Central America's current turmoil. Prolonged upheaval without consolidation is more likely in Central America during the next few years than either revolutionary change or progressive evolution. The United States must decide how it would be affected by extended civil wars and must assess how much capacity it has to influence such upheavals. This report makes it clear, both by what it says and what it fails to say, why it is hard for the United States to face unpleasant realities in Central America and to make hard choices.

Dissent *Dale Good and William Doherty*

We regret that it is necessary for us to dissent with parts of the Atlantic Council's Policy Paper on the Caribbean Basin.

The identification and analysis of the major issues involved present an overall situation calling for U.S. actions adequate to deal with the region's problems. In our opinion, the limited orientation of the Paper results in a failure to come to grips with some fundamental issues.

The Policy Paper is too limited in its orientation to make an adequate contribution to the requirements of steady economic progress and the overall problem of Western security. It does recommend that "the United States should embark on a comprehensive and imaginative program for Caribbean Basin economic development," but it fails to recommend what this would require: a substantial increase in grant and developmental assistance by the United States. Emphasis is placed on trade, and the one-way free trade zone between the U.S. and smaller countries of the region as provided in the Caribbean Basin Initiative. In our view, we should support programs that have as their objectives the stimulation of internal growth and improvement in the living standards of working men and women. Trade diversions do not meet this test. The chief beneficiaries of trade provisions of the Caribbean Basin Initiative will be multinational corporations, which will be encouraged to increase their profits through wage exploitation, and degrading and unsafe working conditions.

We should be prepared to recommend the full cost of essential economic assistance and security assistance programs. We should all be aware of the long-term costs—and the benefits—of reinforcing our own strength by supporting around us a community of resolute, prospering societies. These programs are insurance against the possible necessity at some future date of a vast increase in military expenditures.

We also find the Policy Paper lacking in a full understanding of the nature of the basic political struggle being waged in the area. For example, we disagree with the analysis and conclusions concerning Nicaragua. The early hopes we all experienced with the July 1979 victory of the Sandinista revolution against Somoza quickly were shattered. Nicaragua today is a military dictatorship that has all but destroyed democratic political parties and the free trade union movement. There is no right to strike, no right to bargain collectively, no right to organize. There is no self-determination or right of habeas corpus in Nicaragua. As a matter of fact, Defense Minister Commandante Humberto Ortega has publicly stated that if elections are to be held, they will be "to consolidate revolutionary power, not to call it into question, because power is in the hands of the people through its avant-garde the Sandinista Revolutionary Front."

The paper does discuss the roles of the Soviet Union and Cuba in the region, but it concludes that "the best strategy for containing Soviet influence is to go to the source of the unrest: to treat its underlying social and economic causes." Poverty and social injustice are realities that must be addressed, we should hope primarily for reasons of human rights rather than "strategy" for containing Soviet influence. In any case, whether the roots of the problem lie in social injustice or Soviet interference is an idle argument. If economic development programs to deal with poverty and social injustice are to succeed, we must concurrently with our economic assistance efforts be prepared to cooperate with democratic governments regarding the threat they face of guerrilla movements influenced and supported by Moscow. The post-World War II period clearly indicates that the Soviet Union will use its influence to prevent the correcting of social injustice by reforms, elections, and economic assistance, since these solutions would stand in the way of its objective of one-party Communist rule.

Finally, greater attention needs to be paid to the role of labor movements in country development, as well as in improving the social and economic well-being of working men and women. A primary objective of our assistance programs should be to assure that economic benefits of development are shared equitably, and this requires development strategies that are empoyment-oriented and trade unions through which workers are able to protect their legitimate rights. We need to enlist free labor movements as partners in our assistance programs.

We cannot, however, hope to gain the whole-hearted support of workers in the difficult and burdensome task of national development if they are without rights, without freedom, without justice, without bread. In granting assistance, a major consideration should be the adherence of recipient governments to the conventions of the International Labor Organization, especially those relating to freedom of association, discrimination, and forced labor.

The argument is frequently made by spokesmen of developing countries that emphasizing labor standards constitutes an obstacle to economic progress, and in developing countries labor standards should be limited so as not to jeopardize the nation's capital accumulation and long-term economic interest. But detailed studies show that trade unions historically have pushed up productivity instead of acting as a brake on economic growth. They have been a stabilizing factor, helping to foster a sense of industrial commitment and discipline, and have played an important role in social and economic reforms. There is no substitute for trade unions as the workers' own instruments for obtaining a more equitable share of the fruits of economic progress, and we should encourage governments to support rather than attempt to control or suppress labor movements.

The role of labor in foreign affairs has become more than ever an important factor. The extent to which political stability can be strengthened in many countries depends on the extent to which labor genuinely supports economic and political objectives and programs. U.S. foreign policy depends for success in large measure on the activities and attitudes of labor movements, especially with respect to those countries where cooperative bilateral relationships are important to U.S. interests.

NOTES

1. Robert Leiken comments: "The process described is the 'Sovietization' of Nicaragua, not 'communization.' It goes without saying that 'it is far from certain that the majority of the Sandinistas want to become totally dependent on the Eastern bloc for support.' What counts is (a) how they define 'totally dependent,' and (b) whether their policies will, with or against their wishes, lead to such a relationship. Additionally, the Soviet Union will *not* provide the sort of economic support to Nicaragua that it did to Cuba. Since the mid-1970s the Soviets have been recommending even to regimes of 'socialist orientation' that they should not break their ties with the West or expect major economic aid from the East. What counts for the Soviets is influence in or control of the military, security, and intelligence apparati."

2. David Scott Palmer comments: "The U.S. government was the principal provider of economic assistance to the Sandinistas during their first 18 months in power."

3. Brent Scowcroft notes: "There seems to be an implicit presumption which provides tone to many of the observations throughout the Policy Paper to the effect that there is a more or less inevitable tide sweeping the Caribbean region to the 'left,' a tide to which the United States should be open, and that the chief internal political threat to U.S. interests is likely to result from 'rightist' regimes. The notion of a 'leftward tide' is certainly open to question or even doubt, and the eventual emergence of democracy and respect for human rights through evolution of the 'left,' given the character of some of its constituent elements, is perhaps less likely than through evolution of the 'right.'"

4. Gabriel Marcella comments: "The growing insecurity of the Sandinistas may incline them either in a more authoritarian direction or, what is less likely, a tactical retreat toward toleration of more pluralism."

5. Some members of the Working Group noted that, despite violence and threats of violence by some guerillas, Salvadorans turned out in massive numbers. Some members noted that the elections were marred by an atmosphere of insecurity and the lack of participation of the leftist Frente Democratico Revolucionario (FDR).

6. Some members of the Working Group noted that rapid economic growth can be politically destabilizing. Others noted that democratic regimes are particularly threatened by economic stagnation, especially when coupled with high population growth rates.

7. Robert Foster comments: "U.S. policy should, however, be adequate to achieve U.S. national interests in the area, which are being severely challenged by Soviet-Cuban intervention."

8. As described in an issue paper prepared by Caribbean/Central American Action, "Implementing a Private Sector Based Caribbean Development Strategy," presented to the Atlantic Council's Working Group on the Caribbean Basin.

9. As described in an issue paper prepared by Dale E. Good and William C. Doherty, "Labor Perspectives," presented to the Atlantic Council's Working Group on the Caribbean Basin.

10. Several members of the Working Group believe that the United States should not tolerate the establishment of military bases elsewhere in the Caribbean Basin.

11. Some members of the Working Group believe that the historical record gives no cause for optimism that the current Cuban government would reduce its aggressive activities in the Basin in return for economic ties or political accommodation.

12. Pat Holt maintains that the odds are good that more Caribbean Basin countries will experience revolutionary upheaval during the 1980s.

13. Some members of the Working Group believe that the ideology of the Sandinista leaders make them implacably hostile to the U.S. interests, and efforts at cooperation will fail to alter their behavior.

14. *After Afghanistan—The Long Haul,* Harlan Cleveland and Andrew J. Goodpaster, Cochairmen, and Joseph J. Wolf, Rapporteur (Washington, D.C.: The Atlantic Council, March 1980), p. 41.

15. Robert Foster adds: "The United States should also responsibly assist democratic elements which seek to institute representative government adapted to local conditions."

16. As described in an issue paper by Robert Bond and Marlies Carruth, "Lending to Central America and the Caribbean," presented to the Atlantic Council's Working Group on the Caribbean Basin.

17. Nicolas Ardito Barletta comments: "The majority of the small countries of the Caribbean Basin are keenly interested in pursuing national development policies within the framework of democratic institutions, relatively open and mixed economies, participation of their peoples in the work and the benefits of the development process and closely associated with the rest of the hemisphere and Western community. The United States can identify itself with that goal and support it strongly, in cooperation with other nations, with actions such as the Caribbean Basin Initiative recently approved by the U.S. Congress."

18. Pat Holt comments: "The fundamental problem of the area is social injustice; until this is remedied, massive economic assistance is more likely to make it worse than to start a process of economic growth. Experience with U.S. bilateral aid programs over 35 years suggests that they rarely work anyway."

19. Several members of the Working Group believe that the United States should not tolerate the establishment of military bases elsewhere in the Caribbean Basin.

20. Robert Leiken adds: "Security assistance efforts should supplement the defense perceptions and measures of the countries in question, and they should be directed at real external threats, not internal opposition."

21. Pat Holt dissents: "I am skeptical of the recommendation for a selective increase in U.S. security assistance and particularly the recommendation that NATO and appropriate regional powers should be encouraged to extend military assistance to the region. The region is too militarized now; we ought to be discouraging rather than encouraging the injection of further arms. It is more likely that the region's problems will be resolved, or at least reduced, through political negotiation than through military action. To this end, we should, as the Policy Paper recommends elsewhere, place more reliance on the Contadora Group."

22. At least one member of the Working Group believes that the United States should attempt to revitalize the institutions of inter-American military cooperation for the purposes stated.

    The mechanisms of the inter-American military system include Inter-American Defense Board; Inter-American Defense College; attaché network; periodic conferences of the chiefs of the armies, navies, and air forces of the Americas; periodic exercises and maneuvers; military communications networks; peacekeeping and peace-observer missions (ad hoc only); U.S. military groups; the U.S. Security Assistance Program; U.S. military Latin American specialists; U.S. Southern Command Headquarters in Panama; U.S. military schools (in the U.S. and in Panama); exchanges of personnel, doctrine, and intelligence.

23. Brent Scowcroft maintains that: "There should not be a 'presumption against'

covert action or any other of the operational instruments of policy available to U.S. decisionmakers. All options should be dispassionately analyzed including all advantages and liabilities, in light of the particular situation. Current emotional attitudes aside, the United States should not abjure consideration of those policy options which lie between diplomatic action or security assistance and the use of U.S. troops."

24. Pat Holt comments: "I do not think U.S.–Cuban relations should revolve around Cuban policies in Central America and southern Africa. While important, these are only two of a number of issues between the two countries."

25. Robert Sayre comments: "This paragraph makes two assertions which are dubious: (1) that politically motivated murders in Central American (which to my knowledge are by vigilante groups) represent a violation of human rights by the government of the country; and (2) that human rights abuses in Central America are the most glaring in the Caribbean Basin. The Cuban government, for example, executed a very substantial number of the opposition without any trials and keeps large numbers of political opponents in jail. The Cuban government has not executed any of the opposition recently, but that does not make the early conduct of the present Cuban government any less glaring. It was generally conceded when the Cuban government carried out large-scale executions without trials that it did so for political reasons and that it was in full control. That is not the case, e.g., in El Salvador today where a civil war is in progress, the government does not have full control over its territory or, in some cases, over persons who purport to act for it, and it is not clear that the government is either involved in or condones politically motivated murders."

26. Theodore Achilles comments: "Strengthening existing official and private broadcasting will serve U.S. interests more effectively than the establishment of the proposed Radio Marti."

27. Brent Scowcroft comments: "The IMF is not really suited to deal with the financial crises now occurring. The problems are frequently more deeply seated than the IMF assumes and as a consequence, IMF stabilization programs sometimes require measures so severe as to be politically destabilizing."

Sally Shelton comments: "IMF stabilization programs and commercial bank loan terms should be structured in a fashion concomitant with a country's ability to pay."

28. Brent Scowcroft adds: "Governments and international institutions should intervene with assistance if necessary to insure that this does not occur."

29. Sally Shelton adds that the United States should join the Caribbean Development Bank and fund a "quick disbursing" aid mechanism for the micro-economies of the small islands.

30. Several members of the Working Group, notably Susan Purcell and Robert Sayre, dissent. Robert Sayre notes: "The implication of this recommendation is that the criteria will be overlooked and that Nicaragua should be included in trade arrangements even if it continues its present conduct. The CBI and other special arrangements are not things we do because we have an obligation and another country has a right. They are political concessions and we should not be giving them away unless they serve a useful purpose in achieving the objectives along the lines of the four guidelines set forth in this Policy Paper."

31. Robert Foster dissents: "Amnesty for illegal immigrants currently in the United States is undesirable because it would reward violators of immigration laws and decrease employment opportunities for U.S. citizens."

Chapter 2

Changing Realities and U.S. Policy in the Caribbean Basin: An Overview

Howard J. Wiarda

Among the more serious handicaps faced by the United States and its Western Allies in fashioning coherent, rational, consistent, and publicly acceptable foreign policy strategies is that their peoples—including many journalists, politicians, and even policymakers themselves, as well as the general population—often have only the most rudimentary and superficial knowledge of the foreign areas with which they must deal. The lack of sound knowledge, empathy, and deep understanding of cultures other than its own was a crucial problem—perhaps the single most critical one—for the United States in Indochina, and has been a serious handicap in Africa, Iran, and the Middle East. Because it is a contiguous and a "Western" area, we often assume we know Central America and the circum-Caribbean better; but it may be submitted that the same problems of lack of empathy and understanding that afflicted our policies in these other areas also plague us in dealing with those now-turbulent societies on what we sometimes call our "third border."[1]

America "rediscovered" Central America in 1979–80 when the Nicaraguan revolution led by the Sandinistas succeeded in overthrowing the Somoza regime, when Grenada also came under a leftist government and allied itself with Cuba, and when four church women were massacred in El Salvador. The previous U.S. "discovery" of the circum-Caribbean had occurred precisely twenty years earlier with the coming to power of Fidel Castro and the establishment of a Marxist–Leninist regime in neighboring Cuba, which led to a more or less sustained interest in the area through the mid-1960s. Both the earlier and the more recent "discoveries" of the area spawned a rash of "instant experts" and "instant analyses" that were far too frequently superficial, uninformed, and ethnocentric. The analyses we receive almost make it seem as though Central American history began in 1979, that these countries had no previous background, sociology, or politics. The policies that flowed from such analyses have often been similarly ad hoc and ahistorical.

This study seeks to help fill some of these gaps in our knowledge and understanding by furnishing useful background information, asking the kinds of questions that need to be asked, and providing the forms of interpretation that need to be used. The problems underlying policy for the United States and the Western Allies in Central America and the circum-Caribbean are not just factual but conceptual: they have to do at least as much with the models of interpretation that we use to understand that area as with incomplete factual knowledge. Failure to come to grips adequately with both the situations prevailing in the Caribbean Basin and with the mode and methods we use to map and comprehend the area is a prescription for far worse problems in the future.[2]

THE DYNAMICS OF A CHANGING CIRCUM-CARIBBEAN

The circum-Caribbean region, for the purposes of this study, includes Mexico, the states of Central America, Colombia, Venezuela, Guyana, Suriname, and the islands of the Caribbean. The region includes twenty-six independent states and sixteen dependent territories. There are current and former British and Dutch territories, units that are administratively a part of France, former Danish and Spanish colonies, and one U.S. commonwealth (Puerto Rico). The Basin includes ten mainland countries and fifteen insular countries. It encompasses four larger and emerging middle-range powers (Colombia, Cuba, Mexico, Venezuela), thirteen smaller "city-states" (Jamaica, Dominican Republic, Guyana, Suriname, Haiti, Belize, Guatemala, Trinidad and Tobago, El Salvador, Honduras, Nicaragua, Costa Rica, Panama), and eight "mini-states" in U.N. terminology.

The racial, linguistic, and ethnic background of the area is similarly diverse and complex. Eleven of the countries are Spanish-speaking. These countries have the largest populations by far, the most territory, and the most resources. It is their histories that we usually think of when we think about the area. But the Hispanic countries have recently been joined by nine English-speaking former British colonies; and the relations between these two groups of countries, in the Organization of American States and other international fora, are not always entirely harmonious. Their politics and sociologies are similarly dissimilar.

In the island and mainland Hispanic countries, Catholicism is the dominant religion and Spanish the official or prevailing language; the culture—that is, both the society and the political culture—is strongly shaped by the traditions, customs, and institutions inherited from Spain. The religious and cultural situations—and the institutional arrangements—are quite different in the British Caribbean, to say nothing of the French, Danish, and Dutch.

In the mainland countries the major racial strains are Indian and European, although along the Caribbean rim of Central America, the so-called Miskito Coast (named for the indigenous Indians that inhabited this area), there are sizable minorities of Protestant, English-speaking blacks. Even the Indo-European mix varies greatly, however, between the heavy Indian concentrations of southern Mexico and highland Guatemala and the sparse Indian populations of Costa Rica and Panama. All the countries of this area are predominantly *mestizo*, but the size of their Indian subclass varies enormously. So does the degree of European (primarily Spanish) influence, and the *mestizo* majorities are made up of varying kinds of Indo-European mixes.

In the islands, the predominant racial strains are European and black, as contrasted with the Indo-European mix on the mainland. That is because the indigenous Indians on the islands were all but eliminated by the end of the sixteenth century, as much because of the diseases the colonizers carried as because of force of arms or slave labor. As the Indians died off, Africans were brought in to replace them as manual laborers. Hence the societies and future histories of the islands would be described and written largely in terms of the interrelations between black and white, not Indian and white as in Central America.

But here again, variety abounds. In Cuba and Puerto Rico, the European population has been larger, blacks are a minority, and mulattos are a sizable element of the population. Haiti, in contrast, is 90 to 95 percent black, but its chief institutions—government, land, finance— were historically dominated by a small mulatto elite. In next-door

Dominican Republic, the white Hispanic elite is small numerically but very influential politically and economically, while the vast majority of the population, about 70 percent, is mulatto in varying degrees. Some Dominicans take pride in emphasizing that theirs is the only predominantly mulatto nation in the world, but others would prefer to emphasize the country's Hispanic roots. Jamaica and the other former British colonies also have mulatto elites, a predominantly black mass, and often a small "creole," or white, element, which no longer enjoys political power except sporadically, but still is often financially influential.

There are small pockets of other ethnic/linguistic/racial groups, including Chinese, Japanese, Lebanese, Syrians, Jews, East Europeans, Italians, East Indians, and Americans. These groups often have wealth and influence disproportionate to their numbers. With all these diverse ethnic and racial groups, it should be emphasized that the entire circum-Caribbean, in contrast with the United States, has until recently been quite free of intense racial hatred, conflict, and violence. Fueled by the prevailing economic difficulties of the area, the level of racial tension is increasing, however, and in recent years there have been more race-related incidents and some downright racial clashes.

All the countries of the area are poor, but within that category there is, again, enormous variation. Barbados and Trinidad and Tobago have per capita incomes over $3000 per year, which puts them roughly in the same category as the poorer European countries, Portugal and the Soviet Union. Mexico's per capita income is over $2000 per year, similar to those of Brazil and Argentina; Mexico was long thought to be among the most successful of the newly industrializing countries, (NICs), but now that image is somewhat tarnished. Costa Rica and Panama, in the $1700 range, are nearly twice as well off as Guatemala, Jamaica, and the Dominican Republic, and more than twice as well off as Honduras and Nicaragua. Haiti, with the lowest per capita income in the region ($270), is a virtual basket case, which some believe may collapse, calling for a massive interventionist relief effort, most likely by the OAS or the United States. Table 2.1 provides basic data on all the countries of the region.

As with income, so with various indicators of social and political modernity. Haiti is marked by the absence of viable institutional structures. Cuba is a Marxist–Leninist regime led by a charismatic *caudillo*. El Salvador, Honduras, Nicaragua (now dominated by the Sandinistas), and Guatemala have few stable, well-established institutions, while Costa Rica, Mexico, and Panama have a sizable middle class and some viable political institutions (although they are quite different in the three countries) that may see them through their present

Table 2.1. Representative Country Data

	Size (Sq. Mi.)	1981 Population, Est.	1980 Per Capita GNP, Est. (US$)	1982 Literacy, Est. (%)
Antigua	108	76,000	$1000	80%
The Bahamas	5,389	249,000	3790	93
Barbados	166	256,000	3040	97
Barbuda	63	1,200	1000	80
Belize	8,867	146,000	790	80
Colombia	439,405	26,730,000	1180	82
Costa Rica	19,647	2,271,000	1730	90
Cuba	45,397	9,796,000	1360	96
Dominica	305	79,000	620	80
Dominican Republic	18,811	5,762,000	1160	68
El Salvador	8,260	4,958,000	750	63
Grenada	133	107,000	660	unknown
Guatemala	42,031	7,201,000	1080	47
Guyana	82,978	795,000	690	86
Haiti	10,711	5,099,000	270	23
Honduras	43,266	3,838,000	560	58
Jamaica	4,470	2,198,000	1040	86
Mexico	767,919	68,236,000	2090	74
Nicaragua	49,759	2,480,000	740	58
Panama	28,745	1,940,000	1730	82
St. Lucia	238	124,000	690	80
St. Vincent	150	116,000	380	95
Suriname	70,000	385,000	2130	80
Trinidad & Tobago	1,864	1,250,000	3960	92
Venezuela	352,150	14,313,000	3370	86

Sources: Jon D. Cozean, Latin America 1982 (Washington, D.C.: Stryker-Post Publications, 1982); Inter-American Development Bank, Economic and Social Progress in Latin America 1982 (Washington, D.C., 1982); National Foreign Assessment Center, The World Factbook 1981 (Washington, D.C.: U.S. Government Printing Office, 1981); World Bank, Annual Report 1982 (Washington, D.C., 1982); Hana Umlauf Lane (ed.), The World Almanac and Book of Facts, 1983 (New York: Newspaper Enterprise Association, Inc., 1983).

crises. The Dominican Republic has begun to develop democratic institutions, and Puerto Rico's present commonwealth status represents yet another special case. In general, the former Spanish colonies of the mainland and the islands continue to struggle with an older Hispanic legacy of authoritarianism, hierarchy, and patrimonialism; in contrast, the former British colonies of the Caribbean Basin retain the democratic institutions that are frequently referred to as the "Westminster model" and are among the few democratic nations left in the Third World.[3]

All the countries of the area, however, face severe economic problems that are increasingly being translated into social and political strains. The worldwide economic depression has hurt them badly, markets for their main primary products are drying up, and the twin oil shocks of the 1970s have devastated them. With the exception of Mexico and Venezuela, all are energy-deficient nations who must rely heavily on oil imports, and the sad fact for them is that it now takes two, three, four, or more times as much sugar, coffee, or bananas to buy a barrel of oil as it did only a few years ago.

Economic depression and stagnation—even in some cases contraction—are now being reflected in rising social tensions and political conflict in Central America, the Dominican Republic, Jamaica, Guyana, and Suriname and even Colombia, Mexico, and Venezuela. The economic downturn has occurred at a time of accelerated social change and of heightened expectations for a better life that the governments of the area are unable to provide. In part because of this, the increased social and political pluralism that one finds throughout the area has not produced very many happy, liberal, democratic regimes. Rather, particularly in the Hispanic countries but also in Grenada and Suriname, it has tended to provoke fragmentation, polarization, conflict, and breakdown. Indeed at the base of the political crises now destabilizing much of the region is a profound economic crisis that holds the possibility of undermining many of the democratic and developmental gains made in the Caribbean Basin in the last thirty years.[4]

Although it is not a sovereign nation, Puerto Rico merits special attention in this regard. Puerto Rico enjoys, through its commonwealth status, a "special relationship" with the United States. Yet as neither a U.S. state nor an independent republic, Puerto Rico exists in a certain kind of limbo, which many Puerto Ricans find no longer tolerable. Moreover, it has been affected by the same economic downturn plaguing other nations of the area and is increasingly being caught up in the hurricanes and crosswinds now sweeping the Caribbean. Puerto Rico is not formally a part of this study, but its problems are in some ways comparable to those of other countries here considered, and its internal problems and tensions are certain to reverberate beyond its own shores.[5]

Diversity and Common Features Within the Area

The Caribbean Basin nations that are of chief concern here are enormously diverse and complex. We do neither the area nor our policy analyses a service by lumping them all into one undifferentiated category. Each country requires separate analysis, separate understanding, and separate policy initiatives.

Nevertheless, there is also a logic behind our focusing on the region as a whole. All these nations lie close to the United States, along what has sometimes been termed "our soft underbelly," and athwart major Western trade routes. All of them (with Cuba and perhaps Nicaragua in the future the chief exceptions) are closely tied to United States and Western markets. All are diplomatically, politically, and strategically of importance to us and, to a considerable degree, dependent on us. And all are facing severe economic disruptions that are helping to produce wrenching political traumas that also affect United States foreign policy and produce strains in the Western alliance.

There are other reasons for focusing on the region as a whole as well as on its individual members. All these Caribbean Basin countries face parallel if not similar problems. All lie within what the United States has traditionally thought of as its sphere of influence, its *mare nostrum*. All fall within the same categories—"American Republics," or "Western Hemisphere" divisions—of our major foreign policymaking agencies. They come under the rubric of the Caribbean Basin Initiative, to say nothing of the OAS and other regional bodies. Moreover, they themselves are increasingly cognizant that they have a common destiny, common problems, and a certain psychological as well as geographic *place*. With the major influx of Caribbean peoples to our shores, the region as a whole has had a major impact on U.S. domestic politics and policy.

Finally, this entire area has taken on a new strategic importance for the United States, particularly as political breakdown has occurred in a number of regional states and regimes deemed hostile to the United States have come to power. The fear in the United States is strong that this area can no longer be considered "safe" for U.S. interests, that political instability in some countries of the Caribbean Basin threatens the whole area, and that such chronic instability and potentially widespread upheaval provide opportunities for American and Western adversaries. Since it is seen as a regional problem, the argument runs, there must be regional solutions, and it is up to the United States to provide them. Those reasons for focusing on the common features of the area as well as its diversity are also important.

U.S. Interests and Role Within the Area

The United States has from its beginning had an interest in the Caribbean Basin area, but it was only in the late nineteenth century that the United States acquired both important stakes in the region and the means to play a major role. That is, it was only in the last decades of the nineteenth century that the United States acquired the industrial and military might to make its presence felt throughout the region; and it was around the turn of the century—with the acquisition of the Panama Canal Zone, Puerto Rico, and the Virgin Islands, and a protectorate over Cuba—that the United States acquired major concrete bases, investments, and interests to protect.

The Caribbean Basin has frequently been viewed as both an extension of our earlier expansionist notions of Manifest Destiny, and as an area where vital U.S. interests are affected. Looking over the various nineteenth- as well as twentieth-century American schemes to incorporate, absorb, or dominate all or parts of the region, it is clear that we have always had special concerns in the Caribbean Basin. These stem not just from considerations of self-interest but also from a belief imbedded genuinely and deeply in the American psyche to bring the presumed benefits of our civilization—democracy, elections, capitalism, human rights—to our poor benighted brothers in the Caribbean. That helps explain why in that part of the world particularly, *realpolitik* has frequently been jumbled together with missionary-like political and economic evangelism. Indeed, in U.S. policy toward the area, self-interest and moralism have often been virtually inseparable.[6]

The major U.S. interests in the Caribbean Basin are strategic, political, and economic. That is, the United States is interested in keeping hostile powers out of the area, maintaining its own outposts and base networks throughout the region, maintaining stability in the countries of the area in ways that are amenable to its own interests, and maintaining access to the markets and raw materials of the area. The encouragement of democracy and social, economic, and civic progress has been viewed as part of this overall strategy, as well as an ethical "good" in its own right. These interests have remained more or less constant since the turn of the century.[7] The matter is elaborated later in the chapter and requires no further discussion here.

However, a number of questions arise regarding the U.S. role and interests in the Caribbean Basin that grow out of the changed circumstances of the present and must be raised for further discussion:

1. To what extent, with the massive migration of Caribbean Basin peoples to the United States in recent years, has the United States itself become a partly Caribbean nation, and what are the implications of this for policy?[8]
2. The United States would seem to be a declining presence throughout the area in the last decade, while the Latin American nations have become more assertive and independent. To what extent do these changes affect the U.S. role and interests throughout the Caribbean Basin?
3. New interests and issues—human rights, migration, employment, basic human needs, trade, drug traffic, debt reservicing—have recently come to the fore; to what extent have these affected or supplanted the historical basic interests noted above?
4. To what extent has the presence of other outside powers in the Caribbean—West Germany, Japan, France, Spain, Italy, the Soviet Union, the Scandinavians—as well as the rising influence of middle-level powers within the hemisphere—Argentina, Brazil, Colombia, Cuba, Mexico, Venezuela—made U.S. policy in the region more complex and difficult to implement?

These issues lie at the heart of the analyses elaborated in this study.

Some Major Themes of the Study

That the nations of the Caribbean Basin are facing severe economic and political problems, that the region is in considerable turmoil, and that this has major implications for U.S. and Western policy concerns cannot be doubted. Within this context, however, several themes require special emphasis since they run as currents throughout not only this chapter but the entire study:

1. Whereas there are certain common themes and problems in the Caribbean Basin, the area is also characterized by immense diversity. It has both similar problems and particular ones, unity as well as immense complexity.
2. A great deal of attention is given over to the theme of "crises" in the Caribbean, but the themes of continuity and "normalcy" deserve at least equal emphasis for many countries. Thus, while four or five nations of the region are presently in turmoil, nineteen or twenty of them are not—or at least not yet. Nor is turmoil an unprecedented feature of the circum-Caribbean landscape. The point is that there is as much stability and continuity in the region as there is upheaval.
3. While outside analysts may proffer solutions for the area, the peoples of the Caribbean Basin are increasingly looking toward

indigenous solutions and lesser dependence on foreign forces. How can one blend and reconcile indigenous wants with outside pressures? And can the Caribbean Basin nations find their own way out or perhaps blend these with imported solutions? Are there other hemispheric models (Brazil's developmentalist military, Venezuelan democracy, Mexico's one-party system, Cuban socialism) as well as that of the United States?

4. What policies are appropriate for the United States and the Western Allies in these changed circumstances? Do the older formulas still serve adequately as a basis for policy, or are the new realities of our own situation and that of the Caribbean Basin so changed that new formulations are required?

THE HISTORICAL DEVELOPMENT AND DIVERSITY OF THE AREA

The Caribbean Basin has long been what we may call an "imperial frontier."[9] From the sixteenth through the eighteenth centuries, the fortunes of the major European imperial powers—Spain, France, Holland, England—were also played out in the Caribbean. Every major war fought in Europe during this period had its reflection in the Caribbean Basin, as the great powers jockeyed for colonies and advantage in this strategic region. The rise and decline of Spain, the growth of Holland as a major trading nation, the emergence of France as the dominant power on the European continent, and then the emergence of Britain as the world's dominant nation can all be traced in the Caribbean Basin as well as in Europe. These powers continue to vie for influence and new outposts even in the nineteenth century, after most of Latin America had achieved independence. Despite French efforts to absorb Mexico in the 1860s and Spain's efforts both to hold on to Cuba and Puerto Rico and to reabsorb the Dominican Republic (all of which proved short-lived), by this point Britain had emerged as the dominant imperial power in the Caribbean Basin. Britain in turn began to be supplanted by the United States in the late nineteenth century and on into the twentieth century as the U.S. extended its suzerainty over the area.

Those nations in the area that achieved independence from Spain and France (the case of Haiti) in the early nineteenth century were scarcely more fortunate than those that remained under colonial rule. The internal politics of Haiti, the Dominican Republic, Mexico, and the city-states of Central America were all, from the 1820s to the 1870s, marked by chaos, divisiveness, tumult, and considerable retrogression socially and economically from what had existed under colonial rule. A number of Spain's recently independent colonies reverted to more primitive forms of barter and subsistence, there was no agreed-upon principle of legitimacy, and breakdown and decay rather than "development" were the general patterns.

By the 1870s and 1880s some order had been brought out of the prevailing chaos. The first generation of postindependence *caudillos* or men on horseback had passed from the scene, and some of the early political battles over federalism, church-state issues, and the like had been resolved. This was also a period of growing immigration, some (as yet) limited infrastructure growth (roads, ports, communications), growing foreign investment, and some rising exports of primary goods. Some political institutionalization (new government agencies, political parties, associations) also occurred, and in some countries a modicum of stability was established.

The period 1890–1930 was one of unprecedented development in the region. The population increased, armies and bureaucracies were further institutionalized, investment flowed in, and the economies of the area "took off," largely on the basis of commercialization and the export of raw materials and primary goods to the industrializing world. Four major patterns may be observed:[10]

1. Continued colonial rule in the British, French, and Dutch Caribbean, the stability of which helped stimulate investment and export-financed development.
2. Order-and-progress *caudillos* (Diaz in Mexico, Gomez in Venezuela, Heureaux in the Dominican Republic) who brought development under authoritarian auspices.
3. Oligarchic rule (Costa Rica, El Salvador, Honduras) that nevertheless brought stability and development.
4. Enforced modernization in the early twentieth century, under U.S. Army or Marine rule (Cuba, the Dominican Republic, Haiti, Nicaragua, Panama).

As growth went forward under each of these patterns, new social forces were eventually set loose: a business-commercial elite, a rising middle class, trade unions. These tensions began to be felt in the 1920s, beneath the surface appearances of prosperity and development. With the world market crash of 1929–1930, the elite-dominated systems governing in the area also came under attack.

In the meantime a significant change, already hinted at, had occurred at the international level and involving changed relations of dependence. In 1898 the United States had removed Spain from the Caribbean; at about the same time it came gradually to replace Britain as the dominant economic and military power as well. One can even trace the dates when the United States supplanted Britain as the dominant power in the region: the 1880s in Cuba, 1890s in the Dominican Republic, 1900s in Nicaragua, and 1910s and 1920s in Honduras and Guatemala. The flag, as we know, to say nothing of U.S. customs agents, chewing gum, and baseball, soon followed the dollar. By the time of World War I and on into the interwar period and beyond, although there was still some competition among the major powers, the dependency relationships of the major Caribbean Basin nations were with the United States and no longer with Spain, France, or England.[11]

The period following the world economic crash of the 1930s was politically tempestuous. In a number of societies (Cuba, Venezuela, Mexico) the middle sectors moved to replace the traditional elites and consolidate their own positions; elsewhere (Panama, El Salvador, Colombia) they lived in competition and uneasy tension with them. There were new middle-sector *caudillos* in the persons of Somoza, Trujillo, Ubico, Hernández, Gómez, and Carías; in Cuba, Guatemala, Mexico, Venezuela, and Costa Rica there were new middle class (and often populist–reformist–middle–of–the–road) political parties. But in general one can say that out of the elite-dominated societies of the pre-1930 period came a new societal equilibrium that was either dominated by the middle class or based on a condominium of elite, middle-sector, and (sometimes) emerging labor elements.

The United States had also been influential in pushing change during this period. The formation of Marine-created constabularies in such countries as the Dominican Republic and Nicaragua not only served as the avenues of advancement for dictators like Trujillo and Somoza but also helped to centralize power, to deprive the earlier regional *caudillos* in these countries of their power base, and to accelerate the rise of the *mestizo* middle class. During World War II, U.S. hegemony in the region was further increased and Germany and Britain ceased to be major influences. In the postwar period the United States helped enforce economic liberalization in the region, which also implied greater political liberalization. Often these changes (for example, the creation of centralized, "professionalized" armies as distinct from regional *caudillo*ism) were viewed as alien to the Central American/Caribbean (at least in its Hispanic parts) ways of doing things; many observers are not convinced that enforced liberalization of societies still cast in part in an authoritarian mold was an appropriate strategy. In fact, by *forcing* a false and artificial choice on the region in the post-World War II period of dictatorship versus democracy, the United States may have ruled out various intermediary positions and thereby helped precipitate the very instability it has long sought to prevent.[12]

By the late-1950s and on into the 1960s, new challenges had begun to undermine this middle sector-dominated equilibrium. The Cuban revolution was a major catalyst. But throughout the region new cracks were beginning to appear. Rivalries between and among the various middle sectors were endemic. Organized labor and peasant movements rose up to challenge the prevailing systems. Cuba and Puerto Rico felt increasingly uncomfortable with their histories of frustrated nationalism. Decolonization in the British and Dutch territories set loose new forces and new uncertainties. Revolutionary movements with Cuba as their model, often aided and abetted by outside interests, emerged to challenge the existent legitimacy. Societies began to fragment and political systems had difficulty coping.

For a time the reckoning was put off, through the sheer inertia that governs in most political systems, by living off borrowed economic and political capital, and because there were immense U.S. props and assistance. By the late 1970s these mechanisms of postponement were no longer sufficient or, in the case of foreign assistance, had largely dried up. In some countries (El Salvador) the accommodative model of the past gave way to increased repression and the sclerosis of political institutions. Almost everywhere, including the more democratic countries (Costa Rica, Venezuela, Mexico), a certain ossification had set in, along with immense corruption and/or inefficiencies. The two oil shocks of the 1970s were disastrous, along with the world economic recession that began to deepen in 1979. Rising social tension, racial conflict, violence, and civil war (in some countries) ensued.

Later in this chapter we will present a model of interpretation that shows how the stagnant or sometimes contracting economic pies of the region's nations were reflected in rising political tension and breakdown. It is in this context of crisis and breakdown that the Atlantic Council project on the Caribbean Basin was undertaken.

IMPEDIMENTS TO DEVELOPMENT

The nations of the Caribbean have not been blessed with an abundance of natural resources. Oil in Mexico and Venezuela has proved to be a mixed blessing, although—to paraphrase Sophie Tucker—being oil-rich is still better than being oil-poor. There is bauxite in Jamaica and Hispaniola, an abundance of good land in Cuba, and pockets of gold, silver, nickel, and other minerals elsewhere. But these are scarce riches, and in fact the entire area is poor in natural wealth. The area does not have the minerals—iron and coal—necessary for industrialization, nor are the small pockets of these that do exist present in juxtaposition, as they were in western Pennsylvania during the period of early U.S. industrialization. As Fidel Castro said some ten years ago in a statement he would now just as soon forget, the countries of the Caribbean Basin are so poor that revolution in them may cause only the destruction of the limited wealth that does exist, or only redistribute the poverty.

Geography and nature have been equally unkind. Both the islands and the mainland have steep mountains and mountain ranges that impede development and retard national integration. The mainland countries tend to be divided into *patrias chicas*, out of which unified nations are forged only with difficulty; the islands have rocky spinal outcroppings that often limit settlements to the coasts. Good agricultural land is in short supply, and most of it is not amenable to mechanized farming. Transportation and communications systems are often primitive, designed and built initially by the Marines or large foreign companies for the export of primary products and not necessarily to serve the broader public purpose. And, as an old geographer said, referring to the fact that none of the river systems serve the major urban areas, "The rivers all flow the wrong way."

With the obvious exceptions of Mexico, Colombia, and Venezuela—the bigger nations—none of the countries of the Caribbean Basin have large enough internal markets to be economically viable, except in a quite limited number of products. Unlike populous Brazil or Argentina, for example, most of these city-states or mini-states do not have the potential *ever* to be developed or industrialized nations. Based on their internal market size, they cannot support large-scale industry or manufacturing. It is almost un-American to say so, but realistic policymaking forces us to come to grips with the fact that for the majority of the Caribbean Basin countries, there may be no light at the end of the development tunnel. A few will continue to do modestly well on the basis of tourism, primary goods exports, and small manufacturing; but there will not likely be any developmental "miracle" countries and only a few modest success stories.

Nor did the Central American Common Market or the Caribbean Free Trade Association serve appreciably or over a sustained period to increase the size of potential markets.[13] The fact is, first, that the nations of the Caribbean Basin are competitors in the world market *with each other* for the sale of the same primary products, chiefly sugar, coffee, and bananas. Their economies do not complement each other, as was the case with the French and West German economies after World War II, which is fundamental in explaining the success of the European Common Market as compared with the limited accomplishments of the several Caribbean schemes (trade at one point reached $7 billion). Second, political differences among the countries of the area have kept the common markets from working. El Salvador and Honduras have old and historic grudges, the Spanish- and French-speaking islands of the Caribbean were never enthusiastic about joining the English-speaking part, democratic Costa Rica could not get along with Somoza's Nicaragua, Cuba was ostracized, and so forth. Economists concerned with the area have consistently lamented these political conflicts, but it may be that in thinking over any common market possibilities we should deal with such political differences realistically rather than just as "problems to be overcome."

The small size of the mini- and city-states of the Caribbean Basin has retarded development in other ways. In an excellent series of articles, Roland Ebel has argued that social organization and politics in a city-state are qualitatively different from those in a large nation-state.[14] In Central America politics tends to be highly personalistic, family-, clan-, and clique-oriented, and patrimonialist and organic. Everyone who counts knows everyone else who counts or is interrelated. The institutions appropriate for a larger polity—political parties, mass communications, elaborate and efficient bureaucracies—are not always seen as necessary in the city-state. Institutionalization has hence been retarded, and the agencies and programs created by U.S. assistance have not consistently functioned as intended.

These factors have combined to produce other impediments to development. There are widespread educational and managerial deficiencies throughout the area. Mass illiteracy is still widespread, there are critical shortages of technical and vocational schools, and the universities of the region are ill equipped to provide the leadership elites for the future. Western scholarship and fellowship programs have fallen behind. The number of trained administrators, for either the private or the public sectors, remains abysmally small, although it has risen significantly in the last twenty years in all countries of the region.

The social, economic, and income disparities throughout the area are dramatically visible to all. But perspective is necessary and the over-simplifications that find their way into our media accounts must be corrected. This is not necessarily an area of teeming masses and rich, landed oligarchs. The oligarchies of the Caribbean Basin are nowhere (except perhaps in oil-rich Mexico or Venezuela) so affluent as their American counterparts; in most countries their income and living standards are, rather, at the level of the American upper middle class. The poor are poor by any standards; they want to improve their standard of living but would generally rather be left alone by all potential proselytizers and are not necessarily clamoring for guerrilla action. The middle class, in virtually all countries of the area, has by now not only become sizable but has wrested considerable power from the old elites and now dominates many key institutions: army, church, political parties, labor union leadership, universities, bureaucracy. There are immense social gaps and maldistribution of income, but these must be comprehended in their complex and changing dimensions. Our understanding of the Caribbean Basin nations will not be enhanced if we continue to view it in simplistic, essentially pre-1930 terms.[15]

Six main economic trends in the area command our attention as helping explain the tension and crisis in which the Caribbean nations now find themselves. The first has to do with the long-term balance of international trade and it is this: since roughly the 1920s the gap in the price that these countries receive for the export of their primary goods as opposed to what they must pay to import manufactured goods has steadily widened, making them progressively worse off in comparison to the industrialized nations rather than narrowing much of the gap.[16] Some analyses even suggest that within a decade the United States may be importing *no* sugar from the Caribbean, which would have potentially devastating effects on economies like that of the Dominican Republic. A related fact is that these countries have been subjected to such severe fluctuations of prices for their single crops (whether coffee, fruit, or sugar) that their economies have been like rollercoasters; their governments have often fallen along with the price drops. Second, since approximately the early 1960s, with the emergence of large numbers of newly independent states in Africa and Asia, the nations of the Caribbean Basin have been undercut by these other countries who now produce the same agricultural crops (for example, sugar from Mozambique or Indonesia), but with labor costs that are even lower.

Third, there is a long-term agricultural crisis in the Caribbean Basin area relating not just to lower prices but also to the scarcity of arable land, depletion of soil resources, abandonment of the land, and overemphasis on manufacturing and industrialization often at the cost of agriculture. Fourth, consumer habits in the importing nations have changed dramatically. We now drink more noncoffee drinks than in the past, we have "lite" beer and diet drinks rather than sugared ones, and we use sugar substitutes in all manner of foods. As a nation we are consuming proportionately less of what the Caribbean produces than in the past. That may be beneficial for our collective and individual figures and blood pressures, but it is disastrous for the Caribbean Basin economies whose production of these commodities is largely locked in and cannot be changed quickly.

Fifth and sixth are the catastrophic oil shocks of the 1970s and the severe depression, precipitating a major debt crisis, in which the economies of the nations of the Caribbean Basin as much as our own are locked.[17] The details of these economic crises are treated elsewhere in this volume. Their social and political implications, however, merit attention here.

CHANGE AND BREAKDOWN IN THE CARIBBEAN BASIN

The argument that there is a logic and *system* of Latin American politics often comes as a shock to outside observers. The outsider's images of Latin America, largely shaped by television headlines and *New Yorker* cartoons, are of such constant revolutionary upheaval as to be comic-opera and devoid of all system.

In fact, the politics of the area is quite systematic, although less so in the underinstitutionalized countries of the Caribbean Basin than in the larger and more established polities of South America and Mexico. Moreover, the "system" that exists is quite different from that of the United States. Let us briefly examine what that system is and how it works, as well as the effects on it of the cumulative economic problems discussed above.[18]

In nineteenth-century Latin American society the three main political actors were the church, the army, and the large landowners. Power tended to be centralized, authoritarian, personalistic, patrimonialist, and vertical-corporate. But toward the end of the nineteenth century and accelerating in the twentieth, not only did the older historical groups such as the church and the army begin to change, but new groups began to demand admission to the system. These included the newer business-commercial elites, then the middle class, and eventually trade unions and peasants. Under the rules of the Latin American political game, in which both military and civilian movements could play a role, new groups could be admitted to the system,[19] but generally only under governmental and/or elite auspices and regulation. The Latin American systems gradually became more pluralistic, but this was usually a controlled, regulated, and limited form of pluralism, not the unfettered hurly-burly of American interest group pluralism. Moreover, it is to be emphasized that change could come either through electoral or nonelectoral means—that is, through civilian or military direction. In these ways the Latin American systems could both respond to and accommodate change, albeit limited, without the traditional wielders of power being destroyed in the process.

Two conditions were necessary for the admission of a new group or "power contender" into the system:[20]

1. It had to demonstrate a power capability. That is, it had to show that it was strong enough to challenge the system sufficiently that its voice had to be heard in national councils. In this fashion the business-commercial elites came to be absorbed into the system by the time of World War I, the middle class was accommodated beginning in the 1930s, and organized labor began to make its voice heard from approximately the 1950s on.
2. The group had to agree to abide by certain commonly held rules of the game. It was not permitted to destroy other groups in the system by revolutionary means. And each group had to agree to accept its place in the system and could not put forward exhorbitant demands that could not be compromised.

This system, implying evolutionary change and the gradual absorption of new groups in the political process without the old ones being destroyed or the basic structure of society being upset, worked tolerably well from roughly the turn of the century up to the 1960s. But since then the system has become more and more prone to breakdown. The question is why. What factors have accounted for the fragmentation and polarization that we see all around the Caribbean Basin? Answers to these questions go a long way toward explaining the present crisis in the region and the dilemmas involved in U.S. foreign policy toward it.

The fragmenting and polarizing factors to be emphasized here are long-term and fundamental.

1. *Failures of political power-sharing.* In Nicaragua the Somozas refused to share access to power and its spoils with anyone besides their own retinue; in Guatemala the normal course of sociopolitical development was perverted after the counterrevolution of 1954; and in El Salvador the coup of 1972 denied the strategy of gradual accommodation to new groups that had been followed in the 1950s and 1960s. It is worth noting that in all these cases it was democracy in the Latin American sense (accommodation and "power-sharing," as described in the model above) that was rudely violated, not necessarily or so importantly democracy (elections and party politics) as North Americans understand it.[21]
2. *Economic decline.* The accommodative model of Latin American politics described above is based on one big assumption: an ever-expanding economic pie. To add new groups to the system without sloughing off older ones requires more and more new pieces to hand out to these newer claimants. For a long time in the 1950s, 1960s, and on into the 1970s the Latin American econ-

omies did register impressive growth rates of 3 to 5 percent per year, but since then stagnation and even contraction have set in. One need not go beyond our own society to understand that a zero-sum or negative-sum game in the economic sphere soon gives rise politically to increasing competition, tension, even violence. In the Caribbean Basin, where because of external dependencies the world depression has been even more severe than in the Western industrialized nations, not only are there fewer economic pieces to hand out but this has undermined the legitimacy not just of the existing regime-of-the-moment but of the whole accommodative system described above, provoking sharp, even revolutionary challenges to it.

3. *Mass challenges.* The accommodative model of change worked best in a pre-1960s context where it was the business elites and the middle sectors that needed to be absorbed. These groups shared certain assumptions—i.e., a "gentlemen's" understanding of accepted, permissible behavior. But the newer groups that have risen to prominence since then—organized labor, leftist parties, peasant and guerrilla elements—do not always share these same understandings, are organized on a different basis of legitimacy, and have often explicitly rejected the earlier rules of the game. The accommodative model by which Latin America *historically* adapted to change has proved far more viable and functional in absorbing rising business and middle-sector elites than in handling the rising mass challenges of the last two decades.

4. *The United States as a destabilizing force.* Two factors here command our attention. First, through the Peace Corps, AID programs, and other stepped-up developmentalist activities in the Caribbean Basin in the 1960s, the United States helped raise popular expectations in the area far beyond the capacity of the institutions there to cope with them. Second, when we did turn our attention to institutions, we tended to emphasize those institutions (elections, political parties, apolitical trade unions, and armed forces) reflective of the U.S. polity and not necessarily functional or realistic in the Caribbean Basin context. And in the process of imposing our own institutional preferences on the area, we tended to undermine those established institutions that were functional in that context or that might have presided over some difficult transitions. As a result, we have helped produce in some Caribbean Basin countries the worst of all possible situations: rising, even revolutionary, expectations, coupled with the absence of any viable institutional framework, either traditional or mod-

ernizing, through which these countries might cope with the pressures now thrust on them.[22]

5. *Internationalization of the crisis.* The United States is not the only outside influence in the Caribbean Basin, although because of its might and power and historical role in the region it receives the most attention. The Soviet Union, Cuba, Argentina, Mexico, Venezuela, West Germany, France, and a number of Western European political parties, trade unions, and foundations have also entered the arena, as have transnational church and other groups. Not only does this make policymaking more complex but it also serves further to break down the isolation of the area, to introduce some new destabilizing influences, to involve the area in cold war struggles over which it has no control (and which frequently are of only peripheral interest or importance to the Caribbean Basin nations), and to prevent the possibility that the countries of the area could develop autonomously without outside inference.

These factors help explain not only the recent instability in some Caribbean Basin nations but the profound *systemic* crisis that they are now experiencing. The point needs to be stressed. What we are facing in the Caribbean Basin area is not just another round of coups and revolts seemingly endemic to the region. Rather, we are facing a crisis of a deeper and profounder sort that calls into question the entire developmental model on which these countries have been based since time immemorial, as well as the bases of the strategies on which U.S. assistance and foreign policy have been grounded. Since the crises in the area are so deep and so pervasive, they will not be solved by simple formulas or easy palliatives.

The systemic crisis described here helps explain the increased political tension and violence in the Caribbean Basin area and especially in Central America, the fragmentation and polarization, and the tendency toward breakdown, guerrilla movements, and civil war. That same systemic crisis helps explain the renewed search for self-identity throughout the region (including Puerto Rico) and the effort to find new or altered models of development. It also provides ample opportunity for meddling by a number of outside actors.

POLITICAL INTERACTION AMONG THE CARIBBEAN STATES

Traditionally, the Caribbean Basin nations have existed in a kind of "splendid isolation," cut off not only from the rest of the world but also from each other. Cuba, Mexico, Puerto Rico, and the Dominican Republic had long been enveloped within the orbit of the United States, and other nations of the area have experienced occupations or have been tied to the United States to a greater or lesser extent. In the main, however, the connections with the outside world have, until recently, been minimal and relations with each other almost nonexistent. There was little trade or contact among the Caribbean Basin nations, little in the way of political or diplomatic relations (except for some spectacular invasions and counterinvasions in the 1950s and early 1960s when tensions began to build, the so-called Caribbean Legion launched some armed efforts in the name of democracy to overthrow existing dictatorships, and Cuba made various efforts to export its revolution), and little interest or involvement in each other's affairs.[23] The lack of contact among the Caribbean Basin states was exemplified by the fact that phone calls between the islands had to be routed through a New York exchange; air flights followed a similarly indirect route, with Miami or New York as the major transfer points. Between the islands and the mainland of Central America there was almost no contact whatsoever. All this has very recently begun to change, with major implications for the politics and international position of the area.

Modern communications and transportation have served to break down the traditional isolation of the Caribbean Basin. The changes wrought have been sufficiently treated and need no major elaboration. Radio, television, modern roads, and jet planes have not only brought new ideas, ideologies, and projects (to say nothing of tourists) to previously isolated areas, but they have also served to bind the Caribbean Basin together in new ways and to reemphasize the interdependence of the Caribbean States with each other and with the outside world.

The Cuban Revolution served as a powerful impetus to these changes. Cuba provided not only assistance to guerrilla movements in Venezuela, Guatemala, and the Dominican Republic during an earlier era and more recently in Nicaragua and El Salvador, but it also expanded the range of developmental options available and made the issues starker and more entangled. Instead of the older (1950s and earlier), two-part struggle between the democratic reformers and the conservative defenders of the status quo, both civilian and military, now a third possibility was added: a revolutionary dictatorship that broke with the United States and allied itself with the Soviet Union. The Cuban Revolution enormously complicated not only U.S. policy in the region but also, by providing another and radical developmental option, the domestic politics of every Caribbean Basin state.[24]

In response, in large part, to the Cuban challenge, the United States moved to strengthen its already existing alliance system in the area and to promote regional economic integration. New military assistance pacts were signed with the major states of the area and U.S. military aid was greatly stepped up. These efforts served to bind the Caribbean Basin militaries to the United States—through training programs, arms transfers, provision of military parts—in ways that were not so extensive before. But in recent years military assistance has been down, the military missions (except in crises like El Salvador and Honduras) have been reduced, U.S. military influence has diminished, the military establishments of the area have begun to "shop around" for arms and equipment, and they have sought to diversify somewhat their international ties rather than relying exclusively on the United States.

The revolutionary upheavals, the rivalries, a declining U.S. presence, increasing arms purchases, and a struggle for control and dominance have also led to increasing conflict within the region and between its member states, often quite independent of U.S. strategies and initiatives. If one thinks of the Honduras–El Salvador "Soccer War" of the late-1960s, the Guyana–Venezuela border controversy, the conflict between Guatemala and Belize, the potential for conflict along the Mexico–Guatemala border, to say nothing of El Salvador's civil strife and the outside forces there, Cuba's involvement in various states of the area, and the conflicts along the Honduras–Nicaragua and Costa Rica–Nicaragua borders, there is a strong possibility of even greater interstate turmoil and tension within the region than presently exists. These conflicts have the potential of igniting a regionwide series of conflagrations and of ending the peace that has long kept Latin America, in contrast with other geographic areas, free of major international wars.[25]

The Central American Common market and the Caribbean Free Trade Association have similarly fallen on hard times. The problems are, as we have seen, political as well as economic. The fact that these are competitive rather than complementary economies is not the "stuff" of which successful common markets are made. Political differences among the member states have also kept them apart. There are, of course, some lowered tariff barriers and greater trade in some products; but the notion that these ties would help lead also to greater political and security independence among the Caribbean states has not worked out, except in limited ways and perhaps perversely in the sense of increasing the possibility that chaos and disintegration in one nation may help produce the same conditions in its neighbors.

In addition, the fact that there is no grandiose Alliance for Progress any more and U.S. assistance to the area is greatly reduced has served both to retard economic development in the area further and to give the United States fewer levers to wield. The diminished U.S. presence throughout the region—except in dramatic cases such as El Salvador and the Honduras–Nicaragua situation—has helped encourage other outside actors to enter the Caribbean Basin while also providing possibilities for the Caribbean Basin nations to diversify their trade and international connections. We shall speak to these themes in more detail later in the discussion.

The decreased presence of the United States, to say nothing of the rising sense of crisis—even panic—in some countries of the area, has increased the interconnections among the Caribbean states in ways in which the earlier Alliance for Progress or the common markets did not. There are now non-U.S.-sponsored trade missions traveling between the several nations of the region, and a variety of high-level diplomatic meetings dealing with such common problems as external debt, instability and political upheaval, and the possibilities for negotiation over Central American conflicts. Interestingly, as many of these meetings still occur in Washington—in the think tanks and other research centers—as they do in the Caribbean capitals themselves. Perhaps that is a measure that less has changed than is often thought; it also signifies the continued influence and leverage of the United States throughout the area, despite some loss of hegemony.

With a certain lessened presence of the United States (although the degree thereof and whether the trend is reversible remain topics of hot controversy) and as a reflection also of the new assertiveness, self-confidence, and independence of many of the Latin American states, a number of new regional or "middle-level" powers and power centers have emerged in the Caribbean Basin. These include Cuba, Mexico, Venezuela, and Colombia. For the English-speaking Caribbean it might include Jamaica as well; for the smaller islands, Trinidad and Tobago is often a focal point. The presence of these new middle-level powers and the more active role they are playing (for example, Mexico's and Venezuela's oil initiatives, and their efforts toward resolving the Central American conflicts) add a complex dimension not present in the Caribbean Basin before. For the United States and the Western Allies, this provides both problems and opportunities.

These and other changes discussed earlier have led the Caribbean Basin nations to begin to reassess their attitudes toward the United States. Many see the United States as a declining power, both worldwide and in the region. They reason that it is prudent, therefore, for them to reassess their historical ties to the United States and to begin to diversify their trade, political, and diplomatic relations rather than relying exclusively, or nearly so, on the United States. The thrust toward greater independence from the U.S. is reflected not only in

Cuba's, Nicaragua's, and Grenada's relations with the Soviet Union but also in the application of such countries as Venezuela, Colombia, and Costa Rica for admission to the nonaligned bloc.

On the other hand, most pragmatic Caribbean Basin leaders (including some in Cuba and Nicaragua) recognize realistically the proximity of the United States, its power (albeit somewhat fettered), as well as their dependence on the United States, particularly economically. The United States is so big and the importance of its markets, capital, and technology such that realistic Caribbean statemen come to recognize that they cannot escape from the U.S. orbit, whether they wish to or not. As pragmatists, therefore, with the rhetorical flourishes concerning "dependence," "independence," and "Third Worldism" stripped away, their questions become, how can we retain access to those all-important U.S. markets (including money markets) while also moving toward somewhat greater independence and diversity of relations? And, given the still major U.S. influence, how can we channel U.S. programs and personnel into areas that help rather than harm, while also assuring that we and not the North Americans control our own developmental strategies?[26]

The pragmatic character of the majority of Caribbean Basin leaders, and the way these questions of how to deal appropriately with the United States are raised, make it clear that there is still ample room for U.S. and Western initiatives and policy in the area. But these same questions indicate also how far our relations have come since the 1960s, when U.S. influence was powerful and the U.S. was able almost to dictate both the foreign policies of the Caribbean Basin nations and much of their domestic policy as well. The situation now, in terms of trade relations, security concerns, our need for primary resources, political alliances, and so on, is more strongly one of *interdependence* rather than the one of absolute Latin American dependence on the United States.

One final point merits discussion in this section, and that concerns the relations between the radical and traditional states of the area and whether "ideological pluralism" makes much difference. The answer is yes, but with some qualification. Cuba, Grenada, Suriname, and Nicaragua, the radical states, have by now forged some close ties on a variety of fronts and some common unifying ideological themes. These include suspicion of, fear of, and hostility toward the United States as well as hostility toward the "reactionary" regimes of the area and some assistance to those seeking to overthrow them. The radical states have also been clever in wooing the more moderate states, such as Costa Rica, Jamaica for a time, and the Dominican Republic, with the end goal of separating them somewhat from the United States.

Thus far the more traditional states of the area have not been able to present a similar united front, and their diplomatic initiatives to rally greater international support (often led by the United States) have generally floundered.

"Ideological pluralism" in the Caribbean Basin, which in some quarters has become something of a code term for Marxist–Leninist regimes (while others think chiefly of left-socialist regimes like that of Jamaica's Michael Manley) therefore does make a difference. It also potentially calls into question a key argument often advanced in policy discussions: that the United States can live with "ideological pluralism" as long as that does not translate à la Cuba into an alliance with the Soviet Union. Now, obviously there are different forms of "ideological pluralism," and it makes a major difference if one is speaking of the liberal and democratic socialism of Jorge Blanco in the Dominican Republic and Luis Monge of Costa Rica or the socialism of Fidel Castro or the Sandinistas in Nicaragua. It would be nice if the "ideological pluralism" of *Sandinismo* did not imply an alliance with the Soviet Union, and surely the economic leverage we have over Nicaragua coupled with the Soviets' apparent reluctance to assist the Nicaraguan revolution on a massive scale as it has the Cuban is cause for some lingering optimism that Nicaragua will not become a Soviet satellite.

But one cannot be sure that the Sandinista leadership thinks in terms of such U.S.-style pragmatism. Nor should one forget the frustrated nationalism, the embittered history, and the intense desire for a "place in the sun" of such states as Cuba and Nicaragua. To the United States, our policies toward Cuba or Nicaragua historically are only minor elements in a complex foreign policy that encompasses 150-odd nations. But to the Cubans or Nicaraguans, their relations with the U.S. are all-consuming, and small and often U.S.-occupied countries like these have both long memories and ample reason to be sour toward their northern neighbor. One would hope, therefore, that "ideological pluralism" could be translated, if that is their preference, into *independent* socialist regimes in Cuba and/or Nicaragua, and in the abstract that seems possible. But in the historical experience of this area, with often intense and bitter feelings toward the United States, in such small states with large inferiority complexes, a genuinely independent Marxist–Leninist regime may not prove feasible.[27] Nor it is assured that the United States would allow it to happen. The point is controversial, but it deserves serious consideration and not the pat answers one usually hears. "Ideological pluralism" sounds nice, but the concept should not be romanticized, nor should the difficulties of maintaining a genuinely *independent* socialism in a country like Nicaragua be underestimated.

THE IMPACT OF EXTERNAL ACTORS

In an earlier section we showed how modern communications and transportation have led to an erosion of the traditional isolation of the Caribbean Basin nations, to the increased presence of a variety of new actors both national and transnational, and hence to increased complexity in the international politics of the area. Let us review the lineup of these new actors as a way of providing background for the discussion that follows in other chapters.

The U.S. presence, though diminished from the 1960s, remains considerable. One must distinguish between those countries where the United States maintains "normal relations"—for example, the Dominican Republic—and those where its role is extraordinary—El Salvador, Honduras, and increasingly Costa Rica and Guatemala. In the former countries the U.S. presence in terms of personnel, AID programs, military missions, and so forth is considerably less than fifteen years ago; its leverage hence is also considerably diminished. In the latter countries recent political upheavals have led to a major, renewed U.S. presence both military and civilian, to a considerable increase in the number of U.S. personnel and programs, and to a quite heavy-handed, almost proconsular role being assumed by U.S. ambassadors. Except in these "extraordinary" cases (which we nonetheless must recognize may be becoming more the rule than the exception), the U.S. position throughout the area—politically, economically, militarily, diplomatically, intellectually—is considerably reduced from what it was two decades ago.[28]

A number of the more ideological critics of U.S. foreign policy, unable or unwilling to recognize this declining U.S. presence throughout the area, have suggested that while the political and military presence may be down in some countries, that slack has been more than compensated for by the rising presence of U.S. multinational corporations (MNCs). At least in the Caribbean Basin area, that argument does not seem to be factual. The facts are that in the past few years, even in such "success" countries as Mexico and Venezuela, U.S. private investment has plummeted dramatically;[29] one does not find the hotels of the area jammed as in the past with U.S. businessmen; rather, firms and consortia from other countries—Japan, Germany, France, Italy, Spain, and so on—are getting the contracts for the building of dams, highways, port facilities, and other construction projects. U.S. companies, rather than clamoring to exploit the area, must be induced with much persuasion to invest there and provided with guarantees, as in such major programs as the Caribbean Basin Initiative. Instead of eagerly jumping in, most MNCs have been very reluctant to get involved in the area; their question "Would you invest at present in El Salvador or Guatemala today, or even Costa Rica, Jamaica, or the Dominican Republic?" is difficult to answer affirmatively. The evidence, at least for the Caribbean, provides scant support for the idea that U.S.-based MNCs have simply replaced the U.S. government as the strongarms of our foreign policies. Indeed, the evidence is strong that U.S. firms have decreased their investments in Central America and the Caribbean recently, not increased them.

Into this partial vacuum has come a host of other actors, who are not all of one stripe and whose roles and interests differ. The Japanese presence in the area, for example, is growing, mainly in trade and commercial areas. One reason the Japanese businessmen have been so successful (along with several Western European consortia) is that they are willing to accept contract terms (joint ventures, 51-percent or higher ownership by local interests) that many U.S. firms have not been willing to accept.

Since the mid-1960s there has also been a growing West German presence in the Caribbean Basin region, with both commercial and political ends in view.[30] France, England, Spain, Italy, Benelux, and the Scandinavian countries have established a presence as well. The Spanish role is particularly interesting not just for historical reasons but because Spain would like to couple its entry into the European Community with a kind of mini-Lomé or quasi-commonwealth arrangement vis-à-vis Latin America.[31] In the cases of the other European nations, one finds a considerable mix of trade, diplomatic, and political motives. With regard to the political motives, the feeling is strong that some of the European countries have pursued a vocal and often highly moralistic stance in Central America not only because they see the issues differently but also, in part, to divert attention from domestic politics, to satisfy a left-wing constituency, and because there are no costs involved to them.

Of equal interest are the activities of a number of European political parties, labor unions, and foundations in the Caribbean Basin nations. Until recently, it was U.S. groups of this sort that enjoyed a near-monopoly in the region. That is no longer so. Christian Democratic, Socialist, and Social Democratic groups (chiefly from Germany but not enclusively so) along with the Socialist International have begun to play a major role, providing training programs for young leaders, travel grants, and scholarships. What makes these activities especially interesting is that in many cases it is difficult if not impossible to separate the strategies and programs of these groups from those of their sponsoring governments.

We have already discussed the role of such regional actors as Cuba, Mexico, Venezuela, and Colombia. Mention must also be made of such other "middle-level" hemispheric powers as Argentina, Brazil, and Canada. Argentina's clandestine and semi-surrogate role in Central America has come under strong attack in Buenos Aires. The United States would like Brazil to fill that role, but Brasilia is reluctant and wishes to pursue a more independent course, including new commercial relations with Cuba. Canada has growing interests in the Caribbean Basin, but so far it has not opted for full membership status in the OAS and its desires not to get entangled in the current storms and controversies brewing throughout the area have at least until now overridden the pressures to get more deeply involved.[32]

Other transnational agencies have also become more deeply involved in the Caribbean Basin. There are now so many that one cannot begin to do full justice to the subject matter, but a partial listing provides some indication of their range. On the business side there is the Council of the Americas and Caribbean/Central American Action; on the labor side there is the American Institute of Free Labor Development of the AFL-CIO. Religious and human rights groups have been especially effective in influencing the congressional debate. Think-tanks and university centers like the American Enterprise Institute, the School of Advanced International Studies, the Center for Strategic and International Studies, the Carnegie Endowment, the Institute for Policy Studies, the Heritage Foundation, and the Wilson Center have launched major Caribbean study groups and projects. In addition, numerous special-interest groups, associates of military officers, lobbying agencies, and the like who have plunged into the Caribbean maelstrom. Even the Atlantic Council with its Caribbean Basin Project should be considered in this sense a transnational agency.[33]

In the debate and policy struggle over Central America, the OAS has probably been underutilized, but that regional body may not be equipped to play a much larger role. The Inter-American Defense Board and related agencies have not been significantly involved. But the banks and lending agencies (World Bank, IMF, Inter-American Development Bank) have been heavily involved and their role needs to be examined. Serious questions have been raised as to whether their lending policies, specifically the austerity measures exacted from democratic governments, are appropriate or if they may not prove to be self-defeating. Questions have also been raised concerning the lending practices of the private banks, particularly since in the present crisis it is not just the loans of the big banks that seem to be somewhat at risk but those of smaller, regional and local banks as well. There are also negotiations and policies within the EEC, GATT, and the Lomé conventions that affect the Caribbean Basin nations, but for the most part these have been overwhelmed by the more immediate and pressing military/strategic crises enveloping the area. A number of these agencies are treated in greater detail in other chapters.

But it is no longer the Western and the hemispheric influences alone that are at work in the area. Twenty-five years ago those who raised the specter of Soviet military/political penetration in Latin America were soundly ridiculed, and in fact the notion of Stalinist legions expanding into the area seemed far-fetched. Today that specter, while it should not be exaggerated, should not be entirely ignored. The Soviet presence in Cuba, Grenada, Nicaragua, Guyana, and Suriname is strong and increasing; moreover, with the development of Caribbean air bases, port facilities, and a mobile marine amphibious and landing force, the Soviets now have the strategic capabilities that were entirely lacking a quarter-century back. In addition, their strategy has changed from one of almost blissful disinterest in and ignorance of the area to a much more vigorous, sophisticated, and informed policy of, largely through Cuba, aiding guerrilla elements in their efforts to overthrow existing governments, and of assisting democratic governments to increase their independence from the United States. Thus far, the Soviet activities in the Caribbean Basin have been generally limited and restrained, but neither the United States nor its Western Allies can assume such will always be the case.[34]

Other international currents coursing through the Caribbean merit brief mention here by way of introducing the area. We have spoken of the East–West struggle as it applies in the Caribbean Basin area, and former Secretary of State Alexander Haig once seemed to be arguing that this struggle might be centered there. But there is also perhaps as much of a North–South struggle in the area. Indeed, it may be worthwhile to suggest that the Caribbean Basin is one of those key world regions of conflict where the East–West conflict and the North–South division intersect, with all the potential for discord and contention those terms imply.[35]

Second (and partially obscured by the larger and more dramatic crisis in Central America), the Caribbean Basin nations have been caught up in the movement toward Third Worldism. Third Worldism includes not just the political agenda (nonalignment) and economic agenda (redistribution of the world's resources) with which we are familiar, but also incorporates important and far-reaching intellectual initiatives.[36] Among the latter are various efforts on the part of Caribbean Basin intellectuals and statesmen to divorce themselves from U.S. political and developmental models and to fashion indigenous models more attuned with their own history and traditions. This movement is only beginning in the Caribbean, and any realistic Caribbean politician knows he cannot remove himself or his nation entirely from under the U.S. umbrella. But the significance and long-term consequences of these steps ought not to be ignored.

Third are the themes of dependence, interdependence, and "diversification of dependence." Virtually all the Caribbean Basin nations depend on the United States economically, militarily, politically, and culturally. Most recognize realistically that they cannot sever those ties. But in this era of scarce natural resources, commodities, and primary products, the Caribbean Basin nations see a means by which they can reduce some of their ties of dependence in favor of a more complex and favorable (to them) situation of interdependence vis-à-vis the United States. They would also like to "diversify their dependence" by expanding their trade and other relations with Japan, Western Europe, the Soviet Union and Eastern Europe, perhaps China, the Middle East, Africa, and even other Latin American nations. These steps need not be viewed with hostility by the United States. They reflect, in fact, some quite prudent and realistic steps by the Caribbean Basin nations. Resistance to such initiatives on our part is not likely to be very useful and in fact may be counterproductive. A sounder strategy might encompass adjustment, accommodation, and understanding, combined with a sense of realism as to how far such steps can go in "our backyard" and with a clear idea also of how our own interests can at the same time be served.

In short, the presence of all these new international actors in the Caribbean Basin, national and transnational, has added a complexity to the international politics of the area that did not exist before. Its epitaph has been written before, but with the existence of all these outside forces in the Caribbean and the inability of the United States to effectively remove them or keep them out (even if it wished to do so), perhaps the Monroe Doctrine, as some have argued, is indeed finally dead. It may be recalled that the Monroe Doctrine sought to keep out not only all outside forces but also all outside ideologies. Given the still immense power of the United States in this part of the world and its apparent continued willingness to wield its influence in countries like El Salvador and Nicaragua, it is hard to believe that the Monroe Doctrine is entirely moribund. But it certainly requires rethinking and amendment if it is to survive at all, the first step of which surely requires a realistic assessment of the new international actors present in the Caribbean Basin.

GOALS, INTERESTS, AND PERCEPTIONS OF THE CARIBBEAN STATES IN THE PRESENT CONTEXT

The goals, interests, and perceptions of the Caribbean Basin states in the present context may be summarized briefly since they are quite clear and unambiguous and a number of these have already been discussed. Our concern is not only to list these goals of the Caribbean nations but also to examine preliminarily how and where they are in accord with, or diverge from, the goals and interests of the United States and the Western allies. In outline form, then, the goals of the Caribbean nations are as follows:

1. *Regime viability.* Any regime in the Caribbean area must, in the present circumstances of international upheaval and internal challenges to established ways, pay attention first and foremost to its own survival. The stability of the government in power cannot be taken for granted, as observers from the outside and particularly Western aid administrators are prone to do. Hence the first-order concern, before any public policies can be carried out, must be for securing the government's own power base. That often involves relations with the military, patronage concerns, wholesale bureaucratic reshufflings that are often downright exasperating, if not incomprehensible, to foreign analysts. In short, the private house must be put in order before the public one receives attention.

2. *Sovereignty and territorial integrity.* Ordinarily this factor would have a lower priority, but in the present context of border disputes (Venezuela-Guyana), disputed claims to sovereignty (Belize), armed interventions (Honduras–Nicaragua), efforts at subversion of existing governments (El Salvador, Guatemala), and multiple outside interventions or fears thereof, it must be listed at or near the top. These matters are often frustrating to foreign aid administrators, private economic interests, and lending agency representatives who would rather get on with what they see as the "normal" business of development; however, they are crucial to the Caribbean Basin nations since they involve such fundamental issues as the very existence and integrity of each nation. If leaders in these nations ignore these factors, their own tenure in office (another "first-order" priority) may be quite short.

3. *Economic development and social progress.* Next to maintaining sovereignty, territorial integrity, and its own survival, economic and social development must be among the highest policy priorities of any Caribbean Basin government. This priority, too, is not necessarily or always in accord with U.S. interests that tend to focus heavily on strategic considerations.

4. *Democracy and human rights.* The Caribbean Basin countries want genuinely to have democracy and human rights (as distinct from only paying lip service to these goals), and they wish to have

these in accord with universal criteria and understandings of these terms. But some of their leaders also want that understanding that democracy does not always work well in their context, that sometimes, in emergency situations, democracy and human rights must be suspended. They further wish it were better understood in the United States and the West that democracy and human rights in their countries often imply different meanings, emphases, and institutional arrangements than in the United States and Western Europe. Again, there is considerable room for divergence from U.S. criteria.

5. *Trade, commerce, investments, and markets.* In the international sphere, these may be the highest-order priority of the Caribbean Basin states. Access to U.S. markets, capital, and technology is essential for the very survival of these nations. Such interests run up against the growing pressures of protectionism in the United States, and also against a continuing preoccupation in the U.S. with grand political designs (the East–West struggle, for example), which most Caribbean leaders view as tangential to their main interests. Again, interests and priorities may diverge.

6. *Security, stability, and order.* Caribbean leaders see very clearly the need to resolve what Jeane Kirkpatrick once called the "Hobbes problem" in Central America: the need for order, authority, and legitimacy.[37] They are quite aware of the dangers of outside intervention, as well as of the wrenching, centrifugal forces within their own societies. Generally, however, they would much prefer that, with the proper assistance, they be left to deal with these problems in their own way. Heavy-handed military intervention by outside nations, the subordination of local ways of doing things to some presumably greater war effort, or a foreign ambassador exercising essentially proconsular roles (thus at times supplanting their own president or prime minister) is not acceptable.

7. *A place in the sun.* These small nations have long histories of frustration and a strong sense of inferiority. They wish to be treated not as "banana republics" but with some measure of dignity and respect. They want to see their accomplishments, however modest, recognized, and they insist that they know best how to solve their own problems.

8. *Independence.* The Caribbean Basin nations recognize their dependence on the United States, and most leaders of the region understand and have come to grips with that fact. By diversifying their trade and international connections, however, they seek not to break relations and contacts with the U.S.—an entirely unrealistic step—but to expand their opportunities and to reduce if

only slightly and/or psychologically the uncomfortable reality that they are "sardines" that can at any time be gobbled up by the giant "shark" to the north.[38]

9. *Alternative routes to development.* The era when the United States could dictate the developmental model its neighbors must take, or when the U.S. political and economic system was *the* system to emulate or even inevitably follow (as much of the development literature of the 1960s put it), is fading. Rather than importing U.S. institutions and models that are inappropriate in their own circumstances, Caribbean leaders are increasingly looking to indigenous as well as to other outside models, and seeking to fashion their own route to development. Or they are seeking a more propitious blend between imported institutions and their own local practices. They expect some understanding of these efforts and empathy from the outside. Indeed the fashioning and institutionalization of such indigenous developmental models is likely to be the next great innovative step, in the Caribbean as in other areas of the Third World, and in the social sciences.[39]

GOALS, INTERESTS, AND PERCEPTIONS OF THE NORTHERN, WESTERN, AND INDUSTRIALIZED COUNTRIES – AND OF REGIONAL AND GLOBAL INSTITUTIONS

These goals are stated in summary fashion since they are largely familiar. One of the key purposes is to see the degree to which the goals, interests, and perceptions of the Northern, Western, and industrialized countries are compatible among themselves, and with the Caribbean Basin nations.

United States

U.S. goals, interests, and perceptions toward the Caribbean historically may be summarized as follows:

1. *Security interests:* guarding of our "southern flank," securing access to sealanes, maintaining bases and listening posts, preventing foreign powers from gaining a foothold, securing borders.
2. *Economic interests:* maintaining access to the markets, raw materials, and labor supplies of the area.
3. *Political interests:* maintaining stability in ways that are compatible with our interests, including allowing for change that is not radical or gets out of hand.

4. *Economic development and social progress:* assisting modernization both as a good in itself and because it contributes to 1, 2, and 3.
5. *Democracy and human rights:* emphasizing democratic development and human rights; in times of crisis this interest is often
   subordinated to 1, 2, and 3.

In thinking about U.S. goals, interests, and perceptions in the Caribbean Basin, several questions come to mind. The first has to do with
the traditional sense of superiority, smugness, condescension, and lack
of empathy and understanding toward the Caribbean nations and
peoples that is so deeply ingrained in the American psyche. In this era
of rising Caribbean nationalism and independence, are such attitudes
appropriate and functional, and can they be changed?[40]
Second, what about Puerto Rico and the status question? Many analysts are concluding that Puerto Rico is a potential time bomb for the
United States. What can and should be done with the Puerto Rico
issue at this stage?
Third, as the United States itself has become something of a Caribbean country, what will be the impact of such a large number of
Hispanic-Americans and Caribbean-Americans, with a rising political
consciousness, on our policies toward their native countries? A series
of related questions may be asked with regard to black Americans and
their growing interest in Caribbean affairs. The case of Haiti and Haitian refugees comes quickly to mind.
Fourth, to what extent have the historical and traditional goals of
U.S. policy in the Caribbean Basin as noted above been supplanted by
new goals and interests: human rights, immigration issues, drug traffic, illegal aliens, debt questions, the potential for massive instabilities
on our doorstep, basic human needs concerns, population policy, jobs
and protectionism, foreign labor supplies, and pressures on schools
and social services? How do these new concerns affect American
"bedrock" interests, are they compatible with them, and, if not, what
can give?
Fifth, given our own economic cutbacks, what can be expected in the
way of new aid packages and military assistance programs? Surveys
of public opinion (and, by reflection, of the U.S. Congress) indicate
there will be no grandiose assistance programs as in the 1960s;[41] if that
is so, what levers does the United States have to help shape Caribbean
developments?
Sixth, looking at the Central American imbroglio, as well as the
domestic debate and media coverage of Central American events in the
immediate past years, many seasoned foreign policy observers have
strong doubts that the United States can successfully carry out *any*

rational, sustained policy in the region. When that is combined with our economic difficulties, the lack of funds or public support to carry out any but the most modest of foreign aid programs, our inefficiencies and incapacities both civilian and military, our internal divisiveness, and our lack of will, serious questions must be asked concerning our capacity and ability to fashion and implement any major new Caribbean policy. Recognizing these constraints need not force us into what General Andrew Goodpaster neatly calls the "doctrine of preemptive concession,"[42] but it does, one hopes, introduce some realism into the discussion.

Finally, we must ask how and where and to what degree U.S. goals, interests, and perceptions are compatible with those of the Caribbean Basin states listed earlier. Several glaring contradictions, worthy of further discussion, are immediately apparent. First, U.S. attitudes of condescension, arrogance, superiority, and ethnocentrism are incompatible with the Caribbean desire for respect, dignity, a place in the sun, and a freedom to pursue their own institutional and developmental models. Second, the U.S. emphasis on stability may not be compatible with the Caribbean desire for accelerated change. Third, we seem to be concentrating still on grand political and strategic designs when the Caribbean desire is for trade, trade, and more trade. Fourth, our efforts to resurrect the much buffeted inter-American defense arrangements, and our attempts again to envelop the Caribbean within our sphere of influence may be at cross-purposes with their own efforts to reduce their dependency and diversify their international connections. And fifth, while we continue to talk of U.S. policy *toward* the Caribbean Basin, of their dependence on us, the real situation at present seems to be a more complex one implying far greater *interdependence* than in the past. For example, it is a little-known fact that our trade with the Third World is now greater than that with Western Europe and Japan combined, and that within the Third World category Latin America is by far our major commercial partner.[43]

These questions are difficult and serious; they are addressed in more detail in the chapters that follow. Raising them here serves the purpose of forcing us to begin thinking about what kind of U.S. policies toward the Caribbean one can reasonably expect.

Western Europe, Canada, and Japan

The increasing presence of the other Western, democratic, and industrialized countries in the Caribbean Basin area has already been discussed. For the most part their interests and those of the United States are compatible. That is, they also have an interest in stability and order, economic and social progress, regional security, democracy and human rights, trade, commerce, and investment.

But there are differences with the United States as well. First it is probably fair to say that the interests of Western Europe, Canada, and Japan are concentrated heavily in the trade, commerce, and investment areas, and less so on the strategic and security issues. These differing concerns have to do, obviously, with the fact the Caribbean lies right on the southern border of the United States but considerably distant from these other nations. Nonetheless, it is worth noting that the concentration of the other Western, democratic, and industrialized nations in the trade and commercial area may be closer to what the Caribbean nations want than is the case of the United States.

Second, the foreign policy interests of the other Western democracies with regard to the Caribbean are in some areas at variance with those of the United States. In part this reflects genuinely different perceptions and readings of the situation in the area; an ethnocentrism on the part of these other Western countries that is at least as pronounced as that of the United States; a response on the part of these governments to domestic political pressures; and the luxury not available to the United States of being able to stake out bold initiatives in this foreign policy area without having to pay the price or suffer the responsibilities of their pronouncements.

But there are also sufficiently strong common bonds and interests concerning the Caribbean Basin between *all* the Western industrialized democracies that a more coherent and unified approach might be pursued. Nor should the United States necessarily view the growing presence of these countries in the Caribbean with suspicion and hostility. If the United States is itself a declining presence throughout the area, one can think of far worse scenarios than to have West Germany, France, Spain, Japan, and some other countries fill part of the void. There is evidence that is already happening. A greater European, Japanese, and now Israeli presence will clearly make U.S. policymaking with regard to the area more complicated, but there are useful or potentially useful aspects to these new relationships as well that seem worth exploring.

The Role of Regional and Global Institutions

The United States would generally prefer to work through regional institutions (such as the OAS, the IADB, the Pan American Health Organization, and the Economic Commission for Latin America), which historically at least and to a considerable extent today it can still control, than through global institutions such as the United Nations, where the United States is now a lonely minority. When there are disputes in the region, the first inclination of the United States is to act unilaterally; where that is not feasible or where there is a desire to provide multilateral legitimacy to a unilateral action, the usual advice is to "go OAS." The U.N., in contrast, is often viewed by the U.S. as an interloper in hemispheric affairs, although because of its Third World majorities, some Caribbean Basin states on some issues would equally clearly prefer to "go U.N."[44]

The issue of regional versus global deliberative bodies as sounding boards and conflict-solvers is complicated by several factors. The first is the split within the regional agencies chiefly between the English- and Spanish-speaking countries. The dispute was apparent in the conflict between England and Argentina over the Falklands/Malvinas; it also surfaces in the desire of the small English-speaking countries of the Caribbean to have Canada assume full OAS membership, as a North American counterpoint to the United States and as a kind of "big brother" for the other English-speaking countries. As yet, the English-speaking countries within the OAS have not been fully integrated into the organization, which makes that regional body less effective than it might be.[45]

Second, there is the issue for the United States of a global versus a regional foreign policy, or a "special relationship" with Latin America. Historically there has always been a "special relationship" with Latin America for reasons of history, geography, religion, politics, and culture, but under President Carter that concept was abandoned in favor of a "global" policy and bilateral relations. Obviously there is room for both a global and a regional approach, depending on the issue and the context. A number of the larger countries of South America prefer, in at least some areas, bilateral relations with the United States. But among the smaller states of the Caribbean Basin, a regional forum is often preferred, since in a bilateral negotiation with the U.S. they are woefully at a disadvantage. Clearly a balance between a global and a regional approach would be most useful, but at present that implies efforts to reforge the special relationship as well as a restrengthening of regional bodies like the OAS.

The North–South dialogue, third, also impinges on the regional/ global issue. Since Cancún, there has been little forward motion of the North–South dialogue. In part this is due to U.S. reluctance to resume what is often regarded not as a dialogue but a catalogue of Third World demands. It has also to do in part with discussions within the U.S. government about where the dialogue should take place (GATT, U.N., OAS, or some specialized agency), what issues should be discussed, and how binding the decisions should be.[46]

For their part, the states of the Caribbean Basin are not of one mind on these issues either. Naturally, and in the abstract, the Caribbean nations are sympathetic to and could be expected to champion Third World positions. At the same time some Caribbean states such as Mexico, Cuba, or Venezuela think of themselves as *leaders* of the Third World and not just one among many. The problem is further complicated by the situations of Cuba and Nicaragua, who, if they were to be invited to some North-South forum, could be expected to use the opportunity to castigate the United States rather than for much real dialogue. Finally, having said all this, it must also be stated that most Caribbean Basin nations are rather tepid followers of Third Worldism because as pragmatists they recognize that ideological posturing goes only so far and that in the long run they must deal realistically with the United States.

Fourth, the debt question has posed a major (if not the single major) concern of many Caribbean nations. They must rely on agencies like the World Bank, the IMF, and the IADB, but they would very much like to give themselves a stronger voice in the deliberations and policies of these bodies. And whether global or regional, they believe that their proximity to the United States should afford them special treatment by the lending agencies. The debt question is so crucial that it must now enter into any discussion of appropriate U.S. and Western policy toward the Caribbean Basin.

In all these areas, whether speaking of the goals and interests of the Caribbean Basin nations, those of the United States and its Western allies, or the roles of the regional and global institutions, there are many areas of conflict, discord, and disagreement. But there are also, as made clear in the analysis, opportunities for discussion, dialogue, compromise, and accommodation. This overview should help provide some guidelines for understanding the areas of conflict as well as suggesting where there is room for accommodation.

GROPING TOWARD POLICY

Specific recommendations for U.S. policy are contained in Chapter 1 (the Policy Paper); here let us only summarize the discussion and suggest some general guidelines for policy.

First, it is necessary to reiterate the diversity, as well as the common problems, of the Caribbean Basin. For some purposes this area may be treated as a single unit, for others no. What works in some countries may not work in others. There are immense differences of history, culture, geography, language, politics, society, and economics. There are certain common themes and problems that, with appropriate qualification and nuance, apply to all or most countries of the area; however, it is clear that for policy to be effective, individual and country-specific programs must be fashioned. No one policy blanket will be appropriate for the entire area. The beginning of wisdom in a policy sense is to recognize both the common features and problems of the area and the intense individuality of each case.

Second, we must recognize the nature of the crisis in the Caribbean. It is long-term and systemic, not short-term and easily resolvable. No one U.S. administration can solve this longer-term crisis; a generation or more of a coherent, rational sustained policy will be required. Easy palliatives and panaceas will not do; patience and persistence may. At the same time, we should not overstate the severity of the crisis or assume that its effects are everywhere the same. Most countries in the area are doing reasonably well given the present circumstances; others are limping along but with few prospects of imminent breakdown. Only three or four countries have reached an advanced state of disintegration, commanding dramatic headlines. The crises in these nations are obviously troublesome, but we should be careful neither to understate nor to overstate the severity of the Caribbean situation.

Third, we must come to grips with the new realities of the area. These have to do with the changed, considerably lessened, presence of the United States throughout the area and, at the same time, the fact that we have become something of a Caribbean nation and, to some degree, dependent on that area. The new realities also include changes within the Caribbean Basin nations: their desire for greater independence, their desire to diversify their trade and international connections, the growing assertiveness of some of the nations of the area, their collective and individual desires for achievement and recognition, their Third Worldism, their efforts to fashion indigenous institutions rather than slavishly imitating imported ones, and the accelerated social changes and rising pressures within their own populations. The new realities include the presence of a variety of new outside actors in the area: the Soviet Union, Western Europe, Japan, the middle-level powers of the Western Hemisphere, and a variety of private groups and agencies that may be termed transnationals.

All these "new realities" present both problems and opportunities for U.S. policy and the policies of the Western Allies. They undoubtedly make the situation far more complex than was the case thirty years ago. In addition, they make it far more difficult for the United States to carry out policy. And they certainly raise the specter of failure as well as the possibilities for success.

A useful, albeit simplistic, caveat might be that when faced with new realities, policy also must be reassessed realistically. Simply railing against these new realities and wishing they would go away will not suffice. U.S. policy and that of its Western Allies must adjust to the new *facts* visible throughout the Caribbean Basin nations. We must adjust to our own, generally lessened presence and weaker position throughout the area. We must adjust to the new European presence and that of the other middle-level powers in the area, rather than viewing these consistently as threats. We must take account of the new Soviet presence in the area (and the Cuban one), which is no longer a phantom threat but increasingly real. And perhaps most importantly, we must adjust to the changed realities of the Caribbean Basin nations themselves and their growing assertiveness, independence, and desire for change.

In another paper I have suggested what might be termed a "prudence model of United States-Latin American policy."[47] That stance, the details of which cannot be provided here, implies neither benign neglect on the part of the United States nor what might be called heavy-handed proconsular interventionism. The prudence model is posited on realism rather than romance and wishful thinking in our foreign policy assessments, on restraint and the recognition of limits on what the United States can and cannot accomplish in the area, and on greater empathy and understanding of the Caribbean Basin nations and some unaccustomed deference and modesty on our part that we "know best for them." Nevertheless, it still sees a leadership and catalytic role for the United States primarily in the economic sphere, a renewed "special relationship" with Latin America, and political and strategic leadership that is restrained rather than arrogant and overbearing. These are all happy phrases that obviously need to be fleshed out and to come up against the hard realities of tough policy choices in individual cases. But such a "prudence model" may well serve as a starting point for the discussion.

NOTES

1. Thomas P. Anderson, *Politics in Central America* (New York: Praeger, 1982), as well as the thoughtful review of that book by Don Oberdorfer in the *Washington Post* (June 27, 1982). My own analysis of these problems of empathy and understanding in dealing with Latin America is contained in Howard J. Wiarda (ed.), *Politics and Social Change in Latin America: The Distinct Tradition*, 2nd rev. ed. (Amherst: University of Massachusetts Press, 1982); also see my *United States and Latin America* (Washington, D.C., American Enterprise Institute for Public Policy Research, 1983).

2. Some of the better studies include Richard Millett and Marvin Will (eds.), *The Restless Caribbean: Changing Patterns of International Relations* (New York: Praeger, 1979); H. Michael Erisman and John D. Martz (eds.), *Colossus Challenged: The Struggle for Caribbean Influence* (Boulder, Colo.: Westview Press, 1982); and Richard Feinberg (ed.), *Central America: International Dimensions of the Crisis* (New York: Holmes and Meier, 1982). For a consideration of some of the conceptual problems in interpreting Central America, see Howard J. Wiarda, "The Central American Crisis: A Framework for Understanding," AEI *Foreign Policy and Defense Review* 4, 2 (1982):2-7, as well as Wiarda (ed.), *Rift and Revolution: The Crisis in Central America* (Washington, D.C.: American Enterprise Institute, 1983).

3. Vaughn A. Lewis, "Political Change and Crisis in the English-Speaking Caribbean," paper presented at the Conference on the Caribbean, University of Pittsburgh, October 1982; see also the forthcoming volume edited by Myron Weiner and Ergun Ozbudun, *Elections in Developing Countries*, especially Weiner's introduction.

4. Gary Wynia, "The Economics of the Central American Crisis," in Howard J. Wiarda (ed.), *Rift and Revolution*.

5. Puerto Rico has been the subject of a number of recent conferences and special reports by several Washington-based research centers, including the American Enterprise Institute, the Wilson Center, and the Carnegie Endowment.

6. See two volumes by Lester Langley, *Struggle for the American Mediterranean, 1776-1904* and *The United States and the Caribbean in the Twentieth Century* (Athens: University of Georgia Press, 1976, 1980); see also Howard J. Wiarda (ed.), *The Continuing Struggle for Democracy in Latin America* (Boulder, Colo.: Westview Press, 1980), especially the introduction, "Is Latin America Democratic—And Does It Want to Be?"

7. Howard J. Wiarda, "The United States and Latin America: Change and Continuity," in Alan Adelman and Reid Reading (eds.), *Stability/Instability in the Caribbean* (Pittsburgh: University of Pittsburgh Press, 1983).

8. Jorge I. Domínguez, *U.S. Interests and Policies in the Caribbean and Central America* (Washington, D.C.: American Enterprise Institute, 1982).

9. Eric Williams, *Capitalism and Slavery* (New York: Russell, 1961); Juan Bosch, *El Caribe: Frontera Imperial* (Madrid: Alfaguara, 1970).

10. The developmental patterns are traced in Howard J. Wiarda and Harvey F. Kline, *Latin American Politics and Development* (Boston: Houghton Mifflin, 1979).

11. Howard J. Wiarda and Michael J. Kryzanek, *The Dominican Republic: A Caribbean Crucible* (Boulder, Colo.: Westview Press, 1982).

12. Wiarda, *Continuing Struggle for Democracy*; and Michael Grow, *The Good Neighbor Policy and Authoritarianism in Paraguay: Economic Expansion and Great Power Rivalry in Latin America During World War II* (Lawrence: University of Kansas Press, 1981). A more general article, by Grow and Wiarda, on this theme is forthcoming.

13. For an overview, see Stuart I. Fagan, *Central American Economic Integration: The Politics of Unequal Benefits* (Berkeley: University of California Institute of International Studies, 1970).

14. Roland Ebel, "Governing the City State: Notes on the Politics of the Small Latin American Countries," *Journal of Inter-American Studies* 14 (August 1972):325-346; "Political Instability in Central America," *Current History* (February 1982):56ff.; "The Development and Decline of the Central American City State," in Wiarda (ed.), *Rift and Revolution*.

15. These changes are treated in detail and on a country-by-country basis in Wiarda and Kline, *Latin American Politics and Development*.

16. The evidence is thoroughly presented by Raul Prebisch and in a series of reports issued by the United Nations' Economic Commission for Latin America (ECLA).

17. Inter-American Development Bank, *Economic and Social Progress in Latin America: The External Sector* (Washington, D.C., 1982).

18. The analysis is elaborated in Howard J. Wiarda, *Corporatism and National Development in Latin America* (Boulder, Colo.: Westview Press, 1981); and Wiarda and Kline, *Latin American Politics and Development*, esp. Chapter 7.

19. Howard J. Wiarda, *Critical Elections and Critical Coups: State, Society and the Military in the Processes of Latin American Development* (Athens: Ohio University Center for International Studies, 1979).

20. The analysis follows that of Charles W. Anderson, *Politics and Economic Change in Latin America* (New York: Van Nostrand, 1967).

21. For the different perceptions of democracy in the two parts of the Americas, see Howard J. Wiarda, "Democracy and Human Rights in Latin America: Toward a New Conceptualization," *Orbis* 22 (Spring 1978):137-160; and Wiarda, *The Continuing Struggle*.

22. The arguments are spelled out in greater detail in Wiarda, *Politics and Social Change*.

23. Charles D. Ameringer, *The Democratic Left in Exile: The Anti-Dictatorial Struggle in the Caribbean, 1945-59* (Miami: University of Miami Press, 1974).

24. Howard J. Wiarda, "Cuba," in Ben G. Burnett and Kenneth F. Johnson (eds.), *Political Forces in Latin America* (Belmont, Calif. Wadsworth, 1971), pp. 171-197.

25. Mark Falcoff, "Arms and Politics Revisited: Latin America as a Military and Strategic Theater," paper prepared for AEI's Public Policy Week panel on "The Crisis in Latin America," December 6-9, 1982; forthcoming in 1984.

26. For a treatment of one such effort by a Caribbean state, see Howard J. Wiarda, "The Politics of Population Policy in the Dominican Republic," in Terry L. McCoy (ed.), *The Dynamics of Population Policy in Latin America* (Cambridge Mass.: Ballinger, 1974), pp. 293-322.

27. Mark Falcoff has written provocatively on this theme in his "Arms and Politics," and also in "How to Think About Cuba," *The Washington Quarterly* 6 (Spring 1983).

28. This point is generally conceded by policy analysts; the debate has centered on what to do about it.

29. Mauricio García, "The Impact of Petrodollars on the Economy and the Public Sector of Venezuela," paper presented at the Tenth National Meeting of the Latin American Studies Association, Washington, D.C., March 4, 1982.

30. Wolf Grabendorff, "The United States and Western Europe: Competition or Cooperation in Latin America," *International Affairs* (Autumn 1982):625-637.

31. The Center for Hemispheric Studies at AEI, under a grant from the Tinker Foundation, is doing a book-length study of Iberian-Latin American relations.

32. J.C.M. Ogelsby, *Gringos from the Far North: Essays in the History of Canadian-Latin American Relations* (Toronto: Macmillian of Canada, 1976).

33. For a general treatment, see Robert O. Keohane and Joseph S. Nye, Jr. (eds.), *Transnational Relations and International Politics* (Cambridge, Mass.: Harvard University Press, 1972).

34. Jiri Valenta, "The USSR, Cuba, and the Crisis in Central America, *Orbis* (Fall 1981):715-746.

35. The theme is elaborated in a major AEI research project on "American Vital Interests in Regions of Conflict," directed by Samuel P. Huntington and Brent Scowcroft.

36. For a discussion, see Howard J. Wiarda, "After Cancún: The United States and the Developing World," *PS XV* (Winter 1982):40–48.

37. Jeane Kirkpatrick, "The Hobbes Problem: Order, Authority, and Legitimacy in Central America," *AEI Public Policy Papers* (Washington, D.C., AEI, 1981).

38. The imagery is that of Juan José Arévalo, *The Shark and the Sardines* (New York: L. Stuart, 1961).

39. Howard J. Wiarda, "The Ethnocentrism of the Social Sciences: Implications for Research and Policy," *The Review of Politics* 43 (April 1981):163-167; and Wiarda, "Toward a Non-Ethnocentric Theory of Development: Alternative Conceptions from the Third World," paper presented at the Annual Meeting of the American Political Science Association, New York, September 3–6, 1981, also published in *Dados: Revista de Ciencias Sociais* [Brazil] 25, 2 (1982):229–252, and in *Journal of Developing Areas* (July 1983).

40. The issue is addressed more fully in my congressional testimony, "The United States and Latin America in the Aftermath of the Falklands/Malvinas Crisis," in *Latin America and the United States after the Falklands/Malvinas Crisis*, Hearings before the Subcommittee on Inter-American Affairs of the Committee on Foreign Affairs, House of Representatives, Ninety-Seventh Congress, Second Session, July 20 and August 5, 1982 (Washington, D.C.: Government Printing Office, 1982).

41. John E. Reilly, "The American Mood: A foreign Policy of Self-Interest," *Foreign Policy*, No. 34 (Spring, 1979) 74-86.

42. As communicated to the Atlantic Council Working Group on Western Interests and U.S. Policy Options in the Caribbean.

43. The "new realities" of the Caribbean Basin and Latin America more generally, and their implications for United States policy, are elaborated in Howard J. Wiarda, "Conceptual and Political Dimensions of the Crisis in U.S.-Latin American Relations: Toward a New Policy Formulation," paper presented for AEI's Public Policy Week panel on "The Crisis in Latin America," December 6–9, 1982; forthcoming in 1984.

44. Jerome Slater, *The OAS and United States Foreign Policy* (Columbus: Ohio State University Press, 1967). See also Gary Holten, *The UN and the OAS in the Dominican Republic Crisis: A Case Study of Globalism vs. Regionalism in Peace Keeping and Political Settlement* (Ph.D. dissertation, University of Massachusetts, Amherst, Department of Political Science, 1972).

45. Alejandro Orfila, "The Future of Inter-American Relations," presentation made at AEI, Washington, D.C., November 22, 1982.

46. See the discussion in Wiarda, "Cáncun and After."

47. Wiarda, "Conceptual and Political Dimensions."

Chapter 3

U.S. Policy Issues in the Caribbean Basin in the 1980s: Economic, Social, and Political Aspects

David Scott Palmer

A short paper on as vast a topic as U.S. policy concerns among a region comprising twenty-six independent countries from six major historical-cultural traditions in the areas of economic, social, and political issues can do little more than scratch the surface. A number of approaches might usefully be employed to cut into the subject. The one used here begins with consideration of the context within which U.S. policy evolves or is developed. It then moves to a brief elaboration of the major issues that U.S. policy must address in the social, political, and economic arenas in order to maintain or enhance Western interests in the region. Finally, it considers the major policy alternatives for the U.S. to accomplish its objectives: the "hegemonic," the "collaborative," and the "damage limitation."

THE CONTEXT FOR U.S. POLICY

As I have noted elsewhere, "U.S. foreign policy ... is closely related to four distinct but interacting elements: (1) overarching national interests, (2) the institutions responsible for foreign policy,

(3) underlying national norms and values, and (4) objective realities in the countries and region with which the policy is concerned."[1] By considering each element in turn, we can gain a clearer sense of both the multiple constraints that affect how foreign policy is formulated and carried out and of the specific elements that shape that policy toward a particular problem or part of the world.

Overarching National Interests

In terms of the most fundamental national interests of the United States, none is more important than survival. To this end, great attention is focused on activities and areas from which threats to that survival could be forthcoming, most particularly measures involving defense directed against the Soviet Union. The network of economic and military relationships between the Western European allies and the United States is a basic component of these activities, as are those with other friendly countries and allies in close geographical proximity to the USSR.

Since no such direct and immediate threats have emanated from the Caribbean Basin since the Cuban Missile Crisis of 1962, U.S. relations with the region tend to focus on less vital though still important aspects of our national interests. These include efforts to obtain a dynamic political equilibrium and economic growth in the countries of the region as means of protecting and enhancing the U.S. political and economic system. The major implication for U.S. policy in the region resulting from the absence of grave, immediate threats is the relegating of U.S. relations with the countries of the Caribbean Basin, except Mexico, to a secondary priority, compared to relations with Europe, the Middle East, and the Far East.[2]

The second-level priority accorded the region manifests itself in a number of ways. For example, the U.S. has provided relatively low levels of military assistance to Latin America, including the Caribbean Basin, in the post-World War II period—about $4 billion of some $100 billion provided worldwide.[3] The lower priority also results from the small size of the region compared to the U.S. by almost any imaginable definition. As one illustration, in terms of 1980 gross domestic product, the United States is almost ten times larger ($2.6 trillion)[4] than the rest of the Caribbean Basin countries combined ($282.6 billion, of which Mexico alone accounts for $167.3 billion).[5] To give another example, of approximately $216 billion in U.S. foreign investment worldwide in 1981, less than 10 percent was in the countries of the Caribbean Basin ($17.9 billion, of which $13.8 billion or 77 percent, is concentrated in just six countries—Mexico, Panama, the Bahamas, Venezuela, Colombia, and

Trinidad and Tobago).[6] Concerning trade, U.S. foreign trade is more than four times the total trade of all the other Caribbean Basin countries, and less than 10 percent is with its neighbors in the region (and 76 percent of this is with Mexico, Venezuela, and Trinidad and Tobago).[7]

Such dramatic assymetry in size and disproportionate distribution of U.S. private foreign investment and trade outside the region inevitably focus U.S. public- and private-sector attention elsewhere and relegate the area to a lower-priority status. This is not to say that U.S. interests in the region are insubstantial. As Jorge and Virginia Dominguez have pointed out, they include military security (as a border area), seaborne commerce (65 percent of U.S. maritime commerce), strategic imports (about 50 percent of U.S. bauxite imports and 80 percent of U.S. oil imports transited the Caribbean in 1981), trade (some $21.3 billion in imports from Caribbean Basin countries in 1980, and $24.2 billion in exports to them), and investment.[8] U.S. security concerns have been heightened by Cuba's presence in the Caribbean Basin, with its close relationship with the USSR, and stepped-up Cuban support for guerrilla movements in the region since 1979.

Institutions Responsible for Foreign Policy

Since Graham Allison's groundbreaking study on the bureaucratic politics approach to explaining U.S. foreign policy,[9] analysts and practitioners alike have tended to concentrate on the multiplicity of agencies, organizations, and institutions responsible for formulating and implementing that policy, and on the implications flowing therefrom. The key insight provided by this approach is that policy is the product of multiple interests and concerns, both institutional and individual, and not necessarily a rational response based on the objective appraisal of the national interest concerning a specific issue or problem.

Even though ultimate responsibility for foreign policy rests with the President and the Secretary of State, as a practical matter much is delegated to various agencies and bureaus of the Executive Branch, from the National Security Council (NSC) and special advisors on the White House staff, to the regional and functional bureaus of the State and Defense departments, to other departments such as Commerce, Treasury, and Agriculture, or agencies such as the FBI, CIA, Agency for International Development (AID), Drug Enforcement Agency (DEA), United States Information Service (USIS), and Immigration and Naturalization Service (INS). Furthermore, Congress, in exercise of its constitutional responsibilities for oversight, budget authorizations and appropriations, confirmation of executive appointments, and treaty ratification, also is in a position to play a significant role in foreign policy and frequently does so. Even the judicial system gets involved in the foreign policy process, from antitrust suits for monopolizing foreign trade (e.g., the United Fruit Company in Central America in 1954) to release orders for detained illegal migrants (e.g., Haitians in Florida in 1982).

To complicate matters still further, the nongovernmental sector may also play a significant role in the formulation and implementation of foreign policy. Interest groups or lobbies try to persuade members of Congress or the bureaucracy that their view should prevail on some specific proposal. Many, from churches to corporations, also work directly in the country or region to advance their cause or concerns.

Given this multiplicity of institutions and actors in the foreign policy process, it should not surprise anyone, even its presumed beneficiaries, that the results are invariably complex, often contradictory, and rarely completely coherent. As a result, it probably doesn't make very much sense to speak of *a* foreign policy at all, except at the highest and most abstract level. Multiple actors and institutions normally produce multiple policies, often in tension or even in opposition with one another. Only in times of great crisis can the usual procedures, prerogatives, and protections be short-circuited to produce something quite uniform and complete.

The Caribbean Basin is no less subject to this interplay of U.S. foreign policy actors, public and private, and to the results normally stemming therefrom. In fact, the region may even be more the focus of multiple policies independently formulated precisely because it is not usually viewed as a first-priority foreign policy area. To illustrate the point that many actors are involved, at a recent conference on the Caribbean no fewer than forty-six different U.S. organizations and agencies were represented, public, private, and mixed; federal, state, and local.[10] All have particular interests and concerns, and the task of coordinating them into any single overall approach is immense.

Several components of the long-evolving Caribbean Basin Initiative (CBI) were very controversial, particularly those relating to trade and investment incentives, largely because different actors saw their interests adversely affected by their provisions. Organized labor fears the export of jobs, local units of government fear the continued influx of illegal migrants, Puerto Rico and the U.S. Virgin Islands want guarantees, domestic manufacturers fear unfair competition. Stalemate resulted, delays dampened the extremely high initial expectations and raised frustrations. The eventual product, substantially modified and without the investment incentives provision, was considerably less responsive to the identified needs for which the original proposal was designed.

Even policy responses to problems identified as high-priority and directly related to security issues, as in El Salvador and Guatemala, have been less coherent and complete than one would have expected from a Republican administration that places a premium on the struggle against the spread of Communism in the hemisphere.[11] Congressional subcommittees, church organizations, and academic bodies expressed their concern for human rights violations. Secretary of State Alexander Haig may have focused too much attention on the insurgency in El Salvador early in the Reagan administration, provoking unfavorable reactions both inside and outside government. Sensitive intelligence on covert activities against Nicaragua was leaked to the press in late 1982, presumably by sources opposed to that approach. These leaks forced into the open a broad-scale debate on U.S. policies and goals in the region which had the effect of modifying aspects of those policies. Certainly we cannot attribute all policy adjustments to the interplay of bureaucratic politics by concerned public and private organizations and individuals (after all, intelligent policymakers do change their minds about the best policies to pursue in the face of experience and new information). However, this interplay is important and sometimes vital to understanding why policies evolve in a particular way.

Underlying Norms and Values

The underlying norms and values of the U.S. public play an important role in shaping the country's foreign policy, even though these norms and values are somewhat diffuse and ill defined, and to a certain degree in tension with one another. Historical experience, however, has amply demonstrated that a foreign policy that strays too far from them will likely founder. These norms and values include support for democratic practices, anti-communism, favorable attitudes regarding private enterprise and initiative, and a strong orientation toward domestic issues.[12] One major point of tension occurs when policies against communism simultaneously support dictatorships, or undermine existing democracies. Another relates more generally to foreign policy initiatives that have or are perceived to have adverse implications for domestic concerns. U.S. public opinion is focused primarily on the daily issues that revolve around home, community, and the workplace for numerous historical reasons that have to do with the relative independence of the nation over the years from "foreign entanglements."[13] Few nations have had such a luxury; however, one of the prices paid is a "mass" public with little interest or sophistication in foreign policy matters. Often, therefore, the only way to "sell" a particular foreign policy is to persuade people that it is to their advantage for domestic reasons.

One of the great advantages of recent policies and proposals toward the Caribbean Basin is that, in broad outlines at least, they are consonant with most of these key public norms and values. Counterinsurgency support activities in El Salvador and Guatemala find support on anti-communist grounds, but are in tension with human rights concerns and a general desire to keep the U.S. from military entanglements. "Covert" actions against the established government in Nicaragua also evoke a very mixed popular response for the same reasons. The public and private assistance elements of the Caribbean Basin Initiative drew positive public responses in their support for democracy and private enterprise. But the domestic costs of the trade and investment incentive components were sufficiently controversial to force substantial adjustments in the former and at least temporary abandonment of the latter. Critics greatly exaggerated the cost, and discounted the direct and indirect benefits, including the potential for stemming migration flows through the expansion of local economic opportunities.[14] What policymakers learned through the experience of working to secure passage of the Panama Canal treaties was that popular support increased as the public became more aware of the issues involved and better informed about them. It was not fortuitous that a similar approach to the Caribbean Basin Initiative was followed by such nongovernmental organizations as Caribbean/Central American Action and the Caribbean Council.

The close relationship between foreign policy and domestic issues is also illustrated in the range of interactions with Mexico, particularly in the areas of trade, capital flows, migration, drug smuggling, and energy. While one can agree in the abstract that mutually beneficial policies can be evolved, in practice each area is fraught with negative policy implications for particular U.S. domestic interests.

Objective Realities in the Region

The Caribbean Basin is a study in contrasts. It includes both the largest economy in the world (the United States) and some of the smallest (Dominica, St. Vincent, and Antigua). Economic growth rates over the past decade very dramatically, from a 7.5 percent average in the Dominican Republic to −0.6 percent in Jamaica.[15] In Haiti, over 70 percent of the population is engaged in agriculture, while in the U.S. the figure is about 3 percent (yet there are almost twice as many farmers in the U.S.—6.9 million—as in Haiti—3.8 million).[16] Resource bases also vary widely, from relatively large and important (Venezuela and Trinidad and Tobago) to large and diverse (Mexico, the U.S., and Colombia), to small and limited (Haiti, Jamaica, Guyana, Belize, Suriname, and most of the Caribbean islands).

Most countries are politically stable democracies of one form or another (such as Mexico, the U.S., Costa Rica, Colombia, Venezuela, and most of the English-speaking Caribbean), but some are quite unstable (e.g., Guatemala and Suriname) or not very democratic (e.g., Guyana and Haiti). The number of independent countries in the region has proliferated: in 1950 there were thirteen; in 1983, twenty-six, with still more to come over the next few years. Some entities are still tied to "mother countries," such as the Dutch Antilles, Guadeloupe, Martinique, and French Guiana, Puerto Rico, and a number of small islands.

Countries range in size from 9.4 million square kilometers (km²) (the U.S.) to 280 (Antigua), and in population, from 230 million (the U.S.) to 76,000 (Antigua).[17] Population growth rates are as low as 0.3 percent per annum in Barbados up to 2.8 percent in the Bahamas; and density, from 574 per km² in Barbados to 2 in Suriname.[18] Several nations have quite homogeneous populations (e.g., Colombia, Haiti, Barbados, Venezuela, and El Salvador), while others are quite diverse (e.g., Guatemala, Suriname, Guyana, Trinidad and Tobago, the U.S., and Mexico). Infant mortality rates range from 149 per thousand live births in Haiti and 117 in Honduras to 9 in Mexico.[19] Guyana has only one physician for every 7350 people, while Cuba has one for each 650 (and the U.S., one for each 622).[20] Some 78 percent of Venezuela's population is urban as compared to 32 percent in Guatemala.[21]

While comparisons could be extended indefinitely, these illustrations from the economic, political, and social areas make clear the diversity of the region. A major policy implication of such diversity is that approaches developed to deal with the multiple issues in the region must be complex and multifaceted if they are to have any chance of success. A specific policy urgently needed in some countries will be irrelevant or counterproductive in others. Furthermore, the small size of many countries in the region means that what is perceived as a rather modest policy initiative in a larger contributing country's view can make a major contribution toward solving what from the smaller beneficiaries' perspectives are large problems indeed.

History is another element of the objective realities of the region. Between 1895 and 1961, U.S. policy toward the region and its various countries was set by and large by U.S. priorities and on a timetable set in Washington. As Secretary of State Richard Olney put it in 1895, "The U.S. is practically sovereign in this Hemisphere, and its fiat is law upon the subjects to which it confines its interposition."[22] At least thirty-five direct interventions by U.S. military forces occurred between 1895 and 1933, some lasting several years.[23] By 1929, almost two-thirds of all U.S. direct private investment in Latin America was

concentrated in the Caribbean Basin, some $2.3 billion in all.[24] Wit'ı
the onset of World War II, U.S. activities expanded considerably .n
the region, and included the occupation of several colonies in the Caribbean whose mother governments had been taken over by the Axis.
U.S. domination in the region outside of the European colonies remained largely unquestioned throughout the 1950s.

For a variety of reasons, however, since the failure of the United
States to secure its objective in the Bay of Pigs invasion of 1961,
U.S.–Caribbean Basin relations have been marked increasingly by
what Abraham Lowenthal has called "a loss of hegemony."[25] Some nations in the region are more assertively pursuing their own interests;
some nations outside the region, both friendly and unfriendly to the
U.S., are doing the same within it. Historical colonial power relationships by U.S. allies, Great Britain and Holland, are ending, thus expanding considerably the scope of U.S. concerns in the area. One result
is that it has become increasingly difficult for the U.S. to accomplish
its objectives in the region unilaterally, even on those infrequent occasions when they are pursued diligently and with a high priority (e.g.,
Nicaragua in 1979).

The Utility of Setting Modest Policy Goals
in the Caribbean

Given the second-level priority concern by most public and private
U.S. actors, the nature of the U.S. foreign policy process and this
changing historical context within which U.S. policies are pursued in
the region, the country's goals in the Caribbean Basin are probably
best defined in fairly modest terms. First of all, the United States cannot expect to pursue successfully its policy objectives unilaterally. The
U.S. government needs to work with its allies outside the region, the
governments within it, and with international agencies to promote and
maintain political, social, and economic stability. Such stability is not
defined in static terms, but rather as a dynamic equilibrium within
which change and growth occurs. A multilateral approach in a regional
context of diversity implies a variety of political and economic institutional responses rather than a single "made in U.S.A." mold. Such
variety is not necessarily inimical to U.S. interests.

Secondly, in spite of the strong tendencies by some country leaders
in the area to pursue national development goals by whatever means
they deem appropriate, the U.S. must work to encourage their attainment in a mode that is congruent with U.S. public and private sectors
rather than conflicting or hostile. For in spite of the changes that have
occurred over the past twenty years which make it more difficult

for the U.S. to ensure that its will is effectively carried out in the region, this country remains the most important single actor. The U.S. is still the largest investor in most countries, as well as being the most important trading partner and the most important source of economic assistance, public and private.[26] The resulting economic and political influence is substantial. In principle, therefore, it should be possible for the U.S. to accomplish modest foreign policy objectives in the Caribbean Basin, particularly if they are carried out in a cooperative and multilateral mode with respect to diversity.

Given this context, the major economic goal would be to maintain or secure economic growth and economic development. In the social arena, it would be to keep social mobilization, defined as the incorporation of a country's citizens into the national social system through migration, education, and participation in organizations,[27] within reasonable boundaries. The key political goal would be to foster stable and responsive indigenous systems with reasonable capacities to deal effectively with national problems.

On the assumption that these goals are beneficial both to U.S. and Western interests and to those of the other countries in the region, what are the major issues affecting the attainment or the maintenance of such policy objectives? It is to a consideration of these major issues that we now turn.

THE MAJOR ISSUES FOR U.S. POLICY IN THE CARIBBEAN BASIN

For most countries of the Caribbean Basin, economic issues relate to the basic constraints of small size and small resource endowments, along with the governments' desires to stimulate growth and development. Growth, in turn, depends in large measure on trade and investment for all but the largest countries in the region. Among the most important economic issues are slow, unbalanced, or dependent growth; few new employment opportunities; high imported energy requirements; limited investment opportunities; unfavorable trade balances; large foreign debts and heavy repayment requirements; and low world market prices for most products the region produces.

Economic Issues

Low Rates of Economic Growth. For most countries of the Caribbean Basin, economic growth rates for the decade of the 1970s were lower than for the 1960s. Only Colombia, Trinidad and Tobago, the Dominican Republic, and Haiti countered this trend and only in Guatemala did growth remain at about the same level for both decades.[28] Various factors explain this downward trend for different countries, including political turmoil (Nicaragua, El Salvador) and government policies (Jamaica). However, the single most important one was the sharp increase in oil prices beginning in 1973. Only Venezuela, Mexico, and Trinidad and Tobago among the Caribbean Basin countries, net oil exporters, were able to benefit substantially from this price increase; only Colombia, largely self-sufficient, was not adversely affected to any great degree.

Even so, per capita growth rate averages for the decade equaled or exceeded the U.S. rate of 2 percent for about half the countries of the region. All the larger economies except Venezuela were above the 2-percent average, as were Costa Rica, Guatemala, Panama, the Bahamas, Belize, the Dominican Republic, Haiti, and Suriname.[29] These averages over one or two decades suggest that only a few of the smallest nations in the Caribbean Basin appear to have endemic economic growth problems. However, the most recent world recession buffeted the entire region in 1981 and 1982, and prospects for 1983 and 1984 for most countries are not optimistic.

Unbalanced Growth. The historic dependence of many countries in the region on a single or limited number of exports or services to generate foreign exchange and stimulate growth continues, a function of small size and limited resource base. Although in some cases countries have become more diversified economically over the past decade, they have not overcome their dependence. In 1981, eight of twenty-five, or 32 percent of the Caribbean Basin countries, had single products comprising more than half their exports, including Colombia—coffee, 60 percent; Trinidad and Tobago—oil, 95 percent; Venezuela—oil, 94 percent; El Salvador—coffee, 61 percent; Jamaica—alumina, 53 percent; the Bahamas—oil, 96 percent; Dominica—bananas, 70 percent; and Cuba—sugar, 80 percent.[30] This compares with seven of sixteen, or 44 percent, a decade earlier.[31]

The problem seems to be more one of a general lack of complementarity of the economies of many of the countries of the region; in other words, many tend to produce the same things. The leading export of seven Caribbean Basin countries in 1981 was coffee; of five, petroleum or petroleum products; of three, alumina or bauxite; and of two, sugar. Thus many compete in third markets rather than sell extensively to each other.

Dependent Growth. A continuing problem for most countries in the region, also due to size and resource limitations, is that the sale or use of goods and services produced or available depends to a large degree on factors beyond the countries's borders and thus beyond their direct control. For example, many Caribbean Basin countries depend heavily on tourism, but bad weather, international economic conditions, terrorism, or political turmoil can result in sudden drops in visitors and revenues. Taking exports as a percent of gross domestic product can also suggest the degree of dependence on products destined for foreign markets. With this measure, only the U.S. (8.5 percent), the Bahamas (9.2 percent), and Mexico (9.7 percent) are low. Other countries for which data are available range from 12.2 percent (Panama), 15.8 percent (Haiti), and 16.9 percent (Dominican Republic), to 63.0 percent (Guyana) and 95.9 percent (Trinidad and Tobago), with the median figure 28.6 percent[32] While tourist receipts generally continued to grow in Basin countries during the late 1970s (totaling $13.6 billion in 1975), there were important exceptions. Receipts in Mexico fell from over $2 billion in 1975 to only $800 million in 1976; in Jamaica tourist receipts fell from $129 million in 1975 to $104 million in 1977, and rose to $148 million in 1978.[33]

Relatively Few Employment Opportunities. For a number of reasons, the shift in employment away from agriculture has exacerbated the long-standing unemployment problem in many countries of the area. Some alternatives, as in industry and mining, tend to be capital-intensive and the service sector, particularly tourism, has not been able to absorb much surplus labor. Hence unemployment ranges from 9 percent in Barbados to 27.4 percent in Jamaica,[34] and underemployment estimates run in some countries as high as 50 percent of the economically active population. This inability of the local economies to absorb large segments of the population into the work force is a major stimulus to seasonal, temporary, and permanent migration.

Need to Import Energy to Meet Domestic Needs. Only five independent countries of the Caribbean Basin are either largely energy self sufficient or net exporters—Venezuela, Mexico, Trinidad and Tobago, Guatemala, and Colombia. All the others depend either heavily or totally on imported energy to meet their needs, with the United States by far the largest importer in volume. A few countries, like Costa Rica and El Salvador, have substantial domestic hydroelectric capacity, and Barbados has substantial proven oil reserves. Venezuela and Mexico have responded to the oil import needs of most Caribbean countries by providing for those needs on concessional terms, thereby saving the importers about 30 percent of the world market price. Even with this substantial saving, however, energy costs are high and companies with high energy requirements are reluctant to establish themselves in such countries. Furthermore, foreign exchange needs increased substantially to meet the costs of imported oil, even at the special price. Some relief will be available for oil-importing countries as long as world oil prices continue to be subject to downward pressure.

Limited or Unattractive Investment Opportunities. Total new private direct investment in Latin America has been growing again for several years, from $1.54 billion in 1976 to over $5.9 billion in 1981.[35] However, very small portions of this total have gone to the smaller countries of the Caribbean Basin. Outside of Mexico ($1.14 billion), Trinidad and Tobago ($211 million), Colombia ($209 million), and Venezuela ($160 million), only $264 million (4.5 percent of the total) was invested in 1981 in the rest of the region.[36] This compares with $101 million for the same countries in 1976, or 6.6 percent of total investment that year.[37]

Regular or Sustained Unfavorable Trade Balances. The current account balance for Latin America as a whole has worsened steadily and substantially over the past five years (from −$11.1 billion in 1976 to −$35.8 billion in 1981).[38] The balances of the Caribbean Basin countries taken together have worsened at a slightly more rapid rate (from 35.6 percent of the total to 36.4 percent).[39] If only the smaller countries of the region are considered (excluding Mexico, Venezuela, Colombia, and Trinidad and Tobago), the rate of deterioration of their current account balances is slightly less rapid (from 10.8 percent of the total in 1976 to 10.3 percent in 1981).[40] The implications for the smaller countries may be more serious, however, because of their size and less diversified economies.

To meet the continuing trade deficits and to maintain or generate growth and development, governments resort to foreign borrowing. While such borrowing solves some problems, the increased foreign debt creates others.

Large Foreign Debts Relative to Resource Capacity and Heavy Repayment Requirements Relative to Income. While the total outstanding external public debt for all of Latin America has increased by 4.3 times, from $37.1 billion in 1973 to $159.6 billion in 1980, that for the Caribbean Basin countries has increased slightly more rapidly, from $15.7 billion to $73.0 billion, or 4.7 times.[41] The foreign indebtedness of the smaller Caribbean Basin countries (leaving out Colombia, Mexico, Trinidad and Tobago, and Venezuela) has increased from $3.6 billion to $15.5 billion, or at the same rate as Latin America as a whole. The ratio of debt service to exports has also increased for most countries in the Caribbean Basin, from a median of 6.0 percent in 1973 to 12.2 percent in 1980.[42] Furthermore, whereas only one Caribbean Basin country had an external debt to GNP ratio above 40 percent in 1973 (Guyana, with 56.6 percent), four countries exceeded that in 1980 (Guyana, 93.3 percent; Nicaragua, 71.9 percent; Panama, 71.3 percent; and Jamaica, 54.1 percent).[43] For several countries, over 40 percent of their debt matures within five years—Venezuela (67.4 percent), Mexico (58.8 percent), Trinidad and Tobago (55.7 percent), Jamaica (50.7 percent), the Bahamas (47.7 percent), Panama (44.8 percent), and Costa Rica (47.7 percent).[44]

At this juncture, however, the larger countries of the region, like Mexico and Venezuela, are having as much difficulty in meeting their repayment obligations as such smaller countries as Costa Rica and Jamaica. Those countries with upcoming debt-service payments that are most substantial in terms of recent export earnings also include Mexico and Venezuela and not the smaller countries. While repayment will be onerous for many, particularly if prices for their exports remain low, they seem to be manageable in most cases with some rescheduling.

Falling or Low World Market Prices. Most predictions for the primary goods world market prices produced by the Caribbean Basin countries are quite pessimistic. Prices for sugar, bananas, coffee, and bauxite all were lower at the end of 1981 than they had been at any time in the preceding eighteen months.[45] The overall price index for principal basic agricultural export products declined by 18.6 percent in 1981 from 1980, those for basic mining export products, by 14.8 percent, and forecasts for the next year or two are not encouraging.[46] Even though the composition of exports of most Caribbean Basin economies has become more diversified over the past ten years, declining or flat prices for their traditional primary products makes it harder to earn the foreign exchange income necessary to pay off debts and secure needed imported goods and services.

Dramatic Increase of Foreign Debt to Private Banks. For Latin America as a whole, the financing of the substantial external gap (imports — exports) has come increasingly from private rather than public sources. Bilateral and multilateral official resources declined from 62.2 percent in 1961 to 13.4 percent in 1980.[47] Of total external financing of $22.1 billion in 1980, over $19.1 billion came from private sources and only about $3 billion from official ones.[48] For the Caribbean Basin, the sharp increase in the portion of the external debt with maturity under five years from 1970 to 1980 suggests the degree to which that region follows the general trend for Latin America as a whole. In the Caribbean Basin, only El Salvador, Guatemala, and Nicaragua have succeeded in reducing the portion of the foreign debt maturing within five years.

The major implications of private as compared with public or international institutional lending include shorter-term and higher interest rates, particularly at a time when the London Interstate Bank Offering Rate (LIBOR) is high. This puts some countries, like Mexico (58.8 percent of 1980 debt with less than five-year maturity), Costa Rica (42.7 percent), and Jamaica (50.7 percent) in particularly difficult situations. Although different circumstances obtain, Venezuela (62.4 percent), Panama (44.8 percent), and the Dominican Republic (37.5 percent) will also have some difficulty.[49]

This summary presentation of the major economic issues in the Caribbean Basin indicates that most countries are experiencing difficulties of one kind or another. The fact that those with the most economic problems at present include some of the larger and more important countries, Mexico and Venezuela in particular, suggests that limited size and resource capacity are not the only important factors influencing economic performance. With relatively few grievous economic situations, and those for quite different reasons, special and selective measures for particular cases rather than general approaches are probably indicated. One exception would be in the area of employment creation, which is almost a universal problem. Many countries appear to have taken measures already to deal with economic difficulties, particularly in the areas of economic diversification and foreign debt management. Their prospects for successfully resolving their economic problems are mixed and uncertain.

Social Issues

The major social issues in the Caribbean Basin are tied closely to long-standing historical realities, including patterns of settlement, the capitalistic and extractive nature of the colonial enterprise, and migration flows. They are also closely related to economic concerns, particularly the limited alternatives that exist in the smaller countries and the difficulties of generating both growth and distribution in the larger. They include ethnic and racial tension, the rapid breaking down of traditional relationships, population pressures, class conflict, and crime. To the degree that some governments have been either unable or unwilling to deal constructively with social issues, they have a close political connection as well.

Ethnic or Racial Tension and Rivalry. For historical reasons related to labor force import policies of the colonial powers, some countries of the Caribbean Basin are quite diverse in their social makeup. These include, in particular, Suriname (37 percent Hindustani, 31 percent Creole, 15 percent Japanese, 10 percent Bush Negro, 10 percent other); Guyana (51 percent East Indian, 43 percent Negro, 6 percent other); Trinidad and Tobago (43 percent Negro, 40 percent East Indian, 14 percent mixed, 3 percent other); and Guatemala (58.6 percent *mestizo*, 41.4 percent Indian).[50] In all but the latter, educational opportunities are generally available, which means that ethnicity does not join with class to produce a uniformly poor ethnic group in the society. But backgrounds and socialization patterns remain distinct and are often played out politically as well as socially.

Rapid Social Mobilization. One of the products of the communications revolution of the past forty years, combined with economic growth and conscious government policies, is that most people are now aware of the world beyond their family and their community. Many want to participate in that new world, and increasing numbers are doing so. In the Caribbean Basin as a whole, education levels and urbanization have increased dramatically. Between 1960 and 1977, for example, literacy increased from 65 to 81 percent in Mexico, from 15 to 23 percent in Haiti, and from 45 to 60 percent in Honduras. Between 1960 and 1980 the urban population grew from 30 to 51 percent of the total population in the Dominican Republic, from 48 to 70 percent in Colombia, and from 51 to 67 percent in Mexico.[51] The major implication for society is that once people become a part of it they do not expect to go back to more traditional modes. This means they will be expecting things from society and will begin to make demands on it. Once society has incorporated them, then, it must continue to respond to their needs. Failure to do so may foster social unrest and undermine the legitimacy of existing political and economic institutions.

Given the communications revolution, however, it may also foster migration, which then becomes both a problem and a solution for the countries involved. Migration losses include not only the economically disadvantaged, but also those individuals with skills important for economic growth. While migration of unemployable workers represents a solution of sorts to the losing country, it presents the gaining country with resettlement problems. On the other hand, the loss of skilled workers and professionals who seek better opportunities in another country represents a major loss to the country of origin and a windfall to the gaining country. This ebb and flow of people within the Caribbean and between the Caribbean and outside countries has long characterized regional societies. There is little reason to expect these patterns to change in the short or even medium run.

Population Growth. Increasing populations can be expected as health facilities and sanitation measures improve. Infant mortality rates have declined substantially in the region over the past thirty years. Between 1971 and 1978, for example, infant death per thousand births declined from 63 to 41 in Mexico, from 37 to 24 in Panama, and from 27 to 16 in Jamaica. Total population has increased rapidly as a result. Nicaragua is an exception to this trend: after declining from 45 to 23 infant deaths per thousand births between 1971 and 1976, the infant mortality rate increased to 121 in 1979 and 102 in 1980.[52]

With the exception of most of the islands and El Salvador, the Caribbean Basin countries have substantial areas still outside the effective national territory where new settlement could take place. But few families in modern society wish to become the frontierspeople of years gone by even if governments offer substantial rural settlement incentives. Instead, most prefer the city and aspire to modern amenities and conveniences. The problem for many Caribbean countries is one of distribution rather than of numbers. But in open political systems, forced settlement is not an option. Migration is.

Class Tension and Rivalry. The Caribbean Basin includes some countries in which the gap between rich and poor is quite narrow, as in many of the former Dutch and English colonies. In Haiti and most Spanish-speaking countries, however, the differences are great. By income groups, the bottom 20 percent of households in Mexico divide 2.9 percent of national income; the top 20 percent receive 58 percent. In Trinidad and Tobago, the bottom 20 percent of the population receives 4.2 percent of national income; the top 20 percent of the population divides 50 percent of national income. In Suriname, the poorest 20 percent receives 11 percent of national income; the wealthiest 20 percent, 42 percent.[53]

In several countries the gap between rich and poor appears to be increasing, even in the face of fairly substantial economic growth. Some economists argue that increasing inequality in income distribution is to be expected at the middle stages of economic development, in which most Caribbean Basin countries now find themselves. But because growing elements of the adversely affected sectors of the populations are unwilling to be sacrificed for future generations, the eventual onset of more equitable income distribution is small solace to politicians and key decisionmakers. Conscious efforts at reform—as in Panama, Honduras, El Salvador, and Mexico—have not been very successful to date for a number of reasons, including obstructionism from those in the most privileged positions. One result, as in El Salvador, is an increase in class tension and open violence, both anomic and organized.

Crime, Violence, and Illegal Activities. While the fabric of existing society has held throughout the region, with the exception of Nicaragua due to very special circumstances and the partial exception of El Salvador, it is challenged in a number of countries by sharp increases in criminal activity, from theft to assault to drug smuggling. In some countries, as Mexico, Venezuela, and Jamaica, such activities are primarily illegal profit-making ventures; in others, including Guatemala, El Salvador, and Honduras, the criminal activity has distinct political overtones (Colombia has a good deal of both). This makes the challenge to existing institutions more serious in the latter countries and more likely, if not brought under control, to further weaken the social fabric.

As in the economic arena, the depth and seriousness of major social issues vary markedly among countries and for different reasons. Some countries have severe ethnic and class conflicts that revolve primarily around distributive issues. In others, groups and individuals exploit social issues for political advantage, including the goal of replacement through organized violence of the present social system. In most, however, the very real problems are the result of economic and social change and continue to be handled within the framework of existing national structures, norms, and values.

One problem area, that of drug smuggling, has only indirect consequences in the societies in which it takes place and is much more serious for the United States as the ultimate destination. Another, migration, actually represents a solution of sorts, both for societies with little physical space to accommodate population increases and for others in which it is easier to allow people to leave than to be forced to find jobs for them or open up frontiers for them. But since only two countries, the United States and Venezuela, are the destination of most migrants, what is a solution for twenty-four Caribbean nations is a substantial problem for these other two (except for those small groups of skilled or talented people).

Political Issues

A key to understanding the political issues of the Caribbean Basin is the diversity in political systems within the region. Parts of the area are still under the control of a colonial power, others as ocean-separated parts of a country. One country is a family dynasty, another a one-party capitalist democracy, yet another a one-party socialist democracy, along with several multiparty democracies, several governments with a strong military presence, and several two-party democracies in various states of repair. Policies suitable for one are counterproductive in another. Possibilities for regionwide cooperation are made considerably more difficult with such diversity. But in virtually every case, the countries' future viability depends in large measure on their ability, individually or collectively, to deal with the range of social and economic issues that must be confronted.

Diversity of Political Systems. Of the twenty-six independent countries in the region, several different political systems are present, but the vast majority are democratic in form. This includes all of the former English colonies except Grenada and Guyana; the larger countries of Mexico, Colombia, and Venezuela; and the smaller Spanish-speaking republics of Costa Rica and the Dominican Republic. Honduras has just returned to civilian rule after a ten-year hiatus; both Panama and El Salvador are in the process of doing so, even though the process in El Salvador is infinitely more complicated by a full-scale civil war. Guatemala and Suriname are the only full military regimes left in the region at present, and Haiti is the only family dictatorship. The remaining governments—those of Cuba, Nicaragua, and Grenada—are socialist or socialist-leaning in orientation. So while diversity of regime does prevail in the Caribbean Basin, twenty-one of the twenty-six are "Western" democratic in form, or are in the process of trying to become so.

Uncertain Stability of Democratic Political Systems. Even though a substantial majority of the political systems of the Caribbean Basin are democratic in form, a number of problems beset them. Costa Rica, Mexico, and Venezuela are undergoing the most severe economic crisis in their modern history, and the Dominican Republic may not be that far behind. The El Salvador government's belated attempt to respond to long-standing pressures to make the system more democratic are being threatened by a concerted radical guerrilla movement. In Honduras and Panama, strong military institutions remain poised to return to full political power should civilians misstep.[54] Among the English-speaking Caribbean, most face the difficulty of institutionalizing the Westminster tradition they have inherited in territories that are very small and that have few autonomous power bases outside the government to keep the opposition "loyal" and the majority respectful. Guyana has already made a mockery of democratic procedures and Grenada experienced a civilian "coup" to remove a prime minister who had lost legitimacy. Jamaica's democratic system was sorely tested in the tumultuous period around the 1980 elections, but pulled back to respect constitutional procedure. In a number of the smaller states, the forms continue to be observed amid much grumbling over the way the winners gain their victories and run the countries. Their small size gives them certain advantages—everyone knows each other—but also makes them quite vulnerable to pressures from a determined few.[55]

Presence of Radical Leftist Guerrilla Groups. The victory of the hard-fought Sandinista revolution in Nicaragua and the easy success of a few armed civilians in Grenada has given new hope to those who want to establish socialist states in the Caribbean Basin by force. Guerrilla groups in both El Salvador and Guatemala have been emboldened to mount substantial local and regional offensives toward the goal of final victory for socialism. Several long-standing similar organizations in Colombia have tried to expand their existing bases of operation. Terrorist incidents have occurred in several other countries, including Honduras, Costa Rica, Venezuela, and Puerto Rico. Many of these "popular liberation struggles" receive substantial rhetorical endorsement from Cuba, and there is evidence that some are being supplied with material aid as well. One approach by governments to counter the threat is that which the new conservative government of Colombia is attempting to follow—amnesty and an increase in social welfare programs. Another, followed until recently by Guatemala, is to facilitate radical right responses to physically eliminate all who might give "moral or material help to the enemy." Yet another is to try to combine some political, economic, and social reforms with military operations against the guerrillas, as in El Salvador. The ultimate success or failure of the revolutionaries will more likely be determined by how much popular support they win, which in turn is a function of how well existing governments themselves respond to the needs of their citizens.

In spite of the political diversity of the Caribbean Basin, most countries are democratic in one form or another or have governments that aspire to a mode of open, pluralist political systems. Yet the uncertain stability of many and the challenges from the revolutionary socialist left and/or an intransigent extreme right must be taken seriously. The problems of most countries are multiple and complicated, but have to be addressed by their governments if they are to retain popular support and legitimacy. The most constructive solution revolves around a variety of initiatives that strengthen the democratic process and democratic institutions rather than certain individuals or particular administrations.

POLICY OPTIONS FOR THE
UNITED STATES

The major goals of U.S. and Western policy in the Caribbean Basin were set forth in the preceding section for each of the issue areas. In economic affairs, the overarching objective is to maintain or to secure economic growth and economic development. In social affairs, it is to keep population growth and social mobilization within reasonable bounds. In political affairs, the basic goal is to maintain or secure a stable and responsive political system with reasonable capacity to deal effectively with important problems. One can conceive of a variety of possible policy responses to try to achieve these general goals and to address the specific economic, social, and political issues of the Caribbean Basin. Each implies certain assumptions underlying the policy and a particular view of the region as a whole and its component parts. Three such possibilities are the "hegemonic option," the "collaborative option," and the "damage limitation option."

The Hegemonic Option

This policy option relies basically on U.S. initiatives to deal with the fundamental issues of the Caribbean Basin. It assumes that the United States has both the capacity and the will to carry out its initiatives and that there is a basic consensus among key public and private actors on the main lines of the approach. It also assumes that most Caribbean nations are generally receptive to these initiatives. Its objective is to maintain or increase U.S. influence in the countries of the region, on the premise that the region has become a first-priority policy concern for reasons of national security.

In the economic arena, the main policy instrument would be substantial economic assistance, administered primarily through AID on a bilateral basis. The assistance would be generally directed, as present legislation requires, to infrastructure and self-help projects designed primarily to assist the less privileged sectors of the population in order to effect improved income distribution less painfully and to increase market size. Budgets for the InterAmerican Foundation and the American Institute for Free Labor Development would also be increased. At the same time, Export-Import Bank lending capacity specifically for the region would be strengthened, and other incentives for U.S. private-sector investment and commerce with the region would be provided.

In the social arena, financial assistance would be made available to such agencies as the Population Council and the International Planned

Parenthood Federation and agencies of interested governments in the region to work in the most densely settled countries to help reduce population growth rates. The substantial economic assistance made available for infrastructure would include expansion of educational and health facilities in isolated or ethnically distinct areas, and considerable emphasis would be placed on access roads in those countries with areas now outside effective national territory but suitable for settlement. Relatively more assistance would be made available in countries with greater disparities in income distribution to help the less well off. Legislation would be changed so that direct assistance and technical training can be provided to police and constabulary forces to make them better able to deal with local crime. Collaboration in drug enforcement activities would be strengthened.

In the political arena, support would be maintained in regional and international organizations for the interests and concerns of the democratic countries of the area, and opportunities would be taken advantage of to express U.S. identification with democratic norms and values. Exchange programs would be expanded to permit present and future leaders of countries of the region to study in the United States or to serve as interns or advisors to various types of political organizations. State and local government entities would be encouraged to revitalize "sister" city and state relationships. Serious consideration would be given to reviving 1950s and 1960s programs of official U.S. government support for democratic political party organizations in the countries of the region. Furthermore, substantial assistance would be provided military establishments and other counterrevolutionary organizations to limit and reverse the spread of nondemocratic socialist groups and doctrines.

The Collaborative Option

This policy option operates on the premise that the United States is eager to contribute to the resolution of problems in the area, but that there are institutional and practical limits to what it can reasonably do. It assumes that many countries in the region are in a position to help themselves to a certain degree and to contribute to the improvement of the neighbors' situations as well, and that, within their capacities, this is what they want to do. It sees multilateral rather than bilateral avenues as often more conducive to dealing effectively with most issues. Its goal is to build self-sustaining economic and political development in which the countries of the region themselves have a major stake and to which they make a major contribution. It takes into account national security concerns, but does not see a direct or immediate threat from the region by any country in or outside it.

In the economic arena, U.S. economic assistance would be coordinated with that of other donor countries to avoid overlap and duplication and to ensure that even countries with which the United States did not have very good relations could be beneficiaries. The United States would encourage and support the oil facility arrangement by Venezuela and Mexico, and would work particularly actively with regional and international organizations to channel assistance to where the need was greatest in the areas of social welfare and infrastructural development. International economic institutions would be provided with greater resources so that they could expand their financial assistance capacity. Considerable emphasis would be placed on building regional common markets or free trade areas among smaller countries of the Caribbean Basin and of supporting multilateral efforts to get the necessary transportation and logistical infrastructure in place.

In the social arena, the OAS and the Pan American Health Organization, along with other international voluntary organizations, would be encouraged to expand activities in the family-planning field. New immigration legislation would set clearer ground rules on population flows to the U.S., including a provision to discourage trained persons whose skills are needed at home. Education exchange programs would be available, but with clear and stringent requirement to return to one's own country to put newly acquired capacities to work. Encouragement would be provided to collaborative initiatives to bring people from more populated areas to less populated ones, both within and across national boundaries. Serious consideration would be given to the establishment of a multilateral voluntary organization of residents of the countries to assist with social problems throughout the area.

In the political arena, support or encouragement would be given to public and private initiatives to strengthen democratic practices and procedures, including foundations of friendly governments. Local universities would be strengthened, particularly in the areas where training would be provided to government employees. Multilateral organization efforts to assist political and union leaders would be supported. The fact that democratic practices and procedures predominate in the region would be recognized, and efforts concentrated on trying to make them stronger and better.

"Damage Limitation" Option

This policy option assumes that there is not a great deal the United States can or will do to deal with the major issues of the area and that the best approach is to deal as effectively as possible with problems when they become serious enough to require some kind of response. It assumes that the governments of the countries of the region know best what they need and, by and large, will be able to work things out for themselves. It operates on the assumption that there is no serious crisis in the area that is beyond the capacity of the region's governments to deal with individually or collectively or with the help of international financial institutions. Further, it recognizes that the region is by and large a second-priority area for the United States in economic, political, and national security terms, and that things will likely work out in ways not inimical to U.S. interests.

In the economic arena, private and public multilateral institutions will respond to needs as expressed by the governments of the area. Modest bilateral assistance programs will provide some help, but this is not seen as decisive. Trade and investment will continue to evolve along lines set by each partner. Cartels and common markets will be neither actively opposed nor supported. Special emergency funding will be available for crisis situations, but it will be expected that countries in these kinds of difficulties will work out their own arrangements with the IMF, a regional development bank, or another country.

In the social arena, modest programs will continue, but emphasis will be on nongovernment organizations and on local initiative. A stricter immigration law will be enforced to reduce all types of migration to the U.S., so that countries of the region will have to resort to their own devices to work out problems. If requested, the U.S. would be willing to provide emergency assistance to deal with a particularly pressing social problem in one country or another.

In the political arena, the status quo will be seen as the most desirable situation, and it will be assumed that hostile elements will be repulsed by the energetic action of governments subject to such subversion. If subversion should threaten to win out, then forceful action would be forthcoming to ensure that the status quo would be maintained. In general, policy would be reactive, on the assumption that most governments have or will find the capacity to deal with difficulties in ways most suited to their own national interests.

No option entirely represents either a satisfactory or a likely set of responses to the major issues of the Caribbean Basin. Local or parochial U.S. interests would keep any hegemonic option set of initiatives from being approved, much less carried out. And there is probably a consensus among the foreign affairs community that it is not very realistic to sit on one's hands in hopes that everything will work out in a reasonable way, as the damage limitation option implies—or that if things suddenly threaten to get out of hand and affect the U.S. interests in any fundamental way, the U.S. government will have the capacity to respond quickly and decisively. While some countries in the region explicitly reject the collaborative option if the U.S. is a party, this option represents, on balance, the more reasonable way to deal with the complex sets of issues in the region. To recognize that the United States has interests that it wants to advance, but simultaneously to realize that there are both constraints on independent action and a variety of ways to accomplish them outside of direct U.S. initiatives, is the most practical route for the United States to follow.

NOTES

1. David Scott Palmer, "Military Governments and U.S. Policy: General Concerns and Central American Cases," *AEI Foreign Policy and Defense Review* 4, 2 (1982):24.
2. For another view of U.S. interests in the region, see Margaret Daly Hayes, "Security to the South: U.S. Interests in Latin America," *International Security* 5 (1980). A monograph that illustrates the difficulty of making the case for the importance of the region to the U.S. on grounds other than proximity is Jorge Dominguez and Virginia Dominguez's, *The Caribbean: Its Implications for the United States,* Headline Series 253 (New York: Foreign Policy Association, 1981), esp. Chapter 6.
3. These figures are extrapolations from 1946-1975 totals of $90,476 billion in military assistance worldwide, of which $2562 billion went to Latin American countries (from U.S. government figures compiled in tables in North American Congress on Latin America, *Latin America and Empire Report* 10, 1 [January 1976]: 25, 27.
4. International Monetary Fund, *International Financial Statistics Yearbook,* 1982 (Washington, D.C., 1982).
5. Inter-American Development Bank, *Economic and Social Progress in Latin America, 1980-1981* (Washington, D.C., 1982).
6. Obie G. Whichard, "U.S. Direct Investment Abroad in 1981," *Survey of Current Business* (Washington, D.C.: U.S. Department of Commerce, 1982).
7. Investment figures from Department of Commerce, Bureau of Economic Analysis, Statistical File. Trade figures from U.S. Department of Commerce, International Trade Administration, *Foreign Economic Trends,* country bulletins (Washington, D.C., various dates); and Central Intelligence Agency, *The World Factbook, 1982* (Washington, D.C., 1982).
8. Dominguez and Dominguez, *The Caribbean,* pp, 64-65. Figures on maritime commerce are from the Maritime Administration, U.S. Department of Transportation; Figures on trade are from *Foreign Economic Trends,* and *World Factbook, 1982.*
9. *Essence of Decision: Explaining the Cuban Missile Crisis* (Boston: Little, Brown, 1971), esp. Chapter 5.
10. This was the sixth annual Miami Conference on the Caribbean, December 5-7, 1982. The following organizations, agencies, and companies were among those represented: the City of Miami, Metropolitan Dade County, the State of Florida, Caribbean/Central American Action, U.S. Department of State-Bureau of Inter-American Affairs and Office of the OAS Ambassador, University of Miami, Tesoro Petroleum Corporation, InterNorth Inc., ALCOA, Southeast Bank, Chamber of Commerce of the U.S., Center for Inter-American Relations, Banco Popular (Puerto Rico), Overseas Private Investment Corporation (OPIC), AID, U.S. Departments

of Commerce and Transportation, U.S. Trade Representative, U.S. House and Senate, the White House, Atlanta Chamber of Commerce, PanAm, Gulf & Western.

11. See my "Military Governments and U.S. Policy," p. 25 and *passim*. Also see William Leo Grande, "Drawing the Line in El Salvador," *International Security* 6, 1 (1982):27–28 and *passim*. For another view that emphasizes the consistently counterproductive nature of U.S. policy in Central America, see Walter La Feber, "Inevitable Revolutions," *Atlantic Monthly* (June 1982):74–83.

12. Various poll results reported in *Public Opinion* make this quite evident. For example, 90 percent of a March 1981 national sample agreed that the private business system in the U.S. works better than any other for industrial countries, and 75 percent mentioned freedom and liberty or system of government as what they were proudest of about America (*Public Opinion*, June/July 1981, pp. 30–31). Some 59 percent of a February 1980 national sample felt Communism was the worst form of government (*Public Opinion*, February/March 1981, p. 29), and 83 percent said they would rather fight a war than accept Russian domination in a February 1982 sample (*Public Opinion*, April/May 1982, p. 39). Between the Vietnam War era (circa 1972) and the Iran hostage crisis of 1980, foreign affairs or national defense issues were noted as "the most important problem facing the country today" by 10 percent or less of people surveyed in sixteen national samples (*Public Opinion*, December/January 1980, p. 40).

13. See the pioneering work in this area by Gabriel Almond, *The American People and Foreign Policy* (New York: Harcourt Brace, 1950).

14. There is divided opinion regarding the probable impact of the CBI in the area of migration. Some have argued that the improved economic conditions that should result from the CBI will reduce migration pressures. Others say that the migration urge will actually increase with Caribbean economic growth because economic expansion will not keep up with the rising expectations provided by that growth. From discussion at the Caribbean Migration Policy Conference, Miami, Florida, 8 December 1982, as reported in the *Miami Herald*, 9 December 1982.

15. IADB, *Economic and Social Progress in Latin America, 1980–1981*.

16. World Bank, *IDA in Retrospect*, (Washington, D.C., 1982).

17. CIA, *World Factbook, 1982*.

18. Ibid.

19. IADB, *Economic and Social Progress in Latin America, 1980–1981*.

20. Various sources, including ibid.; UCLA Latin American Center, *Statistical Abstract of Latin America*, 21 (1981); CIA, *The Cuban Economy: A Statistical Review* (Washington, D.C., 1981); and United Nations, *1979/1980 Statistical Yearbook* (New York, 1981).

21. CIA, *World Factbook, 1982*.

22. As quoted in Hubert Herring, *A History of Latin America* (New York: Knopf, 1961), p. 799.

23. From the *Congressional Record*, listed in John Rothchild (ed.), *Latin America Yesterday and Today* (New York: Bantam, 1973), pp. 440–447.

24. United Nations, *External Financing in Latin America* (New York: ECLA, 1965), Table 29.

25. In an open letter to Atlantic Council Caribbean Basin Working Group, November 5, 1982; also see his "U.S. and Latin America: Ending the Hegemonic Presumption," *Foreign Affairs* 55, 1 (October 1976):199–213.

26. Arthur S. Banks et al. (eds.), *Economic Handbook of the World: 1981* (New York: McGraw-Hill, 1982).

27. This definition follows that of Karl Deutsch in "Social Mobilization and Political

Development," *American Political Science Review* 55, 3 (September 1961):493–514.
28. IADB, *Economic and Social Progess in Latin America, 1980-1981.*
29. Ibid.
30. Banks et al., *Economic Handbook of the World: 1981.*
31. Kenneth Ruddle and Donald Odermann (eds.), *Statistical Abstract of Latin America, 1971* (Los Angeles: UCLA, 1972), p. 363.
32. Figures compiled from 1980 merchandise exports and 1980 GDP. IADB, *Economic and Social Progress in Latin America, 1980-1981,* and IADB, *Economic and Social Progress in Latin America, 1982: The External Sector* (Washington, D.C., 1982), p. 376.
33. United Nations, *Handbook of International Trade and Development Statistics* (New York, 1980), pp. 532–533.
34. OAS, *Statistical Bulletin of the OAS* 4, 1–2 (January–June 1982):86.
35. IADB, *Economic and Social Progress in Latin America, 1982: The External Sector,* p. 382.
36. Ibid. Data on several countries were not available, including Barbados, the Dominican Republic, El Salvador, Guyana, Jamaica, Nicaragua, and Panama.
37. Ibid.
38. Ibid., p. 375. Nicaragua data are for 1980.
39. Calculated from ibid.
40. Calculated from ibid.
41. Ibid., p. 387.
42. World Bank, *World Debt Tables* (Washington, D.C., December 1981).
43. Ibid.
44. IADB, *Annual Report, 1981* (Washington, D.C., 1982).
45. IADB, *Economic and Social Progess in Latin America, 1982: The External Sector,* Table 62; Commodity Research Bureau, *1982 Commodity Year Book* (Washington, D.C., 1982), pp. 5, 51–53, 97–98, 329.
46. OAS, *Statistical Bulletin,* Table 3. One forecast summary expects metals prices to increase by 5 percent or more over the next two years, but "commodities prices could be in the doldrums for some time . . . [perhaps] for the next decade" (*Wall Street Journal,* February 1983, pp. 1, 12).
47. OAS, *Statistical Bulletin,* p. 10.
48. IADB, *Annual Report, 1981.*
49. Ibid.
50. CIA, *The World Factbook, 1982.*
51. World Bank, *World Development Report 1982,* pp. 148–149, 154–155.
52. United Nations, *Demographic Yearbook* (New York, 1980), pp. 344–347.
53. World Bank, *World Development Report 1982,* pp. 158–159; I. Adelman and C. T. Morris, "An Anatomy of Income Distribution Patterns in Developing Countries," *Development Digest* (October 1971).
54. See, for example, Thomas P. Anderson, *Politics in Central America* (New York: Praeger, 1982).
55. See the much fuller discussion in several articles on the status of democracy in the Caribbean appearing in *Caribbean Review* 10, 2 (Spring 1981), esp. pp. 4–24ff.

APPENDIX: CARIBBEAN BASIN
STATISTICAL DATA, BY COUNTRY

See the following pages for Tables 3.1–3.13.

Table 3.1. Gross Domestic Product, 1970 and 1980

	1980 GDP (millions $)	Average Annual Growth of GDP		GDP Per Capita		GDP Per Capita Annual Growth Rate (1960–1980)
		1961–1970	1971–1980	1970	1980	
Contributor States						
Colombia	24,068	5.2	5.8	647	922	3.3
Mexico	107,263	7.0	5.6	1,376	1,867	1.3
Trinidad & Tobago	2,644	4.0	4.5	1,669	2,478	2.9
United States	2,587,000	4.5	3.1	4,805	11,363	2.7
Venezuela	37,025	6.1	4.2	2,296	2,470	1.6
Central American Beneficiaries						
Costa Rica	3,395	6.0	5.6	1,150	1,542	3.0
El Salvador	3,227	5.7	4.6	682	688	1.3
Guatemala	8,453	5.5	5.7	928	1,196	2.5
Honduras	2,358	5.2	4.4	571	636	1.6
Nicaragua	2,172	7.0	2.1	950	897	1.9
Panama	3,523	8.0	4.2	1,564	1,918	3.9
Island Beneficiaries						
Antigua	73		3.0		1,000	
Bahamas	2,057		6.2		5,413	
Barbados	661	8.3	1.0	2,326	2,685	2.4
Belize	140		4.0		960	4.5
Dominica	35		-1.4		430	
Dominican Republic	5,705	5.4	7.5	673	1,049	3.6
Grenada	88		-1.0		800	
Guyana	617	3.7	3.3	739	727	0.8
Haiti	1,339	0.3	3.9	214	275	0.3
Jamaica	3,160	5.4	-0.6	1,741	1,406	0.8
St. Lucia	113		0.0		913	
St. Vincent–Grenadines	47		1.0		440	
Suriname	932		4.0	791	2,420	
Other						
Cuba	13,300	2.9	-2.1		1,360	

Sources for GDP: CIA, World Fact Book (Washington, D.C., 1982); Facts on File, Inc., The World in Figures (New York, 1981); IADB, Annual Report, 1981 (Washington, D.C., 1982); IADB, Economic and Social Progress in Latin America, 1980–81 (Washington, D.C., 1982); IMF, International Financial Statistics Yearbook (Washington, D.C., 1982); United Nations, Handbook of International Trade and Development Statistics (New York, 1980); computations based on data from cited sources.

Table 3.2. Annual Variation in the Consumer Price Index, 1961–1980

	Inflation Rate					
	1961–1970	1971–1975	1976–1980	1978	1979	1980
Contributor States						
Colombia	11.1	19.2	24.5	17.8	24.6	26.5
Mexico	2.8	12.3	21.4	17.3	18.2	26.4
Trinidad & Tobago	3.1	13.3	13.0	10.2	14.7	17.5
United States	2.7	6.7	8.9	7.8	11.3	13.5
Venezuela	1.0	5.7	11.3	7.2	12.3	21.6
Central American Beneficiaries						
Costa Rica	2.5	14.1	8.2	6.0	9.2	18.1
El Salvador	0.7	8.9	13.1	13.2	15.9	17.4
Guatemala	0.8	7.8	10.7	8.0	11.5	10.7
Honduras	2.2	6.4	9.1	5.7	8.7	17.5
Nicaragua	1.7		20.4	4.6	48.1	35.3
Panama	1.3	7.3	6.9	4.2	7.9	13.8
Island Beneficiaries						
Antigua						
Bahamas	6.2	8.1	6.9	6.1	9.0	12.1
Barbados	3.0	18.9	10.9	9.5	13.2	18.3
Belize						
Dominica						
Dominican Republic	2.1	11.0	10.0	3.5	9.2	16.6
Grenada						
Guyana	2.3	7.8	12.9	15.2	17.7	14.1
Haiti	2.9	13.4	8.4	-2.6	13.0	17.9
Jamaica	4.2	14.1	22.4	34.9	29.1	26.9
St. Lucia						
St. Vincent–Grenadines						
Suriname	4.2	8.4	11.5	8.8	14.9	14.1
Other						
Cuba						

Sources for annual variation in Consumer Price Index: IADB, *Annual Report, 1981* (Washington, D.C., 1982); U.S. Department of Commerce, *Statistical Abstract of the United States* (Washington, D.C., 1981).

Table 3.3. Balance of Payments (in Millions of $)

	Current Account Balance							
	1973	1975	1976	1977	1978	1979	1980	1981
Contributor States								
Colombia	-54.1	-109.1	-206.6	440.2	321.7	491.0	-23.4	-1,704.0
Mexico	-1,415.1	-4,054.3	-3,410.3	-1,849.3	-3,162.5	-5,469.0	-7,856.1	-11,704.3
Trinidad &Tobago	-35.1	273.2	186.8	146.0	96.3	-39.4	281.0	94.1
United States	7,141.0	18,339.0	4,605.0	-14,092.0	-13,467.0	1,414.0	3,723.0	
Venezuela	860.8	2,169.7	257.5	-3,180.2	-5,735.5	350.1	4,240.4	3,999.0
Central American Beneficiaries								
Costa Rica	-112.1	-217.7	-201.4	-225.3	-363.4	-558.8	-652.6	-391.2
El Salvador	-43.9	-92.8	-5.9	30.4	-238.7	129.2	-61.1	-287.1
Guatemala	7.7	-65.7	-75.0	-31.9	-264.6	-205.4	-163.2	-601.4
Honduras	-34.6	-112.5	-104.6	-128.9	-157.3	-191.7	-319.6	-272.8
Nicaragua	-66.0	-185.0	-39.2	-181.4	-24.9	160.6	-454.2	n.a.
Panama	-111.1	-168.7	-176.2	-155.4	-208.7	-302.2	-302.1	-384.1
Island Beneficiaries								
Antigua								
Bahamas	-145.1	43.4	84.9	180.5	35.4	5.5	-17.3	-64.1
Barbados	-53.0	-29.7	-44.0	-36.2	-31.2	-34.1	-27.0	-87.0
Belize								
Dominica								
Dominican Republic	-96.5	-72.7	-241.9	-262.3	-319.9	-340.8	-806.8	-360.4
Grenada								
Guyana	-63.4	-23.5	-141.2	-95.7	-29.2	-82.7	-128.2	-185.6
Haiti	-1.5	-26.3	-20.2	-37.7	-45.7	-58.6	-77.1	-150.4
Jamaica	-257.6	-282.8	-302.7	-68.2	-87.0	-152.7	-186.5	-457.1
St. Lucia								
St. Vincent-Grenadines								
Suriname	-8.0	131.1	63.3	-3.5	28.0	44.1	15.7	-24.4
Other								
Cuba	-43.0	-246.0	-642.0	-658.0	-276.0			

Sources for balance of payments: CIA, *The Cuban Economy: A Statistical Review* (Washington, D.C., 1981); IADB, *Economic and Social Progress in Latin America: The External Sector, 1982* (Washington, D.C., 1983); IMF, *The Balance of Payments Yearbook* (Washington, D.C., 1980); U.S. Department of Commerce, *Statistical Abstract of the United States* (Washington, D.C., 1981); computations based on data from cited sources.

127

Table 3.4. Total External Debt Outstanding and Disbursed, and Interest on External Debt (Millions of $)

	Outstanding External Debt (millions $)			Interest Payments on External Debt (millions $)		
	1971	1975	1980	1971	1975	1980
Contributor States						
Colombia	1,383.9	2,348.0	4,294.2	49.5	113.7	299.9
Mexico	3,493.7	11,539.7	33,490.0	224.8	832.0	3,844.3
Trinidad & Tobago	101.5	159.4	491.8	4.6	11.9	45.4
United States						
Venezuela	1,026.8	1,261.5	10,866.6	47.1	103.5	1,229.2
Central American Beneficiaries						
Costa Rica	166.9	421.3	1,584.7	8.2	23.4	124.6
El Salvador	92.6	195.8	509.4	3.7	7.0	24.1
Guatemala	109.0	164.1	540.9	7.5	6.4	31.3
Honduras	102.3	264.0	892.1	3.3	10.2	55.4
Nicaragua	188.6	598.4	1,495.7	8.4	35.9	38.1
Panama	244.6	774.2	2,276.3	12.3	41.2	252.7
Island Beneficiaries						
Antigua						
Bahamas						
Barbados	14.3	26.7	78.5	0.7	2.4	5.8
Belize						
Dominica						
Dominican Republic	232.6	411.2	1,185.9	4.8	17.8	96.6
Grenada						
Guyana	147.6	291.4	519.0	3.1	9.6	25.5
Haiti	38.8	56.7	248.6	0.3	1.2	4.3
Jamaica	181.8	690.2	1,299.1	9.6	50.2	107.3
St. Lucia						
St. Vincent–Grenadines						
Suriname						
Other						
Cuba	591	743		35.0	45.0	

Sources for total external debt outstanding and interest on external debt: CIA, The Cuban Economy: A Statistical Review (Washington, D.C., 1981); World Bank, World Debt Tables (Washington, D.C., 1982).

Table 3.5. External Public Debt by Maturities, in % (Based on Total Outstanding Debt at Year End)

	Debt, Maturity 5 Yrs.		Debt, Maturity 5–10 Yrs.		Debt, Maturity 10–15 Yrs.		Debt, Maturity 15 Yrs.	
	1970	1980	1970	1980	1970	1980	1970	1980
Contributor States								
Colombia	24.1	34.9	22.5	37.9	17.1	15.6	36.3	11.6
Mexico	56.5	58.8	24.6	34.4	13.1	5.2	5.8	1.6
Trinidad & Tobago	30.6	55.7	32.9	39.7	14.1	3.6	22.4	1.0
United States								
Venezuela	50.7	62.4	26.1	35.7	17.1	1.8	6.1	0.1
Central American Beneficiaries								
Costa Rica	27.9	42.7	18.8	29.3	20.3	13.1	33.0	14.9
El Salvador	31.1	20.3	17.7	20.6	17.6	20.6	33.6	38.5
Guatemala	40.5	24.3	14.6	25.1	12.0	21.6	32.9	29.0
Honduras	15.8	19.5	18.0	23.8	18.0	18.4	48.2	38.3
Nicaragua	40.2	22.1	16.1	36.3	15.2	19.0	28.5	22.6
Panama	38.4	44.8	12.0	33.5	12.0	11.9	37.6	9.8
Island Beneficiaries								
Antigua								
Bahamas		47.7		26.1		17.1		9.1
Barbados		29.0		27.7		21.3		22.0
Belize								
Dominica								
Dominican Republic	20.6	37.5	23.1	21.6	18.8	13.8	37.5	27.1
Grenada								
Guyana		39.0		20.4		14.5		26.1
Haiti		9.6		13.7		11.7		65.0
Jamaica	40.0	50.7	27.1	20.5	20.0	13.5	12.9	15.3
St. Lucia								
St. Vincent–Grenadines								
Suriname								
Other								
Cuba								

Source for external public debt by maturities: IADB, *Economic and Social Progress in Latin America, 1980–81* (Washington, D.C., 1982).

Table 3.6. Merchandise Trade (Millions of $ FOB)

	1975 Exports	1975 Imports	1980 Exports	1980 Imports	1981 Exports	1981 Imports
Contributor States						
Colombia	1,716.9	1,424.3	4,112.8	3,851.2	3,366.0	4,788.0
Mexico	3,008.8	6,292.0	16,306.9	19,016.7	19,379.0	23,104.4
Trinidad & Tobago	987.4	676.6	2,535.6	1,752.5	2,324.4	1,868.8
United States						
Venezuela	8,853.9	5,461.5	19,280.9	11,318.1	20,078.0	12,378.0
Central American Beneficiaries						
Costa Rica	493.1	627.3	1,017.5	1,375.3	1,029.9	1,092.2
El Salvador	533.0	550.8	968.6	971.7	793.1	980.8
Guatemala	641.0	672.4	1,518.9	1,471.6	1,304.0	1,580.0
Honduras	309.7	372.4	834.5	956.0	804.3	880.5
Nicaragua	374.9	482.2	450.4	847.2		
Panama	330.9	823.1	431.0	1,289.0	339.3	1,374.0
Island Beneficiaries						
Antigua						
Bahamas	116.2	339.0	200.4	784.4	176.0	783.0
Barbados	94.5	196.9	188.5	479.5	196.0	575.0
Belize						
Dominica						
Dominican Republic	893.9	772.7	961.9	1,514.6	1,188.0	1,438.7
Grenada						
Guyana	351.4	305.9	388.9	386.3	345.6	439.8
Haiti	71.4	121.5	211.1	293.8	151.1	357.9
Jamaica	808.7	969.7	1,088.9	1,173.0	980.4	1,296.7
St. Lucia						
St. Vincent–Grenadines						
Suriname	277.2	242.1	514.5	454.1	473.8	511.8
Other						
Cuba						

Sources for merchandise trade: IADB, *Economic and Social Progress in Latin America: The External Sector, 1982* (Washington, D.C., 1983).

Table 3.7. Ratio of Debt Service to GNP

	1971	1973	1975	1976	1977	1978	1979	1980
Contributor States								
Colombia	1.9	2.1	1.9	1.9	1.6	1.7	2.4	1.7
Mexico	2.0	2.2	2.1	3.4	4.9	6.9	8.5	4.9
Trinidad & Tobago	2.7	1.3	1.1	2.9	0.4	0.8	1.1	1.5
United States								
Venezuela	1.1	1.9	1.9	1.3	2.3	1.9	3.2	4.9
Central American Beneficiaries								
Costa Rica	2.7	2.9	3.4	2.9	2.9	6.9	6.5	4.3
El Salvador	1.5	1.6	3.1	1.6	2.5	1.0	1.0	1.2
Guatemala	1.4	0.8	0.4	0.3	0.3	0.5	0.6	0.8
Honduras	0.9	1.2	1.5	2.3	2.8	3.4	5.2	3.9
Nicaragua	4.0	6.7	3.7	4.3	5.0	5.1	3.8	3.8
Panama	3.6	6.1	3.8	5.2	7.7	23.6	14.1	14.5
Island Beneficiaries								
Antigua								
Bahamas								
Barbados	0.4	1.4	1.1	0.9	1.9	1.4	1.8	1.7
Belize								
Dominica								
Dominican Republic	1.1	1.3	1.4	1.4	1.6	1.9	4.6	2.4
Grenada								
Guyana	1.7	3.6	3.3	7.8	7.8	10.0	18.6	12.6
Haiti	1.1	1.0	1.1	1.2	1.2	1.2	0.7	0.9
Jamaica	1.3	2.0	2.8	3.8	4.8	8.0	9.2	7.9
St. Lucia								
St. Vincent–Grenadines								
Suriname								
Other								
Cuba								

Source for ratio of debt service to GNP: World Bank, World Debt Tables (Washington, D.C., 1982).

Table 3.8. Ratio of Debt Service to Exports

	1971	1973	1975	1976	1977	1978	1979	1980
Contributor States								
Colombia	14.1	13.1	11.1	9.5	8.8	9.5	13.2	10.0
Mexico	22.7	22.2	25.1	31.1	43.4	53.4	62.3	32.1
Trinidad & Tobago	6.3	2.9	2.1	5.6	1.0	1.9	2.3	2.4
United States								
Venezuela	3.8	6.0	5.4	3.9	7.6	6.9	9.5	13.2
Central American Beneficiaries								
Costa Rica	10.1	10.2	10.6	9.4	8.8	22.8	22.9	16.4
El Salvador	5.7	5.2	9.0	4.2	6.0	3.0	2.3	3.7
Guatemala	7.9	3.5	1.7	1.4	1.2	2.2	2.6	3.5
Honduras	3.2	3.7	4.7	6.2	7.0	8.4	12.7	9.9
Nicaragua	14.3	21.6	12.3	12.1	13.9	13.4	8.1	14.9
Panama	9.0	14.4	5.9	8.2	11.7	32.9	18.5	14.0
Island Beneficiaries								
Antigua								
Bahamas						1.5	0.4	
Barbados	0.6	2.3	2.7	2.1	2.0	2.1	2.6	2.4
Belize		2.3	1.7	1.6	3.2			
Dominica								
Dominican Republic	6.1	5.6	4.8	6.6	7.5	10.8	21.6	12.2
Grenada								
Guyana	2.7	6.6	4.3	11.2	11.9	15.0	29.8	17.0
Haiti	5.8	5.7	4.6	4.7	4.9	4.2	2.9	4.1
Jamaica	3.2	5.4	6.9	11.2	14.8	16.6	15.9	12.8
St. Lucia								
St. Vincent-Grenadines								
Suriname								
Other								
Cuba								

Sources for ratio of debt service to exports: IADB, Economic and Social Progress in Latin America, 1980–81 (Washington, D.C., 1982); World Bank, World Debt Tables (Washington, D.C., 1982).

Table 3.9. Projected Total Debt Service 1981–1988 (Millions of $)

	1981	1982	1983	1984	1985	1986	1987	1988
Contributor States								
Colombia	795.2	830.7	919.9	1,037.4	1,044.4	968.7	881.5	794.2
Mexico	10,558.6	8,645.8	8,258.0	7,479.1	6,616.3	5,302.3	5,975.4	3,920.6
Trinidad & Tobago	115.8	121.1	202.6	139.2	103.9	93.1	85.3	59.7
United States								
Venezuela	2,933.1	2,667.4	2,548.7	2,596.0	2,042.7	1,854.7	1,577.4	904.7
Central American Beneficiaries								
Costa Rica	344.8	381.5	390.7	382.7	422.3	309.5	254.9	225.0
El Salvador	51.4	71.6	75.5	74.0	67.0	62.8	64.1	65.1
Guatemala	85.4	58.3	77.8	65.7	86.2	72.3	70.1	69.5
Honduras	112.4	132.4	134.2	149.1	140.6	154.3	135.8	130.0
Nicaragua	190.9	234.3	170.1	180.1	163.1	188.2	193.5	196.5
Panama	493.2	467.4	525.7	485.4	422.4	371.5	365.8	269.0
Island Beneficiaries								
Antigua								
Bahamas								
Barbados	15.5	15.0	15.0	15.1	14.5	13.5	13.3	13.3
Belize								
Dominica								
Dominican Republic	254.6	270.8	221.5	211.1	185.9	159.5	142.3	100.0
Grenada								
Guyana	115.4	81.3	73.8	72.5	67.7	51.0	43.5	39.5
Haiti	15.3	8.9	10.0	9.9	11.0	12.4	14.0	15.1
Jamaica	407.4	230.4	233.2	185.6	143.9	123.4	115.9	107.0
St. Lucia								
St. Vincent-Grenadines								
Suriname								
Other								
Cuba								

Source for projected total debt service: World Bank, World Debt Tables (Washington, D.C., 1982).

133

Table 3.10. Development Assistance Annual Averages 1976–1978 (Millions of $)

	Bilateral Aid (Annual Average, 1976–1978)	Multilateral Aid (Annual Average, 1976–1978)	Total Aid (Annual Average, 1976–1978)	Total Aid Per Capita ($, Annual Average, 1976–1978)	U.S. Investment 1970	1975	1980
Contributor States							
Colombia	46.9	19.4	66.4	2.65	584	648	1,012
Mexico	8.0	35.7	43.7	.68	1,912	3,200	5,989
Trinidad & Tobago	1.3	3.7	5.0	4.46	198	—	951
United States							
Venezuela	−15.1	9.7	−5.4	−.43	2,241	1,872	1,908
Central American Beneficiaries							
Costa Rica	20.1	13.2	33.3	16.16	103	169	303
El Salvador	19.7	23.9	43.6	10.23	53	86	103
Guatemala	35.7	30.6	66.3	10.30	158	159	226
Honduras	26.6	36.5	63.1	19.00	151	184	288
Nicaragua	21.3	18.0	39.2	16.99	75	108	89
Panama	23.0	12.3	35.3	19.93	1,190	1,907	3,171
Island Beneficiaries							
Antigua				69.44			
Bahamas	0.1	0.7	0.8	3.77	408	763	2,712
Barbados	4.8	3.3	8.1	32.40	9	19	39
Belize	8.7	4.5	13.1	87.60	4	5	24
Dominica				69.44			
Dominican Republic	13.3	25.0	38.3	7.69	144	222	305
Grenada				69.44			
Guyana	11.5	5.8	17.3	21.32	40	22	7
Haiti	40.5	42.1	82.6	17.39	13	13	33
Jamaica	45.9	14.1	60.0	28.59	507	654	406
St. Lucia				69.44			
St. Vincent-Grenadines				69.44			
Suriname	83.7	2.7	86.4	233.51			
Other							
Cuba	24.4	15.7	40.1	4.17			

Sources for development assistance, annual averages: United Nations, *1979/1980 Statistical Yearbook* (New York, 1981); U.S. Department of Commerce, Bureau of Economic Analysis, Statistical Fields (1982).

Table 3.11. U.S. Military Aid (Thousands of US$), and number of students trained

	Military Aid[a] (Thousands $)					No. of Students Trained		
	1970	1975	1980	1981	1982	1980	1981	1982
Contributor States								
Colombia	2,681	676	258	285	480	444	539	651
Mexico	89	110	126	144	145	43	107	72
Trinidad & Tobago	0	0	0	0	0	0	0	0
United States								
Venezuela	759	668	0	9	29	0	18	31
Central American Beneficiaries								
Costa Rica	0	0	0	33	58	0	37	55
El Salvador	576	1,054	252	25,577	56,318	125	256	747
Guatemala	1,178	565	0	0	0	0	0	0
Honduras	439	1,168	438	533	1,271	166	261	341
Nicaragua	915	1,083	0	0	0	0	0	0
Panama	822	582	278	374	401	202	293	224
Island Beneficiaries								
Antigua	0	0	0	0	0	0	0	0
Bahamas	0	0	0	0	0	0	0	0
Barbados	0	0	58	47	70	13	12	19
Belize	0	0	0	0	26	0	0	16
Dominica	0	0	0	12	17	0	7	8
Dominican Republic	1,846	1,305	248	421	465	47	163	129
Grenada	0	0	0	0	0	0	0	0
Guyana	0	0	0	28	40	0	11	29
Haiti	0	0	119	122	241	10	27	26
Jamaica	0	0	0	49	75	0	8	20
St. Lucia	0	0	0	5	8	0	2	4
St. Vincent-Grenadines	0	0	0	0	0	0	1	0
Suriname	0	0	26	30	23	5	7	2
Other								
Cuba	0	0	0	0	0	0	0	0

Source for U.S. military aid and number of students trained: U.S. Department of Justice, Security Assistance Agency, 1982 Fiscal Year Series Statistical Files.

[a]Includes value of materials, services, training, and education programs for which no reimbursement was received.

Table 3.12. Political Data

	Date of Last Election	Date of Next Scheduled Election	Voter Participation (Last Election) %	Leading Political Party	% of Vote for Leading Party (Last Election)	Second Political Party	% of Vote for Second Party (Last Election)
Contributor States							
Colombia	1978	1982	30	Liberal	55	Conserv.	36
Mexico	1979	1982		PRI	70	PAN	11
Trinidad & Tobago	1981	1986	55	PNM	72	ULF	22
United States	1982	1984	54	REP	50	DEM	42
Venezuela	1978	1983		COPEI	46	AD	43
Central American Beneficiaries							
Costa Rica	1982	1986		PLN	57	UNIDAD	33
El Salvador	1982	1983		PDC	40	ARENA	32
Guatemala	1978	1982		PID/PR	42	MLN	33
Honduras	1981			PLH	54	PNH	42
Nicaragua		after '85					
Panama	1980	1984		PRD		PdD	
Island Beneficiaries							
Antigua	1980	1985		ALP	76	PLM	18
Bahamas	1977	1982		PLP	55	BDP	27
Barbados	1981	1986		BLP	52	DLP	47
Belize	1979			PUP	72	UDP	28
Dominica	1980	1985		DFP	81	DLP	10
Dominican Republic	1978	1982		PRD	52	PR	41
Grenada	1976	unsched.		GULP	52	Coalition	48
Guyana	1980			PNC	77	PPP	20
Haiti	1979			NUP	99		
Jamaica	1980	1985		JLP	59	PNP	41
St. Lucia	1979	1985		SLP	71	UWP	29
St. Vincent-Grenadines	1979	1982		LP	85	NDP	15
Suriname	1977	unsched.		NPK	56	VDP	44
Other							
Cuba	1981	1986		PCC	100	–	–

Source for political data: CIA, World Fact Book (Washington, D.C., 1982).

136

Table 3.13. Population Distribution and Health Statistics

	Total Population (Thousands)	Urban Population (%)	Population Growth Rate	Geographic Area (km²)	Population Density (per km²)	Population Median Age	Infant Mortality (per 1000 live births)	Population per Physician
Contributor States								
Colombia	26,665	76	2.1	1,139,600	23	59.6	61.0	1,970
Mexico	72,270	69	3.4	1,978,800	37	8.9	65.0	1,385
Trinidad & Tobago	1,072	64	0.8	5,128	209	23.9	66.0	1,964
United States	230,000	74	1.0	9,371,829	25		73.0	622
Venezuela	15,580	78	3.4	911,680	17	33.7	66.4	870
Central American Beneficiaries								
Costa Rica	2,282	46	2.6	51,000	45	22.3	70.0	1,390
El Salvador	4,958	40	3.0	21,400	232	53.1	59.0	3,600
Guatemala	7,263	32	3.0	108,880	67	70.2	57.8	4,338
Honduras	3,807	36	3.1	112,150	34	117.0	55.5	3,290
Nicaragua	2,480	58	2.4	147,900	17	12.3	55.2	1,590
Panama	1,875	54	2.1	75,650	25	24.9	69.1	1,335
Island Beneficiaries								
Antigua	76		1.3	280	271		66.0	1,242
Bahamas	254	52	3.7	11,396	22	24.8	68.4	1,446
Barbados	247	56	0.3	430	574	21.0	47.0	3,415
Belize	147		1.8	22,973	6		58.0	4,560
Dominica	80		0.6	790	101		55.4	1,860
Dominican Republic	5,554	54	2.3	48,692	114	31.0	63.0	4,000
Grenada	108		1.0	314	313		69.1	7,350
Guyana	864	47	1.7	214,970	4	45.3	52.2	5,940
Haiti	5,093	25	1.7	27,713	184	149.1	68.5	3,509
Jamaica	2,280	69	1.5	11,422	200		57.0	5,231
St. Lucia	117		1.4	616	190		59.0	
St. Vincent-Grenadines	115		2.9	389	296		65.0	
Suriname	345	50	0.8	142,709	2			
Other								
Cuba	9,693		0.8	114,478	85	25.0	70.0	650

Sources for population distribution and health statistics: CIA, The Cuban Economy: A Statistical Review (Washington, D.C., 1981); CIA; World Fact Book (Washington, D.C., 1982); IADB, Economic and Social Progress in Latin America, 1980–81 (Washington, D.C., 1982); UCLA Latin American Center, Statistical Abstract of Latin America, Vol. 21 (Los Angeles, 1981).

Chapter 4

Issues for U.S. Policy in the Caribbean Basin in the 1980s: Security

Jack Child

INTRODUCTION

The Traditional Approach

The traditional approach to issues of U.S. security in the Caribbean Basin has tended to stress the strategic, military, and geopolitical dimensions of the concept of "security," and to resist the inclusion of broader economic or political dimensions. Historically, U.S. concern over security in the Caribbean Basin has also tended to be crisis-oriented, rising as a threat is perceived and then sinking to a lower level of priority or benign neglect as the crisis passes.

Because real and sustained threats to U.S. security interests in the Caribbean Basin have been relatively few over the years prior to the present crisis, it has been possible to apply an economy-of-force approach, which stressed the need to keep the area tranquil, stable, and safe so that strategic resources could be concentrated on areas of greater threat or priority.

This traditional approach had deep historical and psychological roots that were reinforced by geographic and cartographic perceptions of the area. The psychological root stems from the period of Manifest Destiny and the Spanish-American War, when it was believed that if the United States were to assume its rightful place in the world it must first exercise power and establish order in its own backyard. U.S. naval analysts were especially vocal in expressing this line of thinking, in stressing the need for a canal across the isthmus, and in presenting the Caribbean Basin as an "American Lake" with a strong feeling of U.S. possession and paternalism.[1] In cartographic and geographic terms, the Caribbean was perceived as the United States' third border, a "soft underbelly" that must be secured and protected to safeguard a variety of U.S. interests.[2] There was a tendency to see the Caribbean Basin as a single defensive area or perimeter at the service of U.S. interests rather than as a region with a rich variety of nations and peoples with their own interests and perceptions.

The historical definition of U.S. security interests in the Caribbean Basin that stemmed from these perceptions can be reduced to three interrelated objectives: (1) establishing and maintaining a peaceful, secure, stable, and friendly Southern Flank; (2) guaranteeing U.S. access to the area's raw materials, trade, investment opportunities, and transportation routes; and (3) keeping hostile powers out of the area.

To secure these interests, the United States has followed a variety of policies over the years. Initially, these policies were unilateral, or at best bilateral ones dominated by the U.S. Thus, the Manifest Destiny era of the mid-nineteenth century and the interventionist period of the early twentieth century saw the United States act in defense of its narrow security interests with little regard for Latin American reaction or attempts to obtain Latin American cooperation. This period saw a strong naval interest in controlling maritime choke points (with major emphasis on a trans-isthmian canal) and the sea lines of communications that passed through them as well as the coaling stations, which were the key to sustaining naval power in the age of steam. Hence the attention paid to U.S. bases in the Panama Canal Zone, the Mona Passage (Puerto Rico), the Windward Passage (Guantànamo) and the Straits of Florida.

With Franklin D. Roosevelt's Good Neighbor Policy, this unilateral security approach was abandoned in favor of a multilateral thrust, which would stress that collective security ("Hemisphere Defense") was a necessary complement to the political, diplomatic, commercial, and cultural aspects of the Good Neighbor Policy. Strengthened as a result of the Axis threat to the hemisphere during World War II, collective security approaches were embodied in the 1947 Rio Treaty (Inter-American Treaty of Reciprocal Assistance), in the Inter-American Defense Board, and in the series of multilateral and bilateral institutions that made up what could be appropriately called the inter-American military system.[3] Although this military system had both bilateral and multilateral elements, in practice it was the bilateral Mutual Defense Assistance Agreements and the Military Assistance Program, under firm U.S. control, that dominated security relationships.

This military system declined in strength in the quiescent decade of the 1950s but was greatly expanded in the 1960s in the face of a new threat, that of *foco*-style insurgencies on the Cuban model.* U.S. security approaches toward Latin America in the 1960s (counterinsurgency and civic action) presented an interesting innovation in that they stressed the need to improve social and economic conditions as a way of undercutting the guerrilla's support among the people. The high priority given to this approach in the early and mid-1960s declined with the death of Che Guevara in 1967 and with the increasing U.S. involvement in Vietnam, as well as with the perception that Cuba was no longer actively supporting insurgencies in the area.

Even though U.S. security approaches had shifted from unilateral to a combination of bilateral and multilateral over the years, even the latter were strongly influenced by a sense of overwhelming U.S. power in the Caribbean Basin, which meant in practice that it was the U.S. definition of security threats and interests that predominated.

Challenges to the Traditional Approach

A number of changed circumstances and new realities have challenged the traditional approach to security issues in the late 1970s and early 1980s. A basic challenge is the fact that many of the Caribbean Basin nations are now defining their own security concerns in ways that are less convergent with U.S. security concerns than before. The "Southern Flank" concept as a U.S. defensive perimeter is rejected in favor of a broader concept of the Caribbean Basin as a geographic area in which each nation's own interests and security concerns should be weighed as carefully as those of the United States. Even the term "Caribbean Basin" is seen with some suspicion as a U.S. security concept that harks back to the anochronistic unilateral strategic approaches to the area.[4] Although the U.S. leadership role in security issues is recognized, there is now a greater sense that the security relationships with the

*The *foco* theory argued that a small core of highly trained and motivated cadre supported from Cuba could initiate revolutionary movements in various Latin American countries. The period of the *foco* theory lasted from 1959 until the death of Che Guevara in Bolivia in 1967.

U.S. must be based on true mutual interests rather than on ones defined by the United States.

The old conservative oligarchic order in Central American is crumbling and giving way to new and unpredictable arrangements; the traditional U.S. policy of ensuring stability by supporting the entrenched triad of church-army-landowner is quickly becoming irrelevant or counterproductive. Moreover, one element of the triad—the Catholic church—is undergoing dramatic change as important segments of the church begin to support basic social and economic reforms and independence, and also pose their own challenges to security policies.

In Cuba, U.S. attempts to isolate or pressure the Castro regime have failed to eliminate or limit the threat to U.S. security interests emanating from the island. On the other hand, short-lived attempts to improve relations have not appeared to have had any greater success. The Soviet's military presence and access to facilities in Cuba remains a major geostrategic asset, which they will not give up except in the context of a global U.S.-USSR understanding or confrontation.[5]

Since the late 1970s both security interests and the threats to them in the Caribbean Basin have become increasingly complex and interrelated. Security is perceived as involving economic, social, and political factors as much as military and strategic ones. The previous U.S. support for narrowly based anti-Communist regimes is now seen as self-defeating because of the manner in which such regimes tend to perpetuate conditions that in the long run provide a favorable environment for discontent and insurgency.[6] There remains, however, a realization that Caribbean Basin governments require assistance in facing up to insurgencies, especially if these in turn are supported from outside with direct or indirect Cuban assistance. The contemporary challenge is to provide the necessary security support (economic as well as military) without slipping back to old patterns in which the United States ends up supporting unrepresentative regimes.

Compounding these challenges to U.S. security interests is the realization that the historical overwhelming U.S. influence in the area has declined markedly in the past three decades. Although the United States still has extraordinary influence (actual as well as perceived) in many of the smaller states of the Caribbean Basin, its ability to shape events can no longer be taken for granted. In a sense, U.S. security interests since the late 1970s have faced a situation parallel to that of U.S. energy interests in the early 1970s: just as 1973 saw the end of the era of cheap and easy energy, so did the late 1970s see the end of a long period of cheap and easy Caribbean Basin security for the U.S. (Clearly, the decline had begun many years back, but acquired spectacular momentum with events in Nicaragua, Grenada, and El Salvador, and other areas of the Caribbean Basin in the late 1970s and early 1980s). The Fiscal Year 1983 Posture Statement of the U.S. Joint Chiefs of Staff expressed the following concern:

> It is becoming increasingly clear that a secure hemisphere is no longer a foregone conclusion and that the U.S. must now play a more active and enlightened role in hemispheric affairs. Specifically, the U.S. must continue to build on interests shared with Canada and Mexico, while viewing Latin America not as a Third World area removed from the traditional focus of U.S. strategy, but as a contiguous region whose future bears directly on the security of the hemisphere as a whole.[7]

Implications of These Challenges

These challenges to the traditional approach to U.S. security in the Caribbean Basin suggest that the following should be carefully considered as U.S. interests are reevaluated:

1. The concept of "security" should be broadened beyond the narrow military sense to include economic, social, and political considerations.
2. U.S. security policies should be able to accept change in a positive manner (or at least be able to accommodate to and live with it). The U.S. should be prepared to deal realistically with a variety of ideologies, economies, and sociopolitical systems and accept them as long as they do not threaten their neighbors or U.S. security interests.
3. Potential threats to security interests should be dispassionately and carefully analyzed to avoid overreaction. There should be an awareness of Caribbean Basin resentment over some past U.S. security policies and a sensitivity to avoid reactions rooted in past psychological and geographic perceptions of the area as a "U.S. lake." When differences on security issues arise, the United States should attempt to reassure and avoid the spiraling effect of mutual distrust and rising tensions.
4. Areas of regional and subregional mutual security interests should be found, explored, and emphasized to the greatest extent possible.
5. Approaches to security must be flexible and multilateral as well as bilateral and unilateral; they should be preventative in broad economic, political, and military terms, and not simply curative in terms aimed at containing a specific crisis.

6. The United States must be willing to make concessions to the security interests of other nations, to include those in the Caribbean Basin as well as outside it (Canada, Western Europe).

East-West Versus North-South Approaches to Security*

A useful vehicle for analyzing U.S. security interests involves considering the East-West and North-South approaches to security. These two aproaches differ in their emphasis on U.S. interests, threats to those interests, and policies to protect those interests. Although both approaches have always been present, and are not mutually exclusive, there is a sense of tension and competition between them. The relative priority given to the East-West or North-South approach shapes the emphasis and nature of each U.S. administration's approach to security in the Caribbean Basin.

The East-West approach emphasizes the outside threat and sees that threat as a danger to Latin America as well as to the United States. The Caribbean Basin is defined as a U.S. rear area that must be secured and denied to the adversary. The emphasis is on the U.S. strategic need for the resources in the Caribbean Basin, and on protecting the sea lines of communication, U.S. bases in the area, the Panama Canal, and other U.S. assets. Policies in this East-West approach have a tendency to be unilateral on the U.S. side in terms of securing these assets, although bilateral and multilateral policies are also involved. The bilateral policies are designed to strengthen U.S. relations with strategically key countries, whereas the multilateral ones stress the need for building coalitions against the outside threat.

The North-South approach emphasizes the internal conditions in the Caribbean Basin nations that lead to instability and thus provide opportunities for external adversaries to exploit. In this conception, the Caribbean Basin is seen as an area in which U.S. influence can make a positive contribution toward ameliorating the conditions leading to instability. The North-South approach thus tends to emphasize the political, social, and economic dimensions of U.S. interests. Policy prescriptions are aimed at enhancing development by stressing economic growth, democratization, and protection of human rights. Military aspects of the North-South approach stress nation-building, civic action, and the need to understand the economic, social and political roots of instability.

*The author is indebted to Gabriel Marcella for suggesting and developing this conceptual framework.

As noted previously, both approaches are usually present, but with varying priorities. It should also be noted that it is easier to "sell" the East-West approach to U.S. congressional and public opinion constituencies than the North-South approach, especially during period in which the U.S. economy is depressed.

U.S. SECURITY INTERESTS

This section will analyze the basic U.S. security interests associated with the traditional approach to Caribbean Basin security in terms of how relevant they are in the 1980s as well as how the new challenges to security require a redefinition of these interests. Threats to these interests, and the seriousness of these threats, will be assessed, as well as some special concerns held by individual countries. A more detailed consideration of the military dimensions of threats to U.S. security interests will be presented in the next section.

Establishing and Maintaining a Peaceful, Secure, Stable, and Friendly Southern Flank

This interest remains valid and legitimate, although it requires new analysis and restatement. The significance of this interest lies in the geographic proximity and increasing integration of the United States into the Basin as a Caribbean nation. Ideally, it is in the U.S. interest to have a Caribbean Basin in which outside threats are neutralized, interstate tensions do not reach the conflict level, and internal unrest and dissent find satisfactory outlets within the political system without turning to violence or affording opportunities for destabilizing or subversive activities from outside sources.

The strategic and military dimension of this interest for the United States can be expressed in economy-of-force terms, which have historically permitted the bulk of U.S. military forces to focus on other areas. To use an extreme example, a hostile and unstable Mexico might lead to a sealing of the border and result in a major drain on U.S. military resources. At another level, the cost of assistance programs in the area might rise sharply if widespread insurgencies in the Basin were met by U.S. attempts to aid governments to contain them. The strategic and military dimensions of this interest can also be expressed in terms of U.S. access to the area as well as denial of the area to potential adversaries. The geography of the Basin, and the major trade routes that cross it, put a premium on certain key choke points (See Figure 4-1); access to these points is an important security consideration in terms of a Soviet-Cuban threat to vital sea lines of communica-

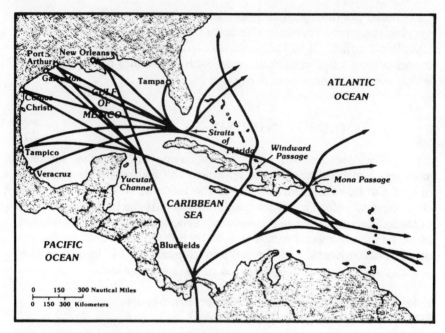

(*Source:* U.S. Secretary of Defense, *Annual Report to Congress, FY 1983*, page II-24.)

Figure 4.1. Primary sea lines of communication in the Caribbean Basin.

tions in case of a European conflict. At a lower level of pirority, the Caribbean Basin offers a number of training, testing, development, communications, tracking, monitoring, and surveillance sites that provide important military advantages to the United States.[8]

The political and diplomatic dimension of this interest lies in the value to the United States of having an immediate set of neighbors with reasonably compatible values and a reasonably convergent approach to regional and global problems. Given the number of nation-states in the Caribbean Basin, their voting power in the Organization of American States, the United Nations, and other fora is important, and their support of U.S. goals is significant. Conversely, the inability of the United States to obtain Caribbean Basin support is a political embarrassment in the international arena. The Basin also represents that segment of the Third World closest to the United States in geographic, economic, and cultural terms, and the ability or inability of the United States to relate positively to the area delivers a message to the rest of the Third World.

The economic dimension of this security interest to the United States lies in the relationship between security and economic development, as well as in the need for a viable economic base on which to build democratic political institutions. A depressed economy, unemployment, undernourishment, an unmanageable external debt, and a sense of dependence on outside economic forces provide a rich breeding ground for unrest and insurgency, whether it is home-grown or stimulated from outside. There is, of course, no guarantee that economic aid will solve these problems; it may in fact have short-term destabilizing effects.

The United States' interest in establishing and maintaining a peaceful, secure, stable, and friendly Caribbean Basin is threatened from a number of sources, some internal and some emanating from Cuba with Soviet support. The fundamental threats are the internal ones, in some of the Basin nations, that stem from the combination of underdevelopment, faltering economies, and unrepresentative political institutions. Specific economic problems find their root causes in a mix of structural and class imbalances, the increasing cost of oil, declining prices for major exports, excessive reliance on one or two sources of foreign exchange, high rates of unemployment and inflation, decline in the GNP, and severe balance-of-payments deficits.[9]

To this internal threat must be added the threat posed by Cuba with backing from the Soviet Union. Although Cuba has obviously not created the conditions for instability, it has seen and taken advantage of these conditions to further its own goals. In contrast to Cuban support for insurgencies in the *foco* period of the early 1960s, the present level and type of support is highly sophisticated and effective. Cuban efforts are now much more carefully tuned to existing conditions within each country, and are supported by a wide spectrum of intelligence, training, ideological, and propaganda activities.[10] Behind these activities lies the Cuban military establishment, now the most powerful in the Basin after the United States, and capable of projecting its power in a number of situations.

The threat posed by Nicaragua in the Central American context of the early 1980s is a more controversial one. To some, Nicaragua is acting as a Soviet–Cuban surrogate in a well-coordinated strategy aimed at overthrowing the existing governments of Central America. To others, the Nicaraguan regime is increasing its military strength (with Soviet and Cuban assistance) in response to a series of threats to its continued existence as a revolutionary government.[11] Regardless of the motivation, it is clear that the impressive increase in the size of its military and security apparatus introduces an important new element into the Central American strategic equation. A particularly destabilizing development would be the introduction into Nicaragua of a major new weapons system with clear offensive capabilities, such as advanced MiG aircraft. To date, the Soviets have acted with some caution on this issue, suggesting a sensitivity to the unpredictable effects of such a provocative step.

A further threat to this interest is the possibility of interstate conflict in the area. Such conflicts might arise from causes unrelated to the two prior sets of threats (that is, internal economic and political problems or Cuban interference), but could have equally damaging effects. Historical border and territorial disputes in the area include those between Honduras and El Salvador, Guatemala and Belize, Nicaragua and Colombia, Colombia and Venezuela, Venezuela and Guyana, and Guyana and Suriname. To this list must the added possibility of conflict in Central American between Nicaragua and Honduras over the activities of groups on the border hostile to the regime in Managua. Several of the possible interstate conflicts in the Caribbean Basin carry with them the threat that one of the parties in the conflict might request the military assistance of Cuba or the Soviet Union, thus setting up the conditions for a superpower confrontation in the region.

These considerations suggest that the original statement of this U.S. security interest can be restated in the contemporary context as follows: *assisting in the establishment and maintenance of a peaceful, secure, stable, and friendly (or at least not hostile) Caribbean Basin that is economically developing, with governments generally accepted as legitimate and respectful of the human rights of their citizens, and with access to effective mechanisms for resolving or defusing interstate conflicts.*

Expressed in this manner, this interest contains a number of different goals that may, in a given situation, be contradictory or mutually exclusive. It may not be possible to pursue economic development, political legitimacy, stability, and peace at the same time, and the policymaker will be forced to make hard choices in the priorities given these elements. Nevertheless, this expression of a basic U.S. interest in the area suggests the complexity and interdependent nature of the economic and political considerations that form the basis for long-term security in the Caribbean Basin.

Guaranteeing U.S. Access to the Area's Raw Materials, Trade, Investment Opportunities, and Transportation Routes

The significance of this U.S. security interest remains high not only in terms of the Basin's own resources, but also in terms of its function as a major transit area for raw materials vital to the United States. The Caribbean Basin itself provides a significant quantity of resources of strategic significance to the United States, especially oil (Mexico, Venezuela), iron ore (Venezuela), bauxite (Jamaica, Guyana, Suriname), and a series of minerals. Approximately 44 percent of the foreign tonnage and 45 percent of the crude oil imported into the United States pass through the Caribbean.[12] U.S. investment in the area (excluding Mexico), while not high in global terms, is important to the United States and vital to many of the economies of the area. U.S. imports from Caribbean Basin nations total about $30 billion a year, and exports about $31 billion (1981). There is some $13 billion in direct U.S. investment; an estimated 6 million U.S. tourists visited the area in 1981.[13]

This U.S. interest is, of course, linked to the previous one in that an economically stable Caribbean Basin would inevitably be closely tied to the United States in terms of its raw material exports, trade, investment, and transportation activities. In a strictly economic sense, these activities are far more important to the Caribbean Basin nations than to the United States since the economies of the Basin depend so heavily on the United States. This suggests that concessions by the United States on matters of tariffs and terms of trade may have an important impact on the Basin at relatively little cost to the United States, and would help achieve some of the security goals that are closely linked to economic development in the Caribbean.

Within the broad statement of this interest, some special concerns have prominence. One of these is Mexico, where levels of U.S. investment and trade are indeed significant, and where the issues of Mexican oil exports and migration are paramount. U.S. interests in a secure, prosperous, and cooperative Mexico have such a priority that in many ways they overshadow U.S. security interests in the remaining countries of the Basin. A second special case, although at a lower level of priority and concern, is Panama. Although the strategic and commercial significance of the canal has declined slowly over the years, it remains an important asset for the United States and many of the nations in the Caribbean Basin.

The U.S. interest in having access to the area's raw materials, trade, investment, and transportation routes is threatened by the internal economic and political factors noted previously as well as by Cuba and the USSR. In assessing the significance of this threat, it should be kept in mind that it is in the interests of the Caribbean nations themselves to maintain these relationships with the United States, and that few viable alternatives are open to them. The Soviet Union has not shown a disposition to support economically a second Cuba in the Caribbean Basin. A more significant threat, from the U.S. perspective, is that chaotic conditions might lead to a breakdown in normal trade and supply patterns. On the positive side, economic terms that the Caribbean nations perceive as fair would contribute toward the foundation of solid security relationships.

We can thus restate the original interest in terms more consistent with the contemporary situation: *permitting the United States reasonable access to the Caribbean Basin's raw materials, trade, investment opportunities, and transportation routes on mutually agreeable terms of price, availability, and volume.* As was the case with the first U.S. security interest, this too represents an ideal goal. But this interest is much more negotiable in terms of price paid and the possibilities of a mutually beneficial economic relationship.

Keeping Hostile Powers out of the Area

Any consideration of this interest must begin by acknowledging that it has been compromised ever since the Soviet presence in Cuba was established in the early 1960s. In one sense, the threat posed by the Soviet presence in Cuba is less than in the early 1960s since Soviet forces can now strike strategic targets in the United States from locations other than Cuba. The current Soviet presence in Cuba, however, poses a series of threats that are complex and at several levels besides the possible use of Cuba (or other Caribbean nations) as potential bases for Soviet strategic weapons. At one level the presence provides optimum surveillance, monitoring, and intelligence installations. The Soviet presence is also a political and military commitment to Cuba and the regime of Fidel Castro. At a third level the presence provides the logistics that have permitted Cuba to emerge as the strongest military power in the Caribbean after the United States and to challenge a series of U.S. interests in the area. Finally, the Soviet Union's access to naval and air bases in Cuba give it an important capability to project power into the area and threaten sea lanes (including those needed to support NATO forces in Europe) and installations in the Basin.[14] This capability is enhanced by having Cuba available as a Soviet forward staging area with large prepositioned stores of military equipment in place before a crisis erupts.

The Soviets have recently embarked on a major increase in arms shipments to Cuba (the 1981 and 1982 totals are the highest since 1962); although part of this total can be attributed to the beginning of a five-year replacement cycle, it is hard to avoid the conclusion that the shipment levels represent a new element in Cuban and Soviet capabilities in the Basin.[15] If Cuban MiG 23 aircraft were to be based in Nicaragua and Grenada, their combat radius would extend to all of Central American, the Panama Canal, northern South America, and most of the Caribbean.[16] Such MiG basing would be intimidating to the nations of the Basin and would heighten tensions in the area. Actual use of these aircraft to close Caribbean shipping lanes or the sea lines of communication (SLOCs) to Europe would trigger an appropriate U.S. response, which must be planned for on a contingency basis. Clearly, Caribbean Basin security issues become rather irrelevant in a scenario involving a full-scale nuclear exchange with the Soviet Union. In scenarios that are non-nuclear or nuclear at a tactical level only, however, the U.S. must prepare contingency plans against the threat from Cuba. These plans would involve a diversion of important U.S. military resources urgently needed elsewhere at the moment of crisis or conflict.

In situations short of a U.S. conflict with the Soviet Union or Cuba, the major concern should focus on convincing the Caribbean Basin nations that it is also in their security interest that the Soviet presence in the area be limited. In this connection the political and economic relations between the United States and the Caribbean Basin nations would be a major factor in persuading them to support these U.S. efforts. In the case of the more radical states in the Caribbean Basin, the U.S. should seek to convince them that the survival of their regime does not require turning to the Soviet Union for military assistance and protection, as long as they do not attempt to export their revolution.

In terms of the reality of the Soviet presence in Cuba, the United States has sought on several occasions to reach understandings with the Soviet Union: 1962, on strategic weapons; 1970, on the use of Cuban ports for missile-launching submarines; 1979, on the presence of Soviet combat troops in Cuba. These understandings form a part of the larger context of U.S.–USSR relations and the mutually tolerated limits of behavior near each other's borders. Despite these understandings, the Soviets have recently threatened to station SS-20 nuclear missiles (with a range of 3200 miles) in either Cuba or Nicaragua as a response to United States plans to deploy Pershing II and cruise missiles in Europe.[17]

With these considerations in mind, the U.S. interest in this connection can be restated as follows: *establishing understood limits to the actions of the Soviet Union in the Caribbean Basin, and obtaining the support of the Caribbean Basin nations in these efforts.*

Additional U.S. Security Concerns

The present context suggests some additional U.S. security concerns in the Caribbean Basin that were not specifically included in the three broad interests considered previously.

1. **Migration.** The United States has a security interest in avoiding situations that would result in massive and uncontrolled levels of migration. These situations could be internal political or economic chaos, revolutions, insurgencies, or interstate conflicts. Mexico is clearly the nation that would have the greatest immediate impact on the United States in these terms, but other Caribbean Basin nations also have this potential. This interest in avoiding massive migration flows is to some extent subsumed in the first U.S. security interest considered (relating to a peaceful, secure, stable, and friendly Caribbean Basin), but its significance is such, and its disruptive potential high enough, that it merits consideration as a separate security concern. Although there is a purely military dimension to the issue (i.e., the possible use of military units to help control the migration), it is clear that the humane and more effective solution is a preventative one focusing on eliminating or ameliorating the circumstances that would give rise to these massive migration flows.

2. **Terrorism.** The general U.S. interest in controlling terrorism has specific aspects in the Caribbean Basin in terms of the Puerto Rico status issue and the possibility of terrorist actions in the United States that have origins in Caribbean Basin tensions.[18]

3. **Narcotics.** The U.S. interest in controlling narcotics traffic in the Caribbean Basin has security implications because of the indications of links to arms traffic and to Cuban involvement,[19] and the way these drugs disrupt and degrade the quality of life in the United States. In the last several years there has been an increasing U.S. military involvement in the control of Caribbean Basin drug traffic using surveillance aircraft, satellites, and ships.

U.S. Basing in the Caribbean

The principal U.S. military bases in the area include the following:

In Puerto Rico:* Roosevelt Roads Naval Station; Ramey Air Force
    Base (inactive); Fort Buchanan (inactive); installations of the
    92nd Infantry Brigade, National Guard.
In Cuba: Guantanamo Naval Base

---

*At the time of this writing (late 1983), there were plans to reactivate Ramey Air Force Base, Fort Buchanan, and other bases in Puerto Rico. These plans were strongly opposed by certain sectors in Puerto Rico that objected to the "remilitarization of Puerto Rico" and its use as a training and operational base for U.S. military activities in Central America and the Caribbean.

In Panama: Fort Amador (193rd Infantry Brigade); Fort Gulick (School of the Americas); Headquarters, U.S. Southern Command, Quarry Heights; Howard Air Force Base.

There are also a number of smaller installations in Panama and on several of the Caribbean Islands. These include an oceanographic research station, missile-tracking installations, navigation facilities, test and evaluation centers, and anti-submarine warfare facilities. Under the 1977 Carter–Torrijos Treaties, the Panama installations and U.S. military presence will be removed by the time of the expiration of the Panama Canal Treaty (year 2000).

Because of the small number of U.S. bases in the Caribbean, it is important to ensure that the U.S. military has access to ports and airfields in other Basin nations; such access relies principally on the political relationship between the United States and the Caribbean nations involved.

THE MILITARY DIMENSION OF THREATS TO U.S. INTERESTS

This section will describe and assess the military dimension of the threats to U.S. interests in the Caribbean Basin, with a primary focus on the Cuban–Soviet threat. A general description of the scope of this threat can be found in the U.S. Military Posture Statement prepared by the Joint Chiefs of Staff:

Cuban military ties with the Soviet Union and the growth of Soviet air and naval presence in Cuba pose the most significant military threats to US security interests in the hemisphere (see Map 1-10 [Figure 4.2]). Although highly dependent upon the USSR, Cuban military forces are large, modern, and increasingly professional. Because of Cuba's proximity to vital SLOCs, the Soviets or Cubans in wartime could attempt to interdict the movement of troops, supplies, and raw materials in the Gulf of Mexico or the Caribbean Sea and could strike key facilities in the area.

Cuban diplomatic and political leverage in Central America, the Caribbean, South America, and with the nonaligned nations has increased, primarily as a result of Soviet political and financial support. Cuba will continue to back insurgent movements and exploit opportunities for revolutionary change, as evidenced most recently in Nicaragua and El Salvador. This threatens collective security throughout the region. Although Jamaica still faces economic difficulties, Cuban influence there appears recently to have suffered a setback.

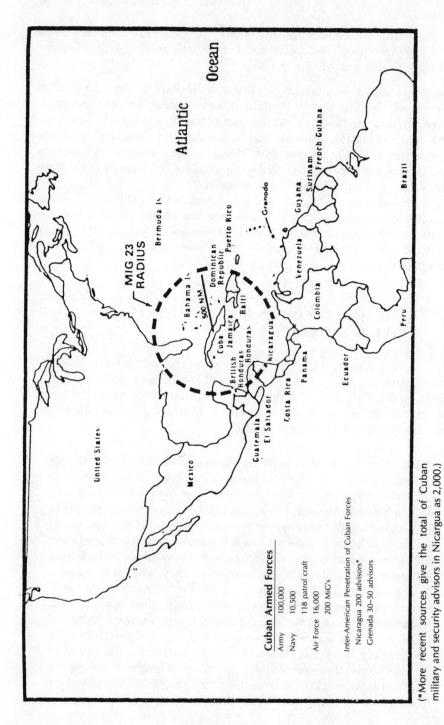

Cuban Armed Forces

Army	100,000
Navy	10,500
	118 patrol craft
Air Force	16,000
	200 MiG's

Inter-American Penetration of Cuban Forces

Nicaragua 200 advisors*
Grenada 30–50 advisors

(*More recent sources give the total of Cuban military and security advisors in Nicaragua as 2,000.)

Figure 4.2. Cuban military influence—Western Hemisphere.

The USSR will continue attempts to weaken US influence in Latin America and exploit opportunities to gain positions of influence through diplomatic, economic, military, and covert means. Close ties with Cuba will facilitate Soviet activities in the area and provide maritime facilities and bases for electronic surveillance and aerial reconnaissance. The Soviets can be expected to continue to upgrade Cuba's military capabilities, and overall Cuban influence could increase further in the Caribbean during the next decade.[20]

One salient characteristic of the military dimension of the threat is the wide range in the size of military establishments in the Basin. The Caribbean Basin contains one superpower and the presence of the second superpower that has built up its principal regional ally (Cuba) to the point where it is the most powerful force in the area after the United States. At the other extreme are the military and police institutions of the new nations of the eastern Caribbean and the remaining colonies. Table 4.1 summarizes this range.

The Soviet Threat

As noted previously, scenarios for a NATO–Warsaw Pact conflict in Europe rely heavily on a massive logistical resupply by sea employing the Caribbean and Atlantic sealanes. Soviet naval forces, especially the submarine, pose a direct threat to these lines of communication. The Soviet Navy, once considered basically a coastal defense force, has grown dramatically in the past twenty years to the point where its ability to project power into the Caribbean and the Western Atlantic is now a major consideration for NATO planners. The threat posed by hostile submarines in the Caribbean is not a new one—in five months of 1942 German submarines sank 114 Allied ships in the Caribbean.[21] What is new is that the present potential adversary has the possibility of using a base within the Caribbean itself; such basing in Cuba greatly simplifies logistical problems for the Soviet armed forces. Furthermore, anti-submarine devices such as the passive SOSUS (Sound Surveillance Underwater System) are generally less effective in the Caribbean, where the islands can provide shelter against detection.[22]

The availability of the Cuban facilities thus provides multiple opportunities for the Soviet Union in a time of crisis or actual conflict:

1. The rapid deployment of more advanced Soviet aircarft to Cuba would put increasingly larger areas of the southern United States inside the combat ranges of these aircraft.
2. The use of Cuba as a recovery and relaunch platform for long-

Table 4.1. Military and Security Forces in the Caribbean

	Military Forces	Security Forces (Police and Paramilitary)
Anguilla	–	26[a]
Antigua	–	327[a]
Bahamas	–	1,156[a]
Barbados	250[a]	822[a]
Belize	(2,300 U.K.)[a]	640[a]
Cayman Islands	–	113[a]
Colombia	67,800[b]	50,000[b]
Costa Rica	–	7,000[b]
Cuba	227,000[c]	15,000[b] (also has a sizable militia)
Dominican Rep.	24,500[b]	10,000[b]
Dominica	–	n.a.
El Salvador	16,000[b]	9,000[b]
Grenada	1,000[a]	300[a]
Guatemala	18,550[b]	11,600[b]
Guyana	7,000[b]	5,000[b]
Haiti	8,000[c]	14,900[b]
Honduras	11,700[b]	3,000[b]
Jamaica	4,000[a]	6,420[a]
Mexico	119,500[c]	n.a.
Nicaragua	25,000[c]	5,000[b] (also has a sizable militia)
Panama	9,000[b]	– (National Guard is also police force)
Puerto Rico	National Guard	7,500[a]
St. Lucia	–	522[a]
St. Vincent	–	n.a.
Suriname	800[a]	n.a.
Trinidad & Tobago	1,950[b]	2,500[a]
Turks & Caicos	–	70[a]
Venezuela	40,800[c]	20,000[b]
Virgin Is. (U.K.)	–	18[a]
Virgin Is. (U.S.)	–	100[a]

[a] From Richard Sim and James Anderson, "The Caribbean Strategic Vacuum," *Conflict Studies* 121 (August 1980):23.

[b] From "Military Balance," *U.S. Air Force Magazine* (December 1982):134-140.

[c] From U.S. State Department, *Atlas of the Caribbean Basin* (Washington, D.C., September 1982), p. 3.

range strategic bombers such as the TU-26 Backfire would greatly increase the threat posed by these aircraft.

3. The refueling and resupply of Soviet submarines in Cuba would significantly increase their time on station and would allow them to avoid NATO interdiction efforts in the Greenland–Iceland–United Kingdom gap.

4. In times of crisis and tension, the USSR could quickly establish missile bases in Cuba as well as deploy tactical and strategic air

assets; these weapons could have nuclear as well as conventional capabilities. While such a step would violate the 1962 (and subsequent) understandings with the United States, the USSR may well consider this step worthwhile as a way of countering the deployment of new U.S. or NATO missiles near its own border and propose a negotiation to arrange a *quid pro quo* for their removal.

The Soviet military presence within Cuba itself is not considered to have a significant offensive capability. The presence involves a ground forces brigade (about 2600 to 3000 troops), a military advisory group (2500), and a major electronic intelligence collection activity at Lourdes, which is the largest outside the Soviet Union. The probable mission of the brigade is a "trip wire" symbolizing the Soviet commitment to defend Cuba, as well as protection for Soviet personnel and installations on the island.[23]

Naval deployments by Soviet combatants are periodically made to the Caribbean, and all but one have visited Cuba. In the South Atlantic the annual total of Soviet ship-days in the area has risen from 200 in 1970 to 2600 in 1980.[24] Such deployments reinforce the reality that the United States has accepted a Soviet naval presence in the area. They also serve an important psychological function by showing the flag and emphasizing the Soviet Union's backing for Cuba and other radical states in the Basin.[25] As expressed by the Soviet Navy's Commander-in-Chief, Admiral Sergei Gorshkov:

> Friendly visits by Soviet seamen offer the opportunity to the peoples of the countries visited to see for themselves the creativity of socialist principles in our country, the genuine parity of the Soviet Union and their high cultural level. In our ships they see the achievements of Soviet science, technology and industry. Soviet mariners, from rating to admiral, bring to the peoples of other countries the truth about our socialist country, our Soviet ideology and culture and our Soviet way of life.[26]

Soviet Tu-95 Bear-D reconnaissance aircraft deploy to Cuba on a regular basis; frequently these flights coincide with U.S., NATO, or Soviet exercises, or with periods of increased international tension. Recently Bear F's (with anti-submarine warfare capability) were introduced to the region, presumably to better observe U.S. Navy exercises in March 1983. The Soviets have also apparently sent pilots to fly Cuban air defense aircraft during periods when Cuban pilots were deployed to Africa in support of operations in Angola and Ethiopia.[27] The possibility of using Cuban airfields for recovery, refuel, and resupply of strategic aircraft gives the Soviets considerable flexibility and significantly complicates the U.S. air defense problem.

Cuba[28]

Cuba possesses today an impressive military establishment capable of projecting power within the Caribbean Basin, assisting its allies, and threatening U.S. interests in the area.

Several factors account for this capability:

1. The sheer numbers in the Cuban armed forces, which are the largest in Latin America after Brazil (which has twelve times Cuba's population).
2. The ability to mobilize reservists and militia to bring the possible total armed forces in a moment of crisis to almost 1 million (out of a total population of just under 10 million).
3. The modernization program carried out by the Soviet Union since 1975.
4. The numbers and types of aircraft, which make Cuba's air force the best equipped in Latin America.
5. The airlift and airdrop capability of its transport aircraft, and the presence of 3000 to 4000 airborne troops.
6. The existence of elite special forces units, the Ministry of the Interior Special Troops, and the Revolutionary Armed Forces Assault and Landing Brigade.
7. Combat experience in Angola and Ethiopia.
8. The naval capability represented by its three submarines, its frigates, and numerous patrol craft.

Although this capability does not pose a serious threat to the continental United States, it is a formidable military establishment in Caribbean Basin terms and could be effectively employed to support a Cuban ally or affect the outcome of an internal or interstate conflict in the area. Cuba also has an impressive air defense capability that would make any attempt to neutralize or invade Cuba a major undertaking that would be very costly in personnel, materials, and money.

The Cuban air strike capability could reach much of the southeastern United States, and this capability must be taken into account in any conflict scenario involving the United States, the Soviet Union, and Cuba.

The Cuban military, including the ready reserves (but not the militia) now numbers more than 225,000 (200,000 army, 15,000 air force, and 10,000 navy), in addition to a large militia, border guards, and other paramilitary organizations. The percentage of the Cuban

Relative Military Strength

For Selected Caribbean Countries

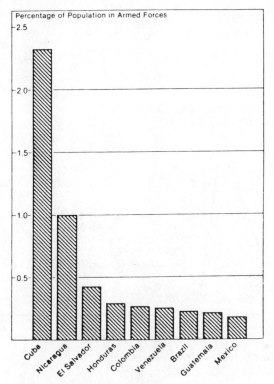

(*Source:* U.S. State Department, *Cuban Armed Forces and the Soviet Military Presence*, Special Report 103, [Washington, D.C., August 1982], p. 2.)

Figure 4.3. Relatively military strength.

population in the active military or ready reserves (over 2 percent) surpasses that of the other Caribbean nations by a substantial margin (their average is about 0.4 percent). See Figure 4.3.

Soviet military deliveries to Cuba increased sharply in 1981 and 1982, an increase that has been accounted for in part by a routine five-year upgrading and replacement cycle, and arms for the new territorial militia, but which also has been seen as a stockpile used to arm Cuban allies in the region. (See Figure 4.4.)

These shipments (especially since 1975 and the 1981–82 surge) represent a major quantitative and qualitative increase for the Cuban military. Ground force equipment has emphasized improvement in

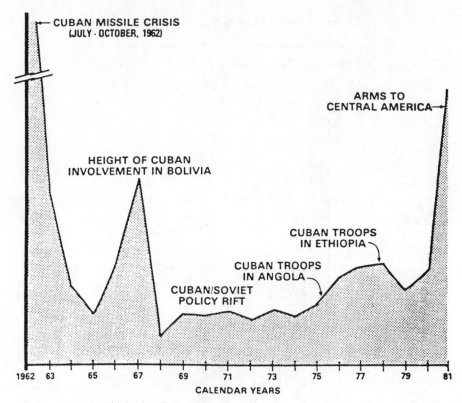

(*Source:* U.S. Joint Chiefs of Staff, *Posture Statement for FY 1983*, [Washington, D.C., 1983], p. 13.)

Figure 4.4. Soviet military deliveries to Cuba.

mechanized and firepower capabilities, and has involved T-62 tanks, BMP infantry combat vehicles, BRDM armored reconnaissance vehicles, antitank guns, towed field guns, BM-21 multiple rocket launchers, and self-propelled anti-aircraft artillery.

The Cuban Air Force has some 200 MiG aircraft in the inventory, to include twenty MiG 23 Flogger F's and fifteen MiG 23 Flogger E's.[29] These aircraft have the range to reach portions of Central America, Florida, and most of the larger Caribbean nations. Air defense missile systems (organic to the air force) include the Soviet SA-2, SA-3, and SA-6, with associated radar and electronic warfare systems. In addition, ground forces units have SA-7 SAMs and sizable amounts of anti-aircraft artillery.

In the context of the Caribbean Basin, Cuba's airlift capability would be able to transport significant numbers of airborne troops and equipment anywhere in the Basin. Cuba has already demonstrated its ability and willingness to commit troops in the 1975 Angolan conflict (although the distances involved required Soviet logistical assistance). Aircraft in the Cuban military and civilian (Cubana Airlines) inventory at present (Il-62 long range, Tu-154 medium range, and An-26 short range) give the Cubans this capability to transport and supply a substantial expeditionary force.

The Cuban Navy is basically a defensive force, although its three Foxtrot class submarines (range 9000 miles) and two Koni-class frigates (range 2000 miles without refueling) give it a limited projection capability. The missile-equipped Osa and Komar class patrol boats and the Turya class hydrofoil torpedo boats can carry out limited interdiction missions. Senior U.S. naval officers have expressed concern over the threat posed by the Cuban submarines and patrol boats to shipping in Caribbean sea lines of communication. They would also pose a significant threat to any seaborne invasion of Cuba.

The problem posed by Cuban conventional capabilities was summed up by UCLA Professor Edward Gonzalez in a recent Rand study: "Cuba could represent a military threat too uncertain to justify a preemptive attack, but sufficiently plausible to tie down a large number of United States naval and air force units."[30]

Cuba's conventional military capabilities described above are supplemented by its support to radical regimes in the Caribbean Basin and to insurgent groups involved in attempts to overthrow the governments of several nations in the region. In contrast with the 1960 *foco* period (see footnote on p. 141), Cuban support for insurgencies is now much more sensitive to existing local conditions and focuses on uniting the various factions, training guerrilla cadres, supplying or arranging for the supplying of arms and equipment, and employing the extensive Cuban intelligence and propaganda system to support the insurgency.

In the case of Nicaragua, Cuba succeeded in uniting the three factions of the Sandinista National Liberation Front (FSLN) in 1978 and supported the FSLN in the critical months of fighting until their victory in July 1979. Since July 1979 the Cubans have provided the FSLN with military and security advisors, and have assisted in the delivery of large amounts of weapons and ammunition, which have made Nicaragua's military the strongest and best equipped ground force in Central America.

Nicaragua

Since the overthrow of Somoza in July 1979, the FSLN has steadily increased its role in the government of Nicaragua at the same time as it built up its military force with Cuban and Eastern European assistance. Soviet and Soviet bloc equipment channeled through Cuba has included the T54/55 tank, BTR-60 armored personnel carriers, artillery, anti-aircraft guns, light aircraft, helicopters, and surface-to-air missiles.[31] One item conspicuously absent from the FSLN inventory is MiG fighter aircraft. Reports circulating in 1982 indicated that Nicaraguan pilots were receiving training in this type of aircraft in Bulgaria, but as of early 1983 no MiGs had been delivered. A number of Nicaraguan airfields have been improved, their runways lengthened since July 1979, and MiGs could be based in a number of locations.

The size of the Nicaraguan armed forces grew rapidly after July 1979. The authoritative *Military Balance* for 1982/83 gives the size of the active armed forces as 21,500 (to be increased) with 20,000 of this in the ground force. To this must be added a border guard of some 5000 (under the Sandinista Popular Army) and a civilian militia of perhaps 50,000. The U.S. Secretary of Defense's *Annual Report to the Congress for FY 1983* indicated that the present level of the armed forces was expected to rise to 250,000, which would mean that one in every ten Nicaraguans would be under arms, in either the regular force, the reserves, or the militia.[32]

The establishment of a strong Nicaraguan military with close ties to Cuba represented by 2000 military and security advisors poses a considerable threat to security in Central America. Nicaragua was used as a major conduit for weapons and logistical support to the Salvadoran guerrillas from late 1980 through the "final offensive" of early 1981; since then the flow of arms has been reduced,[33] although Nicaragua remains an important safe haven and line of communication for the Salvadoran insurgents.

Grenada

With the March 1979 coup, the People's Revolutionary Government led by Maurice Bishop brought Grenada into a close relationship with Cuba, which included military and civilian advisors and substantial economic aid. The pre-1979 army of 250 men was disbanded and replaced with a 1000-man People's Revolutionary Army trained and armed by Cuba; it is the strongest military force in the Eastern Caribbean.[34]

A major security issue involving Grenada was the possible use of the 9800-foot-long runway at the new Point Salines airport, built with considerable Cuban assistance. The Grenadian government insisted that its basic purpose is economic: tourism would be boosted by a modern and more adequate airport nearer to the capital of St. George's that could accommodate jumbo jets.[35] The U.S. government has pointed out that this airport is more than Grenada's needs justify, and that it has strategic significance as a possible staging base for MiG aircraft since it is located near an important oil tanker route, the Trinidad oil fields, the Netherlands Antilles refineries, and major routes to the Panama Canal.[36] Figure 4.5 shows the coverage of the Caribbean Basin by MiG 23 aircraft if they were to be based in Cuba, Nicaragua, and Grenada.

SECURITY INTERESTS OF OTHER STATES

General

Other nations' perceptions of their security interests in the Caribbean Basin show a considerable diversity; "security" means different things to different states. In a general sense, this diversity is reflected in two rhetorical questions: security for whom, and security for what.

As noted in the section on the traditional approaches to security in the Caribbean Basin, the "for whom" question historically has been answered in terms that emphasized security for the United States, or at best for the region as interpreted and defined by the United States. Under the strategic division of labor inherent in the traditional approach, the United States would protect the hemisphere from any outside threat (be it fascism in World War II or Communism in the Cold War), while the nations of the region maintained internal stability with U.S. assistance. This approach was embodied in the U.S. perception that the Caribbean Basin was the "strategic southern Flank," a defensive perimeter in which U.S. strategic concerns were paramount. The numerous contemporary challenges noted above have seriously undermined the validity of this unilateral U.S. definition of security interests in the Caribbean Basin, as nations of the Basin increasingly emphasize their own security interests and concerns. The decline of the predominance of unilateral U.S. strategic approaches does not necessarily lead to a complete fragmentation to the point where each Caribbean Basin nation protects its own narrow national interests. It can be argued that the region or parts of it (including the United States as a Caribbean nation) does have security interests as a region or subregion, which most of the Caribbean Basin nations can support, and which provide a basis for a broader regional or subregional approach to security in the area. Some of these interests and related security issues will be noted later. It is clear, however, that in the contemporary context the "security for whom" question must be broadened to include the nations of the Basin as well as the region as a whole.

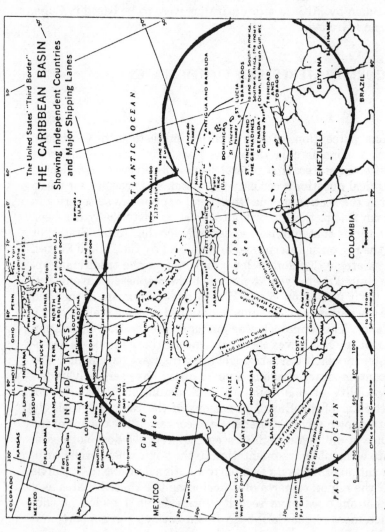

(*Source:* Base map from U.S. Department of State, *Gist: U.S. Interests in the Caribbean Basin* [Washington, D.C., May 1982]. MiG 23 radius coverage added by the author.)

Figure 4.5. Coverage of the Caribbean Basin by MiG 23 aircraft (combat radius of 500 nautical miles) if based in Cuba, Nicaragua, and Grenada.

The "security for what" question can be phrased in terms of "security for status quo or security for change." As noted previously, U.S. definitions of security in the past have traditionally stressed the status quo, or at the most some rather narrow limits to the change that would be tolerated. In the contemporary context of Caribbean Basin security issues, security must be perceived as tolerating nonviolent change to accommodate the broader vision that long-term security is based fundamentally on economic development and democratic political institutions.

A legacy from the past (reaffirmed in some cases by present policies) is the perception held in some Caribbean Basin nations that the United States can, in itself, be a security threat. This perception stems in part from the period of U.S. interventionism and hegemony, and in part from unilateral U.S. overt and covert actions in the Caribbean Basin in recent decades. Although the present ability of the United States to influence events in these ways is undoubtedly exaggerated, the impact of the legacy has been to create a climate of suspicion that U.S. security priorities tend to lead it to take unilateral actions with little regard for the interests of the Caribbean Basin nations.

Because of the important political role the military plays in many of the Caribbean Basin nations, the military's own views on security matters must also be taken into consideration. The so-called first mission of the armed forces, that of defending against outside threats to sovereignty, had been seen as rather hypothetical for many years, but the 1969 Honduras-El Salvador conflict and the contemporary possibility of other interstate conflicts has raised the salience of this concern. A second mission was emphasized in the early 1960s with the threat of externally supported guerrilla warfare: the mission of internal security and counterinsurgency. Many of the Caribbean Basin military establishments (especially the ones with a police role) had been performing internal security functions for many years, but greatly expanded this role with the counterinsurgency thrust of the 1960s and 1970s. The so-called third mission of the armed forces, that of contributing to national development, has received much less emphasis in the Caribbean Basin than in other parts of Latin America.

The paragraphs that follow briefly assess some of the specific national security concerns of selected Caribbean Basin nations.

Mexico

Mexico's security concerns focus on the implications of its financial and political crisis and its relationship with the United States and its Central American neighbors. Internal stability will hinge on the ability of the ruling Partido Revolucionario Institucional (PRI) to meet the economic and political demands growing out of the crisis. Specific security issues for Mexico include internal order, protection of oil fields, and the spillover effects of the Central American conflicts into southern Mexico. Because of the special relationship with the United States and the sensitivity to the issue of U.S. intervention, security cooperation with the United States has been carefully limited. For example, there has never been a U.S. military assistance group in Mexico, although small military exchange programs do exist. The Mexican military establishment, which has been rather small in relation to Mexico's population, has in recent years slowly grown and is now acquiring more modern equipment.

Cuba, Nicaragua, and Grenada

The security concerns of the revolutionary nations in the Caribbean Basin emphasize the basic survival of the revolution in the face of what are perceived to be attempts to overthrow, contain, or isolate the regime. The response to these attempts has been to seek outside guarantors and react to pressure by increasing the intensity of revolutionary rhetoric and, to the extent possible, revolutionary acts. The combination of perceived U.S. hostility and the revolutionary response frequently creates a spiraling effect of mutual distrust and increasing tensions. To some extent, this sense of threat and tensions has served to justify sacrifices and militarization within these revolutionary societies, while at the same time diverting resources and attention from the regime's economic failures.

Central America
(Guatemala, Honduras, El Salvador)

These three Central American nations are going through the difficult transition from the traditonal conservative order to an uncertain future. Security issues are defined quite differently by the different sectors involved in this process, but some common concerns can be identified: the high levels of violence, the disruptive impact of outside actors, the fate of the refugees uprooted by the conflict, and the effects of the accompanying economic crisis. A major security concern is that the civil war in one country (El Salvador) or border tensions (Nicaragua-Honduras) might escalate out of control to become a generalized regional conflict.

Costa Rica and Panama

Because of their political, social, and economic development, Costa Rica and Panama and their security concerns cannot be grouped with the other Central American nations. Security issues for Costa Rica focus on the implications of its economic crisis and the need to avoid becoming involved in a broadening Central American conflict; the same concerns are valid for Panama, with the added factor of the Panama Canal, its security, and the transition process.

Colombia and Venezuela

Security issues in these two South American nations center on the political and social implications of their own particular economic difficulties. For Colombia there is the concern of an endemic insurgency based on a deeply rooted history of political violence, while Venezuela must consider the security aspects of the greater international role it is seeking in the Caribbean. Colombia and Venezuela have had differences over their boundary in the Gulf of Venezuela, and both have territorial disputes with third parties: Colombia with Nicaragua over San Andrés and Providencia Islands, and, more seriously, Venezuela and Guyana over the Essequibo region. Because of Venezuela's heavy dependence on oil exports as a source of income, it shares with the United States a concern over keeping key Caribbean sea lines of communications open in times of tension.

The Greater Antilles (Jamaica, Dominican Republic, Haiti, Trinidad and Tobago, Puerto Rico)

In these Caribbean Basin islands, the major security issues deal with the unsettling impact of current economic conditions and the possibilities for violence that emerge from the inability to resolve economic problems. For Jamaica there is the memory of the strong Cuban influence during the Manley years and the polarization of politics during that period. Haiti and the Dominican Republic have historically had a strained relationship, although there are no indications that this would involve security considerations beyond those stemming from border tensions. The Puerto Rico status issue poses special security concerns in terms of some of the links between extreme violent groups seeking independence and Cuba. Trinidad and Tobago has concerns regarding a possible threat from Grenada to the oil tanker routes.[37]

The Lesser Antilles

Specific security concerns of the states of the Eastern Caribbean stem from their small and troubled economies, limited resources, and minuscule military or police establishments. The severing of the principal colonial links to Great Britain has left many of these new mini-states with a sense of vulnerability in an area of turmoil. The victory of the New Jewel Movement in Grenada and the pro-Cuba posture of the Maurice Bishop regime have had a strong impact.[38] Other security issues focus on smuggling, gun-running, and the exercise of economic rights in territorial waters. Cooperative security efforts would seem to be a logical way of meeting some of these concerns, and there have been some limited preliminary steps taken in the direction of establishing an Eastern Caribbean Regional Security System with U.S. support.[39]

Belize and Guyana

These two Caribbean Basin states share an important security concern involving a major territorial dispute with a much more powerful neighbor. In both cases Great Britain is also involved as the prior colonial power (this fact is now much less relevant in Guyana than in Belize, where Great Britain maintains troops and has a firm defense commitment). In the wake of the outcome of the Falklands/Malvinas conflict, it would seem less likely that either Guatemala or Venezuela would be tempted to try a similar military adventure; nevertheless, the concern over this possibility is felt and expressed in both Belize and Guyana.[40]

Security Interests of Outside Actors

The NATO alliance partners have an obvious interest in maintaining the Caribbean's sea lines of communications open and functioning. U.S. force deployment and logistical support through the Panama Canal, across the Caribbean, and then eastward to Europe would be crucial in the case of a protracted conflict in Europe.

Great Britain, France, and Holland, as European powers with residual posessions in the Caribbean, retain an interest in the security and economic and political development of their colonies. France and the United Kingdom maintain troops in the Caribbean, while the Netherlands has a naval presence.[41] All three nations have important trade, tourism, investment, and aid relationships in the area, with appropriate security interests stemming from them.

Canada occupies a unique position as a hemisphere nation and a NATO partner but not an Organization of American States (OAS) member (although it has observer status and participates in a number of its agencies). In recent years Canada has increased its trade, tourism, and aid involvement in the Caribbean (to include Cuba), and has a series of security interests derived from this involvement as well as from its status as a NATO member. A recent study conducted by the Canadian Department of National Defense concluded that Canada's economic and strategic interests in the area could be threatened by instability and the declining ability of the United States to deal with that instability.[42]

Japan as an outside actor in the Caribbean area maintains a limited but growing interest, primarily in terms of trade (to include trade with Cuba). A recent loan to Jamaica reflected Japan's interest in the economic development of the area and an expression of interest in working with the United States in the region.[43]

THE REGIONAL AND SUBREGIONAL APPROACH TO SECURITY

Attempts to deal with security issues in the Caribbean Basin in the regional context face the basic lack of consensus on regional security matters and the problem that there are no international organizations within the area that deal with the region as a whole on security issues.

At the hemisphere level, the Rio Treaty could conceivably have a collective security and conflict-resolution function in the Caribbean, but has the problem that its membership is not inclusive. Table 4.2 shows the OAS and Rio Treaty status of the Caribbean Basin nations as of mid-1983. Of the twenty-five independent Caribbean nations, only three (Cuba, Belize, and Guyana) are not OAS members. Within the Rio Treaty structure, the membership drops off to only thirteen of the twenty-five nations (Nicaragua is a signatory). This low regional membership in the Rio Treaty severely limits its possible effectiveness in the area.

Despite the inherent difficulties in attempting a regional approach to cooperation in security matters, there are some functional areas where it would seem profitable to attempt to cooperate on a regional basis despite wide divergences in other security matters, for example, avoiding situations that could lead to superpower confrontation; avoiding interstate conflict and seeking peaceful settlement of disputes; avoiding situations that would lead to large-scale migrations; coordinating disaster relief and search-and-rescue operations; controlling terrorism; guaranteeing freedom of navigation; reaching Law of the Sea agreements; and strengthening confidence-building measures.

At the subregional level, security issues become more sharply defined and areas of agreement offer a more solid base for understanding and cooperative efforts. The Caribbean Basin has subregional organizations with a security component to them. The now-defunct CONDECA (Central American Defense Council) was one of them, but it was strongly

Table 4.2. OAS and Rio Treaty Status of Caribbean Basin Nations

	OAS Member	Rio Treaty Signatory
Antigua & Barbuda	Yes	No
Bahamas	Yes	No
Barbados	Yes	No
Belize	No[a]	–
Colombia	Yes	Yes
Costa Rica	Yes	Yes
Cuba	No[b]	–
Dominica	Yes	No
Dominican Republic	Yes	Yes
El Salvador	Yes	Yes
Grenada	Yes	No
Guatemala	Yes	Yes
Guyana	No[c]	–
Haiti	Yes	Yes
Honduras	Yes	Yes
Jamaica	Yes	No
Mexico	Yes	Yes
Nicaragua	Yes	Yes
Panama	Yes	Yes
St. Lucia	Yes	No
St. Vincent	Yes	No
Suriname	Yes	No
Trinidad & Tobago	Yes	Yes
United States	Yes	Yes
Venezuela	Yes	Yes
Total: 25 Caribbean states	22 of 30 total OAS members	13 of 21 total Rio Treaty signatories

[a] Belize is excluded due to a territorial dispute with Guatemala.

[b] The present government of Cuba was excluded in the 8th Meeting of Consultation of Foreign Ministers, 1962.

[c] Guyana is excluded due to a territorial dispute with Venezuela.

criticized for coming under heavy U.S. influence and was generally regarded as being an alliance of right-wing regimes in Central America.[44] At present two subregional organizations exist that do offer possibilities in the security area: the Central American Democratic Community and the Organization of Eastern Caribbean States.[45]

The U.S. government has recently shown an increased sensitivity to the regional approach, as suggested by Assistant Secretary of State Thomas Enders's statement before the House Committee on Foreign Affairs on 4 February 1983, when he outlined U.S. policy toward El Salvador and Central America in regional terms:

A Regional Approach

If power sharing without reference to democratic principles is no solution, what is? The answer is inescapable: the cooperative development of political processes that are democratic and that provide the security as well as the means for reconciliation.

And not in El Salvador alone. For just as the fighting has become a regional problem, the solution must be regional as well. And our objective must be to foster conditions, both political and military, that will bring lasting peace to Central America.

Last October, the Government of Costa Rica helped define a set of principles we believe can help achieve that goal. Both El Salvador and the United States signed the final act of San Jose setting forth eight principles, which single out respect for human rights and the development of democracy and which also include reciprocal measures to reduce and eliminate military conflicts. These principles embody four basic points:

Taking Central America out of East-West competition, through such measures as removal of foreign troops and military advisers;

Defusing tensions among nations in Central America by reciprocal and verifiable agreements on arms imports, frontier control, and assistance to insurgent groups in each other's territory;

Launching a region-wide democratic transformation, by insuring that all citizens who organize politically can have a voice in determining the future of their country; and

Strengthening the economies, by reactivating the Central American Common Market and implementing the economic initiatives of neighboring countries, including our own Caribbean Basin initiative.[46]

U.S. OPTIONS

Option A: A Unilateral U.S. Approach

The unilateral approach to U.S. security in the Caribbean Basin is based on a relatively narrow definition of U.S. interests and a low priority for the Caribbean Basin nations' own security concerns, unless they happen to coincide with those of the United States. In this approach security would have a strong military and geopolitical thrust, would tend toward U.S. isolationism, and would assume that Caribbean Basin security issues could be handled primarily in military terms. The major emphasis would be on control of key sealanes and U.S. borders. The principal sealanes in the area would be protected by U.S. bases, and by the assumption that keeping them open is as much in the interests of the Caribbean nations as it is in that of the United States. Contingency plans would

would be developed for directly confronting any Soviet or Cuban threat to these maritime lines of communications. U.S. security assistance would be available to those Caribbean Basin nations requesting it, to the extent that their requirements are consistent with these U.S. security objectives.

The resources involved in this approach would be rather minimal for the United States, and would be primarily military. The level of resources required could rise in a given country if it faced an insurgency, but even so they would be small compared to the resources required by a regional development program. As a basically unilateral U.S. approach, there would be relatively few constraints on actions by the United States.

The approach has the attraction that it would be relatively easy to sell to U.S. constituencies using the specific and narrow military arguments. On the negative side the approach suffers from its emphasis on immediate crises and the way it ignores the underlying link between security and the basic economic, social, and political environment of the area. Although it might provide for short-term U.S. military security, it would in the longer run lead to an increasingly isolated United States and an increasingly chaotic Caribbean Basin with many opportunities for greater Cuban and Soviet influence. Despite these negative aspects, this is an option that should be considered because of its lower cost in resources and the resulting higher probability that it would be supported by the U.S. Congress and public opinion.

Option B: An East-West Approach

The underlying assumption to this approach is that the principal threats to United States security interests in the Caribbean Basin stem from the Soviet Union or its Cuban or Nicaraguan surrogates. The Caribbean Basin as such is seen mainly as a theater of East-West confrontation and not as an area with its own independent agenda and security concerns. Proponents of this view would hold that if the Soviet Union could be persuaded to restrain Cuba, or if Cuba could be isolated or weaned away from the USSR, the remaining security problems in the Caribbean Basin would be relatively easy to manage.

Protecting U.S. security interests in the Caribbean Basin under this approach implies either reaching an understanding with the Soviet Union or persuading Castro to diminish his military ties to the USSR. The price or resources involved in either of these two possibilities is an unknown, but presumably would be part of a global U.S.-Soviet agreement or an offer to Castro that he would find irresistible.

The approach has a surface attractiveness in terms of the simplicity of dealing with a single source of the threats to U.S. security interests in the Caribbean Basin, but it clearly ignores the broader indigenous economic, social, and political threats to security in the area. It also assumes that the USSR has almost total control over Castro's actions, or that Castro can in fact be enticed to reduce his strategic links to the Soviet Union.

Option C: A Bilateral Approach with Key Countries

This bilateral approach to U.S. security tends to establish priorities among the perceived different threats and countries affected, and devote disproportionate amounts of resources to the higher priorities. In some cases the high priority is acquired by geography, raw materials, or other strategic assets; such would be the case for Mexico, Venezuela, or Panama. In other cases the presence of an insurgency is the justification for a high security priority.

The resources (be they military or developmental) involved in this bilateral approach are more limited than in a broader multilateral approach and can be concentrated on the specific high-priority threat or country of interest. This approach is thus easier to justify to U.S. constituencies because of the apparent clear relationship between the priority or threat and the resources requested. On the negative side this approach tends to ignore the countries or threats not given a high priority, and places emphasis on the military and strategic dimension of security to the detriment of the economic and political dimensions. Lastly, this approach has an inherent tendency to be crisis-oriented and to concentrate on short-range solutions.

Option D: A Broad Multilateral Approach

This approach starts from the assumption that security issues cannot be dealt with in isolation, but must take into consideration the linkages between the military, economic, social, and political dimensions of security; at the same time it takes a multilateral and regional view, acknowledging that the security interests of individual nations cannot be pursued in isolation without due consideration for the interests of the other nations in the region. The approach is also preventative in that it seeks to reduce the possibilities of unrest, subversion, and insurgency through economic and political development. This approach attempts to use a North-South understanding between the U.S. and the Carribean Basin nations as the foundation for security.

The broad multilateral approach places the most demand on resources and creates a complex series of constraints. For the United States the resources required are a mix of development and security assistance, trade liberalization measures and investment incentives. The measures envisioned in the 1982 Caribbean Basin Initiative are a good beginning, but must be strengthened and increased to meet the needs of the region more fully. The United States must be sensitive to different viewpoints on security issues, to the extent of acquiescing to the views of Mexico and Venezuela (and others) that no nation necessarily be excluded. There must be, in effect, a willingness to accept a variety of economic and political systems in the area as long as they agree to abide by principles of nonintervention and not attempt to impose their political systems in any violent way on other nations in the area. To be credible, the nonintervention commitment should also limit U.S. plans to use covert actions to further its goals, except under the most extraordinary circumstances. The determination of what constitutes "extraordinary circumstances" should include careful consideration of the effects of probable leaks, and should come under effective congressional oversight. Some covert actions can in fact be justified as representing the lesser of two evils; others cannot be justified on either moral or pragmatic grounds and should be carefully avoided.

On the political side the U.S. should condition its aid to reasonable compliance with respect for human rights and reasonable progress toward the strengthening of democratic political institutions and social and economic reforms. Regimes that choose not to abide by these norms on a consistent basis run the risk of isolation and being cut off from assistance from the United States and other key regional actors. Judgments on the compliance issue should be as multilateral as possible, taking into consideration the views of the principal nations of the Caribbean Basin as well as international organizations and groups active in these fields.

Because this approach seeks to be all-inclusive, it must strengthen functional areas that can be supported by all the nations of the Basin, in the hopes that agreement and cooperation on these security issues will make it easier to obtain agreement on more controversial issues.

The success of this approach requires also that the revolutionary regimes of the Caribbean Basin can feel that their revolutions are not threatened and do not require a massive military buildup with Soviet support. Unilateral U.S. assurances are not likely to have much credibility in Havana, Managua, or St. George's, and the process of reassuring these regimes must fall on other intermediary states in the Caribbean Basin or outside actors. If effective, these assurances (linked to assurances on not attempting to export revolutions) could result in avoiding dangerous increases in military armaments and in a general decline in tensions.

At the same time, the economic aspects of this approach would, it is hoped, permit a more rational and balanced development of the Caribbean Basin nations and diminish the attraction of violent or radical responses to economic and political problems. The approach would give the Caribbean Basin nations a greater sense of defining and controlling their own security by linking it more closely to economic development and democratic processes.

Although the main thrust of this approach would be multilateral and sensitive to North-South concerns, the approach would not rule out U.S. security arrangements with subregional groupings or individual nations on a bilateral basis. It should also be apparent that the United States could have the option (as would any other state in the region) of resorting to unilateral actions to secure vital interests in emergency situations. For the U.S. such situations could include the presence of offensive Soviet strategic weapons, massive and uncontrolled migration, a threat to the Panama Canal within the provisions of the 1977 Treaty, challenges to Puerto Rico's free choice on the status issue, or threats to vital sealanes in case of a NATO contingency.

Even though realism obviously must permit the use of bilateral and unilateral security measures, choosing these channels over the multilateral ones must take into consideration the possibility that these channels may undercut or weaken the multilateral approach; the credibility of the multilateral channel rests in large part on the U.S. commitment to use it effectively.

The multilateral commitment in the Caribbean Basin will not be an easy one for the United States to support for an extended period. The complexity of the approach, its cost, and the need to reassure revolutionary regimes makes it one that U.S. government and public constituencies will have some difficulty accepting. Its proponents must convince these constituencies that it represents the best option to protect U.S. security interests in the Caribbean Basin in the long run.

SECURITY POLICY ISSUE AREAS
TO BE CONSIDERED

This section will address some specific issue areas that are relevant to the broad multilateral approach.

The Linking of Security and Economic and Political Development

The basic starting point of this approach, as indicated previously, is the linkage between security in its broadest sense and economic and political development. Long-term security cannot be obtained by military means alone, but must be based on meaningful progress in solving the region's fundamental economic, social, and political problems. For the United States this implies a commitment to Caribbean development programs with a range of aid projects, tariff reductions, trade stimulants, and investment incentives, with security assistance available as needed. These measures should be taken in coordination with other major actors in the Basin, and should be tied to the military assistance and tension-lowering measures outlined below.

The political component of this approach involves the encouragement of democratic institutions and processes, and respect for human rights. To avoid ethnocentrism and intervention, this process should be as multilateral as possible, employing institutions such as the Inter-American Commission on Human Rights.

Responses to Insurgencies

The United States should be as forthcoming as possible with military and economic assistance to a Caribbean Basin nation facing the threat of an insurgency. This aid, however, should be clearly conditioned and linked to the legitimacy of the government involved in terms of protection of human rights and progress toward generally accepted democratic processes and economic and social reforms. Judgments on these issues should be as multilateral as the situation permits; as a minimum the U.S. should consult with the region's major actors. Evidence of any involvement of outside elements in the insurgency should be shared with these actors and, if feasible, made public. Regional and subregional institutions and channels should be used as much as possible in responding to insurgencies.

The Role of the Soviet Union

Within the context of the 1962, 1970, and 1979 understandings, and as part of a continuing dialogue with the USSR on a range of issues, the United States should discuss with the Soviet Union the broader question of activities near each other's borders and the level of weapons and presence that are not acceptable. The United States should seek the political and diplomatic support of the Caribbean nations in this process; development and security assistance should be aimed at reducing the likelihood that Caribbean Basin nations might turn to the Soviet Union for assistance. The U.S. should closely monitor Soviet activity in the Basin to ensure compliance with the general understandings. Lastly, U.S. and NATO planning should continue to consider and emphasize the Soviet-Cuban military threat to the Caribbean and Atlantic lines of communication.

The Role of Cuba

As a security issue, the role of Cuba must include consideration of both Cuba's direct military threat and its support for insurgencies and revolutionary governments in the region. The most effective counter to the latter, as argued previously, is to support efforts at economic development and protection of democratic institutions in order to reduce the attractiveness of the violent revolutionary model supported by Cuba. In terms of U.S. relations with Cuba, the United States should explore the possibility of talks leading to a discussion of outstanding differences, using Caribbean Basin nations as third-party intermediaries. As in the case of the Soviet Union, the United States should make clear to Cuba the limits beyond which intervention in other countries in the area is not acceptable.

Security and Diversity

The United States must be prepared to accept the considerable diversity of the Caribbean Basin nations, and the assertive nationalism of some of the more radical regimes. Established revolutionary regimes in the Basin should be persuaded that the survival of their revolution is not threatened by outside intervention and is secure as long as they do not attempt to export their revolutions. The use of intermediaries, to include European nations and political groups such as the Socialist International, should prove useful in bridging some of the differences caused by Caribbean Basin diversities.

Institutions for Security

It would appear worthwhile to attempt to broaden membership in the Organization of American States to include the presently absent Caribbean Basin nations as well as Canada. In the cases of Belize and Guyana, this would require the modification of Article 8 of the OAS Charter, which blocks admission of new members who have pending border disputes with current members. The low number of Rio Treaty signatories in the Basin at present make this an ineffective instrument for conflict resolution, and attempts should be made to increase its adherents.

Subregional security arrangements, such as the Eastern Caribbean Regional Security System, should be encouraged and supported by the United States. The U.S. profile in existing inter-American security institutions (such as the Inter-American Defense Board and the Inter-American Defense College) should be gradually lowered to make them more credible, representative, and effective as multilateral organizations. Care must be taken to ensure that this lowering of the U.S. profile not be interpreted as a lack of U.S. interest; it should be done over time and accompanied by close consultation with all the member nations. The presence of leftist regimes in these organizations is not impossible and should be encouraged in order to open channels of communication. (It should be noted that the Nicaraguan government still has a representative on the Inter-American Defense Board.) The U.S. military training schools in Panama (The School of the Americas and the Inter-American Air Force Academy) should be internationalized using the Inter-American Defense College as a model; the Caribbean Basin nations should be encouraged to make participation in both the staff and student body as diverse and representative as possible.

Conflict Resolution and Avoidance

As indicated previously, there exist in the Basin a number of possible conflict situations stemming from historical disputes and current tensions. The OAS has a long history of reasonably successful conflict resolution and avoidance in the Basin, which functioned as long as the nations involved had limited military potential and as long as the issues involved were border or territorial ones, and not ideological ones. The current range of disputes (Belize-Guatemala, Nicaragua-Colombia, Colombia-Venezuela, Venezuela-Guyana, Honduras-Nicaragua) do not appear to be easily resolvable and thus present a challenge to Caribbean security. To deal with this challenge, the conflict resolution mechanisms of the OAS should be strengthened, membership should be broadened, and the parties involved should make a renewed commitment to resolve them by pacific means.

Peacekeeping techniques can make an important contribution; at present their usefulness is limited by suspicion that they might be used as a "cover" for intervention (the OAS rejected a U.S. proposal to establish a peacekeeping presence during the last stages of the Somoza regime in 1979 for these reasons). OAS peacekeeping faces the dilemma that to be credible and balanced, the U.S. profile in the force must not be excessive, but the success of the peacekeeping mission frequently depends on the logistical, administrative, transportation, and communications support that only the United States can provide in the OAS. Canadian participation in OAS peacekeeping missions could help overcome this problem; so could links to third-party organizations with peacekeeping experience, such as the International Peace Academy (associated with the United Nations).

Confidence-Building Measures

The theory and practice of contemporary confidence-building measures stemmed from efforts to lower tensions between NATO and the Warsaw Pact in Europe. Some of the techniques involved, however, would seem to have applicability in terms of Caribbean Basin security. For example, there could be agreements to notify neighboring states of all significant troop movements and exercises, especially those near border areas; neighboring states could be invited to participate as observers. Joint border patrols could be established in particularly sensitive areas (such as the Honduran-Nicaraguan border), with the participation of neutral third-party observers. A central data registry under OAS supervision could provide information on troop strength, armaments, and installations. Exchanges of military personnel and visits could further break down some of the suspicion and mistrust. The U.S.-USSR "hot-line" concept could be applied to high-tension areas in the Basin by providing communications links between military units on opposing sides of sensitive borders.

Arms Limitations

An important aspect of Caribbean Basin security, and one that is related to confidence-building measures, is that of levels of armament in the area and their limits. The issue is especially delicate in the Central American context because of the short distances involved and the historical balances between the military establishments in the region. Thus the 1979–1982 buildup of the Nicaraguan armed forces is seen as a significant threat by its neighbors; Nicaragua justifies the buildup on the grounds that it is threatened from a number of sources. The Nicaraguan buildup in turn has caused its immediate neighbors to feel that they should also strengthen their armed forces. Apart from the general raising of tension that this produces, there is a considerable draining of funds, manpower, and other resources involved in this process, suggesting that a regional or subregional agreement on limits to arms would contribute to both development and security.

Cooperation in Disaster Relief, Navigation, and Search and Rescue

These functional areas of Caribbean Basin security have the potential of providing areas of mutual interest and agreement even between ideological and military adversaries. As an example, during one of the periods of heightened tension between the United States and Nicaragua in late 1982, a team of U.S. Air Force specialists traveled to Nicaragua to instruct air force, naval, and civilian personnel in search-and-rescue techniques.[47] Apart from the inherent benefits stemming from this cooperation, they provide contacts and possibilities for greater cooperation in other security areas.

Military Assistance

U.S. military assistance in the Caribbean Basin (especially in Central America) has historically been the principal vehicle for establishing and cementing security relationships. In the 1960s and early 1970s, the way this assistance tended to ally the United States with conservative military regimes became a major issue. This situation changed dramatically under legislative provisions of 1976, strongly enforced by the Carter administration, which linked the providing of military assistance to respect for human rights. This linkage can be a powerful tool in the difficult process of persuading a regime under attack from insurgents that it must use restraint. The linkage also serves as a safeguard against the possibility that the U.S. might become too closely allied with repressive regimes in the area. At the same time, the procedure must be used with care to avoid a counterproductive reaction or the total abandonment of a regime under seige from the left.

Military assistance will inevitably remain an essential instrument of U.S. security policy in the Caribbean area as long as there is a threat to the established governments. Such assistance permits access to the military, and, through the human rights provisions, some measure of control over their actions in responding to insurgencies. In the larger states of the Caribbean Basin (Venezuela, Colombia), the focus of military assistance is more technical than tactical, and with considerably less leverage than in Central America because of the greater size and sophistication of their military establishments. The relatively new military assistance programs in the Eastern Caribbean states have focused on their stated security needs for a regional coast guard.

In exploring the possibilities offered by military assistance, it would seem useful to consider employing multilateral channels or at least coordinating the aid with other key states in the Basin. Outside actors with security interests in the area could join the United States as suppliers of military assistance: Canada, the United Kingdom, France, the Netherlands, and other NATO partners could play a useful role in supplementing and multilateralizing U.S. military assistance efforts.

The issue of assisting and training police forces remains sensitive. Such assistance was provided in significant amount to Latin America under the AID Public Safety Program, but was abolished under 1974 legislation in response to charges that it was being used to train Latin American police establishment in techniques to repress and torture their citizens. However, the security needs of a number of the smaller Caribbean nations (especially in the Eastern Caribbean) lie in areas more properly identified as "police" than "military." The Costa Rican security force represents a special case, since it is technically a police force, but it has responsibilities for national defense that go beyond the normal police functions. Thus, some judicious and conditioned U.S. police assistance programs would make an important contribution to security in these countries.[48]

The sheer numbers of Cuban and Eastern bloc military and security advisors in Nicaragua (approximately 2000 Cubans in late 1982) in comparison with U.S. military advisors in El Salvador (approximately 55) gave rise to a U.S. proposal that limits be set on the numbers of foreign advisors in the area, with approximately the same number in each country.[49] The idea was linked to a parallel suggestion concerning levels of heavy offensive weapons in the Central American area. Although no response was forthcoming from the Nicaraguans (or the Cubans), the issue remains one for potential discussion and negotiation.

The Military-to-Military Relationship

A security issue closely related to military assistance is the nature of the relationship between the U.S. military and the military establishments in the Caribbean Basin. The relationship grew into what could be loosely called an "Inter-American military system" during the peak of the counterinsurgency period in the early 1960s, and declined considerably in the 1970s. Nevertheless, a series of institutions and associations from the old system remain: the Inter-American Defense Board, the Inter-American Defense College, U.S. military training schools in Panama, training in the U.S. personnel exchanges, exercises, and so on. In the context of U.S. security programs in the Caribbean Basin in the early 1980s, these institutions need to be reexamined to evaluate their membership, their purpose, the possibilities of making them more multilateral, and their role in implementing new approaches to more integrated security and development programs.

The Role of Intelligence

U.S. intelligence operations in the Caribbean Basin have a legitimate role in the collection and analysis areas, as well as in counterintelligence. However, the category of covert intelligence activities is a potentially counterproductive one on both moral and pragmatic grounds; there is a good possibility that such activities will become publicly known and damage the attempts to build up a regional consensus on security issues and trust in the confidence-building measures. Accordingly, the U.S. should make a commitment to limit intelligence activities to the generally acceptable areas of collection, analysis, and counterintelligence, except in the most unusual and threatening situations. The use of covert actions should be carefully considered on moral, juridical, and pragmatic grounds: the impact of their revelation in the press should be realistically assessed. The responsibility for judging the wisdom and acceptability of such actions should include congressional oversight. Despite conflicting pressures in Congress itself, support for bolder overt action may be easier to obtain than for "covert action," which rarely remains covert for long. A possible test for the decision to use covert means would be to pose the question, "If this covert action became common knowledge and were to be reported in the press at some future time, would U.S. public opinion support it?"

Increased intelligence resources should be dedicated to detecting and publicizing Soviet, Cuban, and Nicaraguan covert intelligence activities as a means of diminishing their effectiveness.

Terrorism

Actions against terrorism (to include hijacking) lend themselves to a multilateral regional approach involving agreements on appropriate measures; the OAS should be encouraged to take a more active role in developing these agreements. Techniques for dealing with terrorists, and training in these techniques, can be shared on a regional basis.

Narcotics

The problem of narcotics traffic to the United States has security implications because of the links to arms traffic and to a possible Cuban connection. U.S. military units should be made available to support the Drug Enforcement Administration and the Coast Guard in attempts to control this traffic. In 1982 military support of the South Florida Task Force included Navy anti-submarine patrol planes, radar surveillance aircraft, and a destroyer; Army helicopters, and Air Force AWACS aircraft.[50]

Migration

Migration becomes a security issue when the numbers and duration of the flow threaten to get out of control. The ideal solution to migration is a preventative one in which economic and political development in the originating nations reduce the incentive to migrate. Failing this, U.S. Coast Guard and military assets can be made available to the INS in emergency situations to assist in control.

The U.S. Military Presence in the Caribbean Basin

As indicated earlier, the U.S. military presence in the Caribbean is low, although it could be reinforced from the continental United States on short notice. The U.S. government should discuss the possibility of access to other bases in the area with the Caribbean Basin nations; should the Soviet Union or Cuba increase the number or capabilities of their installations in the area, the U.S. should be prepared to do likewise if discussions with the Soviets and Cubans do not lead to their removal.

The availability of other bases in the area to the U.S. depends on the nature of the political and economic relationship between the United States and the Caribbean Basin countries involved. At present there are a few possibilities with special significance. They include:

1. The Cayman Islands, because of their strategic location between Cuba and Nicaragua and because they are still under the control of a key NATO ally (the United Kingdom).
2. San Andrés Island, because of its position about 100 miles off the Nicaraguan coast. It should be noted that the island (along with Providencia and a number of small cays) is under Colombian control, but that the Nicaraguan Government of National Reconstruction argued in 1979 that this Colombian claim was invalid and that the islands are Nicaraguan.
3. Honduras, because of its key location between Nicaragua and El Salvador. Honduras has been mentioned as a possible site for the U.S.-run School of the Americas and the Inter-American Air Academy, which are presently in Panama but have to be moved in the near future unless Panama agrees to an extension.

NOTES

1. E. R. McLean, "The Caribbean: An American Lake," *U.S. Naval Institute Proceedings* 67 (1941):948.

2. Louis A. Johnson, "Hemisphere Defense," *Atlantic Monthly* 166 (July 1940):1.
3. John Child, *Unequal Alliance: The Inter-American Military System, 1938-1978* (Boulder, Colo.: Westview Press, 1980).
4. "Caribbean Basin Initiative," *Foreign Policy* 47 (Summer 1982):114-138.
5. U.S. State Department, *Cuban Armed Forces and the Soviet Military Presence,* Special Report no. 103 (Washington, D.C., August 1982) (hereafter cited as "State no. 103"); also discussions with Rene Mujica, Cuban Interest Section, Washington, November 1982.
6. For a discussion of the economic, social, political, and military factors in the Caribbean Basin and their relation to security, see Florentino Diaz Loza, "Importancia Geopolítica del Caribe," *Estrategia* 70 (January–March 1980):33-41.
7. U.S. Joint Chiefs of Staff, *U.S. Military Posture for FY 1983* (Washington, D.C., 1983), p. 11.
8. Margaret D. Hayes, "Security to the South: U.S. Interests in Latin America," *International Security* (Summer 1980):134-138.
9. U.S. State Department, *Background on the Caribbean Basin Initiative* Special Report no. 97 (Washington, D.C., March 1982) (hereafter cited as "State no. 97").
10. U.S. State Department, *Cuba's Renewed Support for Violence in Latin America,* Special Report no. 90 (Washington, D.C., December 1981) (hereafter cited as "State no. 90"); U.S. Congress, Senate, Subcommittee on Security and Terrorism, Committee on the Judiciary, Hearings, 26 February, 4, 11, 12 March 1982, *The Role of Cuba in International Terrorism and Subversion.*
11. For a discussion, see "Forum," *Orbis* 26, 2 (Summer 1982):305-325.
12. U.S. Congress, *Role of Cuba,* p. 88.
13. U.S. State Department, *Gist: U.S. Interests in the Caribbean Basin* (Washington, D.C., May 1982).
14. State no. 103. Also U.S. Joint Chiefs of Staff, *U.S. Military Posture for FY 1982* (Washington, D.C., 1982).
15. *Los Angeles Times,* 20 November 1982, p. 1; State no. 103, p. 2.
16. State no. 103, p. 3.
17. *Philadelphia Inquirer,* 24 March 1983, p. 21.
18. U.S. Congress, *Role of Cuba,* pp. 7, 24-25, 169.
19. *Washington Post,* 12 November 1982, p. A-14; also *New York Post,* 21 March 1983, p. 7, and *Washington Post,* 1 and 10 May 1983, p. A-1.
20. Joint Chiefs of Staff, *U.S. Military Posture for FY 1982.* The figure for 2000 advisors is from State no. 103.
21. U.S. State Department, *Gist,* p. 1.
22. Richard Sim and James Anderson, "The Caribbean Strategic Vacuum," *Conflict Studies* 121 (August 1980):1.
23. State no. 103, p. 5. Also see *DoD/ISA Fact Sheet,* 12 July 1983.
24. U.S. Secretary of Defense, *Annual Report to Congress, FY 1983* (Washington, D.C., 1983), p. II-23.
25. Sim and Anderson, "Caribbean Strategic Vacuum," p. 3-4.
26. The Gorshkov quote is from his book, *The Sea Power of the State* (Oxford: Oxford University Press, 1979), p. 252.
27. State no. 103, p. 5; *Washington Times,* 5 April 1983, p. C-1.
28. This portion draws heavily from State no. 103, as well as from the JCS *Posture Statements* and the Secretary of Defense's *Reports to Congress* for FY 1982, 1983, and 1984.
29. "Military Balance, 1982-83," *Air Force Magazine* (December 1982), pp. 134-140.
30. Reported in *Los Angeles Times,* 28 February 1983, p. 5-B.

31. Ibid.
32. U.S. Secretary of Defense, *Annual Report to Congress,* FY 1983, p. II-23; *DoD/ISA Fact Sheet.*
33. State no. 90, p. 6.
34. Sim and Anderson, "Caribbean Strategic Vacuum," p. 10.
35. EPICA, *Grenada: The Peaceful Revolution* (Washington, D.C.: EPICA Task Force, 1982), pp. 69Z-70.
36. State no. 103.
37. U.S. Congress, *Role of Cuba,* p. 169.
38. Sim and Anderson, "Caribbean Strategic Vacuum," p. 4. Also see F. Clifton Berry, "Cuba's Expanding Power Potential," *Air Force Magazine* (April 1980):44.
39. *Bridgetown Sunday Advocate News,* 31 October 1982, in Foreign Broadcast Information Service (FBIS), 5 November 1982, p. S-4. Also see *Bridgetown CANA,* 14 November 1982, in FBIS, 17 November 1982, p. S-2.
40. *Georgetown CANA,* 26 April 1982, in Joint Publications Research Service, 18 May 1982; *Belize City AFP,* 6 April 1982, in FBIS, 8 April 1982.
41. Sim, p. 23.
42. H. P. Klepak and Captain C. K. Vachan, *A Strategic and Economic Analysis of Canadian National Interests in Latin America,* ORAE Extra-Mural Paper no. 2. (Ottawa: Department of National Defense, 1978).
43. State no. 103.
44. Don L. Etchison, *The United States and Militarism in Central America* (New York: Praeger, 1975).
45. *Bridgetown CANA,* 14 November 1982, in FBIS, 17 November 1982, p. S-2; *Havana Domestic Service,* 8 November 1982, in FBIS, 10 November 1982, p. S-6.
46. U.S. Department of State, *Current Policy #409* ("Progress in El Salvador"), February 1983.
47 *Washington Report on the Hemisphere,* 30 November 1982, p. 8.
48. *Pittsburgh Press,* 1March 1983, p. 14.
49. U.S. Congress, House, Subcommittee on Inter-American Affairs, Committee on Foreign Affairs, Hearings, 20 July, 5 August 1982, *Latin America and the United States after the Falklands/Malvinas Crisis,* p. 160.
50. *Washington Times,* 6 October 1982, p. 2; *Washington Post,* 1 May and 10 May 1983, p. A-1.

Chapter 5

U.S. Security on the Southern Flank: Interests, Challenges, Responses

Robert Kennedy and Gabriel Marcella

The fall of the Somoza government in Nicaragua and its replacement by the Marxist and pro-Cuban Sandinistas; guerrilla movements in Guatemala and El Salvador; the revolutionary upheaval in Suriname; and events in Grenada have marked a decade of increasing turmoil in the Caribbean Basin. Poverty, population pressures, high inflation, deteriorating terms of trade, rising energy costs, inequalities of opportunity, and inequities in the distribution of income and wealth frequently have created pressures for social and economic change. Yet, in a number of countries traditional political structures have been either unable or unwilling to accommodate to needed reform. The resulting environment has been conducive to increased Cuban–Soviet activism, subversion, and open support for revolution, with high potential for the emergence of a Caribbean environment antithetical to U.S. interests. Moreover, expanding Cuban offensive military capabilities and the emergence of a basing infrastructure that might be made available to the Soviets and Cubans pose new challenges to U.S. planners accustomed to the flexibility provided by a secure strategic rear.

This paper will focus on U.S. interests in the Caribbean Basin, current challenges to those interests, and the complex policy choices now confronting the United States.

U.S. REGIONAL SECURITY INTERESTS

There is clearly a hazard in defining U.S. security interests too broadly. By so doing, any difficulties that arise may then be seen as threats to U.S. security. As a result, difficulties may appear to demand an immediate response, when in fact, the threat is so indirect and ambiguous that circumspect responses would be more productive. There is a hazard, however, in narrow definitions of U.S. interests. Such definitions may obscure linkages that do exist between economic, humanitarian, or social interests and the more obvious military or "national security" interests. Narrow definitions, in the absence of clear or overwhelming military threat, tend to encourage a sense of well-being. As a result, the kind of comprehensive planning that may be necessary to deal with developments before they result in serious or critically threatening conditions are frequently postponed. Thus with all the necessary cautions in mind, the authors have opted to address U.S. regional security issues in their broader context.

In the authors' view, the absolute and relative importance of the Caribbean Basin to the United States has increased over the past several decades. More importantly, this trend is likely to continue in the years ahead. Nevertheless, U.S. interests in the Caribbean Basin have been neither clearly defined nor well understood. Examinations of U.S. policy in the region frequently begin with vague statements of U.S. national interests that often confuse rather than clarify significant differences between interests, objectives, and means. We are told what U.S. interests "embrace," what they "focus on," and what they "include." Frequently statements of U.S. interests in the region appear to be more an indication of the environment that the United States is "interested in" achieving to protect its interests in the region than a clear statement of the interests themselves.

U.S. security interests in the region can be broadly defined in terms of the three "P's"—proximity, petroleum, and perceptions.

Proximity

The geographic proximity of the Caribbean Basin to the sea lines of communication (SLOCs) and to the continental United States renders the region vital. The Caribbean Basin sits astride major sea lines of communication (see Figure 4.1, p. 146). In peacetime, 44 percent of all foreign cargo tonnage and 45 percent of the crude oil imported into the United States pass through the Caribbean. In the event of war in Europe half of NATO's supplies would transit by sea from Gulf ports through the Florida Straits and onward to the continent of Europe.

Much of the petroleum shipments and important reinforcements destined for U.S. forces in Europe would also sail from Gulf ports. While cargo could be rerouted to East Coast ports, deficiencies in rail and other forms of surface transportation would severely delay such shipments. Thus, as the Secretary of Defense has noted, "the security of our maritime operations in the Caribbean . . . is critical to the security of the Atlantic alliance."[1]

The physical proximity of the region to the United States also increases the potential for direct attack on the United States. Hostile nations allied with the USSR could provide the Soviets with cost-effective options for direct attack on the United States during times of crisis or conflict. The mere threat of such a possibility is likely to affect U.S. decisionmaking processes during crises. More importantly, the rapid placement by the Soviets of conventional or nuclear cruise missiles or tactical air assets in the region could significantly affect U.S. calculations concerning appropriate courses of political and military actions.

These considerations may appear far-fetched, but Americans responded with alarm to the security threats posed by the emplacement of Soviet missiles in Cuba in 1962, and to the "discovery" of the Soviet brigade in Cuba in 1978. On April 9, 1983, Nicaraguan Defense Minister Humberto Ortega stated that if the Soviet Union put forward the idea of stationing nuclear missiles in Nicaragua, his government "would consider the proposal and make its own decision." Ortega's statement echoed an earlier threat by Soviet official Vadim Zagladin to install missiles in the Western Hemisphere five minutes from the United States.[2] The era of cheap security in the Caribbean—which permitted the United States the flexibility for forward defense and power projection in Europe, the Middle East, and Asia—has ended.

In addition to the more obvious strategic value of the region, the United States has a wide range of bases and facilities in the Caribbean.[3] These are:

The substantial port and logistic facilities at Guantanamo Bay.
The facilities in Puerto Rico, including Roosevelt Roads for fleet training and support operations, the logistics and administration facility at Fort Buchanan.
In Panama, the U.S. continues to operate and maintain a range of bases and facilities, including Howard Air Base, with its long jet runway; Fort Gulick, home of the U.S. Army School of the Americas; and Fort Clayton, headquarters of the 193rd Infantry Brigade for Canal defense. Moreover, U.S. Southern Command has its headquarters at Quarry Heights in Panama City.
Elsewhere there are such facilities as the Eastern Test Range missile

and space support facilities on the Grand Bahamas Island, at Grand Turk, and in Antigua; oceanographic research facilities in Eleuthera, Grand Turk, Antigua, and Barbados; long-range navigation (LORAN) facilities in San Salvador and the South Caicos; and the U.S. Atlantic Underseas Test and Evaluation Center in the Bahamas.

Economic Interests

The world crisis brought on in part by the marked increase in price and the real or contrived shortages of petroleum in the mid- and late 1970s has highlighted the importance of petroleum as a strategic resource in time of peace or war. Petroleum, though, is not the only U.S. economic interest in the region, nor can overall U.S. economic and military security best be understood through a narrow focus on petroleum. Rather, in the authors' view, U.S. policymakers as well as the general public are best served by an understanding of this nation's broader economic interests in the region.

Markets. Mexico and Venezuela are clearly America's dominant regional trading partners. Today, they account for over 70 percent of all U.S. exports to the region and over 60 percent of all U.S. imports from the region. While it might be considered an overstatement in a short-term sense, stability and development in the region will affect the long-term future of these markets. Moreover, the Caribbean market place *is* of significant importance to the United States. Today, when Mexico and Venezuela are included, the Caribbean Basin is the world's fourth largest market for U.S. products, following the European Economic Community (EEC), Canada, and Japan; it currently accounts for about 13 and 11 percent of total U.S. exports and imports, respectively. Since 1973, imports from the Caribbean Basin have been a steady 77 percent of all U.S. imports from Latin America. U.S. exports to the Caribbean, however, have increased in absolute and relative terms to nearly 75 percent of all U.S. exports to Latin America. As a percentage of U.S. worldwide trade, U.S. trade with the Caribbean has increased since 1973, while it has generally declined with the EEC, Canada, and Japan.[4]

Investment. The United States is the largest foreign investor in the Caribbean Basin. U.S. private investment, which is mainly in manufacturing, trade, and services, represents over 50 percent of all U.S. private investment in Latin America. While the growth of U.S.-Caribbean investment, although substantial, has not kept pace with the growth of U.S. investments elsewhere, approximately 8 percent of

U.S. worldwide investment and 32 percent of U.S. investments in developing countries are located in the region. Again, U.S. investments in Mexico and Venezuela predominate.

Resources. Compared to other developed countries, the United States is relatively independent of foreign sources of basic mineral raw materials, except for fuel. Currently, the United States imports only about 15 percent of its domestic nonfuel mineral requirements compared to Western Europe and Japan, which import about 80 and 95 percent, respectively.[5] The Caribbean Basin, however, is rich in two strategically important resources—bauxite and petroleum—and has an abundance of less critical resources.

Bauxite is the only raw material currently used in the United States in the commercial production of alumina, an intermediate stage in the production of aluminum. U.S. domestic sources of bauxite (300 to 325 million tons) are inadequate to meet long-term demands.[6] Today Jamaica is second only to Australia as the world's largest producer of bauxite and alumina. Along with Jamaica, three other Caribbean nations—the Dominican Republic, Guyana, and Suriname—supply about 85 percent of U.S.-imported bauxite and about 39 percent of imported alumina. While the United States has virtually inexhaustible alternate resources for the production of alumina other than from bauxite, research to produce alumina from non-bauxite resources is in its infancy.[7] Thus the United States is likely to remain dependent on bauxite imports in the foreseeable future.

An even more critical strategic resource in the Caribbean Basin is petroleum. Venezuela and Mexico are among the world's leading producers of crude oil. Although production has dropped as a result of the recent oil glut and world recession, in 1980, Mexico, Venezuela, and Trinidad and Tobago produced, respectively, an estimated 1.96, 2.15, and 0.215 million barrels per day (mbd) of crude oil and supplied the United States with approximately 10, 3, and 2 percent of its crude oil imports.[8] With its proven reserves estimated at 45 billion barrels and beyond,[9] Mexican oil reserves are exceeded only by those of Saudi Arabia, the Soviet Union, Kuwait, and Iran. While Mexico probably could not and probably would not sustain high production levels beyond fifteen or twenty years, if demand for petroleum warranted expansion and Mexico decided to expand production rapidly, Mexican crude oil production could exceed levels of 6 mbd by the early 1990s.[10] Such production levels compare favorably with the 1980 estimated Mexican production of 1.9 mbd and Saudi Arabia's 9.6 mbd.

Taking into account the high expectations for offshore discoveries along the Gulf and Caribbean coasts and the potential of Venezuela's

Orinoco Tar Basin, the Caribbean Basin could rival the Middle East as the largest supplier of oil to the United States and could become a major supplier to the world community.

In addition to crude oil production, the Caribbean Basin is currently a very important source of refined petroleum products. Oil refineries in the Caribbean Basin account for about 70 percent of the total refined petroleum products imported by the United States.[11] This represents about 8 percent of total U.S. daily consumption of refined petroleum.

Besides bauxite and petroleum, the Caribbean Basin is also a significant supplier of fluorspar. The United States acquires about 60 percent of its total fluorspar requirements from Mexico. Used in the iron, steel, aluminum, and chemical industries, fluorspar currently has limited substitutability and has no generally accepted substitute when used as a flux in the manufacture of steel.[12] Principal alternate sources are in Spain and Italy.

The Caribbean also supplies the United States with such less critical resources as silver, zinc, gypsum, cadmium, iron ore, antimony, mercury, manganese, bismuth, selenium, barium, rhenium, and lead.

Perceptions

Perhaps even more significantly, the Caribbean Basin is important in terms of our own self-perception and the perceptions of others. Events in the Caribbean are a significant manifestation of the effectiveness of the United States as a world power. Thus, much of the world regards U.S. actions in the Caribbean as important indicators of U.S. maturity, confidence, and determination in dealing with complex international issues. Failure to deal maturely and effectively with events at the doorstep is likely to be taken at home and abroad as yet another sign of declining U.S. power.

THE CHALLENGES

While the Caribbean has increased in importance to the United States, challenges that are undermining U.S. influence in the region are becoming more pronounced. In recent years the Caribbean has been experiencing a new dynamism. Advances in transportation and communication have brought a view of the modern world to the most remote villages. The resultant desire for rapid socioeconomic improvement now fuels instabilities and revolution in a number of countries of the region. Inadequate domestic infrastructure, insufficient capital formation, underdeveloped markets, and lack of economic diversification complicate developmental efforts and add to internal political pressures. Furthermore, a latent and frequently manifest suspicion that private initiative and private enterprise not only may not be the most efficient path to rapid economic development and a fair distribution of income, but rather may be instruments of repression and resistance to change, adds to the labrynthian complexities that confound developmental efforts. In some countries the less privileged are now challenging what they perceive as unresponsive governments and political structures and are seeking the political means to alter their status.

Lack of social, economic, and political development, however, is not the only cause of dissidence, disorder, and political disintegration. Cuba, the Soviet Union, and Sandinista Nicaragua have been actively exploiting demands for social and economic improvement and political participation. This has added an East–West dimension to what was essentially an internal problem in the North–South context. In some countries Cuban and Soviet support for revolutionaries has led to a crippling political polarization, seriously complicating efforts designed to achieve social, economic, and political progress (see Figure 5.1).

Propaganda emanating from Cuba, the Soviet Union, and Marxist groups in the region has played on perceptions of capitalist exploitation and on an undercurrent of resentment of the United States. This resentment by the underprivileged for what they perceive as historical American economic imperialism, military interventionism, and support for traditional elites who perpetuate economic impoverishment has impeded U.S. efforts to develop balanced policies in support of long-term social, economic, and political reform. The dilemma for American leadership is twofold: on the one hand, the United States is sympathetic to demands for immediate socieconomic and political reform; on the other hand, the radicalization of reform movements with Soviet and Cuban assistance suggests a high probability that should an *immediate* collapse of the old order occur, it will simply be replaced by a new Marxist–Leninist order likely to be even less capable of fulfilling the social and economic aspirations of the people, inclined to impose an even more narrowly based political system along totalitarian lines, and hostilely anti-American. There is also a high probability that emerging Marxist–Leninist states will seek security in the Soviet alliance system.

One of the more compelling challenges to the interests of the United States and its regional partners is the new form of revolutionary warfare and the internationalization of conflict. The romantic emphasis of the 1960s on isolated violence has been replaced by the more sophisticated revolutionary strategy of prolonged, revolutionary warfare. To-

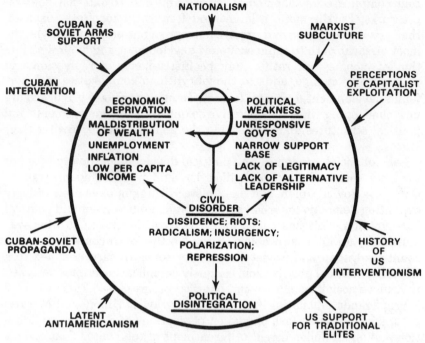

Figure 5.1. The cycle of crises.

day's Marxist–Leninist revolutionaries, taking advantage of the demand for social and economic reform, employ broad-based groups, popular front coalitions, image building, and the nurturing of international alliances for political support and resources. Solidarity groups, the media, church, and academia are all a potential part of the tactical arsenal of the new revolutionaries. The task is to polarize the Central American societies and simultaneously internationalize the conflict in an attempt to diminish the leverage of the United States and to weaken the national institutions.[13]

These techniques of achieving power were clearly evident in the rise of the Sandinistas in Nicaragua. According to Cesar Sereseres and others at the Rand Corporation, through the *Terceristas,* Cuba and the Sandinista hard-core Marxist–Leninists deliberately sought to involve moderate Latin Americans and West European governments in supporting the revolutionary struggle to topple Somoza and to isolate the United States. The pattern is being repeated, with variations, in El Salvador and Guatemala.[14] Likewise, such techniques are part of the current strategy of the Farabundo Marti National Liberation Front (FMLN) in El Salvador.

The Insular Caribbean

The problems of the insular Caribbean are fundamentally economic. High population growth rates, declining terms of trade, widely fluctuating commodity prices, rampant inflation, high energy costs, lack of skilled manpower, high levels of unemployment, and inequitable income distribution patterns are placing increasing strains on fledgling democratic institutions.

Diversification. As the English-speaking states of the insular Caribbean struggle to achieve economic development, to widen their internal basis of support, and to avoid the appearance of close alignment with the United States or with their former colonial rulers, they are attempting to diversify their international relations. The potential for wider patterns of economic interchange, including economic relations with Eastern bloc countries, is being explored. Association with the nonaligned movement and identification with African liberation movements have been among the avenues chosen by several of the states of the region for enhancing their international prestige and their own self-esteem.

Nevertheless, a close relationship between the countries of the insular Caribbean and the United States remains. The United States still is the principal source of capital investment, technology, public- and private-sector assistance, and the main market for the region's products and excess labor. Shared experiences in democratic government, the result of British colonial tutelage, suggest affinities between the United States and the English-speaking Caribbean that extends beyond economics.

Socialist Experimentation and Radical Reform. In their efforts to build more integrated, economically healthy nation-states, several Caribbean leaders have resorted to an eclectic blend of capitalism, state capitalism, socialism, mobilizational politics, and benevolent authoritarianism, while retaining the form and substance of the English parliamentary political system. This Caribbean blend, expressed vaguely as "democratic socialism" by former Prime Minister Michael Manley of Jamaica and labeled "cooperative socialism" in Guyana, has been attempted to generate economic growth, coopt the more radical reform elements in these divided societies, and provide an overarching symbolism to rally the people.[15] Generally, the results have been disappointing, especially in the area of economic growth. For example, in Jamaica the prodigious deficit-spending policies of Manley and his People's National Party, coupled with a decline in national productivity and a decline in the world price of bauxite, led to a 57-percent decline in the Jamaican Gross National Product (GNP) over the last decade. Concomitantly, investment capital, both internal and external, dried up while violence increased in that country.

More radical solutions have also been called for. In Grenada, opposition leader Maurice Bishop seized power from the eccentric, corrupt, and autocratic regime of Prime Minister Sir Eric Gairy in March 1979. This marked the first instance of a coup in the English-speaking Caribbean—an area where the parliamentary system is deeply rooted. Bishop's New Jewel Movement, described as Marxist and reformist, installed a dictatorship with close ties to Cuba. Although Cuba was not directly implicated in the overthrow, it stepped in quickly to provide economic and security assistance to the Bishop government. Fears of similar leftist takeovers in the insular Caribbean (whether through the ballot box or through violent overthrow) abated as a result of the moderate redirection in the wake of recent insular Caribbean elections in Jamaica, Dominica, St. Lucia, and St. Vincent. Grenada, however, was a potential threat to regional security until the October 25, 1983, collective action by the United States and the Organization of Eastern Caribbean States. Cuba maintains a flexible policy to take advantage of opportunities that may arise.

Grenada. Since Bishop's 1979 coup, Grenada has followed a pro-Cuba, pro-Soviet foreign policy line. While Bishop himself was infatuated by the Cuban revolutionary model, the New Jewel Movement did not consolidate a Marxist-Leninist system. Cuba was active in extending assistance in areas that affect the security of Grenada and the island's strategic value to Cuba. Along with assistance from the Socialist bloc, Cuba provided military, technical, security, and propaganda assistance to the Bishop government. A number of Grenadians were sent to Cuba for training in military and security-related fields.[16] Cuba also aided in the construction of a 75-kilowatt transmitter for Radio Free Grenada. The new transmitter was used to beam Cuba and Soviet propaganda into the Carribean and South America.

Perhaps the greatest security concern was the expansion of facilities at Point Salines Airport. The Bishop government contended that the planned 9800-foot runway was necessary for tourism. Grenada, however, ignored requests for a standard project analysis of economic benefits. The planned runway would have had a clear military potential. Such a runway would have permitted the operation of every aircraft in the Cuban and Soviet inventory. It would have been adequate to handle the Libyan Illyushin transport aircraft and C-130s, such as those that were detained by Brazilian authorities in early 1983 because they were carrying armaments destined for Nicaragua. It also would have accommodated Soviet and Cuban MiG aircraft and thus offered the Soviets and their Cuban allies a greater radius of operation, including the potential for operations into South America and the South Atlantic.[17] The potential Cuban–Grenadian threat was one of the principal concerns of the Venezuelans and was a reason for their purchase of highly sophisticated F-16 fighter aircraft from the United States in 1982.[18] The growing Cuban–Soviet influence raised concerns among Grenadians and other members of the Eastern Caribbean community. The urgency of these concerns and the deteriorating internal security situation resulted in the collective action of October 1983.

In a bloody episode reminiscent of the brutal events nearly a year earlier in Suriname, Maurice Bishop was murdered on October 19, 1983, and replaced by a Revolutionary Military Council headed by General Hudson Austin. Out of concern for the collapse of the internal security, and the safety of approximately 1000 U.S. citizens, the United States intervened with military force in a collective action with Antigua, Dominica, St. Lucia, and St. Vincent. According to official statements the objectives were "to restore peace, order, and respect for human rights; to evacuate those who wish to leave; and to help the Grenadians reestablish governmental institutions."[19]

Central America

Nicaragua. After overthrowing the Somoza dictatorship in a bloody and highly destructive civil war, the Sandinista National Liberation front (FSLN) faced the twin tasks of economic reconstruction and political consolidation. The United States supported Nicaragua's efforts to establish a more just social order. It also hoped Nicaragua would preserve a pluralistic political process. The Marxist–Leninist-dominated FSLN, however, has been attempting to establish a one-party political system of unanimity. Consistent with the classic approach to establishing single-party domination, the FSLN has established control over key government positions and the security apparatus and is continuing its efforts to isolate and emasculate democratic forces by limiting the freedom of the media, controlling public dissent, diminishing the influence of the Catholic church, reducing the role of the private sector, and dominating the labor movement.

While the political evolution of Nicaragua is still incomplete, the Party of the Sandinista Popular Revolution has established itself as the single embodiment of the revolution and integrator of the many diverse interests. In this respect, Nicaragua is rapidly becoming a Marxist-Leninist state. For the time being, the Sandinistas bear the mantle of legitimacy based on their role in the overthrow of the universally despised Somoza. They are using this mantle to promote a new revolutionary mystique that justifies their sociopolitical programs and foreign policies and undermines the opposition. Opposition is considered "counterrevolutionary."[20]

Thus, the emergence of a full-fledged Communist state with formal security ties to Cuba and, indirectly, to the Soviet Union remains a serious potential threat. In this worst-case scenario, the installation of Cuban or Soviet air and naval power in Nicaragua in peacetime or during a crisis would complicate U.S. defense planning on the Southern Flank and contribute largely to the elimination of the "economy-of-force" approach the United States has taken with respect to Caribbean security.

Even in the absence of a formal security arrangement with Cuba or the Soviet Union, the emergence of a Marxist–Leninist dictatorship in Central America would continue to focus the attention and resources of the United States and its regional partners on conflict potential elsewhere in Central America. The Sandinistas have been active in their support for revolutionaries in Central America, and they feel that their security is directly tied to the triumph of revolution in Central America—a "revolution without frontiers."

Between October 1980 and February 1981, Nicaragua was the staging site for a massive Cuban-directed flow of arms to Salvadoran guerrillas. Periodic reports indicate that arms destined for Salvadoran and Guatemalan guerrillas continue to pass through Nicaragua (presumably with the full authorization of the Sandinista National Directorate).[21] Nicaragua also serves as the support and command base for the Salvadoran guerrillas. The guerrillas' Unified Revolutionary Directorate has its command center near Managua and, with the help of Cuba and Nicaragua, coordinates logistical support for the guerrilla movement.[22]

Cuban influence remains pervasive in Nicaragua. A great many Cuban advisers are believed to be there. According to Department of Defense estimates, about 5500 Cuban civilian advisers and some 2000 Cuban military and security advisors are in Nicaragua.[23] Cuban advisors are believed to be serving in key posts throughout the government. With Cuban assistance as well as advisors from East Germany, Bulgaria, North Korea, and the Soviet Union, the Sandinistas are not only improving internal security but are reported to be in the process of building the largest standing army in the region.[24] Today the Popular Sandinista Army numbers 25,000, supported by 25,000 reservists, a militia of about 80,000, and 8000 police and security forces.[25]

The Sandinistas have also been lengthening landing strips, which will be able to accommodate sophisticated jet aircraft. Nicaraguans have also been trained as jet pilots and mechanics in Bulgaria.[26] While there is no evidence of MiGs in Nicaragua yet, any future emplacement of MiG aircraft in Nicaragua would greatly increase the potential for total coverage of the region by hostile combat aircraft. Furthermore, such improvements, coupled with significant increases in the size of the Sandinista Army and current Sandinista support for radical groups, are rightly perceived as a threat by Nicaragua's neighbors. As a result, other Central American countries are likely to feel the need to pump additional money into their armed forces to counter the Nicaraguan threat, reducing the funds that might otherwise be available for internal socioeconomic programs. This is particularly true for the contiguous states of Honduras, El Salvador, and Costa Rica.

Despite such factors, it is neither imminent nor inevitable that Nicaragua will emerge as a full-fledged Communist state with formal security ties to Cuba or as a fully totalitarian Marxist–Leninist state. Several obstacles remain to the communization of Nicaragua. First, while Castro is highly regarded by the Sandinista leadership and Castro's magnetic personality clearly captivates many of those who supported the revolution, it is far from certain that the majority of the Sandinistas are ready to become totally dependent on the Eastern bloc for all forms of support. Further, to date the Soviet Union apparently has been unwilling to provide the sort of economic support to Nicaragua that it did to Cuba. Without a clear indication that such support would be forthcoming, it is unlikely that Nicaragua would willingly break its economic ties with the West. Second, if the Sandinista leadership wishes to avoid a serious economic disruption and consequent economic downturn, which might undermine its support, it must rely on the existing mixed-enterprise economy (including the private sector) that directly depends on the Western economic system. Today Nicaragua still depends on Western sources of capital and assistance for its post revolution reconstruction. This fact, however, must be balanced against the Marxist–Leninist approach, which subordinates economics to the political objective. Third, movement toward more authoritarian government controls is meeting some vigorous opposition from the church and other groups within and outside of Nicaragua. Furthermore, armed insurgents in the North (the National Democratic Front) and in the South (the Democratic Revolutionary Alliance under Eden Pastora) constitute a definite threat to the Sandinistas. Finally, some elements within the Sandinista government have publicly declared their intent to maintain pluralism in Nicaragua. In this regard the decision in mid-August 1983 of the Sandinista-controlled Council of State to relax controls on political parties in preparation for the elections promised for 1985 is promising. Whether this relaxation as well as previous statements of support for pluralism is simply a tactic being pursued by the Sandinista to disarm internal opposition and relieve the pressure from the United States remains to be seen. Nevertheless, this slackening of the pace of revolutionary consolidation may well provide the United States with time to develop and implement policies that increase the probability of achieving a greater degree of democracy in Nicaragua.

Its close association with the deposed Somoza regime has made it difficult for the United States to develop close relations with the new Nicaraguan government. The United States provided military assistance and considerable political support to the Somozas since the 1930s. Inevitably, the Sandinista revolution developed an automatic anti-imperialist, anti-U.S. thrust that merged easily with the Marxist–Leninist framework of its leadership. The United States is resented for its past role and it is feared for its anti-Sandinista posture. The Sandinistas, moreover, have, under Cuban advice, deliberately pursued a policy of eliminating U.S. economic and political leverage over the consolidation of their revolutionary process. This has been done by diversifying their sources of foreign economic and military support and by internationalizing the conflict in Central America. Thus the task of reversing the trend toward a one-party Marxist–Leninist state will not be easy. The United States must not only obtain the confidence of the democratic sectors that remain in Nicaraguan society, but also it must offer the Sandinista leadership alternatives that permit them to adopt more pragmatic, less ideological approaches to the solution of Nicaragua's current difficulties. Ultimately the Nicaraguan leadership will have to convince themselves of the advantages of not following the Cuban path.

El Salvador. El Salvador is the scene of a brutal revolutionary conflict between right and left, with a number of reformists caught in the middle. A critical factor in shaping the evolution of contemporary El Salvador has been the role of the military institution. Since the early 1930s, the military has been in power. In 1932 the Salvadoran military came to power in the wake of a Communist-inspired peasant uprising, one of whose leaders was the now-famous Farabundo Marti. The revolt was brutally suppressed (some 30,000 peasants were killed in a massacre, which became known as the *matanza*), and the threat to the existing order was effectively eliminated. Calls for some measure of social and economic reform, however, continued to surface. By the late 1940s a number of military officers began to believe that internal order could be assured only if reforms were forthcoming. Following the Revolution of 1948, a group of young officers, impressed by the Mexican revolution model, took power and embarked on a program of moderate modernization. Thus, the Salvadoran military became what could be called the first reformist military institution in Latin America. Their programs, however, though well intentioned, only tinkered with the status quo. No sweeping reforms that might seriously challenge the privileged classes were undertaken. On the other hand, the very moderation of their programs seemed to guarantee the support of the oligarchy, who, in a classical Latin American response to demands for social change, believed that modernization without structural change, guided by the armed forces, offered the promise of effective security from serious threats from the left.[27]

Between 1948 and 1970, the Salvadoran military lost much of its reformist direction, isolated itself from its own society, and developed into a closed institution known for its high degree of unity, staunch but undifferentiated anti-Communism, and ideological uniformity. Challenges to the traditional order were frequently considered to be Communist-inspired. Moreover, the "success" of the *matanza* suggested to many in the military that internal stability was best served by an immediate suppression of potential threats to the existing order.

By 1970, Christian Democracy, a movement that was calling for reforms similar to those advocated by the United States during the Alliance for Progress years, had become the principal opposition. Concerned that the Christian Democrats might come to power, the military intervened in the elections of 1972 and through electoral fraud and repression succeeded in defeating Jose Napoleon Duarte and the Christian Democrats. Following the election, the Christian Democratic Party was suppressed and its leadership driven into exile, further forcing the rank and file to the left.

Continued political repression in the face of calls for an opening of the political process coupled with a failure to achieve social and economic reforms contributed to the undermining of the government's moral legitimacy. Opposition continued to grow and violence became an institutionalized feature of the political scene. In response to demands for reform and leftist violent revolutionary activity, elements within the right, with the tacit if not explicit sanction and assistance of elements within the government, organized paramilitary forces to eliminate political activists, peasant and labor leaders, and activist members of the clergy. The increasing incidence of revolutionary violence, repression, and political assassination led to a greater polarization of society and to a growing international isolation of El Salvador. The fall of Somoza in Nicaragua and the cutoff of U.S.

economic and military assistance to the Salvadoran government further encouraged the left and contributed to the development of a siege mentality among traditional conservative elements, which in turn further polarized society and resulted in a slide toward political disintegration.

In the midst of escalating violence on October 15, 1979, a bloodless coup installed a new government of younger officers and moderate civilians committed to reforming the country's "antiquated economic, social and political structures." The government promised to end repression, create a democratic political system, and implement agrarian reform. Even though the coup resulted in the retirement of approximately 40 percent of the more senior officer ranks, the so-called October Junta could not muster sufficient support from the generally conservative military and security forces to carry out its bold program. A new junta, which included Jose Napoleon Duarte and other Christian Democrats, was formed in January 1980 and soon announced sweeping banking and agrarian reforms. The new government was immediately confronted with a number of formidable challenges. To implement reforms likely to lead to social and economic change, a strong government based on either a broad consensus or a monopolization of the means of violence was required. The junta was neither. Its reform programs were attacked from the left as insufficient and by the right as threatening. The polarization and subsequent militarization of society left the government in a position where it could neither effectively control right-wing terrorism nor put an end to the terrorism and guerrilla activities of the left.

In spring 1980 it was feared that the fragile government coalition could not survive these challenges. Some believed that a Marxist–Leninist takeover of El Salvador was imminent. Many thought the coalition would be toppled by the right or overwhelmed by the combined efforts of the Farabundo Marti Liberation Front (FMLN). Neither happened. The insurgency's "final" military offensive of January 1981, the result of a strategic miscalculation about a popular uprising, was defeated by government forces. Rightist coup efforts were blunted. In March 1982, close to a million and a half Salvadorans went to the polls[28] to elect a new constituent assembly tasked to write a constitution and set up full presidential elections. Those elections are now scheduled for 1984.

The significance of the popular vote in the 1982 elections for the constituent assembly has been the subject of multiple interpretations. As a minimum it would seem that the elections demonstrated the popular yearning for an end to the bloodshed. The right under Roberto D'Aubuisson won control of the National Assembly and attempted to turn back the reforms. These efforts largely failed, but the government of provisional President Alvaro Magaña has been unable to build a cohesive coalition, take advantage of the legitimacy provided by the remarkable March 1982 elections, launch an effective counterinsurgency effort, or improve its international image.[29]

Thus, the violence of the right and left remains as the immediate grave threat not only to the existence of current government, but also to the prospects of socioeconomic and political reform along democratic lines. Right-wing "death squads" and the brutal repressive acts of elements within the National Guard, the Treasury and National police, and the civil defense forces, although now apparently less frequent, continue to alienate the *campesinos* as well as worker, teacher, and student groups and thus lend credibility to the revolutionary left's contention that real reform can take place only through revolution and a total reordering of the political and security apparatus. On the other hand, violent terrorist and guerrilla actions of the left not only beget rightist reaction but also constrain the government's ability to pursue reform as it is forced to devote increasing resources to containing the insurgency. Gross domestic production has declined 25 percent since 1980.

The left is clearly able to mount strikes against government security forces and highly visible infrastructure targets, disrupt harvests, pin down a large portion of the army in static defense, and deprive the government of a decisive victory. In certain areas of the country, such as Morazan, guerrilla dominance is practically unchallenged. The guerrilla strategy is to lengthen the conflict, exhaust government forces, destroy the economy, and politically isolate the government, as a prelude to victory. Nevertheless, the revolutionary left confronts some formidable realities. First, the government has not been totally discredited as was the Somoza regime. It has the conditional support of the church and apparently has (if the elections of 1982 meant anything) the support of a substantial number of citizens. Thus, the FMLN has not yet won the widespread support of the peasants and, to date, has had only limited success in recruiting.

Second, even though the principal guerrilla groups united under the FMLN in 1980,[30] the left is hardly monolithic. Events surrounding the slaying of Melida Anaya Montes, a leading member of the Popular Liberation Forces (FPL), the April 1983 "suicide" of Salvador Cayetano Carpio, the FPL leader, and the periodic internecine violence that has characterized the various groups now united in the FLMN indicates that differences of tactics, strategy, and personalities exist within and between the groups.[31] Such differences as do exist among the various guerrilla and front groups are likely to be exploitable.

Third, despite the continued and highly visible actions of the insurgents, the elections of 1982 provided the government of El Salvador an edge in the "legitimacy" test and thus an edge in the continuing battle for international recognition and support.

Regardless of these insurgents' problems, however, the government and the military have not been able to prosecute an effective counterinsurgency, often permitting the FMLN cheap psychological victories, such as the taking of the city of Berlin in early 1983. Part of the problem is that the military and civilian authorities do not coordinate the political, economic, and military components of policy well. Just as serious are the structural deficiencies of the armed forces: ineffective command and control system; poor departmental and brigade command organization; a static defense mentality and incapacity for small-unit operations; lack of tactical intelligence; poor logistics, transport, and communication; lack of well-trained middle-grade officers; an outmoded promotion system based on time in grade only; poor coordination between the Ministry of Defense and units in the field; and the fragmentation of security functions between the National guard, the Army, Treasury Police, and the civil defense and territorial guards.[32] These deficiencies will not be remedied quickly since they require not the reforming of but literally the building of a professional military organization. This will require time and outside assistance. The new Defense Minister, General Carlos Eugenio Vides Casanova, is expected to improve the command structure and has begun to implement a more vigorous counterinsurgency strategy, relying more on small-unit and offensive operations. There are some indications of growing government military successes in the field.

In the midst of the civil strife, the government continues to make progress in agrarian reform. In 1979, 40 percent of the land belonged to less than 2 percent of the families. By the third quarter of 1983 the land reform program had redistributed more than 20 percent of all arable land, benefiting about 500,000, or, one in ten Salvadorans. This achievement contrasts with the lack of progress in other areas, particularly in altering the ineffective and corrupt system of criminal justice. As presidential elections in El Salvador approach in 1984 and in the United States later that year, the Vietnam analogy shadows the policy debate. While some contend that the war can be lost in the U.S. Congress, the reality is that it can be won only in the political, psychological, and military battlefields of El Salvador. And, in the final analysis, it can be won or lost only by the Salvadorans.

Guatemala. On the heels of the Sandinista victory in Nicaragua and the insurgency in El Salvador, the intensification of insurgency in in Guatemala in 1979–1982 refocused attention on the problems of one of the most strategic countries in Central America. Guatemala is a country of approximately 7.5 million, endowed with a wealthy and diversified economy. It has been burdened by a rigid sociopolitical order presided over by a leadership structure that frequently has waged a relentless, undifferentiated "anti-Communist" domestic campaign against all reformist elements. In the process, the political center has been virtually eliminated and opportunities for the development of more broadly based alternative leaderships have been seriously diminished. The level of political violence has been high in Guatemala. In the past, political violence frequently appeared to have the tacit or, in a number of cases, the explicit support of the government.

Recent problems in Guatemala can be understood in terms of an aborted social revolution. Guatemala developed a highly stratified and inequitable social order, based on racial lines and the sharp cleavages between Guatemala City and the rural areas. In the late 1940s and early 1950s under Juan Jose Arevalo and Jacobo Arbenz, Guatemala appeared to be attempting to emulate Mexico and its social revolution. Political and economic rights were extended to the Indians. Land reform was pursued and minimum-wage laws passed. Arbenz relied heavily on the support of the Communists. Furthermore, he implemented land reform through expropriation and seizure of the large estates. A counterrevolution organized in Honduras and aided by the United States swept out Arbenz and the Communists. Seen in the context of the Cold War, the United States feared the establishment of a Communist government. Since then, Guatemalan governments have been hard put to accommodate demands for social change, often considering them as Communist-led or Communist-inspired, or both. In the 1960s a counterinsurgency effort liquidated the social ferment in Zacapa and in the urban centers. It did not, however, eradicate the desire for social reform that led to the appearance of an entirely new form of insurgency in the 1970s.

Evidencing a more sophisticated form of revolutionary warfare, the Guerilla Army of the Poor began to establish the bases for prolonged revolution in 1972. Its strategy contained four elements: prolonged popular warfare, popular front organization, internationalization of the conflict, and maintenance of external support. In tactical terms this meant building a logistic infrastructure, widening the support base among Indians, gaining Cuban support, and increasing its international diplomacy through solidarity groups, the news media, church and academic groups, activists, and the heterogeneous critics of U.S. "interventionism" in the Third World. The insurgent strategy differed from the less effective romantic strategies of the 1960s. The government responded with repressive counterinsurgency methods and thereby swelled the ranks of the opposition. The outcome was the deterioration of internal security, the elimination of moderates, and the progressive domestic and international isolation of the government.[33]

The insurgents were able to widen their support base because of structural inequities in Guatemalan society. Some of the more salient: only about one-third of the population has benefited from Guatemala's economic growth in the last thirty years; 80 percent of the land is held by 2 percent of the farm families; nine of ten rural inhabitants live on plots of land too small to support a family; 25 percent of the rural families have no land at all; 20 percent of the population earns about 65 percent of the national income; the lowest 20 percent earns less than 4 percent; and 5 percent earn about 33 percent of the gross domestic product. These figures give Guatemala the most skewed distribution of wealth in Central America. Unemployment reaches 33 percent of the labor force and in some rural areas 40 percent. Such inequities are compounded by stark differences between rich and poor in life-expectancy mortality rates, health services, nutrition, and education.

The social inequities, the violence, economic mismanagement, and electoral fraud added up to what the young officers who rebelled in March 1982 called *desgobierno*. They stated:

> The government has no strategy to deal with the guerrillas. It has used the tactic of disorganizing society, labelling any vocal leadership as subversive, and attempted to use brute force against a political problem. The guerrilla would not be a serious military problem if not for the corruption, inability to govern, exploitation, and violence that provides the guerrillas with recruits and legitimacy.[34]

Today, the exponents of change—mostly students, professors and other professionals, new urban classes, and many military officers—want better treatment for the Indian, social and economic reform, and a more open and competitive political system that involves the military less directly in politics. In the recent past, the aspirations of such groups were stifled by an elite power structure that like Salvadoran elites, essentially regarded reforms as Communist. As one business leader put it, "We call the Christian Democrats the 'watermelon people. . . . They're green on the outside but red on the inside.' "[35] This tendency to consider those who call for reform as subversive led to increasing violence and polarization during the later days of the administration of President Romero Lucas Garcia (1977–1982). It also did much to assure that concern over Communist influence in the reform movement became a self-fulfilling prophecy. Members of student and labor groups, the clergy, educators, lawyers, doctors, journalists, community workers, as well as the urban poor and peasantry were all subjected to violence. As a prominent observer of Guatemalan affairs has stated, "Between the guerrillas, the security forces and paramilitary groups, virtually every organized segment of society and leadership group became the target of violence, usually physical, but sometimes psychological."[36]

As is the case elsewhere, Cuba has been active in exploiting the situation in Guatemala. By the end of 1981, the then Chief of Staff of Guatemala's armed forces, General Benedicto Lucas García, put the insurgents' armed strength at 2000 to 4000.[37] By February 1982, under Cuban urgings, the four major guerrilla forces had formed a coalation called the National Patriotic United Front[38] and were reported to be increasingly effective in securing support from among the Indian population.[39] In the past, insurgent opposition to the government had not received much support from the traditionally passive Indians. However, successes in recruiting from the Indian population (which comprises nearly 50 percent of the total population of Guatemala) early in the decade were a serious setback for the government.

In March 1982, the fraudulently reelected Lucas government was removed from power in a bloodless "coup" led by a group of reform-minded young officers who then turned to retired General Efraín Rios-Montt to lead the new government. Since then the government, through various means, has appeared to be bringing peace to the countryside.[40] Rios-Montt, who himself was removed by a coup in August 1983, implemented the strategy of "rifles and beans." It included socioeconomic assistance, arming the Indian militia to serve as a buffer against the guerrillas, and striking the guerrillas directly. As contrasted with the Salvadoran counterinsurgency, the Guatemalans apparently are succeeding in defeating the guerrillas by applying an integrated concept of security and development. "Rifles and beans," according to Rios-Montt, meant 20 percent military effort and 80 percent socioeconomic assistance. The program provides peasants emergency food, medical aid and sanitation, public services, roads, resettlement of displaced villagers (estimated to number 250,000 to 500,000), seeds, fertilizer, tools, technical aid and instruction, and materials for reconstruction. These measures, along with dealing hard blows to the insurgents, permitted, according to the government, the reestablishment of ninety local governments and the resumption of productive activity in the zones of conflict. By the end of 1982 the government claimed that the guerillas had been defeated and their leaders driven abroad. Moreover, for the first time in history Indians participated in the Council of State as advisors to the president. It nonetheless remains to be seen whether

Guatemala can integrate its diverse social groups into a nation and eliminate the causes of insurgency. The insurgents may have been dealt a serious setback, but they have not been eliminated. The new government of General Oscar Humberto Mejia has pledged to legalize political parties and hold elections for a constituent assembly by July 1984. These optimistic developments were counterbalanced in the fall of 1983 by a new round of violence. Some observers in and out of Guatemala have advocated that the military leave politics as soon as possible.

The Cuban Threat

Twenty years of revolution have brought Cuba no closer to socialist utopia. Indeed, Cuba's socialist economy requires a daily Soviet subsidy estimated to be over $8 million—the equivalent of a quarter of Cuba's GNP.[41] Moreover, in December 1979, Fidel Castro acknowledged Cuba's economic difficulties and promised twenty more years of austerity.[42]

Despite poor economic performance, however, the Cuban revolution has had some successes in health, sanitation, education, and housing (although in some instances not as pronounced as some other countries of the region). Moreover, there is an apparent deep dissatisfaction with the quality of life in some quarters, as evidenced by the 127,000 or more who left Cuba in April–May 1980. In an objective sense, Cuba does not appear to be attractive as a model for economic development for most societies in the region.

Economic failures, however, have not diminished Cuba's willingness to project itself into regional and worldwide activities. Today, according to State Department estimates, Cuba has about 35,000 military personnel serving in combat and security assistance roles in Africa alone.[43] As has been noted earlier, in the Caribbean Basin Cuba has been active in supporting guerrilla efforts. The Cubans have worked to unite traditionally splintered radical groups behind a commitment to armed struggle in return for Cuban advice, intelligence, and material assistance. They have trained revolutionaries in urban and rural warfare; supplied or arranged for the supply of weapons to support guerrilla efforts in the region; and encouraged terrorism in efforts to provoke indiscriminate violence and repression in order to weaken governments and attract converts to armed struggle.[44]

As noted earlier, Havana worked clandestinely with the *Tercerista* during the Nicaraguan war to channel weapons to diversify the Sandinistas' international sources of support. Cuba has at least 2000 security and military advisors in Nicaragua. In El Salvador Fidel Castro played a key role in unifying the five guerrilla groups under the

Farabundo Marti Liberation Front and accomplished the same in Guatemala with the establishment of the National Patriotic United Front. In Costa Rica a special legislative commission documented Cuba's role in establishing a supply network during the Nicaraguan war. The network was later used to supply Salvadoran insurgents. Cuba was implicated in training M19 guerrillas in Colombia and is active in nurturing an insurgency in Honduras.

As a long-term investment, Cuba and the Socialist bloc are offering university scholarships to highly motivated lower- and middle-class students in the Caribbean, implying far-reaching consequences for the future of the region. The scholarship program for the Caribbean alone involves thousands of students each year.

Today, Cuba's highly sophisticated regional policy operates at two levels—overt and covert—maintaining normal state-to-state relations with other governments and forging contacts and developing flexible options with revolutionary movements through clandestine assistance and training. It is the latter effort—growing Cuban military capabilities, Cuba's apparently well-coordinated anti-U.S. psychological warfare campaign, and its close relationship with the Soviet Union—that threatens U.S. interests in the region.

Also of concern is the more remote but no less troubling implications of growing Cuban military capabilities should a war occur involving the United States and the Soviet Union in Europe or elsewhere. The combat radius of Cuba's MiG 23s now permits Cuba to strike targets throughout much of the Gulf, to threaten approaches to the Panama Canal, and to attack installations in the United States as far north as Savannah, Georgia. The radius of air and sea interdiction would expand to include almost the entire Caribbean Basin if Cuban and/or Soviet aircraft were permitted to operate from bases in Grenada and Nicaragua (see Figure 5.2). Moreover, if the Cubans were provided more advanced aircraft such as the Fencer (Su-19), they would be able to strike targets deep in the United States. In a conventional conflict with the Soviet Union in Europe, the United States would be required to divert significant military resources if it wished to neutralize the Cuban threat. One can envision a requirement for U.S. air and naval forces, just at a time when they were urgently needed in Europe, having to stop en route to Europe to neutralize Cuba. The Cuban threat would be even more serious if nuclear weapons, including cruise missiles, were placed in Cuba in the possession of either the Soviets or the Cubans.

Cuba also could be used as a logistics base, recovery point, and turnaround facility for Soviet aircraft, ships, and submarines operating in the Gulf of Mexico, the Caribbean Basin, and the Atlantic. Backfire (Tu-26) bombers launched from the Kola Peninsula and recovered and

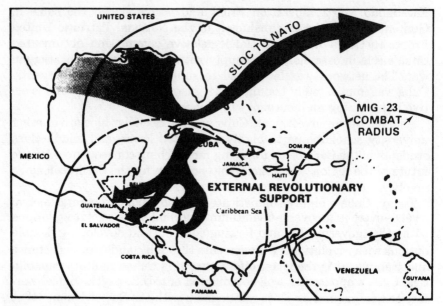

(*Source:* Joint Chiefs of Staff, *United States Military Posture for FY 1983* [Washington, D.C.: U.S. Government Printing Office, 1983], p. 12. Circles of potential coverage of MiG 23 aircraft operating from Nicaragua and Grenada added by authors.)

Figure 5.2. Potential area coverage of MiG 23 aircraft.

relaunched from Cuba would permit strategic surveillance and attack throughout much of the North and South Atlantic. In a strategic nuclear conflict, it would also permit the Soviets to strike targets deep in the United States. Similarly, Soviet submarines could use Cuba for refueling and ammunition resupply and thus avoid interdiction by U.S.-NATO anti-submarine warfare forces (ASW) operating in the Greenland–Iceland–United Kingdom gap.

THE COMPLEXITIES OF POLICY DEVELOPMENT

While rhetoric and relative emphasis have differed from time to time, both President Carter and President Reagan have followed similar paths in their attempts to meet the challenges confronting the region. Both have stressed the need for democracy, development, and nonintervention. Differences between the two administrations and between each administration and its critics have been rooted less in disagreements over fundamental national or regional objectives than in disagreements over principal or underlying causes and most promising cures for the current round of instabilities in the region. Yet the U.S.'s apparent inability to deal effectively with the events in the Caribbean and to achieve a domestic consensus for concerted action is as much a product of the lack of clarity of its goals and differing judgments over current trends as it is the product of differing views on the efficacy of policies designed to address the problems the region confronts.

Clarity of Goals

There is some consensus for our stated goals for the region—democracy, development, and nonintervention. In the absence of clarity, however, these broad goals are virtually meaningless as guides to policy and furnish no basis on which to judge the efficacy of U.S. efforts. We support democracy, yet we have but a dim view of what it is we intend to promote and why. We believe that democracy and the freedoms and personal incentives that democracy promotes have been the key to Western economic success. Yet history has marked some authoritarian governments with great economic successes from the days of the Roman Empire to Imperial or even Nazi Germany, and more recently under the Shah of Iran. Are authoritarian governments prone to excesses? Or is it that despite historical and cultural experiences that might suggest something to the contrary, the peoples of Latin America have demonstrated an increasing demand for political participation over the last several decades?

Furthermore, what do we mean by democracy and what kind of democracy do we wish to promote? Is it the European parliamentary model of democracy, on occasion pluralistic to distraction, or the U.S. model of representative government that we seek? Is it an eclectic form of democracy that borrows from both but grafts to the European and American forms the unique historical and cultural experiences of each of the many countries involved? Or is it a new form of democracy, possibly the outgrowth of historical cooperative political experience, capable, however, of aggregating at the national level the wishes of the many? Over what time frame must the change to democracy take place? How do we judge when a government is democratic in substance as well as form? Must it have elections? Must the press be totally free? Must there be active political parties? What were our own experiences in this regard? Do trends count? Is Panama on the road to democracy? Is Mexico, dominated by one party, democratic? If so, in what sense of the word? Have the people of El Salvador made truly revolutionary advances toward democracy since 1979 or only minor, cosmetic changes undeserving of American support? What is the acceptable pace of democratic evolution and what are the measures? Is Guatemala now making progress toward democracy?

We support economic and social development, yet we are uncertain how that is to take place. We frequently argue for a free-enterprise model. We emphasize private initiative and private enterprise. Some in Latin America believe central planning is necessary to avoid the inefficiencies of an unconstrained marketplace. Participation of the state in the development process has frequently been an attractive alternative to leadership groups in the region who have been unconvinced that the mechanisms of the free marketplace are capable of promoting quick and equitable development. What balance between market and central planning mechanisms should be sought? Will they differ from country to country? Who will determine the appropriate balance and thus set the direction of development policy? How does one deal with economies judged to be economically inviable?

What do we mean by social development? Do we mean an end to class structures and common structures that perpetuate the class systems? Are we calling for a redistribution of the wealth through such measures as agrarian reform? Is agrarian reform conducive to economic development, or is it a political measure to reduce pressures on central governments in times of crisis which is likely to be counterproductive over the long run?

We emphasize nonintervention and self-determination, yet again we apparently understand the terms only vaguely. Is nonintervention an active or a passive policy? Should it include the collective efforts of others to actively preclude military intervention in the hemisphere? Should the United States practice nonintervention? Or does the United States have a special right to act unilaterally in the region to preserve democracy? Likewise, do the Soviets have a similar right in Eastern Europe? What do we mean by intervention? Does nonintervention mean that other powers should not be involved in assisting the militaries of duly constituted governments? Some have suggested that U.S. military assistance to the governments of El Salvador and Guatemala constitutes U.S. intervention in the internal affairs of these states. Is U.S. assistance to NATO countries considered interference? Or is it intervention only when the right of constituted governments is challenged by revolutionaries?

The fashioning of effective policy has also been hampered by disagreements over the nature of the overall problem, and over judgments concerning the nature of change sweeping the hemisphere and the immediate and long-term policy actions indicated.

North–South Versus East–West

A number of critics of current policy see instabilities in the Caribbean and Central America essentially as a North–South issue. That is to say, they view social inequities and economic deprivation as fundamental to the current wave of unrest. While they recognize the role that Cuba and the Soviet Union have played in exploiting revolutionary trends, they believe that long-term stability can be achieved only by assisting and encouraging the countries of the region to resolve their social and economic problems.

On the other hand, others, including a number of those serving in the current administration, see instabilities essentially as an East–West issue. They recognize the underlying social and economic causes of revolution. However, they believe that the strength and effectiveness of the current round of terrorist activity and guerrilla warfare can be attributed directly to Cuban and less directly to Soviet arms shipments and interventionist activities in the hemisphere. They further believe that needed social reforms and economic development can take place in the long run only if the shorter-term security problem is resolved.

Neither of these perspectives captures the reality that confronts the hemisphere today. The problem is neither essentially North–South nor East–West. It is both simultaneously—with all the complexities that two simultaneous problems of such significant proportions entail. Policy formulations that emphasize the East–West aspect will in the short and long runs be as counterproductive as will approaches that focus principally on economic and social reform and ignore the essential fact that the Soviet Union and its Cuban allies are aiding and abetting revolution in the region.

The choice of the geopolitical framework determines the policy choices, influences the mix of resources to be employed, and affects the responses by the American people and by the varying publics in the region. A choice in the East–West framework emphasizes improving war-fighting capabilities against the Soviets. It entails expanded basing arrangements, security assistance to modernize the capabilities of regional allies, coalition defense of sea lines of communication, intelligence sharing, and streamlined command arrangements. The North–South framework stresses the developmental imperative, internal defense, civic action, and nation-building. Given the intrusion of the East–West conflict into the region, the defense of U.S. interests in the Caribbean necessarily involves both approaches. The task of policymakers is to strike a balance between both frameworks, one that is credible to the U.S. people, to allies, and to friends and foes.

The Nature of Change

The continued inability to achieve a consensus among policy elites in this country for action to secure U.S. interests in the region also has been the result of disagreements over the nature of the changes that are taking place in the hemisphere. It has been the tacit, if not explicit, position of the two previous administrations—indeed, the general position of the United States since the days of the Alliance for Progress—that given the political and economic structures in several countries of the region, democracy, development, and social change would for some nations represent nothing less than a revolution. The task therefore has been to bring about revolutionary change in the absence of revolutionary violence.

On the other hand, some have argued that revolutionary change will inevitably be accompanied by revolutionary violence and that the United States should not be on the side of reaction. Yet, those who argue for such a stance, presumably in keeping with our own historical traditions and ideals, have failed to mark clearly the course of U.S. action. Are they suggesting that the United States should actively support revolutionaries when their proclaimed aim is democracy, development, and social justice? Or rather, should the United States simply withdraw its support for the current government? At what point should it make the decision to do either? What are the factors that indicate a revolution is taking place or perhaps will take place in the near future? Is it the lack of democratic forms or the substance of democracy? Or the lack of economic and social development?

Is it when the government is repressive? If so, how do you measure repression? By the number killed? kidnapped? Do trends count? Is a government repressive if there is evidence of a hard-core group of revolutionaries? Does the size of the group count? At what point should the United States shift its support? Is it when the revolutionaries constitute 10 percent (or 20 percent or 50 percent) of the population? How do you determine who are the good guys deserving of U.S. support and who are the bad guys? In El Salvador, is it the Duartes, the Magañas, the Vides Casanovas, or the Villalobos, the Handals, or the Ungos? Is a government repressive if in its "postrevolutionary" phase through the use of fear and totalitarian controls it need not exercise the more obvious forms of repression? If repression is an important variable, should our support for revolutionaries be limited only to countries that have been our neighbors or is there a greater moral good to which we aspire? If so, should our policies also be applied to Poland, Afghanistan, Czechoslovakia, the Soviet Union? Should our decision to support the revolution be affected by judgments concerning the nature of the revolutionary movement in terms of the likelihood that the form and substance of the government that is likely to emerge in the postrevolutionary phase will fulfill the people's aspirations for real political, economic, and social development? If our judgment is that the old order will simply be replaced by a new order likely to be even less capable of fulfilling the aspirations of the people and inclined to impose an even more narrowly based political system along totalitarian lines, should our actions be different?

If, however, we believe that revolutionary change can take place in the absence of revolutionary violence, then what policies should the United States pursue that are likely to have the highest probability of encouraging appropriate change while reducing the level of violence? Where movement toward democracy, economic development, and social change appears to falter, should the United States deny military and security assistance? What effect will this have on the militaries of the countries involved? If repression has been an issue, will the U.S. ability to influence the methods and tactics of the military—however minor and indirect that ability has been—be enhanced or diminished? What will be the effect on the level of violence if military assistance is cut off? Will revolutionaries be heartened or discouraged? Where a government's security interests are involved, will the government simply divert funds from needed economic and social programs to cover its military needs?

Should the United States deny both economic and military assistance to regimes that appear to be moving too slowly toward necessary reforms? What are the probabilities of affecting the kinds of changes desired through such an action and upon what framework do we make our judgments concerning probabilities?

FASHIONING A STRATEGY FOR THE 1980S AND BEYOND

Given the challenges that confront the region, a comprehensive U.S. strategy for the Caribbean Basin should be based on six broad guidelines. These guidelines will help maximize the probability of achieving U.S. short-term as well as long-term regional objectives and will demonstrate to the rest of the world a maturity in dealing with the complex problems that beset the region.

Support for Socioeconomic Development

Support for socioeconomic development should be the cornerstone of U.S. policy. It is not a simple call to idealism, however; rather it should be understood as a pragmatic approach in seizing the initiative, expanding the number of policy options available, and improving the probabilities of favorably influencing events in the region. While the United States has generally supported reform, it has frequently vacillated between emphasizing reform and emphasizing stability within the context of the Cuban-Soviet threat. Policy statements should consistently underscore U.S. support for social and economic reform, emphasize efforts to help the governments of the region bring about reform, and highlight the failings of the Cuban–Soviet model as an effective mechanism for economic development.

Such an approach would clearly signal to the region as well as to other countries, especially in the Third World, a U.S. commitment to social and economic development, and serve to underscore the fact that the United States recognizes that the principal underlying causes of the region's instability are social and economic. Such an approach would also assist in seizing the initiative from Cuba, the Soviet Union, and the far left. Moreover, it would serve to strengthen moderate elements who recognize the need for reform. It would signal the far right that the United States believes that reform must come if the societies are to avoid imminent collapse, and that in the absence of a commitment to reform, the far right can no longer count on U.S. support. Lastly, support for development would improve the probability of achieving domestic consensus for other policies in the region.

Support for Broadly Based Representative Forms of Government

In conjunction with an emphasis on social and economic reform, the United States should support and assist the further development of representative political institutions and processes. Seymour Martin Lipset wrote over two decades ago that "stability . . . depends not only on economic development but also upon the effectiveness and legitimacy of its political system."[45] Today, authoritarian governments in some countries of the Caribbean Basin lack the political legitimacy necessary to ensure long-term stability in the region. Legitimacy comes from process as well as performance. Thus, in modern political cultures, a government that can link its existence to the will of the governed is generally viewed as legitimate by those it governs as well as by outside observers. Similarly, a government's political legitimacy can be established through effective performance in responding to the demands of the governed. Authoritarian governments in the Caribbean have failed on both counts. Generally speaking, they have neither been "freely" selected by the governed nor responsive to the demands of the people. Rather, they have been representative of a narrow sector of the polity that has generally been resistant to change.

While it is frequently argued that one should not attempt to impose American democratic values on people whose history and culture suggest quite a different political heritage, the postwar history of Latin America suggests an increasing popular demand for political participation. In recent years, this trend has been reflected in Central America, especially in the wake of the failure of traditional authoritarian systems to achieve real social and economic progress. The democratic elective process appears to offer the most promising solution to the legitimacy crisis. In this regard, the warning of Mihajlo Mihailov, the anti-Communist Yugoslav writer, appears to be pertinent: "Right wing dictatorships are essentially the fifth-column of totalitarianism. . . . Practically every present-day totalitarian country was authoritarian or partly authoritarian before the Communists came to power."[46]

The United States can best assure a rejection of Communism and the long-term stability of the region not only by assisting the Caribbean Basin countries in their quest for economic development, but also by supporting those elements in each of the countries in the region that are attempting to promote democratic government. In much of the English Caribbean, such an approach would contribute to strengthening the existing democratic institutions, the legacy of British parliamentary influence. In the Spanish-speaking countries, U.S. support for the continued development of broadly based representative forms of government would provide order and direction to current trends.

Further development of democratic institutions and processes is likely to serve to promote social and political integration, as mechanims are developed for interest articulation. It would enhance the legitimacy of governments of the region and provide a vent for popular frustrations when, as is almost inevitable, governments fail to achieve all the social and economic goals set by rising expectations. Finally, it would provide an institutional mechanism for orderly change of government. The United States, however, must also recognize that while there are many who are dissatisfied with the pace of social and economic reform and are now demanding some form of political participation as a means of achieving reform, there are also many who are skeptical about the efficiency of democratic government. Hence, movement toward democracy may at times be slow and should not necessarily be expected, in all cases, to mirror European or American parliamentary models.

Support for International Conventions that Protect the Rights of Individuals as Well as the Social Whole

While it is beyond the scope of this paper to address the many aspects of the debate over the role of human rights in U.S. foreign relations, carefully constructed policies that support human rights and human dignity can be powerful tools in the international community. A human rights standard, however, should not be the *sine qua non* for interstate relations. It is not in our relations with the Soviet Union or its allies. It should not be with other countries, especially our neighbors. Moreover, the human rights standard should not be applied any more rigidly to countries who historically have been friends and neighbors than it is to those who have consistently been violators of human rights.

By working through international organizations and conventions rather than through unilaterally imposed restrictions on states based on their adherence to human rights standards, the United States can take a balanced position that offers the opportunity to pressure, in a visible way, consistent violators such as the Soviet Union and its allies. It also offers the opportunity to pressure indirectly more friendly governments. Since a wide variety of factors affect a country's approach to human rights, direct U.S. restrictions placed on traditionally friendly governments may well be counterproductive not only in terms of the ability of the United States to influence those governments in other areas of concern to the United States, but also in terms of the probable effect of the restrictions on human rights violations. Where restrictions may be useful, they should be applied with discretion by the Executive Branch acting in concert with Congress.

Support for Efforts Designed to Separate the Moderates from the Far Left and Far Right

In a number of countries the normal bell-shaped curve that defines the political spectrum has been distorted by radicalization and reaction. The task is to assist countries so affected in their attempts to recreate the center and a new political consensus. This will not be an easy task, nor will success always be assured. The extremes in such countries as El Salvador and Guatemala, however, are not monolithic. Nor, in the case of the left, is it totally controlled by Havana and Moscow. Policies should be pursued that maximize the probability of producing friction among extremist groups with the objective of separating the more moderate elements from the extremists. Deprived of a support base from within the moderate left, the far left is likely either to go back underground (thus reducing the immediate threat to the governments in question) or to become even more radical and violent, increasing the probability of further alienating itself from the bulk of the population. Likewise, as more moderate elements break away, the extreme right will be more exposed.

Promote Bilateral and Multilateral Cooperation

In an age of increasingly interdependent relationships across the spectrum of human endeavor (social, economic, political, and security), the difficulties that confront the nations of the region are problems that can best be resolved through community efforts. In this respect, the Caribbean is remarkable for the complexity of multilateral interests involving a variety of international actors. Bilateral relationships lay the groundwork for continued influence. Multilateral relationships, while often difficult to orchestrate, frequently offer greater promise of long-term success and stability and provide a cushion where bilateral efforts fail. By promoting a climate of multilateral as well as bilateral cooperation conducive to dealing with common social, economic, and political concerns and the resolution of conflicts through peaceful means, the United States will be advertising its willingness to cooperate with nations of the region and to deal with them as sovereign. Such an approach will also increase the prospects for assisting in bringing about revolutionary social, economic, and political change in the absence of revolutionary violence. The members of the Contadora group in Central America—Mexico, Panama, Venezuela, and Colombia—fall into this category and are deserving of U.S. support and cooperation.

Weaken the Soviet-Cuban Alliance

The Soviet-Cuban relationship is one of a convergence of interests. Both parties derive benefits, and in the regional context, the relationship affords Cuba the political, economic, and military assets required to carry out its activist role in support of Marxist-Leninist revolutions. While the relationship is currently a firm one, it need not be for the indefinite future.[47]

Decoupling the Cubans from the Soviets is not in the cards in the short and perhaps not even in the medium term. The United States, however, should avoid policies that strengthen Cuba's reliance on the Soviet Union for its security and economic viability. Just as importantly, American governments must adopt policies that alter the ideological and generational rigidity of the current Cuban leadership and invest in the pragmatism and idealism of future leaders.

SPECIFIC POLICY RECOMMENDATIONS

Economic Policy

While the specific problems that confront each of the countries of the region will vary as they attempt to develop economically, most of the countries suffer from the combined impact of inadequate domestic infrastructure, underdeveloped national markets, lack of competitiveness in world markets, lack of economic diversification because of extreme dependence on a few key sectors (e.g., agriculture, tourism, and natural resources), insufficient capital formation, and the combined effects of the current world recession.

As a result, the pace of economic development of Caribbean Basin countries continues to fall short of natural expectations. The combination of depressed world prices for key commodity exports and upwardly spiraling prices for imported oil during the 1970s and early 1980s seriously affected the balance-of-payments position of the countries of the region. Debt burdens have grown and foreign exchange reserves have shrunk. Concomitantly, the ability to generate the capital necessary for socioeconomic development has diminished and development hopes have been frustrated. Although international agencies are providing some financial assistance, the servicing of an increasing external debt is draining domestic capital markets. As a result, capital from private as well as public sources is in extremely short supply.

High inflation and growing political instabilities are compounding the problem of capital formation. Personal savings and investment, essential to the supply of money to capital markets, has decreased as inflation erodes purchasing power and forces increased expenditures to maintain living standards. Moreover, where savings and investment capital is available, it frequently finds its way to locations abroad that are relatively free of political and economic risk. Likewise, foreign investors, concerned over the potential for hostilities and/or economic collapse and fearful that pressures from the radical left will force a leftward drift to government policies toward foreign investments, have been reluctant to invest in countries marked by increasing instability.

In an effort to constrain demand for imports, generate funds to service the external debt and control inflation, a number of the governments of the region have pursued moderately restrictive monetary and fiscal policies that have further reduced the funds available for investment by the private sector. The net effect of the general constriction in the overall supply of money available to the capital markets has had perhaps an even greater impact in the Caribbean Basin than it would have had elsewhere. For many of the countries of the region, the private enterprise structure is dominated by small, conservative family-owned businesses, which for cultural reasons are generally disinclined to borrow outside of the family membership. The short terms, high interest rates, and high collateral demanded by lenders further reduce incentives for borrowing. As a result, growth in the private sector is generally limited, jobs are not created rapidly enough to keep pace with the growth of available labor, under- and unemployment abound, additional socioeconomic and political demands are placed in the system, capital seeks safer refuge abroad, and the cycle continues.

Under such circumstances, central planning often appears to offer an opportunity to break the cycle. Participation of the state in the development process is attractive to frustrated leadership groups in the region because they lack faith in the interplay of the mechanisms of the free market to promote quick and equitable development. This feeling is reinforced by the anticapitalism of the British type of socialism found among the leadership in the English Caribbean, by anticolonialism, by the Marxist subculture, and by belief in the dependency theory of unequal and exploitative economic relations between the developed and developing countries. Moreover, an anticapitalist, procorporate state bias rooted in Hispanic values runs through the Spanish-speaking nations. This mixture of attitudes is in turn captured by the concept of developmental nationalism, which urges the mobilization of all sovereign resources to development. In sum, the state is viewed more favorably as the pivot for national development and assigned a substantial role in the ownership, production, and distribution of goods and services.

It is frequently argued that where in capitalist economies investments are frequently diffused and guided by profit, in a socialist centrally planned economy, limited investment capital can be concentrated in areas likely to produce specifically desired social and economic outcomes. Moreover, through central planning capital flight abroad can be more effectively controlled, consumption patterns altered, and inflation reduced. Ultimately, it is argued that economic growth can be achieved in those sectors best able to contribute to an improvement of the balance of payments and subsequently to the formation of capital necessary to foster improvements in domestic infrastructure and further economic and social progress.

While in theory there may not be anything inherently evil or wrong with central planning, central planning has generally had a dismal record. Nevertheless, the continued failure of Caribbean countries to achieve rapid socioeconomic progress has resulted in increasing pressures from the left for greater central planning. Such pressure, as noted earlier, chill the business communities and more conservative elements who generally believe that central planning, which is likely to come at their expense, will not only stifle incentive but also exacerbate rather than alleviate the economic problem confronting the nations of the region.

The Caribbean Basin Initiative (CBI) launched by President Reagan is a step in the direction of assisting the countries of the region in solving their economic difficulties. The offer of one-way free trade, supplemental emergency economic assistance for several key countries, efforts to supplement the noncommercial investment risk insurance operation of the Overseas Private Investment Corporation (OPIC), expanded protection through the U.S. Export-Import Bank for short-term credit from commercial banks to the regional private sectors for critical imports, and general efforts to assist private-sector development in the Basin will all contribute in the near term to alleviate some of the problems that plague the region.[48]

The legislation finally passed Congress on July 28, 1983, reduced the impact of the original concept. Textiles, apparel, footwear, petroleum products, luggage, handbags, and canned tuna were deleted from the list of eligible items. Moreover, qualifying nations can export duty-free if 35 percent of the value of the goods originated there, as opposed to the originally proposed 25 percent. Judgments on the impact of CBI vary. One State Department economic officer estimated in 1982 that as the result of the free trade, regional exports to the United States would increase by as much as $2.5 billion annually. A subsequent analysis, which took into consideration changes to the original plan, estimated that eliminating tariffs would stimulate exports from eligible nations by a scant $45 to $90 million.[49] The wide gap between the two estimates clearly counsels caution about the CBI's impact. In addition, much depends on economic recovery in the United States.

If the region is to achieve lasting social and economic progress, if the nations of the region are to become full partners of the community of Western nations in a political, social, and economic sense, then a more visionary effort of longer-term focus must be adopted. In this regard nothing less than a mini "Marshall Plan" effort is called for. It is recognized that it will be virtually impossible to muster support in Congress or with the U.S. taxpayer for such an effort. Nevertheless, it is the charge of the executive and Congress to guard the future as well as the present. A mini Marshall Plan investment in the region now will help reduce the probabilities of having to invest heavily in the future in a region that will have lost confidence in the Western political and economic model. The authors recognize the enormous complexities involved in attempting to assist the countries of the region in their economic development efforts. Nevertheless, the following broad elements of a more comprehensive plan for Caribbean Basin economic development should be considered.

First, the United States should undertake, in cooperation with key regional partners, a Caribbean Basin program for economic infrastructure development. Most of the countries of the region suffer from inadequate transport facilities such as ports and roads, inadequate public utilities, poor communications, underdeveloped credit facilities, insufficient skilled manpower, an inadequate pool of managerial talents, poor health and sanitation facilities, and an inadequate understanding among the elites of advantages and disadvantages of public-sector versus private-sector approaches to development and the approaches to achieving proper balance. In agriculture, for example, there is a need for research and extension services. There is also a need for feeder roads and warehousing facilities. In tourism, poor air transport facilities often inhibit rational development. In manufacturing, a lack of managerial talents and skilled manpower frequently inhibit expansion. In international and intraregional trade, mechanisms are lacking for facilitating an expansion of commerce. Assistance in infrastructure development would enable the countries of the region to increase the efficiency and productivity of these industries and thus enable them to build additional capital for economic expansion.

As part of the program of infrastructure development, the United States should nurture "Institutes for Democracy and Economic Development." One of the fundamental tasks of these institutes would be to increase the awareness of the elites in the countries of the region (businessmen, educators, government, etc.) of the approaches that have been pursued within the Western community to forge an effective balance between private- and public-sector efforts in order to foster economic development and expansion. Institutes should be located in every country of the region willing to assist in their establishment. Lecturers should be drawn from countries that represent the many and diverse economic models available in the Western community of nations.

Second, for economic as well as psychopolitical reasons, the United States should increase its bilateral and multilateral assistance programs. While an emphasis on private enterprise may be economically sound, many in the region, unconvinced of the role of private enterprise as a mechanism for real economic advancement, are likely to view an approach that appears to place primary or sole emphasis on improving the climate for private enterprise as a forerunner to yet another round of exploitation by multinational companies. As a result, U.S. support for economic development in the region will be seen by many as disingenuous.

In addition to such efforts, the United States should sponsor and fund projects that bring together government as well as private interests in an attempt to identify and resolve country and the more general regional development requirements (e.g., capital formation, energy alternatives, foreign investments, and trade market development). To this end, the United States should promote the establishment of "international trading centers" in the Caribbean and in Central America. Such centers could be funded as part of the infrastructure development program and could serve to bring together U.S. corporate investors, high-level U.S. and foreign officials, members of the business communities from the countries of the Caribbean Basin, and national and international banking and financing institutions. Such centers could serve as centralized facilities for activities related to international trade. They could function as focal points for spawning other development projects in the areas of energy, foreign investment, and technology transfer. The centers could also serve as a mechanism for forging ties between officials and businessmen of the Caribbean Basin countries and those of the United States.[50]

Third, the United States should promote the transfer of technology to improve the productivity and worldwide competitiveness of existing and developing national industries in the region. The United States also should encourage most countries to create a favorable environment for foreign investments and encourage the continued expansion of U.S. private investments in the region. Most U.S. technology transfer is in the form of capital goods (e.g., manufacturing equipment) and takes place as a result of U.S. direct foreign investment. Such transfers help Caribbean Basin countries upgrade their industrial base, improve the comparative advantage of their exports, and reduce the cost to the consumer of import substitutes. Improvements in the efficiency of export industries are likely to contribute directly to export earnings and an improved balance of payments. Improvements in the efficiency of import-substitution industries is likely to assist in reducing the portion of inflation that can be attributed to increasing costs. The net long-term effect of technology transfer, although somewhat indirect, is likely to be an increased availability of capital for economic expansion and diversification. New jobs will be created rather than lost through the acquisition of technologically intensive goods.

Furthermore, the aforementioned international trade centers could be used to acquaint prospective regional buyers with the technologies available and to illuminate the potential financing alternatives.

Finally, the United States should seek a general expansion of trade in the region. While development assistance, technology transfer, and foreign investment are important in assisting countries in overcoming problems of domestic capital formation, the long-run economic success of the Caribbean Basin countries also requires an expansion of trade. In this regard, CBI efforts to achieve one-way free trade for twelve years are likely to help. While certain American business and labor interests have objected to the free-trade idea as potentially injurious, a safeguard mechanism to protect domestic industry from serious injury is a part of the plan. Moreover, the long-term benefits to the United States, the result of economic development in the region, are likely to outweigh the potential short-term costs to business and labor.

The expansion of the export sector in Caribbean Basin countries also depends on, among other things, improved market intelligence and an increased foreign awareness of and demand for Caribbean Basin products. The "international trading centers" may be helpful in this regard.

Information Policy

The Soviet Union spends in excess of $3 billion annually on building its worldwide image through information programs. The United States spends about $550 million on cultural exchanges, Voice of America, films, speakers, exhibits, and other aspects of "public diplomacy," including $90 million in a separate fund for Radio Free Europe and Radio Liberty. The Soviet Union and Cuba broadcast approximately 480 hours weekly in ten languages, including Quechuan and Guarani. The U.S. broadcasts eighty-one hours a week in three languages. While Voice of America broadcasts enjoy a high reputation as a timely and dependable source of information, Soviet and Cuban information programming is becoming more sophisticated and subtle and appears to be well integrated with the overall Soviet-Cuban foreign policy effort.

In addition to the classic forms of public diplomacy, the Soviet Union and its Eastern European and Cuban allies sponsor thousands of scholarships for the less privileged for study in Eastern Europe, Cuba, and the Soviet Union. These programs are frequently of long duration and high political content. While many students from the region study in the United States, most are privately or personally funded. Programs that are funded by the U.S. government (1) are at the postgraduate level; (2) are frequently of short duration for specialized training or conferences; (3) do not specifically consider political effect; and (4) frequently favor middle- and upper-income groups whose families already have strong American connections. An official in one U.S. embassy in the region commented that upper-class children frequently are educated in the United States. Upon their return, their newfound business and technical skills make them particularly attractive to the business community. On the other hand, children from the lower classes are frequently educated through scholarships from Communist countries. In time, he fears that there could be a Marxist-oriented bureaucracy in the country confronting a democratically oriented middle-class business sector. In a similar vein, one foreign minister in the region stated that the graduates of Soviet schools are packing the departments of mining and agriculture. He expressed a fear that they might be hindering government development programs in such a fashion as to promote the growth of Communist influence among rural and working populations.

The potentially adverse effects of such a situation are obvious. U.S. influence in the region is currently being challenged. There appears to be a well-coordinated, well-financed program on the part of the Communist countries to carry the ideological struggle in the Caribbean down to the grass-roots level. By their very nature, over 60 percent of the current U.S. government programs provide opportunities to the upper- and middle-class elements within the region, already favorably inclined toward the United States. In addition, U.S.-sponsored exchanges and scholarship programs for the Caribbean Basin are inadequate in two respects. First, they are not competitive with those sponsored by the Communist countries in terms of the number and duration of opportunities provided. Second, their design is more appropriate to developed than to developing countries in terms of the participant groups. In contrast, the Soviet Union and its allies offer their scholarships to bright, seemingly qualified undergraduate students from the low- to middle-income population groups who live primarily in small towns or rural areas. The scholarships are offered on a four- to six-year basis, with the first year usually a study of Russian or another Eastern European language. Recipients are usually free to pick their field of study from a variety of academic options. Students taken to Cuba for education include even primary- and secondary-level students. The Soviet Union and its allies recognize that such efforts are a long-term investment that will repay them when these foreign students move into positions of responsibility in their own nations in the years to come, either through advancement or through revolutionary upheaval.

One public affairs officer at a U.S. embassy in a key Central American country remarked that neither the U.S. government nor the American public are yet convinced of the necessity of competing in the battleground of ideas. Past levels of spending for public diplomacy would tend to support this judgment. A former secretary of state remarked, "All of us are concerned—and rightly so—that we not slip into military weakness. . . . Yet cutting back our other international programs contributes to another kind of weakness, every bit as dangerous. It cuts back our arsenal of influence." And the chairman of the U.S. Advisory Commission on International Communication, Cultural and Educational Affairs stated in the commission's 1980 report that

USICA [U.S. Information and Communication Agency, now the U.S. Information Agency], as this government's principal resource in public diplomacy, is not a luxury item in the Federal budget. It is indispensable to our national security and warrants far more than existing inadequate levels of support. Public diplomacy is as important to the national interest as is military preparedness, and it ought to be treated with the same degree of concern. We believe that public diplomacy programs can decrease the probability of military involvement.

In response, the U.S. must increase the number of hours of broadcasting to the region and expand the broadcasting efforts to include programs in key indigenous languages. In addition, the United States should expand its government-sponsored scholarship porgram and ensure that the majority of funds are available to the underprivileged for study in the United States.

Military Policy

The current emphasis in U.S. defense planning on warfighting overshadows the central fact that the security concerns of the Caribbean Basin countries are focused internally—on economic development and political stability. The best way for the United States to secure its Southern Flank for the longer term is to address these North-South concerns before they become enmeshed in the East-West as the result of opportunism by adversaries and Marxist revolutionaries.

In this regard, security assistance remains an important instrument of U.S. foreign policy. Used well, it can further U.S. interests by increasing the effectiveness of friends and allies to deal successfully with internal disorders and external threats as well as provide a means of access to, and ultimately influence, decisional elites. Until the late 1960s, the United States was the main source of military technology, training, and doctrine for the region. During the fifteen years from 1966 to 1980, however, the Foreign Military Sales (FMS) Program fluctuated widely, reflecting the varying moods of Congress toward Latin America and changes in policies of different administrations. Such fluctuations suggest an inconsistency that was likely to try the most patient of friends and closest of allies. Of the worldwide totals, all of Latin America, including the Caribbean nations, received only 2.8 percent of total security assistance monies appropriated by Congress during that period. Moreover, only 2 percent of the FMS credits were allocated for the region and, of this small amount, the eastern Caribbean received nothing.[51] The Latin American International Military Education and Training (IMET) program also declined drastically in the 1977–1980 period, from $10.2 million in 1976 to $2.5 in 1980, and from 3948 students in 1976 to 1689 in 1980. In recent years there has been an effort to reverse this trend. Such efforts should be given strong support. The figures for 1982 and 1983 were $10.9 million and $11.6, with $13.6 proposed for 1984, affecting 2481, 3046, and 3892 trainees, respectively.[52] Of the proposed 1984 budget, $5.1 million is intended for Caribbean Basin countries.

The general decline in security assistance to Latin America during the past decade has been the product of a number of factors and has had mixed results. During the 1960s, U.S. policy emphasized that arms purchases should be limited to those required to equip Latin American military forces for internal security and civic action activities. Major purchases of sophisticated military equipment designed to defeat external aggression were considered by the United States to be unnecessary and economically harmful since they retarded national development by consuming scarce resources.[53] The sale of sophisticated weapons was tacitly prohibited at first, then later specifically prohibited by Congress. Tension created by U.S. unresponsiveness to requests for arms from Latin American nations and the growing obsolescence of major weapons systems held by Latin American countries was initially held in check by cost considerations and political uncertainties. However, as as result of continued U.S. reductions in security assistance allocations and further restrictions on sales to Latin American nations, Latin leaders began to look elsewhere for armaments. The presence of alternative arms suppliers from Western Europe, many of whom were riding the crest of European economic recovery and were being given aggressive governmental support, thus limited the ability of the United States to control or influence Latin American arms acquisitions.[54]

Concerned with the great increase in worldwide U.S. military sales from 1971 ($952 million) to 1977 ($10 billion), President Carter announced a new conventional arms transfer policy that further aided the decline in U.S. security assistance. Marking a distinct break with the past, Carter stated that arms transfers henceforth would be a policy of exception, with the burden of proof on the proponent to justify why the transfer should be made. Furthermore, arms transfers would be used to promote human rights; transfers had to contribute to U.S. national security; and the United States would not be the first supplier to introduce new advanced weapons systems into a region. While the IMET program was not directly affected by the President's restraint on arms transfers, the size and value of the program also continued to decline throughout the period of the Carter administration. In an effort to promote greater respect for human rights, however, the Carter approach may well have been politically counterproductive. In Central American countries beset by serious internal problems, reductions or suspensions of security assistance weakened the confidence of governments in the U.S. commitment to their national security, reduced U.S. access to the host country military, surrendered a capability to affect decisions made by the military (which ultimately affected the political development of countries), increased their sense of insecurity (and thus perhaps contributed unwittingly to greater human rights violations), and may well have enhanced the confidence of leftist insurgents. Moreover, the general reduction in U.S. military sales to Latin America has not reduced the arms expenditures by countries of the region.

Finally, the general decline in security assistance over the last fifteen years has been the product of a persistent uncertainty concerning the value of security assistance as a means of advancing U.S. interests. Today, there are two distinct schools of thought on the issue. Security assistance optimists see a variety of benefits: regional stability, professionalization of recipient institutions, and the increase of U.S. influence over decisional elites. Pessimists, however, have questioned the benefits to professionalization and influence, warning that the definition of professionalization is a function of culture and that influence is itself a difficult value to measure. Both schools claim to speak with authority over issues that unfortunately are not amenable to rigorous scientific analysis. All agree, however, that to be effective security assistance must be an element of the comprehensive bilateral relationship that exists between the United States and the recipient country, a relationship balanced by economic and political components. When the comprehensive relationship deteriorates or does not exist, the effectiveness of security assistance is correspondingly reduced, and any benefits derived are at best short-term.

A detailed analysis of the effect of security assistance is not within the scope of this effort, but some general observations are in order. U.S. bureaucratic expectations of the immediate effectiveness and utility of security assistance in Third World environments are unrealistically high, particularly on the notion of influence. Influence is not an end in itself. Moreover, influence is not synonymous with access, which is the proximate and easily more achievable goal.[55] If the United States promotes security assistance on the basis that it influences behavior, it has neither specifically structured programs to influence future behavior nor decided how it hopes to influence officers to do what. Moreover, influence is not the only objective of security assistance. Training and developing allied and friendly military capabilities are also objectives.

Countless studies of U.S. security assistance have amply indicated that the United States is poorly organized to administer security assistance. Bureaucratic coordination between elements of the departments of Defense and State, Congress, the country team, and the regional military command creates bottlenecks and delays that unnecessarily increase costs, discourage prospective clients, and emit the wrong signals about U.S. commitment to mutual security. The complex apparatus must also be seen as a reflection of the widespread and honest misgivings about the utility of security assistance in furthering U.S. interests. Nonetheless, there is a pervasive feeling that the United States must modify its procedures to improve the implementation of security assistance, to improve the hopes of making it a more useful instrument. To do this will require adopting a more pragmatic approach to the issue. Security assistance must be regarded as a long-term and two-way interactive process. It ought not be considered ad hoc or exceptional. Security assistance must address the continuing needs of Caribbean Basin states, especially in view of their poverty and the frequent lack of professional military institutions.

In Central America and the Caribbean countries, military forces are generally small with inadequate budgets and are in need of basic training in the fundamental areas of combat, logistics, management, communication, intelligence, and leadership. They often lack a professional corps of noncommissioned officers, a deficiency that seriously handicaps their counterinsurgent capability. They are in a category quite distinct from such highly developed militaries as those of NATO. It would be appropriate for the United States to anticipate these needs and be prepared to assist across the spectrum of their military requirements. With the exception of Mexico and Costa Rica, the military plays a central role in the Spanish-speaking countries. In recent years there has been an awakening social conscience on the part of some younger officers, an awareness of the urgent need to solve the problems threatening to overwhelm their societies and institutions. Indeed, many Central American military officers consider democracy to be the only salvation for their institutions and societies. This openness creates an opportunity for the United States to communicate its skills and expectations to help promote socioeconomic and political development as well as military professionalism.

In the English Caribbean, military assistance requirements are different from those in the Hispanic countries. In the English Caribbean, democratic values are already well established, and the military occupies a subordinate position in national affairs. The need is for law-and-order forces: police, constabulary, and coast guard forces. Promoting their development serves the interests both of the countries concerned and of the United States. Assistance to security forces of the region can help promote the range of U.S. objectives such as regional stability, maritime security and navigation safety, search and rescue, antismuggling and illegal immigration control, and fisheries law enforcement. It can also reinforce already existing democratic values, demonstrate U.S. support for regional stability, encourage participation in regional forces such as the Regional Coast Guard, promote professionalism of the defense forces, foster development of indigenous training capabilities, provide a counterweight to continued Cuban support for radical political movements, lessen the attraction of "free" Cuban military training, demonstrate genuine U.S. interest in helping close neighbors meet their legitimate security needs, and establish a U.S. military presence in the region in the face of a reduced British presence.

Thus, for both Central America and the insular Caribbean, current efforts to increase moderately our security assistance efforts in the Caribbean Basin should be supported. In the longer term, the United States ought to develop a North-South security policy and a supporting military strategy. The military strategy should be tailored to the real requirements of the United States and recipient nations. It ought to be consistent with their nation-building goals, consistent with their aspirations for maneuver room from the superpower contest, and conducive to a relationship of cooperation rather than needless confrontation with the United States.

Country-Specific Policies

The task confronting the countries of the Caribbean today is not unlike the task that has often confronted countries elsewhere in Latin America and in the world: to manage change without incurring violence. The question confronting the United States is which policies, if pursued, have the greatest probability of assisting the countries of the region in bringing about change (where change is demanded and imminent) with a minimum of destabilizing violence and, as a consequence, have the greatest probability of securing and enhancing U.S. interests and influence in the region.

The English Caribbean. In the English Caribbean, which is characterized by strong democratic political institutions but weak economies, the United States should focus its attention on assisting the countries of the area in their attempts to develop economically. Jamaica, the largest and most influential nation of the subregion, should be identified as a model of democratic mixed-enterprise development for the other countries to emulate. The United States must also be aware that the potential for instability remains in the English Caribbean. Hence, the United States should be prepared to work with existing democracies to enhance their ability to limit the flow of arms and assistance to potential terrorist groups within their borders.

Guatemala. Despite the laudable objectives of America's policies on human rights, their application in Guatemala in the late 1970s reduced U.S. influence among Guatemala's decisional elites, aided in exacerbating the paranoia among rightist groups and elements of the government and the military, heartened the resolve of the insurgents, and, consequently, may well have contributed to the very repressions the United States sought to eliminate. The task today is to assist in strengthening the democratic process in Guatemala. A number of officials in the current government, as well as the previous government of Rios-Montt, appear to have recognized, perhaps not as perfectly as we who live at some distance from the tough problems of everyday decisions, the need for social and economic reform and assistance for the less privileged. The Guatemalan government has eliminated much, if not all, of the violence of the death squads and paramilitary forces and moved to give a voice to the Indian communities in national policymaking. Moreover, plans are being studied for electoral and political reforms. It has also largely defeated the guerrilla insurgency, or driven it underground or into exile. All of this has been done without the help of the United States. It is time, therefore, for the United States to support an expansion of the democratic process as a foundation of longer-term stability. While it is critical to reestablish communication with military officers who have been out of touch with the United States for a generation, the United States should move cautiously on resuming military assistance. Emphasis should be placed on economic assistance in order to signal support for the government's social and economic programs and in order to underscore the U.S. commitment to economic development. It is imperative that the United States reestablish and sustain a dialogue with the Guatemalan military.

El Salvador. El Salvador is the linchpin of Central American policy. The United States should continue to work with the current governing coalition to stem the tide of leftist insurgency, reduce rightist repression, and institute social, economic, and political reforms in order to assist the Salvadorans in their efforts to build a more democratic political order. If long-term stability is to be achieved, however, moderate elements of both left and right must be brought into the democratic political process. To achieve this, the United States should underscore its role in providing economic assistance and the importance of socioeconomic reform and development as a solution to the underlying problems that plague El Salvador. Such an emphasis should be evident in all policy pronouncements, including those identifying the military threat and the nature of U.S. military assistance. This approach would build consensus by emphasizing the U.S. commitment to economic development and social reforms, enhance the prospects for broadening U.S. domestic support for all U.S. programs in El Salvador, and more nearly align the policy of the United States with that of its allies and friends.

A second pillar of the Salvadoran strategy is to continue to denounce the violence and repression by the right as well as the left in order to make it clear to the more moderate elements that, indeed, they have a constructive role to play in a new political order. Concurrently, the United States ought to continue to support the counterinsurgency program of the government and efforts to reduce the flow of arms to insurgent forces.

With the appointment of Richard Stone as U.S. ambassador-at-large to search for a peaceful solution, a momentum developed for negotiations. Negotiations, if properly managed, appear to offer the best promise of breaking the stalemate. Moreover, as the "suicide" of Cayetano Carpio demonstrated, the revolutionary left is not monolithic and there appear to be exploitable tactical and ideological differences among the various leftist groups. Some argue that negotiations will legitimize the left by granting it what it was unable to win either on the battlefield or at the ballot box, weaken the current government, heighten the probability of a rightist coup, and offer the guerrillas time to rearm. There is some validity to each of these concerns. No policy is risk-free. On the other hand, negotiations need not legitimize the radical left. Moreover, they offer El Salvador an opportunity to win at the conference table what cannot be won on the battlefield, namely, a re-creation of the center. To serve this purpose, however, negotiations must be truly "unconditional." They must not be designed so as to automatically bring the "left" as a single force into the government. They must not be structured to focus on ways of dissolving El Salvador's current security forces. Rather, they should focus on ways to achieve social reform, economic development, to expand political processes, and to eliminate violence of the far right and left.

Nicaragua. Today there is no doubt that the government of Nicaragua is dominated by Marxist-Leninists. Total power, however, has not yet been consolidated in the hands of the Sandinistas. The United States has attempted to encourage Nicaragua to reduce its dependence on Cuba, and to restrict the movement of arms through Nicaragua to revolutionaries in El Salvador and elsewhere. At the same time, the United States has expressed support for the government's stated objectives—reconstruction, social justice, economic development, and political pluralism. These efforts have produced mixed results. The level of internal dissatisfaction is rising in Nicaragua, as the population begins to question the meager results of four years of revolution, particularly in the area of human dignity. Moreover, the Sandinista leadership has demonstrated an inflexibility in dealing with dissent, thereby offending the Pope, the Nicaraguan Catholic church, and other elements. These are definite indications that the consolidation phase is not going well.[56] An organized armed opposition has appeared. Several thousand guerrillas are now active in Nicaragua. Contrary to the Sandinista disinformation campaign, most of the guerrilla leaders are not former supporters of Somoza. The larger group is the Frente Democratico Nacional, whose directorate includes Lucia Salazar, the widow of Jorge Salazar, an anti-Somoza businessman murdered by the Sandinistas in 1980; Alfonso Callejas, a former Vice President of Nicaragua who broke clearly with Somoza in a 1978 attempt to oust Somoza; and others who were decidedly anti-Somoza. The second major group, the Alianza Revolucionaria Democratica, is headed by anti-Somoza hero Edén Pastora, and includes former post-Somoza junta leader Alfonso Robelo, Miskito Indian leader Brooklyn Rivera, and former anti-Somoza fighter Fernando Chamorro.

There should be no illusions about the Sandinista capability to deal with these new Nicaraguan revolutionaries. The prospects for the new revolutionaries depend on the deterioration of the popular base of the Sandinistas. A totally confrontational attitude by the United States toward the Sandinistas at this moment is likely to provide them with further justification for an anti-U.S. bias (if that is needed), reinforce the interventionist image of the United States in the region and worldwide, strengthen Sandinista unity,[57] diminish the legitimacy of the opposition, perhaps drive the Sandinistas farther into the embrace of the Cubans and Soviets, legitimate the export of revolution as a defensive measure, and justify measures to repress domestic opposition.

Current U.S. policy has attempted to maintain military pressure on the government of Nicaragua through shows of force and support for those elements in Nicaragua striving to ensure that the original revolutionary goals of social-economic development and political pluralism are achieved. The United States also has attempted to draw Nicaragua into negotiation and dialogue over regional issues that concern the Central American community and the United States. To this end, the San Jose group (Costa Rica, Honduras, El Salvador, Panama) invited Nicaragua to agree that the area should be freed from East-West competition, that the armaments race be reduced, and that the democratic institutions be encouraged. Nicaragua refused to consider the proposal, and in April 1983, Interior Minister Tomas Borge stressed the subjects his country would not negotiate: the principles of the Sandinista revolution, the overall Central American situation, and "counter-revolutionaries." The United States should, in conjunction with the Contadora group, continue to seek a negotiated solution with the current Nicaraguan government. It should emphasize that the United States is not intractably hostile to the Sandinistas, but that any negotiated solution must rest on some movement on the part of current leadership in Managua in fulfilling the revolutionary objectives of the original Sandinista movement—reconstruction, social justice, economic development, and political pluralism, and in adhering to the international principle of nonintervention in the affairs of their neighbors. By midsummer 1983, the Sandinistas were displaying more flexibility toward the United States on regional security.

Cuba. Because of Cuba's location in the Caribbean and because it is a Communist state in the backyard of the United States, U.S. policies with respect to Cuba are among a number of the more visible messages sent not only to the nations of the hemisphere, but also elsewhere, particularly to the Soviet Union. Such messages convey an image of the United States, as well as the substance of U.S. policy toward Cuba and toward others. Thus, U.S. policies toward Cuba contribute in a significant way to communicating to others, especially to the nations of this hemisphere and to the Soviet Union, America's sense of direction and purpose, its understanding of the complexities of international interaction, and the confidence it has in its ability as a nation to apply to meaningful ends the range of its political, economic, and military capabilities: in short, its maturity as a great power. U.S. policies toward Cuba also serve as a signal to other nations concerning such substantive matters as the view held by the United States concerning what constitutes acceptable behavior between states of unequal size and importance. It also demonstrates what Cuban and Soviet behavior the United States will tolerate in its sphere of influence. U.S. vacillation, weakness or absence of response in the face of challenging Cuban-Soviet behavior, or inconsistency or apparent failure to recognize its own best interests is likely to prompt further aggressive behavior on the part of the Soviets or Cubans and cause dismay among friends, allies, and neutrals alike.

The significance of such linkages should not be understated. Images of the United States and the substance of its policy form the basis for the perceptions of the United States by the leadership elites in other countries. Such perceptions will determine their willingness to support U.S. objectives. Thus perceptions of the United States in large measure determine the degree of influence the United States is likely to have at a given time. Given the history of U.S.-Cuban interaction since the Cuban Revolution and the importance of ensuring consonance between future policies toward Cuba and U.S. worldwide objectives, just how should the United States deal with Cuba?

The central long-term objective of U.S. policy toward Cuba should be nothing less than changing the behavior of the Cuban government, including a reorientation from its alliance with the Soviet Union, and its replacement by a government that respects the basic human freedoms and is willing to cooperate in the solution of the common problems that will confront the nations of the region in the decades ahead. This objective is not likely to be achieved in the short or medium term. Cuba's dependence on the Soviet "sugar daddy" for economic and military assistance, the fundamental hostility toward the United States and the generational rigidity of the Cuban leadership, and Castro's self-perception as a leader of the Third World all work against a quick change in Cuban behavior. In the past, U.S. policies have generally been short-term and inconsistent. The United States has supported the use of force against Castro, has threatened the use of force, and on several occasions has even proffered more normal relations. Such inconsistencies may well have contributed more to strengthening Cuba's peculiar Castroite Marxist-Leninist system and Cuban-Soviet ties than to weakening them.

The absolute range of policy alternatives available to the United States spans the spectrum from conciliation to direct military confrontation. Both ends of the spectrum, however, are unrealistic given the current state of U.S.-Cuban relations and regional affairs. Direct confrontation has failed in the past, often has been counterproductive, probably has strengthened the internal cohesion of the Cuban leadership elite, and is likely to be perceived as overreactive by the world community and by the American public. The unqualified resumption of normal relations with Cuba would provide little incentive for Castro to change, confuse friends and neutrals in the region, and reinforce the contentions of some that the United States is simply unable to forge a coherent strategy for the region.

A less direct approach is likely to be more effective in the long term. In this regard, the United States must seize the moral high ground of social and economic reform and democracy in the region. There must be no mistake at home or abroad that the United States is genuinely interested in socioeconomic progress and democratic development in the region—not just in keeping the region safe for U.S. business. This will appeal to the American public's ideals, to the peoples of the region, to our allies and friends abroad. It will also assist in recapturing the moral initiative from Castro. The United States should also engage the Cubans in a dialogue, not rhetoric, on the future of the Caribbean Basin and hemispheric security issues. Heated rhetorical exchanges, even when provoked, should be avoided. Great nations do not engage in such exchanges with lesser powers. Patience, calmness, and deliberation should mark the U.S. strategy for dealing with Cuba.

Cubans must be encouraged to recognize the costs of the Cuban-Soviet military relationship, the underlying reasons for the failed Cuban economy, and the possible benefits of resumed trade and cooperation with the United States and other countries of the region. The task is to plant doubts in the minds of current and future Cuban leadership concerning the long-term value of the close Cuban relationship with the Soviet Union and East European allies. This requires a long-term and consistent diplomatic carrot-and-stick effort that fundamentally seeks to alter the predispositions of the leadership about the United States, about the Soviet Union, and about the efficacy of Socialist centrally planned economies.

To this end, the United States should also pursue policies that strengthen Cuba's chances of exercising greater autonomy in its relations with the Soviets and of developing options for reforming the inefficient and repressive political and economic system. Such an approach will require the United States to place greater emphasis on Cuban national interests in the context of Soviet-Cuban relations. It will require the United States to *identify* and target those interest groups that aspire for system reform and for greater autonomy from the Soviet Union—two fundamental drives, the result of the robust nationalism that characterizes most Communist and non-Communist societies, which dovetail with U.S. policy interests. As long as the Soviets are perceived as indispensable for Cuba's survival, the chances of weakening Soviet-Cuban ties are minimal. Such an approach also must include a consistent and sincere interest in improving U.S.-Cuban relations, must avoid direct attacks on Fidel Castro, must factually report the nature of the Cuban economic failure, must underscore the relationship between that failure and Cuba's unfortunate choice of economic models, must lament Cuba's subservience to the Soviet Union, must underscore the potentially positive role Cuba could play in this hemisphere and elsewhere were it not for the unfortunate ties to a blatantly aggressive Soviet Union, and must consistently illuminate, where clear evidence exists, Cuban interventionism.

There is, of course, no guarantee that such a policy will work. There is, however, the historical record of increased Cuban adventurism in Africa (and losses in conflicts on that continent), a dismal economic record, increased Soviet-Cuban cooperation and increased intervention in the Caribbean. These are powerful factors that can and should be used in our efforts to foster change over time in Cuba. The task before us is to increase the probability of favorable change in Cuba over the long run so that in twenty-five years American policy toward Cuba will be marked by greater success than it has been over the past twenty-five years.

CONCLUSIONS

The United States is now facing one of the most difficult of its challenges in the post-World War II era—how to help the countries of the Caribbean region bring about revolutionary changes in their societies without the concomitant revolutionary violence. Assisting the peoples of the region in bringing about such change is, however, more important for U.S. long-term interests than is the elimination of violence. Thus, what the United States does to meet the challenges now confronting the region and how it does it are of paramount importance. Today the United States still has a significant degree of influence in the region. It can help the peoples of the region and influence the direction of events by working with *existing* governments.

In so doing, however, the United States must consistently underscore its support of social and economic progress, encourage movement toward democratic government, emphasize its commitment to human dignity, reject violence as a solution to the problems that beset the region, condemn outside intervention in support of terrorism and violence, and build bridges to leadership elites across the political spectrum. Such an approach holds the greatest promise of recreating a center in those societies that have been polarized by conflict. It also has a high probability of bringing about desired change in the region. Moreover, such an approach is likely to be accepted by the majority of the American people.

NOTES

1. Caspar W. Weinberger, Secretary of Defense, *Annual Report to the Congress, Fiscal Year 1983* (Washington, D.C.: Superintendent of Documents, February 8, 1982), p. II-23. Also see Joint Chiefs of Staff, *United States Military Posture for FY 1983* (Washington, D.C.: Superintendent of Documents), pp. 12–13.
2. Hedrick Smith, "US Warns Soviet on Missile Threat," *New York Times*, April 19, 1983, p. A–5.
3. For a more comprehensive view of U.S. facilities in the region, see Congressional Research Service, Library of Congress, *United States Foreign Policy Objectives and Overseas Military Installations*, a report prepared for the Committee on For-

eign Relations, United States Senate, 96th Cong., 1st sess. (Washington, D.C.: U.S. Government Printing Office, April 1979), pp. 198-205.

4. See International Monetary Fund, *Direction of Trade Statistics Yearbook 1982* (Washington, D.C., 1982), pp. 380-382.

5. For example, see Michael Calingaert, "Minerals and Foreign Policy," *Materials and Society* 4 (1980):247.

6. U.S. Congress, Joint Economic Committee, *Special Study on Economic Change, Volume 2: Energy and Materials: A Shortage of Resources or Commitment?* 96th Cong., 2nd sess. (Washington, D.C.: U.S. Government Printing Office, December 1, 1980), p. 218.

7. Ibid.

8. See Larry Auldridge, "World Oil Flow Sumps, Reserves Up," *Oil and Gas Journal* (December 29, 1980):79.

9. George Baker, "Mexico's Energy Plan Puts Exports at 1.5 MMbopd in 80's," *World Oil* (March 1981):110.

10. David Ronfeldt et al., *Mexico's Petroleum and US Policy: Implications for the 1980's: Executive Summary* (Santa Monica, Calif.: Rand Corporation, June 1980), pp. 3-4.

11. See E. L. Peer et al., *Trends in Refinery Capacity and Utilization* (Washington, D.C.: U.S. Department of Energy, Assistant Secretary for Resource Applications, Office of Oil and Natural Gas, December 1980), p. 55.

12. Some foreign steelmakers have been using dolomitic limestone, with good success, as a substitute flux for fluorspar.

13. The authors are indebted to Cesar Sereseres, David Ronfeldt, Edward Gonzales, and Yoav Ben-Horin of the Rand Corporation for developing this concept in their ongoing research project, *Geopolitics, Security, and US Strategy in the Caribbean Basin*, draft, March 1983, pp. 52-55.

14. Ibid., p. 55.

15. For a classic statement of Michael Manley's political philosophy, see his *Jamaica: Struggle in the Periphery* (New York: W. W. Norton and Company, 1982).

16. U.S. Department of State, Bureau of Public Affairs, *Cuba's Renewed Support for Violence in Latin America*, Special Report No. 90, (Washington, D.C., December 14, 1981), p. 10.

17. Ibid.

18. The F-16 sale was also an effort to recognize Venezuela's strategic, political, and economic importance in the region, see James L. Buckley, Under Secretary for Security Assistance, Science and Technology, *Statement Before the Senate Foreign Relations Committee*, February 5, 1982, published in "Proposed Sale of Aircraft to Venezuela," *Current Policy No. 369* (Washington, D.C.: U.S. Department of State, Bureau of Public Affairs, February 1982).

19. U.S. Department of Defense, *Grenada: October 25 to November 2, 1983* (Washington, D.C., November 1983), p. 1.

20. In an interview in 1980, Minister of the Interior Tomas Borge said, "We did not carry out a revolution merely in order to allow it to end. . . . Frankly, we are the only people with moral authority in this country. It is the Sandinista front which made a sacrifice here." *Cambio 16* (Madrid), December 22, 1980, pp. 77, 79, 80.

21. See *Cuba's Renewed Support for Violence*, p. 6, also see Leslie H. Gelb, "US Aides See Need for Big Effort to Avert Rebel Victory in Salvador," The *New York Times*, April 22, 1983, p. A-10.

22. "The US and Nicaragua," *Gist: U.S. Interests in the Caribbean Basin* (Washington, D.C.: U.S. Department of State Bureau of Public Affairs, April 1982).

23. Office of the Secretary of Defense, International Security Affairs (OSD/ISA), "Last Sheet on Threat to Latin America," (Washington, D.C., July 12, 1983), p. 2. Also see "President Reagan's Address to Joint Session of Congress on Central America," New York Times, April 28, 1983, p. A-12.
24. According to the Department of Defense, the Sandinistas are attempting to build the Nicaraguan Army from an estimated strength of 60,000 into a force of 250,000. See Weinberger, Annual Report, p. II-83. The Sandinistas have already increased the numbers in uniform to about 138,000.
25. OSD/ISA, "Last Sheet on Threat to Latin America," p. 2. Also see "President Reagan's Address," New York Times.
26. Weinberger, Annual Report, pp. II-23, II-26.
27. See William Leo Grande and Carla Ann Robbins, "Oligarchs and Officers: The Crisis in El Salvador," Foreign Affairs 85 (Summer 1980):1086.
28. There has been some dispute over the numbers of voters during the election, the extent of any possible fraud, and the meaning of the elections themselves. For example, see Raymond Bonner, "Fraud Is Reported in Salvador Vote," New York Times. June 4, 1982, p. A-5. Nevertheless, despite guerrilla efforts to keep polling places closed and threats of death to those that voted, most reports of the elections indicated that the Salvadorans voted in great numbers. See, for example, Warren Hoge, "Salvadorans Jam Polling Stations: Rebels Close Some," New York Times, March 29, 1982, p. A-1.
29. On the March 1982 Constituent Assembly elections, see Enrique Baloyra, El Salvador in Transition (Chapel Hill: University of North Carolina Press, 1982), pp. 167–179.
30. As a result of Cuban and Soviet insistence, the various major guerrilla groups combined their efforts in 1980. The new combined military command assumed the name of the United Revolutionary Directorate (DRU). See Cuba's Renewed Support for Violence, p. 6.
31. See Richard J. Meislin, "Top Salvadoran Rebel Dies in Mystery," New York Times, April 22, 1983, p. A-1.
32. See Philip Taubman, "Salvador's Ability to Win Doubted in Report," New York Times, April 22, 1983, p. A-11; Leslie H. Gelb, pp. A-1 and A-10, and Lydia Chavez, "Vides' First Target Is Army Brass," New York Times, April 24, 1983, p. E-2.
33. For an excellent analysis of these developments, see Cesar D. Sereseres, "The Guatemalan Legacy: Radical Challenges and Military Politics," paper presented for discussion by the Study Group on U.S.-Guatemalan Relations, School of Advanced International Studies, The Johns Hopkins University, Washington, D.C., January 12–13, 1983.
34. Ibid., pp. 19–20.
35. See "Guatemalan Keeps a Step Ahead of Rightist Gunmen," New York Times, May 4, 1981, p. A-2.
36. Sereseres, "Guatemalan Legacy," p. 29.
37. Raymond Bonner, "Guatemalan Army and Leftist Rebels Are Locked in a Growing Civil War," New York Times, December 4, 1981, p. A-14.
38. "Guatemala Leftists Say They Are Joining Forces," New York Times, February 11, 1982, p. A-6.
39. See Bonner, "Guatemalan Army and Leftist Rebels."
40. See Richard J. Meislin, "Uneasy Peace Comes to Rural Guatemala but Disquiet Lingers," New York Times, December 22, 1982, p. A-1+.
41. Cuba's Renewed Support for Violence, p. 3.
42. See Marcel Niedergang, "Dependence and Survival," Le Monde, transcribed in Foreign Broadcast Information Service (Latin America), April 15, 1980, pp. K-7–K-9.

For assessments of the Cuban economic situation, see the articles by Carmelo Mesa-Lago, Cole Blasier, Theodore H. Moran, and Jorge F. Perez-Lopez, in *Cuba in the World*, ed. Cole Blasier and Carmelo Mesa-Lago (Pittsburgh: University of Pittsburgh Press, 1979).

43. *Cuba's Renewed Support for Violence*, p. 3.
44. *Cuban Support for Terrorism and Insurgency in the Western Hemisphere*, Current Policy No. 376 (Washington, D.C.: U.S. Department of State, Bureau of Public Affairs, March 12, 1982).
45. Seymour Martin Lipset, *Political Man* (Garden City, N.Y.: Doubleday, 1959), p. 64.
46. Quoted in Raul Manglapus, "Security, Stability, and the Philippines," *Worldview* 24 (March 1981):16.
47. For a discussion of this relationship, see Gabriel Marcella and Daniel S. Papp, "The Soviet-Cuban Relationship: Symbiotic or Parasitic?" in *The Soviet Union in the Third World*, ed. Robert H. Donaldson (Boulder, Colo.: Westview Press, 1981), pp. 51–68.
48. For a summary of the original Caribbean Basin Initiative, see U.S. Department of State, Bureau of Public Affairs, *Background on the Caribbean Basin Initiative*, Special Report No. 97 (Wasington, D.C., March 1982).
49. Richard Feinberg, Richard Newfarmer, and Bernadette Orr, "The Battle over the CBI," *Caribbean Review* (Spring 1983):16.
50. The authors are indebted to Robert Stevens, formerly with the Strategic Studies Institute at the U.S. Army War College, for his ideas on this issue.
51. Derived from data appearing in Agency for Industrial Development, *US Overseas Loans & Grants* (Washington, D.C., 1981) and in U.S. Department of Defense, Security Assistance Agency, *Foreign Military Sales and Military Assistance Facts* (Washington, D.C.: various years).
52. Defense Security Assistance Agency, *Congressional Presentation, FY 1984* (Washington, D.C., 1983), p. 315.
53. See, for example, Herbert Y. Schandler et al., *Implications of President Carter's Conventional Arms Transfer Policy* (Washington, D.C.: Congressional Research Service, Library of Congress, September 22, 1977), p. 37.
54. See Luigi Einaudi et al., *Arms Transfers to Latin America: Toward a Policy of Mutual Respect* (Santa Monica, Calif.: Rand Corporation, R-1173-DOS, June 1973), p. 3.
55. For a more complete treatment of security assistance and influence, see Gabriel Marcella, "Security Assistance Revisited: How to Win Friends and Not Lose Influence," *Parameters* (December 1982):43–52.
56. For more information on Sandinista problems, see Stephen Kinzer, "Nicaragua: The Beleaguered Revolution," *New York Times Magazine*, August 28, 1983, pp. 22–28+.
57. While in the authors' view there is a greater probability of strengthening Sandinista unity if the United States pursues a totally confrontationist policy, they also recognize that such a policy would result in stresses and strains within the FSLN that could lead to fragmentation—as a minimum over the tactics of dealing with such a U.S. approach.

Chapter 6

Issues for U.S. Policy in the Caribbean Basin in the 1980s: Migration

Robert H. McBride, Harry E. Jones,
and David D. Gregory

BACKGROUND

Is the United States being unwillingly pressured by international events to revise its view of immigration policy as a simple domestic matter? The traditional goal of U.S. immigration policy has been to recruit permanent citizens. Beginning in 1959, however, new waves of legal and illegal international labor migration surged out of the economically stagnant areas of North Africa, the Mediterranean, and the Caribbean Basin into the expanding economies of Western Europe and North America. During the 1960s the Western Europeans tried to legalize these flows into temporary movements. On the other hand, U.S. immigration policy sought to restrict legal entry from the Caribbean Basin at a time when the demand for the migrant's labor was increasing. Male workers, and later their families, ignored these restrictions and continued to respond to employers' needs in the U.S. The result was the creation of what is now viewed as the "illegal alien problem."

Stimulated by economic opportunity, fueled by population pressures, and confused by political instability, immigration from the Caribbean Basin to the U.S. across our porous and contiguous border has generated a new, fearful, nativistic response in the American public. The public's largely incorrect view of the current situation is that the movement of Latin Americans into the U.S. is a relatively recent phenomenon; the number of illegal immigrants in the U.S. is equal to the number of unemployed citizens; these migrants have little or no education and are from the bottom and most desperate social classes in their countries; they perform only the most menial work in this country for which they are all cheated and underpaid; they are an excessive drain on our educational, medical and other social services; and, finally, their removal would be a positive step in improving our current high unemployment.

Inadequate data, competing interest groups, the advocacy positions of most academic studies, and the fluid nature of the problem keep us from any clear-cut answers as to the costs or the benefits of this current pattern of migration. As we try to deal with the interrelated issues of migration, economic growth, national security, international trade, diplomacy, and population replacement, it is clear that the situation is far more complex than commonly believed. It may also be more serious if addressed in a purely nationalistic way. Today, combined legal and illegal entries into this country account for almost half of our total population growth. With the projected U.S. economic recovery and the aggravated economic, political, and population problems of the Caribbean Basin, there is every reason to suspect that immigration pressures will continue throughout the 1980s.

The questions remain: Can our own international migration policies be formulated in such a way as to take into account our special relationship and growing interdependence with the countries of the Caribbean Basin? Can immigration policy be employed as a short-term instrument of economic and educational development to our mutual advantages; or, as is more commonly the case, must these policies be characterized by negative objectives and restrictions?[1]

Intraregional Migration

The massive transfer of populations in the Caribbean Basin is an old phenomenon. European diseases and labor practices halved the native populations on the mainland and eradicated them throughout the islands by the seventeenth century. In 1650 the white settlers repopulated the islands with slaves from Africa. This uprooted black population was unable to perpetuate itself until the abolishment of the slave trade in the nineteenth century; for example, it required the importation of 3 million slaves throughout the eighteenth century to obtain a growth in the black population of 1.5 million.[2] Only with the end of the slave trade did the black population become self-sustaining for the first time. By the mid-1800s the Caribbean governments of Jamaica, St. Lucia, and Barbados enacted legislation encouraging emigration to ease population pressures, despite the strong objections of the plantation owners who feared the loss of cheap labor.

Then, as today, the pattern and volume of migration were largely determined by outside economic forces. Robert Bach divides the movements into four periods.[3] The first period, between 1835 and 1885, consisted of short jumps between islands and adjacent countries in Central America by former slaves moving away from the old plantations and patterns of servitude. The migrants were single males who worked with seasonal contracts in the new plantations which offered higher wages. Where land was available for settlement, the former slaves tended to remain in their own countries. During the second period, from 1855 to 1920, the migrants were largely recruited and contracted by U.S. companies to work in sugar production in Cuba and the Dominican Republic and to build railroads and the Panama canal. At this time "remittance payments" became an important source of developmental capital for the home countries. The Great Depression during the third period, between 1920 and 1940, halted emigration throughout the region. Contracts were revoked and migrants were forcibly "repatriated." Much of the social and political turmoil in the Caribbean during the 1930s has been directly attributed to this forced return and the shutting off of the emigration "safety valve." The final period, from 1940 to the present, was stimulated by labor shortages during the Second World War and has been sustained by expanding postwar economies. The new waves of migrants went to the United Kingdom until 1962, the United States (to be discussed in the following section), and between neighboring Caribbean Basin countries. Initially, the intraregional migration pattern of this last period was into the rural regions of contiguous countries. By the 1960s these migrants were likewise caught up in the urban explosion that began to depopulate vast areas of the countryside.

To date, the two greatest exporters of labor within the region have been Colombia and El Salvador. More than a million Colombians have crossed the easily penetrated border into Venezuela; it has been estimated that Colombians currently comprise 10 percent of Venezuela's population. Another 150,000 Colombians migrated to the Dominican Republic, 60,000 to Ecuador, and a large but undetermined number to Panama. Even before the present violence, over 350,000 Salvadorans had migrated to Honduras, of whom 267,000 returned to their own country after the Soccer War with Honduras in 1967.[4] Since the recent civil strife, Salvadorans have continued to seek escape in neighboring countries: 100,000 in Mexico, 100,000 to 180,000 in Guatemala, 30,000 in Honduras, 20,000 in Nicaragua, 10,000 in Costa Rica, 7000 in Belize, and 1500 in Panama. Hondurans have also pursued seasonal migrations to Guatemala. Guatemalans, however, have sought seasonal work in southern Mexico. Their numbers have been significantly increased by the 50,000 Mayan Indian refugees seeking to escape the genocide in the northeastern provinces. Among the island populations, the Haitians continue to constitute most of the migrants. They are considered the most docile and easily exploited of all the current migrants. Because of their government's policies—or lack of them—the dividing line between voluntary and involuntary, economic and political migration is the most confused. Approximately 40,000 Haitians reside in the Bahamas and another 200,000 in the Dominican Republic.

Much of this intraregional movement is directly stimulated by the continued demographic instability in the Caribbean Basin. A population growth rate of 2.9 percent per year for the region ensures that overpopulation and underemployment will worsen throughout the rest of this century. This is not a view shared by the U.S. Bureau of the Census, however, which indicated in 1978 that the falling birth rate for much of Latin America heralded a marked improvement for the future. While it is true that there has been a marked decline in the "rate" (births per 1000 women) of increase, the increase of population in absolute terms makes the problem worse than it was a decade ago. Robert Fox demonstrates that Mexico, Central America, and the Caribbean contributed over 5.8 million people per year to the world population between 1970 and 1980. In absolute numbers, Mexico yearly adds two-thirds more people to its total population than the U.S. Even if by some miracle Mexican fertility rates were to drop to replacement level, the population would increase by 40 percent over the next twenty years.[5] Updated forecasts project that the current Mexican population of 72 million will mushroom to over 100 million by the end of this century.

Compared to Mexico, El Salvador is in even worse shape. The smallest nation in Central America (about the size of Massachusetts), it has 4.2 million inhabitants. Its population density is nearly 500 people per square mile. Unlike other Latin American countries, its yearly population growth rate has remained high at 3.5 percent. Around 58 percent of this population earns as little as $10 per month. It is estimated that 73 percent of the children under five years of age suffer from malnutrition.

Haiti, with a population of nearly 6 million, is the most densely populated nation among the Caribbean islands. It is ranked among the thirty poorest countries in the world. Unemployment is well over 50 percent and at least 75 percent of the population is illiterate. Even though life expectancy at birth is a mere forty-nine years and the island has one of the highest infant mortality rates in the world (between 130 and 150 per thousand), its total population will more than double by the year 2000.

The situation does not improve when we move away from total population figures to a narrower consideration of the growth in the labor force. Excluding the islands and the Caribbean rim of South America, the growth in the potentially economically active population in Mexico and Central America has been projected from 11 million in 1950 and 22 million in 1975 to 53 million in 2000. What this means is that 1.2 million new jobs must be created annually from now until the end of this century. The magnitude of this task is more easily grasped when it is compared to job creation in the United States, where, with considerable difficulty, nearly 2 million new jobs were created per year during the 1970s. How can Mexico and Central America, with economies that are 6 to 8 percent the size of our own, even approach meeting the projected need? Can Mexico support the projected economically active population of 174 million, El Salvador the 15 million, and Haiti the 18 million people by the end of the next seventy years?[6]

For a pathetically short time the oil boom of the 1970s created a mirage of development that promised to alleviate some of the employment problems, particularly in Venezuela and Mexico. Venezuela attracted ever-increasing numbers of temporary migrants from a greater diversity of Caribbean countries. Mexico appeared to be creating the necessary economic infrastructure that would ultimately provide its people with needed jobs in the future. And yet in August 1982 Mexico was hit by its worst financial crisis since the years of the 1910 Revolution. During the following months, the credibility of Mexico's political system was severely shaken. By March 1983, after repeated international loans, many financial experts believed that Mexico would once again have to devalue its currency. However, the "free" exchange set by the Bank of Mexico remained at about 149 pesos per dollar until September. Since September 23, the "free" rate has been depreciating by 13 centavos per day. The programs imposed by the International Monetary Fund, while easing the financial crisis, have created a desperate situation for the poor workers and peasants who can hardly afford "a little more austerity." During the "good times" from 1978 to 1981, the purchasing power of these classes was actually eroded by the oil-inflated economy. Since the beginning of the recent devaluations, the apprehension of aliens along the U.S.-Mexican border has increased from 20 to 50 percent a month; February 1983 was a near-record with nearly 70,000.

Similarly, falling demand for Venezuelan oil highlights the relationship between oil and international migration in the Caribbean Basin.

Just as in Mexico, falling oil prices undermined confidence in the economy, the first signs of which were a flight of capital. In February 1983, the Venezuelan government responded by suspending the sales of foreign currencies and then imposing strict controls. The bolivar was devalued by 78 percent and imports were severely restricted. The migrants—who for the past years have filled the less attractive jobs in services, agriculture, and construction—have always been viewed by the Venezuelans as "temporary" workers. Because of the internal Venezuelan economic situation, the normal tension between Colombia and Venezuela over immigration has increased. While some "temporary" workers have already voluntarily returned to their countries because they can no longer save enough money to send home, the majority will hold on until they are expelled. It is quite probable that these workers from Colombia, Ecuador, the Dominican Republic, Trinidad, and Guyana will find themselves in a similar plight to that of the million workers (largely Ghanaians) thrown out of Nigeria in January 1983 as a result of that country's dramatic decline in oil revenues. How many of these workers, like the Mexicans, will turn to the North?

Migration to the United States

The immigrants coming to the United States in the late nineteenth and early twentieth centuries were still largely Europeans. They were the last swell of a series of earlier waves of immigrants—over 34 million people in all since the opening up of North America—who would experience relatively few restrictions until the onset of the First World War. (Table 6.1 depicts the magnitude of legal migration from all countries to the U.S. from the 1860s to the present.) Little attention was paid to the Caribbean Basin because of the relatively small number of legal migrants originating from the area. Actually, during this period there was considerable free and unregistered movement back and forth across the U.S.-Mexican border. As late as 1853 large sections of the American Southwest belonged to Mexico.

During the early part of this century, particularly after the end of World War I, and continuing to the 1940s, ethnic prejudices were whipped up in the United States against immigrants of all kinds. The word "alien" was used derogatorily in both political cartoons and writings. Legal immigration from the Caribbean Basin region was impeded by the overall restrictive legislation passed for the first time in the 1920s. These laws sought to fix the racial, national, and ethnic makeup of the U.S. population by imposing immigration quotas in proportion to the national origins of the then-present U.S. population. This new system gave preference to Great Britain while discriminating against

Table 6.1.   Immigration to the United States, 1860s to the Present

1861–1870	2,314,824
1861–1870	2,812,191
1881–1890	5,246,613
1891–1900	3,687,564
1901–1910	8,795,386
1911–1921	5,735,811
1921–1930	4,107,209
1931–1940	528,431
1941–1950	1,035,039
1951–1960	2,515,479
1961–1970	3,321,677

Source: U.S. Immigration and Naturalization Service.

countries like Poland and Italy. These new laws also had the effect of blocking immigration from other areas such as the Caribbean Basin. Restrictive laws, combined with the Great Depression and the tendency of totalitarian governments to view emigration as "treasonous," drastically limited all migration during the 1930s. Again in the 1950s, when the United States revised its immigration laws, the overall policy continued to be prejudicial against Latin America and the Caribbean Basin. Many inhabitants of European colonies and now independent territories migrated to Great Britain and the Netherlands.

Most of the early illegal and legal immigrants to the U.S. from the Caribbean Basin were primarily Mexicans (who moved into the Southwest) and Cubans (who moved to Key West). It was not until the early 1940s that a major change began to take place. Because of the labor shortage during the war, the U.S. instituted the Bracero Program which brought in 220,000 Mexican workers between 1942 and 1947. Workers were also encouraged to come temporarily from the Caribbean islands through the H-2 (temporary worker) Program. In the 1940s and 1950s approximately 500,000 Puerto Ricans took advantage of inexpensive air fares and moved to the U.S. mainland. A half million Cubans immigrated to the United States between 1959 and 1969 for a combination of political and economic reasons. During the 1960s and 1970s immigrants from the Dominican Republic began to arrive in increasing numbers. In the late 1970s President Carter authorized the one-time entry of over 100,000 Cuban refugees. The Haitian "boat people" who began to appear off the coast of Florida in 1972 totaled nearly 80,000 by 1982. By 1977 nearly 22 percent of the Jamaican population, 24 percent of the Puerto Rican population, and 11 percent of the Dominican population lived in the United States. Even so, undocumented Mexican workers composed the largest group of illegal immigrants. Even after the Bracero Program ended, their numbers steadily climbed upward.

Oscar Handlin reports that as of 1945, 2.5 million Mexican-born immigrants were living in the United States, principally in Los Angeles, El Paso, and San Antonio.[7] Many of these people were actually U.S. citizens. In 1970, 28 percent of the 4,247,377 legally registered aliens in the United States were from the Caribbean Basin countries, primarily from Mexico (714,509), Cuba (288,718), Colombia (52,903), Jamaica (51,496), and the Dominican Republic (65,503). The number of legal aliens remained fairly constant during the 1960s and 1970s at between 3.5 and 4 million. Naturalizations, deaths, and departures effectively balanced the number of new arrivals. There is every indication, however, that the number of illegal aliens in the U.S., as well as of foreign-born naturalized citizens, was steadily growing and outnumbered the registered aliens.

Since the residents of Puerto Rico are U.S. citizens, they are rightly not included in the above statistics reflecting immigration by aliens. The Puerto Rico Planning Company has compiled data demonstrating that movement between Puerto Rico and the mainland is not a one-way flow. Between 1972 and 1977 over 115,000 more individuals returned to Puerto Rico than moved to the United States. From 1978 through 1981 the trend was again reversed, with over 130,000 more people coming to the U.S. than returning home to Puerto Rico. It is instructive that the country with the greatest degree of freedom in its coming and goings between its island and the United States manifests the highest percentage of return movements. One can find a comparable circular pattern in the movements between Italy (a major exporter of labor) and its member countries (formerly importers of labor) in the EEC.

A contemporary feature of illegal immigration has been the movement of El Salvadoran and other Central American nationals through Mexico into the United States. Since 1980 over 200,000 Salvadorans entered this country seeking refuge and economic betterment. The Immigration and Naturalization Service (INS) considers them illegals, not refugees. Therefore, the INS, enforcing U.S. immigration law, has been apprehending and deporting between 800 and 1000 Salvadorans a month. Like the more recent undocumented Mexican workers, these new illegal immigrants move out of the southwestern states and are found increasingly in large eastern cities.

Until recently, changes in U.S. immigration laws continued to reflect a bias against the Western Hemisphere. In the 1960s, a new law provided for hemispheric quotas—170,000 per year from the Eastern Hemisphere and 120,000 from the Western Hemisphere—which continued to ignore the reality of the situation. Not until 1977 did the Western Hemisphere countries receive the same national limitations and preference categories as the Eastern Hemisphere. The system established a 20,000-immigrant quota for any one nation, although certain close relatives and refugees might be admitted above the quota. This quota was well below the potential and annual immigration from countries like Mexico. In 1981 a remedial bill sponsored by Senator Edward Kennedy, known as the "Immigration and National Efficiency Act," was passed which allowed slightly increased immigration from Mexico and Canada. Because of the enormous demand for immigrant visas and U.S. policy, which gives preference to relatives and certain categories of professional and skilled workers, those individuals with no special qualifications will still be effectively barred from legal immigration for the foreseeable future. Therefore, it will be from this very group—by far the largest—that the flow of illegal immigrants will continue to come.

THE SITUATION TODAY

Grasping the Problem

Although the number of immigrants from the Caribbean Basin has been growing steadily, we should realize that not everyone from these countries seeks entrance into the United States. Regardless of the push factors described in the previous sections, the majority of citizens remained in their own countries. In the past, family reunion and real economic opportunities in the United States played the crucial role in attracting those who did come. Will this continue to be true to the same degree? Or are population pressures, failed economies and hopes, and increasing political instability in the region combining to stimulate new waves of illegals whose major goal is "escape"? In the area of policy, there is really very little that the U.S. can do directly to influence birth rates and total population size or national employment patterns in other countries. Migration policy, however, is an area where the U.S. *can* play a direct role. Nevertheless, we have failed to formulate a coherent migration policy during the last four administrations. Our inability to deal with the situation stems less from the lack of information in these areas than it does from the conflict between special-interest groups and popular prejudices that cloud the issues and make the search for a rational immigration policy so difficult. Nonetheless, enough has been learned to draw some conclusions.

How Big Is the Problem?

We know the exact number of people legally processed for immigration each year by the Department of State and the Immigration and Naturalization Service. These people either apply for immigrant (permanent resident) visas in other countries or they arrive here in some temporary status and apply for a legal adjustment to that of permanent resident. Between 1970 and 1979, 4,336,003 immigrants legally entered this country. During earlier decades beginning with 1900–1910, foreign-born residents in the U.S. steadily declined until, in 1970, they constituted a low of 4.7 percent of country's total population of 203 million. The 1980 census shows the first upturn: the 13,956,077 residents born outside the U.S. now compose 6.2 percent of our total population of 226 million. Even more significant in terms of its effect on North American popular culture is the fact that 22,973,410 persons over age five lived in homes where a language other than English was frequently spoken; 11,117,606 of these individuals said the language spoken was Spanish.

Illegal immigrants enter the United States by surreptitiously crossing land borders or by arriving as temporary visitors and remaining to work illegally. Antiquated control methods give only a rough estimate of the number of alleged tourists, students, and other temporary visitors who disappear into U.S. society. Those who successfully steal across borders are never counted. During the 1970s, Commissioner Leonard Chapman, Jr., of the Immigration and Naturalization Service estimated that there were between 12 and 15 million illegal aliens in the United States at any given time. He repeated this assertion—particularly during budget requests—in testimony and public speeches without fear of contradiction. No one had the facts. A number of recent studies carried out independently in both Mexico and the U.S. provide convincing evidence that the real figures are closer to the 3–5 million range. Over 50 percent of these illegals are Mexican nationals. Of course, most estimates of illegals are based on the number of people who are arrested by the INS patrols along the border where apprehension activity is concentrated. Some of these Mexicans are caught and counted repeatedly throughout the year as they enter the U.S. or return home. Many of these same studies estimate that eight out of ten Mexican workers voluntarily return home each year.[8]

Who Are the Immigrants?

Obviously, we know more about legal immigrants than we do about the illegals. Contrary to popular conceptions of immigrants as poverty-stricken peasants, 12 percent of employed immigrants are professional, technical, and managerial people. A considerable number of the 60 percent of the immigrants categorized as "unemployed" are wives and children of these people. In addition, we know where they came from. Although INS figures are not publicly available for any year later than 1978, current State Department data on immigrant visa issuance gives a good picture of the national origin of new immigrants from the Caribbean Basin. Table 6.2 gives the breakdown for fiscal year 1981—excluding refugees.

Elsa Chaney and others provide evidence indicating that the illegal immigrants arriving in the United States, though unskilled, are selected from among some of the most energetic, capable, and ambitious samples of their countrymen.[9] A detailed survey by the Mexican agency CNIET showed that the migrants sampled had a median education higher than the Mexican average and at least three out of four had jobs before being attracted to the U.S. Most viewed their moves as temporary and intended to return to their native countries after having earned targeted amounts of money.[10] A quarter of a million aliens are naturalized as U.S. citizens each year, at which point they drop out of the statistics maintained by INS. Children born to either deportable or legal aliens after they arrive in this country automatically become U.S. citizens and are excluded from the official tabulation of aliens. Department of Commerce figures released in 1982 show that people of Mexican origin in the United States (both aliens and U.S. citizens) doubled during the 1970s to 8,740,439; Puerto Ricans numbered 2,013,945, and Cubans, 803,226. Since these figures include everyone from new arrivals to third- and fourth-generation Americans, they are more indicative of the cumulative effects of migration than of actual current or recent trends.

Where Do They Go?

Two sets of statistics are maintained by two different government agencies, the Department of Commerce and the Department of Justice (INS). Commerce's Bureau of the Census enumerates people by national origin, consolidating them all into a few selected nationalities. INS tabulates responses to its alien registration program. Illegal alien counts are estimates based on the number of arrests. These combined figures indicate where immigrants from the Caribbean Basin settle.

Newcomers tend to pursue patterns of "chain migration," by following the path of earlier immigrants. Friends and relatives inform them about opportunities and provide temporary shelter. The overall result is to cluster the new immigrants in specific regions and cities. Gradually, international migration becomes a regional problem in the

Table 6.2. Caribbean Basin Sources of Immigration to the United States, FY 1981

Independent	Countries	Colonies and Dependencies	
Bahamas	396	*France*	
Barbados	2,080	Guadeloupe	50
Colombia	8,791	Martinique	36
Costa Rica	1,255		
Cuba	6,159	*Great Britain*	
Dominica	696	Anguilla	142
Dominican Republic	16,960	Antigua	684
El Salvador	7,686	Belize	831
Grenada	985	British Virgin Islands	210
Guatemala	3,542	Turks and Caicos	25
Haiti	6,238		
Honduras	2,241	*Netherlands*	
Jamaica	22,450	Netherlands Antilles	165
Mexico	95,051		
Nicaragua	2,214		
Panama	4,063		
St. Lucia	648		
St. Vincent	694		
Trinidad	4,224		
Venezuela	725		

Note: The apparent discrepancy between issuances and country limitations, most obvious in the case of Mexico, is the result of a court decision in which it was determined that the U.S. government improperly used Western Hemisphere quota numbers to process the Cuban refugees admitted during the Carter administration. These "recaptured" Cuban numbers are being issued *in addition* to the normal worldwide quota and account for the abnormal rise in Western Hemisphere visa issuances over the past several years. This program is now coming to an end.

United States, in that not all areas of the country are affected equally. While the immigrants provide important economic benefits to a region, they also have a unique impact on housing, education, medical services, and so on. This regional concentration indirectly adds to the difficulty of formulating a national consensus on immigration policy. Perceptions of the Haitian "boat people" in southern Florida or the Central American "Mercedes-Benz people" in southern California are quite different from the perceptions in the Midwest.

In 1978 INS received the address reports of 4,280,364 legal aliens. More than 75 percent lived in only six states: California (1,283,598—30 percent); New York (796,454—19 percent); Texas (392,094—9 percent); Florida (370,238—9 percent); Illinois (287,777—7 percent); and New Jersey (275,852—6 percent). The top two registered nationalities were Mexicans (989,265) and Cubans (354,725).

Census Bureau figures on people of Hispanic origin corroborate INS findings. Of the 8,740,439 persons of Mexican origin in the United

States in 1980, 3.6 million resided in California and 2.8 million in Texas, while 408,000 lived in Illinois and another 396,000 in Arizona. Of the 2,013,945 Puerto Ricans, almost a million lived in New York and 244,000 lived in nearby areas of New Jersey. Another 129,000 Puerto Ricans lived in Illinois. Of the 803,226 persons of Cuban origin, 470,000 lived in Florida, 81,000 in New Jersey, 77,000 in New York, and 61,000 in California. Of the large group of Hispanics not broken down by nationality in the initial report, 753,000 resided in California, 557,000 in New York, with the remainder concentrated in New Mexico, Florida, Texas, New Jersey, and Colorado. Most of these Hispanics have a national origin within the Caribbean Basin.

Impact on the Sending and Receiving Countries

In the developed and developing areas of the world, both legally sanctioned and illegal immigrants have played an increasingly important role. John Kenneth Galbraith has shown migration to be the oldest solution to poverty: "It selects those who most want help. It is good for the country to which they go; it helps break the equilibrium of poverty in the country from which they come."[11]

Since the mid-1950s the Organization for Economic Cooperation and Development, the International Labor Organization, the EEC, and the governments of Europe have evolved programs and policies developing from the concept of the liberalization of manpower movements in the late 1950s, through the relaxation of regulations in the 1960s, to current ideas favoring the international concentration of manpower policies. In the case of Europe, Germany's and France's economic growth in the 1960s was fueled by this necessary labor supply. The sending countries in turn were able to ease regional unemployment temporarily and improve their foreign cash reserves dramatically. At the peak of Spain's economic development in the early 1970s—when it had become the tenth industrial nation in the world—migrants' remittances and receipts from tourism continued to be the government's two most important sources of income.

Emigration has been, on balance, beneficial to the countries of the Caribbean Basin. These governments regret the loss of valuable skilled and professional people. Nevertheless, they believe that the disadvantages are outweighed by the hard-currency remittances sent home. Furthermore, migrants returning after years in the United States bring savings to invest, lifelong pensions, and/or Social Security benefits. Emigration can provide important and beneficial short-term solutions. Even so, long-term, random, and extensive immigration to the

U.S. can have serious effects if seen only as a means of postponing serious thinking about solving economic problems at home.

In receiving countries, like the United States, the impact of immigration is unevenly spread throughout the country. For example, the number of Haitians arriving each year is minuscule relative to the total number of immigrants, but they are perceived as an exaggerated problem because of their dramatic entry from across the sea in frail craft and their concentration in southern Florida. Conversely, the larger number of Mexicans crossing into the U.S. each year cause fewer problems than expected. They are easily assimilated into already-existing large Mexican communities.

In Atlanta, where the foreign-born population is only 2.3 percent of the total, the immigrants have little "apparent" impact. Yet in cities like Miami (where 53.7 percent of the total population is foreign-born), San Francisco (28.3 percent), Los Angeles (27.1 percent), and New York (23.6 percent), many types of businesses could not survive without them. In Washington, D.C., garage attendants, domestic servants, kitchen help, and so on are recruited (legally and illegally) from Central America and the Caribbean despite the high level of local unemployment. Businesses contend that they are the most reliable applicants for the job. The State of Vermont generally seeks to bring in temporary H-2 workers from Jamaica to pick the apple crop. In 1982, however, the growers cooperated closely with the U.S. Labor Department and the Vermont State Employment Service Division to hire unemployed Americans. Of the 10,000 unemployed contacted, only 395 said they might be interested. Fewer than 25 percent of these respondents actually showed up to work. Similar cases are repeated throughout the southwestern states.

How Much Can the Melting Pot Hold?

Looking backward through rose-colored glasses, the period of massive European immigration to the United States is seen as an exciting and colorful time in our nation's history. The fresh supplies of immigrants were greeted with open arms. Ethnic neighborhoods happily filled with people seeking, and realizing, a new and more rewarding life. The truth is that most new classes of immigrants were initially treated with suspicion and hostility; we have always been a diverse culture ridden with racial and ethnic prejudice. The problems of assimilation were greater where the cultural differences between the established Americans and the newer immigrant groups were the most extreme. Many U.S. citizens believed that the country was already overpopulated when it was still only half its present number.

A public opinion survey by the Roper Organization in March 1982 showed that Americans had a more positive attitude toward earlier immigrants, with a mixed or negative attitude toward recent arrivals. Respondents were shown cards listing various nationalities. They were then asked if this group has been a "good thing" or a "bad thing" for the U.S. They could also respond with "mixed feelings" and "don't know." The highest approval rating went to the English, with 66 percent saying their arrival was a "good thing" and only 6 percent a "bad thing." Trailing close behind were the Irish, Jews, Germans, Italians, and Poles; all received a majority opinion that they had been good for the country. Moreover, far more people felt that the Japanese, blacks, and Chinese had been good rather than bad for the country. Except for the English, all had been treated with varying, but marked, degrees of hostility when they first arrived. Countries listed from the Caribbean did less well in the survey. Only 25 percent of the respondents thought the Mexicans had been good for the country; 34 percent considered them bad. Puerto Ricans received only a 17-percent "good" response, Haitians, 10 percent. Cubans were at the bottom of the survey with 9 percent responding that they had been a "good thing" and 59 percent believing they had been definitely bad for the country. Of course the poll has nothing to do with the actual information as to the real costs and benefits resulting from immigration. What the poll shows is a nice correlation with the media coverage of immigration—especially Haitian and Cuban. The press during this period created the myth that many of the Cubans were criminals or insane. Actually, fewer than 2 percent of the 120,000 Cubans had been jailed or committed to mental institutions. Nevertheless, 66 percent of the respondents said they would like to see the number of immigrants to the U.S. reduced.

This last opinion echoed the conclusions of the 1972 U.S. Commission on Population Growth and the Future, which recommended that North America's population be stabilized and immigration levels not be increased. Neither this commission nor any other group to date has answered the question, how many new arrivals do we actually need or can we effectively absorb?

The 1980 Census presents a trend whose importance has not reached the level of public consciousness: namely, the near-record low fertility rate of the previous decade. The number of births was 17 percent below the Census Bureau's 1971 projection. By 1976 the number of 1.8 children per women in the U.S. was the lowest in our history, despite an increase in women of childbearing age. A recent report by the Rand Corporation demonstrates that the actual 11-percent increase in U.S. population during the 1970s fails to call attention to important differences among individual age groups. The student population (5–14 age group) declined by 14 percent. The college and military group (18-21 years) increased by 17 percent. Homebuyers (25-34) grew by 49 percent. The major consumers of health care, persons 65 years and older, was up 28 percent. The report's major conclusion is that as a result of the decline in fertility rates among our native-born population since the 1960s, our population of young adults will soon begin to shrink and will remain small for the remainder of this century. This will in turn cause labor markets to tighten in the 1980s and 1990s. Wages will rise and unemployment fall as business competes for young workers.[12]

Admittedly, this trend strikes one as counterintuitive when looking at current unemployment figures. Nevertheless, the Labor Department's February 1983 report, which registered the rate of unemployment at 10.4 percent, shows a drop from the December 1982 rate of 10.8 percent. This drop seems to have less to do with the awaited economic recovery than with the drop in the number of teenagers in our population by 400,000 in 1982. If the number of workers in the labor force had just remained constant since the beginning of the year, the unemployment rate would have climbed to 10.9 percent.[13]

Our low fertility rates should make us more acutely aware of the significant impact immigration can have on this country—both positively and negatively. Calvin Beale, of the U.S. Department of Agriculture, calculates the net legal immigration and refugees made up a third of the 2.3 million increase in our 1981 population.[14] The Rand report, combining both legal and illegal immigration, believes that the figure is closer to one-half the total U.S. population growth. They further predict that population pressures plus worldwide political instability will increase immigration to the United States. Leon Bouvier, writing for the Population Reference Bureau, shows in Table 6.3 the effects of different fertility and immigration rates on the size of the U.S. population.[15] The staff and other guest experts at the bureau have come to the conclusion that immigrants will account for all the population growth by the 2020-2030 decade if U.S. fertility rates continue at the present low levels.[16]

ISSUES AND OPTIONS FOR THE U.S. IN THE 1980s

Four Key Factors

Four key factors are crucial to the final policy decision in the field of immigration reform: (1) we must be sure we understand why refugees and migrants come to the United States; (2) we should decide who is

Table 6.3.   U.S. Population: The Next 100 Years

Total Fertility Rate	Year			
	2000	*2030*	*2050*	*2080*
	No Immigration			
1.8	243.7	244.8	227.3	201.6
2.0	250.3	267.8	265.9	260.8
2.2	257.7	295.0	311.6	341.3
	Annual Net Immigration = 500,000			
1.8	255.5	277.6	274.1	268.2
2.0	262.3	302.1	315.0	335.1
2.2	269.9	331.0	365.6	425.1
	Annual Net Immigration = 750,000			
1.8	261.3	294.1	297.5	301.5
2.0	268.3	319.2	340.0	372.2
2.2	276.0	349.0	392.6	467.1
	Annual Net Immigration = 1 million			
1.8	267.1	310.4	320.9	334.8
2.0	274.2	336.3	365.1	409.3
2.2	282.1	367.0	416.6	509.1

Source: Leon F. Bouvier, *The Impact of Immigration on U.S. Population Size* (Washington, D.C.: Population Reference Bureau, 1981), Table 2. Used with permission.

Note: The above figures only give an idea of total numbers. They do not provide information on population composition (age structure and sex).

needed and if it is prudent to continue with equitable quotas for all countries; (3) we have to take into account our governmental structure to deal with immigration and the political pressures that influence its administration; (4) finally, we have to be aware of the effects our immigration policies have on our neighbors in the Caribbean Basin.

Refugees and Migrants – Why Do They Come?

People coming to live permanently in the United States arrive either as immigrants (legal or illegal) or as refugees. To date, with the exception of those nonworking immigrants who come to join close family members, the majority come for economic reasons. Regardless, our fear of the population growth in the Caribbean Basin has led us to concentrate on the supply side of the equation. This causes us to overemphasize the favors that we are doing countries like Mexico, making us believe that our primary role is as a "safety valve" for their over population and underemployment. Nevertheless, it is our contention that since the 1950s the movement of immigrants into the U.S. has been determined by the demand of U.S. employers. This is particularly true in the case of illegal immigration.

Contrary to American perceptions that desire to see all immigrants seeking citizenship, millions actually prefer a temporary sojourn in this country. A critical study by Renaldo Baca and Dexter Bryant indicates that a high percentage of undocumented Mexican workers would rather keep their native citizenship.[17] Most of the surveys of undocumented Mexican workers in the U.S. show that eight of ten workers return home within nine months to a year.

All things being equal, people prefer their own countries rather than a permanent move to a relatively alien and hostile culture. Of course, all things are not equal. The result is that minimum-wage, dead-end jobs unacceptable to American citizens offer economic opportunities to people from countries where the economic rewards are fewer. The average American makes seven times as much as the average Mexican performing a similar job in his own country. We have seen how migration of all kinds slows during recessionary periods in the host country.

Refugees ostensibly come for other than economic reasons. The U.S. definition of a refugee is anyone who would be persecuted upon his return home after flight from his country. It is common enough to assume that people are refugees if they come from countries with governments that *we find oppressive*. When one looks into individual cases, one often sees that people who consider themselves refugees are in fact defined as economic immigrants by the INS. Even before the current conflict in El Salvador, however, hundreds of thousands looked for work outside the country. All Haitians returning home after attempting to enter the U.S. illegally do not face persecution. For that matter, neither do most "refugees" from Eastern Europe.

Throughout Latin America there are outspoken opponents of both rightist and leftist repressive regimes who are in real danger. They are normally granted refugee status in the U.S. if there is not a routine way of admitting them. But their numbers are very few. One of the exceptions made to our refugee policy was Cuba. We can ask how many of the more than 100,000 who arrived in the late 1970s were in real danger in Cuba? How many initially left Cuba because of a refusal to live under Castro and Communism for moral reasons, and how many simply foresaw their hopes for a better life disappearing under the new regime?

Until recently, it is probable that the majority of migrants out of the Caribbean Basin could be categorized as "economic migrants" rather than "refugees." Beginning with the flight of the Southeast Asians in the 1970s, however, the number of refugees has climbed sharply over the years. By 1980 the U.S. admitted 370,000 refugees—135,000 being Cuban and Haitian. Another 217,000 refugees came in 1981. Although this annual average of 200,000 refugees admitted to the U.S. from 1979 to 1981 seems high to us, it is nothing compared to the millions of refugees admitted by West Germany after World War II. As a nation we respond much more emotionally to refugees than we do to immigrants. Of late we have been in the danger of allowing our reactions to a few Haitians and Cubans to set the negative tone of our need for immigration reform. In any case, while economic incentives continue to be the major driving force behind immigration to the United States, the number of refugees should continue to increase as a result of the current political and economic situation in Central America. As political instability feeds off unresolved population pressures, we can expect new and massive transfers of people both within and from this area.

Whom Do We Want?

All people should have the freedom to migrate. Alternatively, all countries have the right to decide which, as well as how many, people to let in. Annual immigration quotas reflect the official position that some amount of annual immigration is a good thing. This, in itself, makes the United States different from many countries in the world. It is also indicative of a sort of national schizophrenia on the subject. The Roper poll and our attitudes toward refugees mentioned earlier shows that most Americans do not think the annual influx of immigrants is a "good thing." When we look at individual cases—the Audi dealer who needs a German mechanic, the household needing a live-in domestic, the Japanese restaurant needing a Japanese chef—most of us agree that exceptions should be made. We might likewise agree that exceptions should be made for the foreign-born spouse of an American citizen or for a noted Soviet dissident. It is through this yearly accumulation of thousands of "exceptions" that our present laws seem to have been shaped.

These laws also imply that we want some kinds of people and not others. Through a system of preferences, we give top priority to close relatives of Americans and permanent residents (spouses, children, and parents), and to highly skilled professionals, such as scientists, doctors, and successful creative artists. To a lesser extent, we allow for the entry of more distant relatives and workers whose skills are in short supply. As presidential administrations change and crisis situations come and go, we also make varying provisions for refugees. Relatively few legal immigrants have come from the Caribbean Basin because of their professions or job skills—fewer than 10,000 in 1981. The majority of legals enter on the basis of family relationships.

All these preferences are abused from time to time. Illegal aliens marry U.S. citizens solely to become citizens. Workers obtain false documentation showing skills they do not have. Birth certificates are altered, or false ones obtained, to prove that children have parents who are U.S. citizens, or that they themselves were born here. On the whole, however, the system has worked fairly well for legal entrants to the United States.

The U.S. Immigration Control System

The United States attempts to enforce its immigration laws and manage the flow of immigrants at its borders and overseas. It does so via a system of dual controls in which State Department officers in foreign embassies and consulates screen applicants and issue visas. When travelers arrive at U.S. borders, they are again screened and either admitted or turned back by the Immigration and Naturalization Service. Aliens apprehended while entering surreptitiously are deported by the INS Border Patrol. Although a small INS staff conducts investigations and makes arrests throughout the United States, finding and deporting undocumented aliens is an overwhelming task in so large and complex a country. Actually, 50 percent of the undocumented aliens apprehended are arrested crossing our border and another 20 percent are located a short distance inland. Nevertheless, our overall border control system is ineffective. By one estimate, if an alien attempts to cross into the U.S. illegally three times, he will make it. Apprehension thus becomes a nuisance rather than a deterrent. There are no effective legal sanctions against either employers or the undocumented aliens for working in the U.S.

Alternate Views of the Future

Until recently, an extremely optimistic view of immigration in the 1980's was that the situation would gradually improve as the recession in the U.S. disappeared and trade with the Caribbean Basin increased. Oil production would spark the Mexican economy and provide additional jobs at home. Tourism, food exports, and investments in the area would rise. As the employment situation improved, fewer people would immigrate to the U.S. and the illegal alien problem would lessen.

The status quo view sees things remaining unchanged. It basically does not believe that immigration is the problem it is made out to be.

In times of recession, immigration will normally drop. Otherwise, aliens will continue to fill jobs, essential to keep business going, that Americans will not take. Research tends to substantiate that even illegals contribute more than they take from the society: they pay into the Social Security fund, do not evade taxes, and do not place a burden on welfare funds. They are a positive addition to the U.S. economy and should not be shut out.

The extreme pessimistic view is that low and falling prices for oil and the one-crop exports of the countries will keep the economies of the Caribbean Basin depressed. The growth of the total population, on top of weak economies and endemically high levels of unemployment and underemployment (over 50 percent in Mexico) will impel ever greater numbers of illegal migrants to come north. The Hispanic portion of the U.S. population, legal and illegal, will soon become the largest minority group in North America. Its size, combined with greater job aggressiveness, greater family stability, and continued prejudices, will weaken the economic position of American blacks. Ethnic conflicts between blacks and Hispanics will become commonplace in large coastal cities. The democratic structure of the country will be weakened by the large influx of people from countries devoid of real democratic traditions. The emphasis on bilingualism will weaken the assimilative effect of traditional, popular American culture. The Southwest will create regional problems similar to those of Quebec in Canada.

The Position of the Reagan Administration – The Caribbean Basin Initiative

The Reagan administration recognizes that the objective of the United States is to have economically healthy and friendly neighboring countries abroad—especially in our own backyard. The initial Caribbean Basin Initiative (CBI) took the position that the best way to solve the problems of the area was to help develop the economies of the individual countries. The long-term effect of a successful initiative would, it is hoped, reduce emigration out of the area. The original $350 million of aid, however, was targeted for El Salvador and Costa Rica, two countries that contribute relatively few immigrants to the U.S. The desire to improve the economies by increasing American business incentives to invest in the area is being undermined by the spreading political turmoil. El Salvador had been one of the most successfully industrialized countries in Central America. The business community's recent negative experience in Mexico, plus the economic failure of Venezuela, has also dampened investors' enthusiasm. In fact, the effectiveness of our type of capital, rather than labor-intensive, industrial development in keeping people at home, is debatable. During better years, it did little to retard the movement out of the Dominican Republic or Mexico. Ideally, the CBI should have the effect of forcing us to overtly incorporate immigration policies into a long-range plan for economic development and manpower training in the Caribbean Basin. In August 1982, when the CBI was being debated, the Senate passed the Simpson–Mazzoli Immigration Reform and Control Act, which seeks to paralyze all movements out of the area.

CONCLUSION

Immigration Control

The volatile nature of the contemporary economic and political world order requires a fluid and versatile immigration policy that can more readily adapt to America's shifting, enlightened self-interests. While there are indications that the situation could change, the present number and negative effects of illegal aliens in the United States has been exaggerated. They are not a drain on the U.S. economy. They play an important role in agriculture, hotels and restaurants, health care, the garment industry, and assembly operations. Serious questions exist regarding the extent to which illegal aliens suppress wages and job opportunities for certain classes of Americans and legal resident aliens in some regional labor markets. By and large, however, they are hardworking, productive, ambitious people who benefit both the North American economy and the economies of their homelands.

The existing immigration control mechanisms of the departments of State and Justice work well enough for legal immigrants. Attention, however, should be focused on illegal immigration. The United States has the right and the obligation to its citizens to monitor who crosses its borders. To use our present system more effectively, INS should be given greater economic and political support. It should be increased in size and its personnel upgraded by higher entry standards, better training, and higher grades and salaries. The 350 Border Patrol agents on duty at any one time are understaffed, underpaid, and underequipped. To improve the efficiency of the overall system, INS policies should be jointly developed by the departments of State and Justice. Immigration must be viewed more as a matter of foreign policy and less as a criminal activity.

Numbers of Legal Immigrants

Any reforms in our immigration policy should seriously consider the demographic and international economic implications of its proposals.

In particular, they should be economically rather than ideologically based. There are definite limits to the number of immigrants the U.S. can absorb. The ceiling, however, should be adjusted to the country's total fertility rate and labor needs. The current rate of 1.9 should set annual net legal immigration at around 650,000.

Refugees

The admission of large numbers of people outside of the annually established immigration quotas should not be subject to passing political whims of successive presidential administrations. While refugee admission should be the result of consultation between the administration and Congress, the actual number admitted should be factored into our overall immigration needs. Refugees should, however, be individuals who in fact will suffer for their political or religious beliefs if they remain in, or are returned to, their homelands. Economically strong allies should be encouraged to take a share of the people displaced from countries undergoing extremes in political violence.

System of Preferences

We should try to develop a more flexible system of preferences. Finer differentiations should be made between refugees, illegals seeking permanent residence, and temporary workers. Legislation should not cause many otherwise temporary workers to seek permanent residency out of anxiety and fear. When immigration slots desired by true permanent immigrants are temporarily taken, the overall process of the assimilation of immigrants is impeded.

Regularization of Status

As long as there is a demand for foreign workers to fill the jobs that U.S. citizens refuse, illegal immigration (especially from Mexico) will continue. As long as the economic opportunities are here, punitive legislation will not stop the flow. It will, however, continue to aggravate the worst aspect of the undocumented worker's status: namely, his definition as the member of a criminal subclass in U.S. society. It is this status that causes these workers to be more easily exploited and negatively effects local labor markets.

It is potentially dangerous for the United States to have millions of people living and working outside of the law. "Operation Wetback" in the 1950s and "Operation Jobs" in the 1980s demonstrated just how impractical, as well as ineffective, it is to round up and deport these people. The pragmatic alternative is to allow them to regularize their status. Some could be granted amnesty; some could become permanent resident aliens; and others could be designated as temporary workers. In any case, the granting of amnesty might be reserved as a bargaining chip in our relations with certain governments.

Temporary Worker Program

The nature of the U.S. economy has always required immigrant labor to compete effectively. This labor will become more essential as a result of our declining birth rate and our unfavorable position in the competition for international markets. Provisions should be made for the development of a variation of a Western European temporary worker program. A program should be designed that can meet the needs of American business and respond to the transitory nature of current immigration patterns between the U.S. and the Caribbean Basin.

The number of temporary workers should be verified by the existing labor certification program of the Department of Labor. The burden of proof, however, should be on the employers. They should first be responsible for seeking out all alternatives for training and hiring our own citizens and legal aliens. The temporary workers should at first be recruited from the pool of illegals already in the U.S. who seek to regularize their status. Next, arrangement for other temporary workers should be conducted through bilateral relations explored by the Department of State.

The program should be designed in the form of an international labor treaty. A strong emphasis should be placed on manpower training. Training and remittances could provide an important component to our foreign assistance programs. The program could also be used as a strong negotiating factor when more than one country is capable of supplying the needed labor. The bilateral nature of the programs would also require that the sending country take some responsibility for its workers who are temporarily in the United States.

Substituting an expanded H-2 program, which emphasizes short-term agricultural employment, for a temporary worker program ignores the fact that undocumented workers are now employed throughout the economy. It is doubtful that even a slighlty expanded H-2 program could handle the demand for agricultural workers if the growers were to lose their present source of labor. The system processes nearly 28,000 immigrant workers a year. Most are recruited from the English-speaking areas of the Caribbean. Fewer than 1000 per year come from Mexico.

Employer Sanctions

Since the 92nd Congress (1971-1972), bills have been introduced to halt illegal immigration. Most have been based on the premise that the influx of illegals can be effectively blocked by eliminating job opportunities for them in this country. Invariably, the cure-all solution is "employer sanctions." Wayne Cornelius has shown that this remedy has been unsuccessfully tried in a dozen U.S. states. Nowhere have the penalties reduced the hiring of illegals. After studying twenty other countries, the GAO concluded that "laws penalizing employers of illegal aliens were not an effective treatment to stemming illegal employment."[18]

If employers are assured legal means to recruit the type of labor needed for the job, employer sanctions would not be necessary. Many experts are skeptical of the effectiveness of employer sanctions because it places them in the position of monitoring and enforcing legislation that runs contrary to their own self-interest. Such a proposal increases the employer's costs without providing any alternatives to solving capital and labor needs. It is a negative rather than a positive incentive that will aggravate the existing situation. It will not stop the hiring of the undocumented. It will, however, increase their vulnerability, making them more easily exploitable.

Identity Cards

At this time the suggestion to create 230 million counterfeit-proof national identity cards, to deal with between 4 to 6 million transitory illegal immigrants, seems like overkill. The potential dangers and discriminatory abuses of such "internal passports" far outweigh the advantages. Rather, over the next decade new, counterfeit-proof Social Security cards—for those who need them—should gradually replace the older variety.

Relations with Countries of the Caribbean Basin

In the final analysis, the formulation of immigration policy at this time should be strategically pursued as a means of creating a powerful international labor and trade area between the U.S. and the countries of the Caribbean Basin—particularly Mexico. Regardless of Mexico's current setback, the continued flow of people, products, money, and energy will forge an interdependence between our two countries. Together we will ultimately play a crucial role in the direction of the development of the entire Basin.

NOTES

1. G. Tapinos and P. Piotrow, *Six Billion People: Demographic Dilemmas and World Politics* (New York: McGraw-Hill Book Company, 1978).
2. A. Rosenblat, *La Poblacion Indigena y el Mestizaje en America*, 2 vols. 1954.
3. Robert Bach, "Caribbean Migration: Causes and Consequences," *Migration Today* 10, 5 (1982):6-13.
4. S. Diaz-Briquets, "International Migration within Latin America and the Caribbean: A Review of Available Evidence," unpublished paper. (Washington, D.C.: Population Reference Bureau, 1980).
5. R. Fox and J. Huguet, *Population and Urban Trends in Central America and Panama* (Washington, D.C.: Inter-American Development Bank, 1977); Robert Fox, "The Downhill Slope's Slope," paper presented to the Conference on Population for Non-Governmental Organizations, United Nations Fund for Population Activities, 1982.
6. Robert Fox, "Population Issues and the Pace of Change in Latin America," paper presented to the Conference on Inter-American Coordination in the Development of Latin American Instructional Materials in Geography and Related Social Sciences, Austin, Texas, 1981, pp. 8-9.
7. Oscar Handlin, *A Pictorial History of Immigration* (New York: Crown Books, 1972).
8. Manuel Garcia y Griego, *El Volumen de la Migracion de Mexicano no Documentados a los Estados Unidos* (Mexico City: CNIET, 1980).
9. Elsa Chaney, in *The Restless Caribbean*, by Richard Millet and W. Marvin Will (New York: Praeger, 1979).
10. Garcia y Griego, *El Volumen de la Migracion.*
11. John Kenneth Galbraith, *The Nature of Mass Poverty* (Cambridge, Mass.: Harvard University Press, 1979), p. 136.
12. William Butz, Kevin McCarthy, Peter Morrison, and Mary Vaiana, *Demographic Challenges in America's Future* (Santa Monica, Calif.: Rand Corporation, 1982).
13. Gene Koretz, "Economic Diary," *Business Week*; March 28, 1983, p. 24.
14. Calvin Beale, *U.S. Population: Where We Are; Where We're Going* (Washington, D.C.: Population Reference Bureau, 1982).
15. Leon F. Bouvier, *The Impact of Immigration on U.S. Population Size* (Washington, D.C.: Population Reference Bureau, 1981).
16. Beale, *U.S. Population*; "World Trends and Forecasts: Population," *The Futurist* 16, 6 (December 1982):72.
17. Renaldo Baca and Dexter Bryan, "Citizenship Aspirations and Residency Rights Preferences: The Mexican Undocumented Worker in the Binational Community," special report to the Select Commission on Immigration and Refugee Policy (Washington, D.C., 1981).
18. Wayne Cornelius, "Simpson–Mazzoli vs. the Realities of Mexican Immigration," unpublished paper, University of California at San Diego, 1983.

Chapter 7

Caribbean Energy Issues and U.S. Policy

Edward F. Wonder and J. Mark Elliott

Energy problems in the Caribbean Basin have rarely drawn the sustained attention of U.S. policymakers. This is partly because of the marked diversity of the countries in the region (e.g., oil importers vs. exporters, economic "haves" vs. "have-nots"), which complicates the formulation of a Basin-wide policy on energy. More importantly, the United States has tended traditionally to view the region as a natural sphere of influence. This has allowed policy resources—and, in this paper, specifically energy-related policy resources—to be devoted to regions where access to oil cannot be taken for granted. Where initiatives have been taken in the Basin, they have been very specific in scope and narrow in their impact on the region (e.g., lifting oil import quotas on heavy fuel oil from the region in 1963). What broader arrangements have been considered have tended to focus on supply, which immediately limits the potential U.S. partners to Mexico and Venezuela.

The urgency of the supply issue in the U.S. has now faded in the wake of another allegedly permanent oil glut and the apparent crippling of OPEC. What has taken the place of "energy diplomacy" is the Reagan administration's faith in "market-based" solutions to U.S.

energy problems. This faith in the market may be well placed in a weak oil market where the region's two chief oil exporters, Mexico and Venezuela, have strong economic incentives to boost output. With respect to other energy-related issues, however, such as resource development and balance-of-payments support, strict reliance on the market and the private sector may be insufficient. In viewing Caribbean Basin energy issues confronting U.S. policymakers, it is clear that the "energy problem" cannot be reduced to that of supply alone, that ability to pay for imported energy is just as, or more, important for many countries in the region, and that the linkages between energy policy and trade and economic policy are of major significance.

Energy policy, and the conceptual framework on which it rests, must continually be tested against reality, and, importantly, against identifiable trends that may transform the context in which policy is to be implemented. U.S. policy vis-à-vis energy relationships in the Caribbean Basin is no exception. Is the traditional U.S. preoccupation with supply sufficiently comprehensive to address adequately the most pressing energy and energy-related issues in the region? Will a steady and even increasing flow of oil and other energy resources from within the region be assured by reliance on the market and private capital? Can the ability of the region's oil import–dependent countries to pay for oil be assured without compromising their economic growth? Can the U.S. and other Western states take for granted their access to the region's oil?

It is admittedly difficult, as others have noted, to characterize the Caribbean Basin in terms of energy relationships because it does not form a coherent, identifiable system in itself, a point that will become clearer later in this paper.[1] The historical importance of the region in energy terms to the U.S. and the West is nevertheless clear. It is the contention of this chapter, however, that the nature of this importance, which traditionally has been viewed in the U.S. as a function of supply, will change over the coming decade. The economic problems of the region that are related to energy form a cluster of issues that will have lasting and major significance for U.S. and Western political as well as economic interests. These energy-related economic problems will rival supply questions in their eventual impact on those interests.

This chapter spends considerable time defining and discussing the key issues, but the hierarchy of issues is just one part of the conceptual framework demanding reexamination. Just as important is the structure of key relationships. For the past two decades, energy relationships and policies in the region have been shaped in large part by the dominant actor in the region (the United States), on the one hand, and external events and actors on the other (e.g., Persian Gulf suppliers, embargoes). The key characteristic of these shaping factors is that they were largely beyond the influence of the two principal oil suppliers in the region and the economically adversely affected states. The continued validity of this statement over the next two decades is at least open to question. Significant change in this situation carries potentially major importance for U.S. policy toward, and influence in, the region.

PRINCIPAL ENERGY ISSUES

The number and diversity of countries and energy situations in the region make it difficult to identify and define a coherent list of policy issues that the energy problems found in the region pose for the U.S. There is no doubt that, at the level of practical policy implementation, there is a high degree of country-specificity with which U.S. policy must deal. Nonetheless, it is possible to identify a cluster of region-wide issues that are of fundamental importance to both the countries in the region and U.S. interests.

Paying for Oil Imports

Rising oil import prices, particularly in the 1978–1979 period, have had a markedly deleterious impact on nearly all the economies of the region. For many of the countries, the ability to pay for energy without compromising economic growth prospects is the most serious "energy" problem. How to get these countries through the next few years until economic growth and export trade pick up, correspondingly, becomes a major area for policy attention.

Although the impact of the first round of oil price increases in 1973–1974 was ameliorated by petrodollar recycling, the groundwork was laid for the much more serious oil "shock" experienced in the wake of the 1978–1979 price hike. Expansionary economic policies delayed internal adjustment to higher oil prices while fueling inflation.[2] Export growth largely compensated for higher oil prices, rather than stimulated economic growth. (For many of the countries, fuel imports expanded at a faster rate than imports of any other goods.) Very importantly, foreign borrowing encouraged by relatively flat real interest rates and the ready availability of capital became a major means to cover current-account deficits. The shorter amortization periods and variable interest rates of this debt made countries vulnerable to the drop in economic growth and higher interest rates encountered at the end of the decade. As a result, when oil prices skyrocketed in

1978–1979, mounting foreign debt became a serious constraint on economic growth. Not only did countries have to export more to pay for oil, they now had to worry about servicing the added debt.

The impact of the recessions of 1974–1975 and 1980 can be seen in Table 7.1. The table shows the current account deficit as a proportion of the gross domestic product (GDP) of countries in the region during the two recessions. In only six of thirteen non-oil-exporting countries was the proportion smaller during the second period, and for most of the six the improvement was marginal. For some of the worse-off countries, the deterioration of their situations was substantial. If one considers average annual growth rates over the entire period, except for Jamaica and Nicaragua, all countries in the region experienced some GDP growth during the 1975–1980 period. However, only Trinidad and Tobago, an oil exporter, showed a higher GDP growth rate in 1975–1980 than in 1970–1975. The GDPs of Mexico and Venezuela grew at the same rate over both halves of the decade. As might be expected, countries in the Caribbean Basin that import all their oil *and* whose economies are largely dependent on the external sector suffered the greatest adverse effects during 1980.

While higher oil prices do not explain totally the economic ills of the region—national economic policies, falling commodity prices, and recession in trading partners also played a major part—the region now finds itself having to adjust to the effects of the economic policies of the 1970s, despite the recent fall in oil prices. Whether existing institutional mechanisms will suffice to provide balance-of-payments support where energy costs remain a major underlying problem, or whether additional measures are needed is thus critical.

Role of the Region's Suppliers in the World Oil Market

The two principal Caribbean Basin oil producers, Mexico and Venezuela, have played a crucial role in the functioning of the world oil market. This has been especially true during the past two years, when expanding Mexican exports (over 1.7 mbd at the end of 1982), together with North Sea output and falling demand levels, have substantially weakened the market power of the Organization of Petroleum Exporting Countries (OPEC). Venezuela, while a cofounder of OPEC, has not adhered to OPEC production ceilings, thus contributing to the disunity within OPEC so apparent in early 1983.

Both countries possess oil resources (proven plus potential) that, if exploited, potentially assure them a continuing major role in world oil trade. Mexico's total hydrocarbon resources (both oil and gas) exceed,

Table 7.1. Comparison of the Deficit on Current Account, as a Proportion of the GDP of the Countries of the Region in the World Recessions of 1974–75 and 1980

Country	1974–75 (%)	1980 (%)
Nicaragua	14.03%	20.91%
Guyana	3.89	20.77
Costa Rica	13.76	19.04
Dominican Republic	5.48	14.07
Honduras	9.24	13.63
Panama	9.85	8.58
Mexico (oil)	5.50	6.02
Jamaica	7.37	5.90
Haiti	3.13	5.60
Barbados[a]	5.86	4.09
Guatemala[b]	1.99	1.93
El Salvador	5.49	1.84
Colombia	1.94	0.10
Trinidad and Tobago (oil)[c,d]	+20.91	+10.63
Venezuela (oil)[e,f]	+20.10	+11.40

Source: Inter-American Development Bank, *Economic and Social Progress in Latin America: The External Sector* (Washington, D.C., 1982), p. 51.

[a] Maximum in the decade, 10.68 percent in 1976.

[b] Maximum in the decade, 4.02 percent in 1978.

[c] With balance-of-payments surplus.

[d] Maximum deficit in the decade, 17.82 percent in 1971.

[e] Maximum in the decade, 9.86 percent in 1979.

[f] Maximum deficit in the decade, 18.2 percent in 1978.

by official estimate, 250 billion barrels. Venezuela, which until recently faced a potentially serious squeeze on its conventional oil reserves, has in excess of 1 trillion barrels of oil (considered "unconventional" because of the need for special recovery and processing technologies) in the Orinoco heavy oil belt. Only 5-10 percent may be recoverable, however. Leaving aside questions of timing and expense of development, resources of this magnitude suggest that a significant flow of export oil from the Caribbean Basin might help keep some slack in the world oil market, and may prove to be especially important later in the decade if higher economic growth in the industrialized world leads to a tightening of the oil market.

The refineries in the islands also play a critical role in the regional oil system. The major refinery capacity exceeds 4 mbd, not counting the smaller "tea-kettle" refineries (range of 10,000 bbl/day), found in a number of countries which may be economically marginal. Desulfurization capacity in the Caribbean (important because of U.S. environmental limits on the sulfur content of fuel oil) far exceeds that in the U.S. The major refineries serve both regional and European customers. A spot market also flourishes in the region. While small in comparison to the Rotterdam spot market, the region's poorer countries use this spot market to purchase crude consignments below contract crude prices.

In light of this importance, the policies of the two principal suppliers regarding production and export levels are of major significance for Western interests. Maintenance of a healthy refining industry is also important to the health of the host-country economies. The important roles of the region's suppliers raise the issue of whether the U.S. should seek to establish preferential access to Venezuelan and Mexican oil, or whether it can rely on market forces to assure its access to that supply.

Energy and Economic Growth

Despite the apparently greater decoupling of economic and energy demand growth rates in many industrial countries, developing countries still confront a situation in which greater economic growth means large jumps in energy consumption. Many of the early stages of economic development (commercialization of agriculture, transportation, urbanization) are energy-intensive. In more tropical areas, energy growth is highest in the commercial and transportation sectors that are of major importance to economic growth rather than the household sector because there is no space heating requirement and there is less inadvertent waste. Capital and foreign exchange shortages frequently limit the availability of more energy-efficient technology, and substitution possibilities may be more limited. Over the long run, economic development strategies must stress greater energy efficiency, yet this may well require pricing systems that reflect all or nearly all the real costs of energy. Adopting such policies may be politically very difficult.

A number of countries in the region have established energy policy commissions or revamped the traditional ministry of mines to include energy. Nevertheless, energy planning and related intellectual resources are rudimentary in many cases. Are market-based energy policies the solutions to these countries' problems, or does there remain a legitimate need for planning? Is the current U.S. energy assistance effort adequate?

Development of the Region's Resources

As already indicated, the Caribbean Basin possesses considerable oil resources, but these are concentrated in two countries. What about the rest of the countries? One finds a much less promising picture. In addition to the "oil problem," a number of countries face a shortage of firewood, making better use of traditional fuels a pressing matter. Several of the Central American countries have untapped hydroelectric potential that could meet electricity needs more cheaply than imported oil and could offer an exportable commodity as well, although the unrest in the region precludes development of a regional electricity grid at this time. A few countries may possess as yet undiscovered or undeveloped oil resources, but the chances of any major discoveries occurring are remote. Nevertheless, there may be enough in places like Honduras to meet at least domestic demand, thus relieving balance-of-payments pressures attributable to oil imports and taking a country, however small, out of the world oil market. The solar and biomass potential of a number of the countries may be significant, but time, technology, and money are needed to develop these resources. Development of these resources will not have a major impact on oil imports for some time, and even then this impact will be limited unless alcohol fuels can be developed to substitute for oil in the transportation sector. (Such a development could, as a by-product, offer an additional economic outlet for sugar cane producers.)

In view of the limited financial, human, and technical resources available within many of the countries, the kind of strategy to promote development of these resources takes on added importance. Is there a legitimate need for multilateral financial assistance programs, or will private-sector investment, in response to market signals, be sufficient to assure adequate resource development? Can the countries of the region be assured of stable access to sufficient quantities of capital on acceptable economic terms? Is there a need for coordination of resource development projects, especially if large-scale investment in and use of heavy crude upgrading facilities (to make a larger share of lighter, more premium-use products per barrel of crude) might threaten the economic underpinnings of U.S. synthetic fuel projects?

Supply Security

In contrast to Middle Eastern sources, the Caribbean is widely perceived in the U.S. to be a much more stable, secure source of oil for not only the United States but the entire hemisphere. In Venezuela the steady decline of reserves and production in recent years apparently has been arrested by new offshore discoveries and wider use of enhanced recovery techniques. Venezuelan authorities now believe that conventional oil reserves are large enough to cover both domestic demand and exports (1.5 mbd in 1982) into the 1990s. Mexico would clearly like to increase its production and sale of oil (at a stable price) to finance economic development. Both countries have sought to develop with the U.S., as well as other developed Western economies and Japan, a stable, long-term export market for oil at market prices. Indeed, Mexico supplanted Saudi Arabia in 1982 as the leading supplier of U.S. oil imports.

Against these opportunities lie an array of problems ranging from economic and technical constraints on development of reserves in the region to a lack of a consistent, reasonable, and acceptable (to the region) U.S. policy. Over the past two decades U.S. domestic pricing policy, market intervention, regulatory impediments to imports of natural gas, oil "back-out" legislation, and so forth have had adverse effects on the economies of Caribbean suppliers and on the stability of the U.S. market for their products. To these countries, a "market-based" U.S. energy policy offers them treatment no better (and also no worse) than that offered the least reliable sheik. This situation raises the question of whether U.S. diplomatic initiatives, such as negotiating "special relationships" with Mexico and Venezuela to ensure U.S. access to their supply, are needed or could better recognize the differences between the behavior of these countries and, say, Libya.

While political and economic events will undoubtedly have the greatest influence on the security of Caribbean oil suppliers, it is also worth considering the possibility of intentional overt or covert attempts to disrupt by force the production, refining, and transportation of oil within the region. Unlike nuclear facilities, which have been attacked by terrorists in Spain, France, and South Africa, for example, oil facilities (rigs, pipeline, tanks, refineries, etc.) have not been particularly attractive targets for such groups. In full-scale hostilities, (e.g., the Iran–Iraq war) oil facilities have been prime targets for attack, however. Because the production and refining capacity of the region is geographically dispersed, it is unlikely that terrorist attacks on refineries or other facilities in one or two locations could significantly affect the supply security of the United States. Should such attacks actually present problems at some point in the future, physical-security technology is readily available for implementation by facility operators with assistance from national authorities or through bilateral arrangements with the U.S. For example, the U.S. Department of Energy has transferred security technology developed in its nuclear defense programs to protection of the Strategic Petroleum Reserve (SPR), and the experience developed through such programs could be useful at some point in time.

Security of transportation routes and carriers is another aspect of physical security of supply, since the major transportation links the region are susceptible to disruption by hostile forces at sea. While the possibility exists for disruption of oil transportation at sea as a result of terrorist acts, the likelihood of such disruptions and the overall impact on the supply picture within the region should be small. Even if major hostilities were to erupt so as to give rise to threats to the security of the region, the U.S. would be better able to maintain security of routes in the Caribbean than in the Persian Gulf or the Indian Ocean. Physical security of supply does not, at this time, appear to be threatened within the region.

CHARACTERIZATION OF THE REGION IN ENERGY TERMS

Several of the other papers in this study have pointed out the cultural, political, and economic diversity of the countries in the region. The diversity of energy circumstances is less marked, however. The most important difference among countries is whether they import or export oil. This is a key difference, though, as whether a country is also an economic "have" or "have-not" tends to relate closely to oil status.

Key Energy Parameters

Table 7.2 lists four key energy parameters for selected countries in the region. With the exception of Venezuela, Trinidad and Tobago, Mexico, and Jamaica, the per capita energy consumption figures are relatively low in comparison to industrial countries. However, the table also shows that energy consumption more than doubled for many countries during the period covered and that the share of energy in total merchandise imports also rose dramatically in a number of cases.

More importantly, for most of the countries in the region, energy (at least that traded in the market place) means oil and little else. With the exceptions of Mexico, Venezuela, Trinidad and Tobago, and Colombia, where natural gas and/or coal play significant roles, both commercial energy demand and supply involve oil (typically in the range of 85 to 100 percent of total demand and supply). The Central American states have developed hydroelectric sources of electricity, but even there oil satisfies over 80 percent of total energy demand. In the island states virtually all electric capacity is oil-fired.

Of the countries in the Caribbean, only Mexico, Venezuela, and Trinidad and Tobago are net exporters of energy (oil). The large majority of countries depend on imported energy sources. Overall, however, the *region* (excluding the U.S.) is a net exporter of energy (oil).

Table 7.2. Energy Data for the Caribbean Basin

| | Average Annual Growth Rate (%) | | | | Energy Consumption per Capita (kg of Coal Equivalent) | | Energy Imports as % of Merchandise Exports | |
| | Energy Production | | Energy Consumption | | | | | |
	1960–74	1974–79	1960–74	1974–79	1960	1979	1960	1979
Haiti	—	13.7	1.5	20.8	34	63	—	15
Honduras	29.4	6.4	7.7	1.7	149	238	10	13
El Salvador	5.1	24.3	7.7	8.4	143	338	6	9
Nicaragua	26.4	−16.3	10.4	2.7	176	446	12	14
Jamaica	−0.7	−2.0	11.0	−5.4	424	1,326	11	39
Guatemala	9.9	2.4	6.2	1.6	167	229	12	12
Dominican Republic	1.8	−5.1	14.4	−1.1	156	490	—	37
Colombia	3.5	2.0	5.7	7.1	494	914	3	10
Costa Rica	9.5	3.5	10.1	7.5	304	812	7	20
Mexico	5.8	15.7	7.7	7.8	713	1,535	3	3
Venezuela	1.1	−3.3	7.1	5.5	1,521	2,944	1	1
Trinidad and Tobago	2.8	3.9	10.5	6.2	1,619	4,872	35	23
USA	3.4	0.7	4.4	2.0	7,981	11,681	8	37

Source: World Bank, World Development Report, 1982 (Washington, D.C., 1982), p. 122–23.

The Caribbean Basin is one of the three major oil-producing regions in the non-Communist world (excluding North America). While the Middle East produces far more crude oil than the Caribbean Basin, the discoveries in Venezuela and Mexico were historically among the first major finds outside the U.S., predating the discoveries in Saudi Arabia. Table 7.3 indicates the size of the region, in relationship to the U.S. and the rest of the world in terms of crude oil production and refining capacity in 1982. On both indicators, the Basin constitutes less than 10 percent of world totals, a factor of no little importance in evaluating the Basin producers' ability (or lack thereof) to determine the functioning of the world oil system.

In 1982, Venezuela, an original member of OPEC, ranked eighth among all producing countries in the world, while Mexico ranked fourth.[3] Of the OPEC nations, Venezuela accounted for about 10 percent of total crude oil production. In terms of proven crude oil reserves, Venezuela was ninth (with 21.5 billion bbl) and Mexico fifth (with 48.3 billion bbl of crude) in the world, with the world total being 670 billion in 1982. Estimates of Mexico's total hydrocarbon (oil and gas) reserves reach in excess of 250 billion bbl.

The influence of the region on the Western Hemisphere is substantial. For example, the Caribbean Basin accounts for about 30 percent of the total crude production and 20 percent of the total refining capacity in the hemisphere. For the U.S., imports of crude oil from the Caribbean states in 1982 surpassed those from the Persian Gulf. When the East Coast of the U.S. is considered separately from the remainder of the country, the Caribbean sources provide about 8 percent of all refined petroleum products.

Unlike the Middle East (with Saudi Arabia), no country in the region is in a position to determine how the world market behaves, but Mexico and Venezuela are in a position to affect market dynamics in the Western Hemisphere. Venezuela in particular has played an important role in mitigating the consequences of the Arab oil embargo in 1973 and the 1978–1979 supply "shortfall." Despite a decline in Venezuela's production due to the depletion of that country's conventional reserves, particularly lighter crudes that are refined into distillates, Venezuela's production increased in 1973 and 1979, periods that saw significant cutbacks in oil deliveries from the Middle East as a result of conflicts in that region. Specifically, during the cutback in Iranian crude oil exports in late 1978 and early 1979, increased exports to the U.S. from Venezuela helped offset the impact of the loss of Iranian crude. For example, in the fourth quarter of 1978, Venezuela increased its export to the U.S. by 4 percent over the quarterly average of the first three quarters, and in the first quarter of 1979 the increase was

Table 7.3. Comparison of Key Oil Parameters for the Caribbean Basin, the U.S., and the World

	1982 Crude Oil Production (bbl/day)	1982 Refining Capacity (bbl/day)
Caribbean	4,748,400	5,244,100
U.S.	8,655,000	16,800,000
Non-Communist world	38,352,000	60,268,447
World total	53,002,000	77,141,447
Caribbean as % of world total	8.9%	6.7%

Source: Oil and Gas Journal, January 31, 1983.

6 percent over the same quarter in 1978. (Total Venezuelan production in 1979 was about 9 percent higher than 1978, decreasing in 1980 to levels below that in 1978.)

Mexican production has climbed steadily since 1976, reaching 2.7 mbd in 1982, up from 984,219 bbl/day in 1976. More than half of total production is exported (approximately 1.7 mbd at the end of 1982) with 800,000 bbl/day going to the U.S., making Mexico the leading U.S. supplier.

Both Venezuela and Mexico have strong economic incentives to develop stable and secure access to markets for their oil. In some cases, such as with France, intergovernmental agreements include provisions for oil supply. In others, such as the U.S., long-term contracts have been used. Moreover, Venezuela, which has publicly expressed a desire to be a stable, secure source of crude oil and refined products for the U.S., has planned to spend $2.3 billion during the 1980s to convert its refineries to maximum distillate production, thus enabling the refining of heavier crudes to meet the broader demands of the U.S. market.

Energy Costs and Regional Economies

Most countries in the Caribbean were able to keep their energy costs relatively low compared to the balance of trade until the end of the decade. In fact, most countries in the region were able to maintain a strong external sector during the rise in oil prices in the 1970s. However, the size and structure of the external debt continues to be a problem for several countries in the region, including the oil exporters. Table 7.4 indicates the external indebtedness situation for countries in the region. One must point out that several of the countries in the Caribbean have a substantial (relative to total gross external debt) fraction of their financial assets invested abroad, such that the ratio of interest received to interest paid is rather high. These countries include Venezuela, Trinidad and Tobago, Barbados, and Guatemala.

Finally, for most countries in the Caribbean during the 1970s, the real interest rate paid on their external debt was very low, making it advantageous for countries to increase their external indebtedness in order to pay for higher-priced imports (including oil). The 1980 recession, however, was accompanied by more restrictive monetary policies, which caused the real rate of interest paid to increase. Continuation of high interest rates would have an obviously adverse impact on the economies of the region and would inhibit economic growth. Reluctance of private banks to renegotiate payment periods, let alone grant new loans, could confront these countries with a credit crunch just as softer oil prices eased the economically depressing impact of oil imports. Because the smaller countries, even collectively, account for a relatively small share of the region's total commercial borrowings, private banks will likely attach a low priority to their problems in the face of much more serious ones (when viewed in a global context) found in Mexico, Venezuela, Chile, Argentina, and Brazil. This leaves the smaller countries little alternative but to appeal to official multilateral and bilateral financial assistance.[4]

IMPLICATIONS OF THE ISSUES
FOR U.S. INTERESTS AND POLICIES

The glut of oil that now threatens the stability of OPEC has encouraged a belief that the energy "crisis" is past, that what residual U.S. concern remains is largely one of security of supply (with less than 20 percent of U.S. imports coming from Arab suppliers, one wonders how seriously even this issue is being taken), and that energy prices, which are now lower in real terms than 1979 levels, are no longer an economic factor of overriding concern. Part of this picture may be accurate—for now. The validity of this view depends on the impact of economic resurgence in the industrial world on energy demand, which no one knows, and on favorable assumptions regarding the stability of Saudi Arabia, which could be easily disproved. Moreover, the optimism expressed in industrial countries over oil prices does not fit the situation for developing countries, for which even $28 to $30 for a barrel of oil is a serious burden.

The U.S. can ill afford to assume that energy is no longer an important issue in its Caribbean Basin relationships. Possible political instability arising from prolonged economic distress and defaults on debt are just

Table 7.4. Structure of the External Public Debt[a] of Caribbean Basin, by Type of Creditor, 1960, 1970 and 1980 (Percentages on the basis of total outstanding balances at year-end)

	Official Multilateral			Official Bilateral			Suppliers			Banks[b]			Other Loans[c]		
	1960	1970	1980	1960	1970	1980	1960	1970	1980	1960	1970	1980	1960	1970	1980
Bahamas	n/a	–	26.1	n/a	38.0	22.7	n/a	18.0	2.3	n/a	44.0	48.9	n/a	–	–
Barbados	n/a	–	69.7	n/a	18.8	18.7	n/a	–	0.6	–	–	11.0	n/a	81.2	–
Colombia	36.3	38.7	43.1	28.7	42.3	18.8	10.3	11.3	7.2	10.9	5.3	30.3	13.8	2.4	0.6
Costa Rica	12.7	46.7	38.9	36.4	35.7	16.5	9.1	4.4	2.4	21.8	8.8	37.7	20.0	4.4	4.5
Dominican Republic	–	9.7	33.4	–	72.3	37.2	150.0	7.0	0.2	–	11.0	29.2	–	–	–
El Salvador	93.9	51.6	64.4	–	34.9	33.2	–	1.7	–	–	11.1	2.4	6.1	2.4	–
Guatemala	31.4	30.7	70.0	47.0	34.1	30.0	–	–	–	21.6	25.6	–	–	7.9	–
Guyana	n/a	9.9	29.0	n/a	72.5	39.9	n/a	–	3.1	n/a	5.4	17.2	n/a	12.2	10.8
Haiti	7.9	2.2	71.3	71.1	64.5	26.2	10.5	24.4	1.3	10.5	–	2.5	10.5	8.9	–
Honduras	78.3	70.8	63.3	13.1	26.4	24.7	4.3	2.8	2.3	4.3	–	10.7	–	–	–
Jamaica	n/a	24.0	26.3	n/a	24.0	41.7	n/a	–	0.9	n/a	8.8	24.6	n/a	43.2	5.1
Mexico	16.2	29.7	13.5	33.9	12.9	5.5	15.2	10.1	0.9	25.8	36.6	72.9	8.9	10.7	7.2
Nicaragua	65.8	40.5	32.3	29.3	33.6	31.2	–	4.5	1.0	4.9	21.4	35.5	–	–	–
Panama	11.8	32.4	23.5	44.1	31.0	11.9	–	24.5	1.3	–	2.1	50.4	44.1	10.0	12.9
Trinidad and Tobago	–	34.4	12.2	–	20.5	21.7	14.3	3.3	–	38.1	12.3	60.2	47.6	29.5	5.9
Venezuela	–	35.1	1.9	14.3	13.8	2.1	25.1	15.0	3.2	60.6	32.0	61.8	–	4.1	31.0

Source: Inter-American Development Bank, Economic and Social Progress in Latin America (Washington, D.C., 1982), p. 74.

[a] Public and publicly guaranteed debt, payable in foreign exchange and with a maturity of more than one year, includes the undisbursed portion at year-end.

[b] Includes other financial institutions.

[c] Includes nationalization and bond issues.

– Zero or not significant.

n/a: Not available.

two examples where the contributing effect of energy problems in the Caribbean Basin can have a serious impact on U.S. and Western interests. This importance is independent of whatever is the current health of OPEC. The region will undoubtedly continue to play a major role in U.S. energy supply, and possibly that of several of its major allies, in the coming decade. Even if Mexico diversifies its customer base so as to reduce economically and politically sensitive dependence on the United States, it still will be one of the top two or three sources of U.S. oil imports. In addition, France is using Mexican oil as a way of obtaining some diversification of supply, as is Japan. Venezuela will continue to supply 400,000 to 600,000 bbl/day of oil to the U.S., and by the end of the decade could begin sizable production in the Orinoco. The Panama Canal (or a possible trans-isthmus pipeline) will remain an important transit point for Alaskan oil. The island refinery system will remain closely integrated into the product supply system for the East Coast.

It is clear, then, from a number of standpoints, that energy issues in the Caribbean Basin will retain their significance over the next ten years. Both by itself, in terms of oil supply, and in combination with other factors, in relation to the region's economies, energy will remain an important item on the agenda of U.S. policy toward the region.

Paying for Oil

For most of the countries in the region, the foremost energy problem will remain that of "ability to pay" for imported oil. The record of the 1980–1982 period demonstrates the seriousness of the problem. In 1980, 60 percent of the Dominican Republic's export earnings had to go to pay for oil (vs. 11 percent in 1973). In that same year, the Dominican Republic's current account deficit was 14 percent of GDP, as opposed to 5.5 percent in 1974–1975. The case of Costa Rica is even more disheartening. Largely under the weight of higher oil prices, that country slid from relative prosperity to actually negative economic growth in 1981. The ratio of interest payments on external debt to GDP for most of the Central American countries more than tripled over the 1970–1980 decade, when borrowing to help finance oil imports increased. The picture is not much better in most of the other oil import-dependent countries. Economic recession in the U.S. and elsewhere, and depressed commodity and raw material prices, have further compounded the ability of these countries to expand exports to help ease the oil import burden.

The existing institutional mechanisms can cope only partially with the problem of oil cost. The principal oil-financing facility at work in the Basin, established jointly by Venezuela and Mexico in 1980 to ease the financial burden on their customers in the Caribbean and Central America, has made a useful near-term contribution in this area. Almost $400 million was lent in FY82, but at possible long-term cost. (Trinidad and Tobago also has a smaller oil-financing facility intended for use by the island countries, but its importance is overshadowed by the Mexican-Venezuelan facility.) Under the 1980 San Jose accord, the two countries have agreed to share the regional markets, while charging market prices for their oil, and to finance 30 percent of the bill at 4 percent over four years, or at 2 percent over twenty years if the funds are invested in energy projects. These interest rates will likely be raised in 1983, but presumably will still be kept below the rates available from private banks.

To date, the recipient countries have used the facility principally as a means of balance-of-payments support. Only two energy projects, one entailing purchase of a refinery, have been initiated. Most of the countries lack the capability to identify projects for possible long-term financing, and prefer to use other sources of concessionary financing that, unlike the loans from the Mexican-Venezuelan facility, are not earmarked for a specific purpose.

The beneficial short-run impact of the facility has proved especially important in such places as Costa Rica and El Salvador, where the facility accounted for approximately 30 percent of the capital account, offsetting a current-account deficit that otherwise could have crippled the Salvadoran economy even more had El Salvador had to pay the full bill for its oil. The potentially adverse long-run impact of the facility stems from the fact that it may discourage adoption of alternate fuel sources. In Barbados, the electric utility is reluctant to shift to non-oil-fired capacity because the facility eases the cost of oil. The same problem can be found elsewhere, and nearly all of the Island electrical capacity is oil-fired. The long-term impact could be to retard shifting from oil in a sector where alternative fuels (such as coal-water mixtures) might be usable, and has not contributed to new capital formation, only to the overall debt burden.

How long both countries can afford, in the face of their own economic problems, to continue the facility is another matter. Although neither country has abandoned or curtailed its commitment to maintain the facility, continuation of serious economic pressures could force those governments to reexamine the facility. Should the facility be cut back or terminated, it is not so clear that alternate sources of balance-of-payments support will be forthcoming. It is highly unlikely that private banks will lend for this purpose, as no new productive assets are being created. Some countries, such as Costa Rica, simply have no access to private capital due to debt-service problems. If true, this means that either multilateral or official bilateral assistance must be made available.

Under the proposed terms of the Caribbean Basin Initiative, the U.S. Agency for International Development was to use Economic Support Funds primarily for balance-of-payments support, as well as to stimulate local private enterprise. The impact of the program in the balance-of-payments area was admittedly limited, and it was envisioned that other countries, including Canada, Mexico, Venezuela, and Colombia, as well as the International Monetary Fund and multilateral development banks, would have to carry a large share of the burden. Obviously, the viability of this approach presumes that the other parties have sufficient resources to meet foreseeable needs. Ultimately, the focus of efforts to strengthen international mechanisms for balance-of-payments support must shift to the International Monetary Fund. U.S. support for augmenting the funds available to the IMF takes on added importance in light of the possibility that an additonal sharp fall in oil prices might discourage Mexico and Venezuela from continuing their oil facility.[5]

Over the long run, there is no substitute for expanding the Basin countries' exports which, due to limited intraregional markets, must for the most part go out of the region. The Caribbean Group for Cooperation in Economic Development, meeting in June 1982, reached just this conclusion. Recovery from economic recession in the U.S. and elsewhere is a prerequisite for the success of this approach. In the meantime, many of the countries will continue to require balance-of-payments assistance.

Resource Development

The resource development "issue" is, in fact, several issues. First, there is the problem of access to capital for energy projects, which for the oil importers is a serious matter, and which raises for them the issue of whether more extensive energy lending by multilateral institutions is required. In the case of the two principal oil exporters, however, resource development may be less a matter of access to capital and technology, to which they have ready access in the market, than it may be one of access to stable markets for their products. The issue of technical assistance also arises in the context of resource development, as does the equally as important task of developing human resources—technically and administratively skilled manpower—without which a program of technology transfer cannot be successful.

Multilateral Energy Lending

By far one of the most controversial areas of the Reagan administration's views on development assistance has been its opposition to establishment of a separate World Bank energy lending affiliate. First proposed by the Bank in 1980 following discussions with a number of governments, including Venezuela, the concept of the Energy Affiliate was to entail a major expansion of the Bank's energy lending (from $13 billion in the FY81–85 lending program to $25 billion) and establishment of a new institutional mechanism for energy lending purposes to prevent the enlarged energy program from distorting the overall sectoral balance in the Bank's lending program.[6] In addition, the focus of Bank lending for energy would shift from the traditional emphasis on electric generating capacity toward a relatively greater role in funding oil and gas exploration, coal exploration and development, refinery modernization, and development of renewables, especially those related to firewood. The rationale for this expansion rested on the beliefs that high energy prices would persist, with crippling effects on developing-country economies; that these countries would not have sufficient access to private capital to meet their needs; that energy policy had to be better integrated with economic strategy; and that recipient countries would need impartial advice (i.e., the Bank and contractors hired with Bank money) in developing energy policies and dealing with concessionaires.

Although reaction to the proposal from energy experts was mixed, with skeptics questioning the propriety of the Bank's assuming exploration risks normally the province of the corporate sector, it was the Reagan administration that launched the strongest attack on the concept. The administration argued that the case had not been made for a specific level of investment in LDC energy, that the Bank's subsidized interest rates skewed the allocation of capital on both global and local levels, that projects financed by the Bank might not advance U.S. objectives, and, importantly, that Bank lending, if to governments, would displace the private sector in recipient countries.[7] The administration also questioned the Bank's purported assumption that private-sector investment would be insufficient to develop resources meeting the "test of the marketplace." Where private investment was insufficient, the administration asserted that it more than likely was a result of ill-conceived domestic policies in the recipient country, especially below-market energy pricing and failure to provide assurances against nationalization. The Bank subsequently dropped in 1983 the idea of a specific energy-related facility due in part to U.S. opposition, but continued to explore other institutional options to obtain more leverage from its lending resources for use in a number of fields, including but not limited to energy.

The World Bank's Energy Affiliate has not been the only institutional mechanism proposed or debated. The Inter-American Development Bank, making many of the same arguments as did the World Bank, increased its energy lending, and its director proposed the creation of a new institutional entity for a larger program.[8] Venezuela, in 1980, proposed the establishment of a Hemispheric Energy Fund to provide seed capital for energy projects in energy importing countries. Significantly, Venezuela proposed to its regional neighbors that U.S. and Canadian participation would be essential to the success of such a fund. However, as the Latin American Energy Organization (OLADE) developed its own Latin American Energy Cooperation Program, Canada and the United States were not invited to participate in its drafting. Some U.S. Agency for International Development funds have been contributed to OLADE energy workshops.

The IADB lending program for oil and gas exploration and development began in 1980. Through 1982, $45 million had been lent for oil and gas exploration in Bolivia, Jamaica, and Costa Rica. This was a little less than half of the FY82 World Bank lending to all of Latin America and the Caribbean for oil, gas, and coal projects.[9] Although the thrust of World Bank lending in oil and gas has been toward Africa, Panama was awarded a loan in the $6 million range to strengthen indigenous institutional capabilities in energy planning and administration and to hire independent contractors to gather and interpret past exploration data, carry out additional surveys and assist government authorities in dealing with concession holders, and help negotiate exploration agreements. Costa Rica was awarded a $3 million loan to develop a national energy plan and to carry out geological studies. The national oil company of Jamaica received the largest World Bank loan to the region to finance oil exploration.

The relative merits of expanding multilateral energy lending and establishing a World Bank energy affiliate depend very much on the perspective one adopts toward the nature of the energy problems in the region and how they can best be addressed. From a strictly "energy policy" perspective, in which oil imports are considered the problem and the emphasis is on exploration, development of new energy technologies and sources, and conservation, attention is going to focus principally on what can be done within the energy sector itself to lessen oil dependence. Frequently, this will mean oil exploration projects as the most direct way eventually to decrease such dependence, and that is precisely what one is seeing in such countries as Jamaica, Panama, Honduras, and the Domican Republic. If one approaches the energy problems from a "balance-of-payments" perspective, however, in which serious current-account deficits rather than oil imports per se are viewed as the problem, the range of options expands to include not only measures in the energy sector, but other economic policy measures designed to reduce these deficits as well. In this perspective, energy problems are viewed not in isolation, but as part of a broader economic problem calling for far-reaching measures within the countries and in the international monetary system to get out of the debt hole they have dug for themselves.

It is not at all clear, when viewed from this broader perspective, that funneling limited World Bank resources into oil exploration or refinery modernization represents a cost-effective use of the money. While granting that a successful exploration program may yield enough oil to take a country out of the oil market and that the large oil companies will likely not be interested in projects with little or no export potential, the marginal returns to money spent on oil exploration, when compared to alternative uses of the money, may still be insufficient.

Operating as a lender of last resort, in addition to the market but not subject to the same cost-benefit calculus, could easily place the Bank in the position of supporting the highest risk or lowest payoff projects. Rather than acting as an alternative to private capital, the Bank could focus on those areas where market dislocations prevent otherwise worthwhile projects from being funded. In some instances, this may be because private banks have cut back lending to developing countries; in others it may be because necessary institutions or capabilities to implement projects are inadequate or nonexistent in the country. The resulting Bank role in projects on both the demand and supply sides of the energy equation may still be extensive, but the economic justification would be stronger. Just what kinds of projects could benefit from Bank support would depend on the specific circumstances of a particular country or case, but they could range from helping to fund conversion of utility boilers to coal to devising new institutions (public or private) to facilitate planning or technology transfer. Excluded would be such areas as retrofitting of refineries or oil exploration, which have received Bank support in recent years.

The objective of these energy measures, in combination with economic policies directed at both the current account and capital account, would be not to eliminate energy imports, but to make their economic impact more manageable. Over time, the rate of growth of oil consumption might be moderated by both supply- and demand-related energy measures, but energy autarky would not be a policy goal. Both macroeconmic policy and "energy policy" would have to be closely integrated to achieve these objectives if the same old spiral of rising debt and inflation is to be avoided. Indeed, measures specific to the energy sector are likely to have little overall impact if macroeconomic policies perpetuate the current economic situations in these countries.

The view espoused here, that the problems can best be approached from a "balance-of-payments" perspective in which energy policy becomes a subset of macroeconomic policy, presumes a far better capacity for integrated energy-economic planning and policy implementation than is frequently encountered in the region. A scarcity of energy experts, poor interagency coordination, and, often, political interference with planners obviously handicap govenments in this endeavor. The World Bank and the IADB, by directly supporting energy planning through financial and technical assistance and by using their potential leverage over recipient governments, may have greater impact on these countries' ability to cope with the economic problems posed by oil imports than they would by funding high-risk exploration programs.

If the World Bank and IADB energy lending programs can be criticized, so too can the position of the Reagan administration. As the administration has acknowledged, there are areas where such lending clearly is justifiable. Bank participation in project preparation in the electricity area and pressure on the borrowing government to adopt economic pricing policies can make a project more attractive for private capital. Bank participation may also have a "catalytic" effect (i.e., attracting additional financing by assuring thorough project evaluation and reducing risk to cofinancers). Technical assistance loans can be used to hire private companies, while "Letters of Cooperation," which commit the Bank to consider financing development resulting from privately funded exploration, can help encourage exploration work, leaving decisions to commit economic resources to exploration, and the risks thereof, to state or private oil companies.

On the other hand, the administration's position is too narrowly drawn. It is too quick to assume that because multinational energy companies have shied away from certain projects that those projects are therefore uneconomic. Investment decisions made within a more global framework do not necessarily demonstrate that a specific project is economically unjustifiable. Moreover, Bank loans, even to public-sector entities, frequently provide a means for hiring private companies on a contractor basis. In some cases, the indigenous private sector is underdeveloped, and the public sector is the only entity capable of planning and carrying out (albeit inefficiently in many cases) major projects, as is the case in the utility sector. Lastly, in the Caribbean Basin, where public-sector responsibility for energy is extensive (with the exception in some cases of oil refining and marketing), development of the energy base may be a prerequisite for private-sector commercial investment in energy-intensive industries, such that restricting energy lending to the public sector could inhibit private investment.[10] An almost theological belief in the efficacy of the market and the private sector is not a good guide to policy where development of the public sector and better government planning may be needed.

While it is clear that multilateral agencies cannot and should not supplant private capital, the least resource-advantaged countries in the Caribbean Basin may well find their access to sufficient private capital blocked by their larger neighbors in Mexico and Venezuela. Where they do obtain access, interest rates and risk premia are likely to be relatively high, raising serious questions as to whether these countries will slowly sink in a sea of debt. Perhaps the U.S. policy of opposing an increase in World Bank lending or establishment of the energy affiliate while actually abstaining on votes on specific loans is an acknowledgement that the issue is more complicated than "let the market take care of it" rhetoric suggests.

Technical Assistance

U.S. bilateral energy programs in the Basin region, most of which are administered and funded by the U.S. Agency for International Development (AID), provide technical assistance, manpower training, and financial assistance. The technical assistance tends to take the form of pilot and demonstration-scale projects for renewables (wind power, solar cookers, etc.), resource analysis, provision of cost-free technical experts from the United States, assistance in developing national energy plans and planning infrastructure, and, in some countries, large AID missions staffed by engineers and other energy experts. AID funds training courses in energy management and planning and in renewable energy sources, and will fund participation in non-U.S. courses (e.g., the International Labor Organization's course in coal technology, the Barriloche Foundation course in energy economics). The AID-sponsored courses are global in makeup rather than regional, and AID has recognized a need for a more regional focus to its training efforts.

AID has also provided financial assistance for energy-related projects, such as the purchase of small, more efficient buses to replace old jitney cabs in Santo Domingo, and has funneled money through the Caribbean Development Bank to fund wind turbines in Antigua and a mini-hydro project in Dominica, and is helping to fund, through Caricom, a series of country energy assessments. Large AID missions in the Dominican Republic and Jamaica can provide technical assistance directly to the host government. As a general matter, however, AID leaves the task of meeting large-scale capital requirements to multilateral institutions.

A prospectively interesting and useful asset in the technical assistance area is the U.S. system of national laboratories. The Los Alamos National Laboratory (LANL) is interested in providing technical services throughout the Basic region. LANL already has established a relationship with the Mexican National Institute for Nuclear Research, and has consulted in the geothermal area in Mexico and St. Vincent and St. Lucia. LANL is interested in consulting on geothermal development and assessment of resources, especially as yet undeveloped mineral resources that could provide a new export product. Brookhaven National Laboratory for a number of years has provided considerable analytical support for LDCs in the energy area. The national labs have not, to date, been extensively used for technical assistance outside the nuclear area, but the availability of non-nuclear expertise from these sources merits closer attention.

Any technical assistance program to the region will encounter a number of formidable obstacles. Energy-planning and project-management capabilities in many of the countries are meager, and coordination of specific projects within one agency, let alone on an interagency basis, is poor. In the Dominican Republic, for example, the utility has started over seventy-five projects and not yet completed one. The pool of skilled personnel is small. Utility and industry officials are frequently reluctant to switch from tried-and-true but energy-inefficient technologies. The political systems themselves, in which there may be no stability at the top administrative levels, impede efforts to plan and execute projects having more than two-year lead-times.

The more difficult problems may thus be institutional rather than technical in character. Overemphasis on technical assistance per se should be avoided. In many countries, scarcity of appropriately skilled manpower is a major obstacle to the development of energy policies and projects. No program of technology transfer and assistance will succeed in the absence of developing a cadre of trained experts capable of assuming programmatic and planning responsibilities. Low-capital-cost, "low-technology" options that do not require expensive retrofitting or construction of entirely new facilities for their use merit attention. One example of a promising technology meeting these requirements and nearing the commercialization phase is a coal-water mixture that could substitute for fuel oil in electric utility boilers. However, attitudes that resist change can effectively block use of better technologies.

Resource Development in Venezuela and Mexico

While most of the discussion in this paper has focused on the import-dependent countries in the region, an equally critical but very different resource development issue is found in Venezuela, Mexico, and Colombia. These countries possess substantial oil (or coal, in the case of Colombia) resources. The problem in these countries is to generate sufficient cash flow to support both exploration and development, to attract capital to cover costs not supportable by internal cash flow alone, and to develop stable markets of sufficient size to make resource projects economically viable. The latter point may seem a bit strange against the background of a tight oil market as recently as 1981, but it nevertheless remains that oils exports are absolutely critical to the Mexican and Venezuelan economies (oil revenues account for more than 90 percent of total export revenues in both countries) and, by extension, to the stability of their political systems. These countries can ill afford substantial and prolonged economic retrenchment necessitated by a precipitous drop in those revenues. Coal exports will likely become equally as important to the Colombian economy over the next two decades.

The relationship between oil revenues and the economies of Venezuela and Mexico, and the role declining oil revenues has played in the serious economic problems currently confronting both countries, are too complicated and too well documented elsewhere to require a lengthy discussion of these topics here.[11] The focus here is on how these problems, and the solutions thereto, may effect the pace of resource development and thus oil output over the next decade or two.

At the beginning of 1983, Mexico was earning about $48 million per day from oil exports of 1.7 mbd, and an increase in these exports to over 2 mbd in 1983 was thought to be possible. The $48 million finances the $35 million in daily interest payments on the external public debt of $60 billion, leaving some money for government and Pemex budgetary requirements. Petroleos Mexicanos (Pemex) is caught in the middle, in that as an increasingly important player in world oil trade, it must be sensitive to market trends, while, on the other hand, domestically it is a major instrument of economic policy and thus subject to strong political pressures.

The problem is that Pemex has pursued four contradictory goals: (1) to sell at prevailing world—that is, OPEC—prices; (2) to increase overall exports while retaining some ceiling on the amount going to the U.S.; (3) to keep low prices inside the country; and (4) to finance social development with oil revenues. Already, the new de la Madrid government has acted to raise domestic oil prices, and Pemex has had to show some flexibility on price and crude quality in its export policy. However, it has also been forced to curtail, in the short-run, its exploration and development and refinery programs. To keep the oil sector growing, Pemex will have to spend $20 billion over the next six years on exploration and development, refineries, and the distribution and transportation system. It is not clear that Pemex can do this and fund economic development without large-scale foreign borrowing. Another fall in oil prices would be a serious blow to these plans and would rock the Mexican economy.

Venezuela actually saw its oil export earnings in 1982 fall for the first time in a decade, dropping over $2 billion in 1982. Although Venezuela's external debt is smaller than Mexico's, its economy is very dependent on oil revenues, and its conventional oil reserve situation, which is heavily weighted toward less profitable heavy oil, puts Venezuela in an unenviable market position. On September 27, 1982, the Venezuelan government seized the $5 to $6 billion of Petroleos de Venezuela's foreign exchange holdings and those of other state-owned entities and placed them under the Central Bank as a means of improving Venezuela's creditworthiness. This action has raised doubts as to Petroleos' autonomy and its future ability to carry out the multi-billion-dollar investment program for developing the Orinoco. (In 1980, it was estimated that the first 125,000-bbl/day tranche of Orinoco production capacity would cost $5 billion, and that is for a relatively easy region of the Orinoco). The move was denounced by the opposition parties, and management of the economy was an issue in the 1983 presidential election campaign.

Venezuela's circumstances also differ in one important respect from those of either Mexico or Colombia. The latter two countries possess substantial fossil fuel resources that are economic at current foreseeable prices. Venezuela's Orinoco oil is more vulnerable to soft oil prices, however. Orinoco oil will be expensive (production costs in the $18–$20 range or more) and requires investment in expensive upgrading equipment at refineries. The Venezuelan government itself, in the late 1970s when synthetic fuels were attracting attention in the U.S. and elsewhere, portrayed Orinoco oil as a cheaper alternative to those fuels, but not necessarily to more conventional crudes. This is part of the dilemma Venezuela confronts in a much-changed oil market. Orinoco oil's synthetic fuel competitors have collapsed, while lower oil prices and lower refinery capacity discourage investment in new billion-dollar upgrading plants. Venezuela's strategy for dealing with this has been to negotiate joint investment arrangements with refiners for building these facilities, gaining access to the refiner's market while giving the refiner an assured source of crude. Both strictly commercial and government-to-government arrangements have been negotiated, although no U.S. refiners, who have largely shelved major new projects, have participated.

Soft oil prices, new additions of conventional oil resources, slower growth of domestic demand, and severe capital constraints led the

Venezuelan government, in June 1983, to cut back sharply the Orinoco development plan. Rather than having a 240,000-bbl/day production capacity in 1988, the target is now 130,000 bbl/day by 1990. The goal of mbd for the end of the century has disappeared from sight, although the Orinoco plan has not been formally scrapped. Thus, the fate of the Orinoco has come to resemble that of many other synfuel projects.

The situation in Colombia is somewhat different. Unlike Mexico and Venezuela, Colombia is not attempting to develop its coal resources, estimated to be 10 billion tonnes, by itself, but has brought in Exxon as the concessionaire. Colombia's coal represents anywhere from one-half to two-thirds of all coal in Latin America. A recently released International Energy Agency study of the world coal trade indicates that Colombia will have marginal costs substantially below U.S. coal exporters (an advantage of over $20 per tonne in North European markets), and could be selling 47 million tonnes of coal in all markets in the year 2000 at prices in the range of $70 to $80 per tonne.[12] Colombia has recently signed an agreement to supply Puerto Rico's coal needs for the next eleven years.

U.S. policy on multilateral lending in support of energy projects clearly must distinguish between the circumstances facing the poorer, oil-import-dependent countries and the oil (or coal) exporters. The latter, to the extent that their resources are economically competitive in world markets and their economic and political systems remain stable, can attract foreign capital and technology through existing corporate and private bank mechanisms. The former, however, frequently do not enjoy the same access to private capital. For them, capital arrangements may pose serious obstacles to energy projects, especially in the public sector where capital-intensive electric utilities are generally found. Having these countries shut off from private capital or charged exorbitant risk premia, resulting in economic dislocations leading to potential political instability, does not serve U.S. interests.

A recent study of lending problems in the Basin concludes that "In the 1980s, the Central American/Caribbean region will have to rely heavily on official rather than commercial resources of financing."[13] Multilateral financing is not necessarily incompatible with the development of the private sector. Indeed, World Bank lending can lay the foundation for private project. The goal is not to make countries energy self-sufficient—even if possible, it would be too expensive—but to cushion their economies against external oil price shocks and possible loss of supply, and, over time, to develop diversified economies better able to pay for energy.

Supply Security

Concern for supply security has been a prominent theme in U.S. energy policy since 1973.[14] Certainly until 1980, there was widespread acceptance of the premise by the administrations in power from 1973 onward that the existence of supply security concerns made energy policy a matter of national security and foreign policy, and that there could and should be "energy diplomacy" aimed at preserving security of supply. The Reagan administration, however, has defined the issue principally in terms of responses to disruption of supply rather than stability of access to supply, in the sense of being in the good political graces of the supplier on a day-to-day basis. With the partial exception of the Persian Gulf, there has been less emphasis on energy diplomacy and access to oil.

During 1978–1979, when events in Iran and Iraq sent oil prices skyrocketing, the concept of a "special relationship" with Mexico for oil, even a North American Common Market, began to draw attention in the U.S., including from then presidential candidate Ronald Reagan. The purpose would be to assure U.S. access to Mexican oil. Critics attacked these concepts, however, for being undesirable or unnegotiable in themselves, inconsistent with the preferences of the Mexican government, or for sending the "wrong signals" to U.S. allies and adversaries (i.e., that the U.S. was cutting a special deal for itself and would no longer care about Persian Gulf stability). With the advent of the latest oil glut, the "special relationship" concept no longer seems so urgent.

The idea of a regional oil supply accord is not new. Venezuela proposed the establishment of such an accord in 1957 and has raised the issue again on several occasions since then. The exemptions granted Canadian and Mexican crude from the Mandatory Oil Import Quota Program constituted an accord of sorts. A preferential arrangement with Mexico was, from one perspective, a logical extension of the past record.

The concept of an oil accord with Mexico, Venezuela, or both, still does not make much sense, if viewed as a means to secure a large share of their exports. Both countries have strong economic incentives to boost their output (at a rate that one hopes will not send their domestic inflation any further above the roof), and will continue to have these incentives for years to come. This is especially true of Mexico. Venezuela, while not in a position to increase its exports markedly, has incentives to continue to use a more flexible pricing policy.

U.S. interests will be served by these developments even if the U.S. share of exports from these countries does not increase. More oil on the market keeps the pressure on the Persian Gulf suppliers and makes more non-Arab oil available to U.S. allies. A conscious U.S. strategy of increasing its relative share of their exports could inflame nationalist sentiments in Mexico, whereas letting economics push up overall exports means that, even if the U.S. share is constant, a greater volume will reach the U.S.

Moreover, if there is one central lesson to be learned from the 1970s, it is that overdependence on one region or one country is potentially dangerous, regardless of how stable that country or region might appear at the outset. Exchanging dependence on one region where instability has already caused serious problems for dependence on another country(ies) where continuation of economic malaise could undermine political stability in the future hardly seems to be wise policy. While Mexico's proximity might be viewed as an advantage to those who would intervene militarily to protect the oil fields in Chiapas and Tabasco, it is just this prospect of becoming the U.S. strategic petroleum reserve that can severely complicate diplomatic relations with Mexico.

Already, Mexico supplies most of the contract crude going into the Strategic Petroleum Reserve (SPR). Although the most recent contracts were implemented on a government-to-government basis, the SPR purchase has yielded considerable diplomatic benefits to the U.S. The availability of SPR purchases gives the U.S. an effective policy instrument without having to resort to difficult-to-negotiate and likely untenable formal bilateral or multilateral accords. These purchases can be especially useful from a diplomatic standpoint in circumstances where, due to a soft market, Mexican exports through normal commercial channels are subject to downward pressures.

An alternative to a formal government-to-government accord would be a differential tariff on oil imports, under which all imports would be subject to a levy except those originating in designated "secure" countries. In the case at hand, Mexico, Venezuela, and Trinidad and Tobago could be so designated. The objective of the differential tariff would be to create economic incentives to import from the secure countries, while avoiding the potential diplomatic problems encountered in a formal energy supply accord. The end result—a preferred relationship with these three countries—would be the same.

While the differential tariff concept has attracted attention at various points since October 1973, it suffers from many of the same defects as a formal accord. It offers no guarantee that more oil would be forthcoming from the favored supplier than would have been the case without the levy, nor would it preclude dependence on insecure sources if economic recovery were to push up demand substantially beyond what "secure" countries could meet. Steering import patterns toward favored suppliers could create technical problems if the quality of the crude does not fit the capacity of the refinery system to handle it, or if the products from that crude do not match the pattern of product demand in the U.S. The differential tariff, as does the special relationship approach, downplays the importance of the fungibility of oil in world trade, which the events of 1973 and 1978–1980 demonstrated helps considerably to mitigate the effect of boycotts and loss of supply due to local war or unrest. From a diplomatic standpoint, a differential tariff could still send ripples through the Western Alliance, possibly encourage intra-Alliance competition for oil "sanctuaries," and would fail to insulate the United States from the political and economic repercussions of maltreatment of U.S. allies and trading partners by less reliable suppliers.

As Richard Neustadt observed of the "special relationship" between the U.S. and Great Britain in the defense sector, at times it was neither special nor much of a relationship.[15] The implied admonition is relevant here as well. Supply security, in the cases of Venezuela and Mexico, is one area where the market works in the U.S.'s favor. The market acts as a buffer between the U.S. government and supplier-state governments. A more realistic and effective U.S. policy for supply security is to fill the Stategic Petroleum Reserve at maximum rate (especially when prices are soft) and to negotiate quietly emergency supply arrangements with Mexico and Venezuela, assuring equitable treatment of U.S. allies in such arrangements. The special relationship approach can be justified only if the United States is willing to undermine whatever symbolic and treaty commitments it has made to solidarity with its allies in the face of energy emergencies and blackmail (one must not overlook that the U.S. is bound by treaty to share oil under specified circumstances with its fellow members of the International Energy Agency). That kind of tradeoff is too great to warrant imposing a preferential arrangement on the oil market.

Energy and Economic Development

The relationship between energy and economic development is a pervasive and complicated one, as discussed earlier. It is beyond the scope of this paper to engage in an extended discussion of this topic. The point to be made here, however, is that, given the impossibility of achieving energy self-sufficiency in a cost-effective manner in the countries of the region, economic development strategy must, while encouraging the most efficient use of energy, promote the country's ability to pay for the energy that it must continue to import. This means that the export sector of the economy must expand and diversify away from dependence on one or two primary earners of foreign exchange.

One of the major weaknesses in the countries of the region is energy-pricing policy. The real cost of energy is hidden from the consumer by domestic prices that are substantially below market levels. Although some countries, notably Jamaica and the Dominican Republic, have raised domestic energy prices, a sudden lifting of all controls on energy prices could seriously harm economies in the short run, and possibly cause, due to the economic dislocation that could follow, political problems.

This does not mean, however, that there is no alternative to extensive price controls. Even if a sudden freeing of prices is unwise, a system of differentiated prices could be established that motivates consumers and investors to make decisions in the direction of energy efficiency (or use of non-oil fuel sources) or that favor, directly or through rebates, key export industries (such as sugar cane or raw materials). Admittedly, such a system would require a stronger administrative apparatus than many of the countries now possess, and would entail the politically chancy task of picking economic winners and losers, but it also might ease the transition to eventual freeing of energy prices. An inflexible U.S. insistence on freeing energy prices immediately misses the point that such prices frequently cannot be freed overnight.

Any discussion like the one above is academic, however, if the economies of the industrial world do not recover. While intraregional trade must be promoted, the U.S. will remain the principal export market for many of the countries. Thus, U.S. economic policy must be just as important to the rate of economic growth in the Caribbean Basin as is energy pricing or other energy-related concerns.

CONCLUSIONS AND POLICY RECOMMENDATIONS

The linkage between energy and U.S. and Western interests vis-à-vis the Caribbean Basin is a very important one and will remain so regardless of whatever short-run weaknesses in price or market conditions may do to encourage the belief that concern over energy is a thing of the past. Both directly, in terms of supply, and indirectly, in terms of the impact of oil prices on the region's economies, energy constitutes an important strand in the web of U.S. interests in the region. What is clear, however, is that neither the emphasis of past administrations on supply issues and little else, nor the current one's belief in the ability of "market" solutions to take care of all but the most obviously national security-related issues provide an adequate policy framework for dealing with energy issues in the Caribbean Basin.

The discussion of the issues here leads to several conclusions that can serve as points of departure for U.S. policy:

The principal energy problem facing oil-import-dependent countries is that of paying for energy without mortgaging prospects for economic growth. However, rather than viewing this situation from an "energy policy" perspective, in which the problem is oil imports and the focus is on measures specific to the energy sector intended to reduce or eliminate oil imports, approaching the problem from a "balance-of-payments" perspective, in which the problems are serious current-account deficits and heavy external borrowing, emphasizes the necessary linkage between energy measures and macroeconomic policies intended to improve ability to pay for energy and generate formation of capital.

Continuation of oil supply from the region's oil exporters is strongly encouraged by market forces and the economic incentives these countries have to expand or maintain exports and be reliable suppliers.

U.S. capacity to influence and shape energy-related developments in the region is being challenged by the growing economic and political influence of Mexico and Venezuela, who are able to use energy relationships as diplomatic instruments, and by the important roles played by multilateral financial institutions in addressing the region's economic problems.

The soft oil market prevailing in early 1983 does not detract from the importance of the above. While lower oil prices offer some relief from balance-of-payments pressures, the impact of the 1978–1982 period, in which oil prices and foreign debt spiraled, lingers on. The permanency of this market softness is not assured, as the implications of economic recovery in the industrial countries and of the altered economic viability of alternate fuels and high-cost resources for future oil market behavior are not clear. Thus, a relaxation of U.S. concern due to the current softness of the oil market is not warranted.

Adoption of a balance-of-payments perspective toward energy problems in the Caribbean Basin provides a frame of reference for developing a U.S. policy position. This perspective suggests that efforts to lessen oil dependence in the energy sector must be viewed as part of a broader effort to bring the balance-of-payments and debt situations under control. Accordingly, U.S. policy on specific issues such as World Bank lending should be based on how those issues relate to the achievement of this objective.

The most immediate issue to arise in this regard is that of direct balance-of-payments assistance. Mexico and Venezuela already have established an oil-financing facility that has provided short-term balance-of-payments support. If this is to be something other than a subsidy, the long-term development aspect of the facility must be utilized. Existing U.S. balance-of-payments support through AID neatly complements this facility. Where additional U.S. activity can help is in discussing with officials of the two donor countries and officials of recipient countries how the facility can be better used for energy-development purposes.

The existence of the Mexican–Venezuelan facility, though, is by no means sufficient in itself to address the broader issue of balance-of-payments support, and how to bring balance of payments under control without aggravating the debt situation. As the Atlantic Council's Working Group on International Monetary Affairs has observed, a whole host of measures for dealing with international indebtedness are needed.[16] These measures must include steps entailing economic adjustment in debtor nations and augmenting IMF resources.

Lowered oil prices only partially ameliorate this situation. Ironically, lower oil prices may ease current-account pressures on importer countries while they simultaneously weaken Mexican and Venezuelan ability to maintain their facility. A sudden reversion to higher oil prices, however, could easily undermine measures intended to cope with debt. It is this indirect importance of energy—through the impact of oil prices on national economies and, in turn, on the stability of the international financial system—that energy may have its strongest impact on U.S. interests in the Caribbean Basin.

The adoption of a balance-of-payments perspective also provides a different focus on the resource-development/multilateral lending issue than the more traditional emphasis on oil import reduction allows. The benchmark for evaluating projects in oil importer states would not necessarily be how much oil they displace, but how they contribute to a process of bringing the balance of payments under control. In some instances, measures that do allow substitution of less expensive fuels for imported oil may make sense, such as conversion of electric utility boilers to coal or coal-water mixtures. Development of renewable sources, as well as more efficient utilization of energy, can be economically justified in many instances. In others, however, projects outside the energy sector that offer the prospect of new export items may be a more cost-effective measure. The point here is not to downgrade the importance of the energy sector, but to suggest that a wider net must be cast to capture the full range of potentially effective measures.

This view of the issue suggests that establishing a World Bank Energy Affiliate, if it leads the Bank to assume predominantly high-risk or low-payoff projects, or ones that simply involve the transfer of assets from one owner to another rather than creating new ones, might not represent good energy policy. By the same token, however, the view that multilateral banks should concentrate their resources on those areas where market dislocations prevent funding of otherwise worthwhile projects suggests that the Reagan administration's opposition to lending to the public sector and its belief that private-sector investment decisions accurately demonstrate the creditworthiness of a particular project are not good guides to policy. The U.S. government could make a more useful contribution if it were to place greater emphasis on finding more innovative ways in which public- and private-sector actors can work together to assure the most effective use of multilateral lending and to promote capital formation within recipient countries.

Simply viewing the World Bank and IADB as another set of windows dispensing loans is not going to have much beneficial impact on the economic situations of the recipient countries if all those countries do in the end is run up their debt. Greater attention should be given to carrying out projects without resort to debt. For example, a large and potentially cost-effective dent in oil consumption could be made if electric utility boilers were converted to coal, which, though still imported, would be cheaper than oil. A major obstacle to coal conversion in the past has been the capital cost of converting the boiler to use coal. New technologies producing coal-water mixtures (Atlantic Research's coal-water technology, Mitsubishi's M-coal technology) offer a way around this obstacle by avoiding or minimizing necessary changes to the boiler. The developers of these technologies, and/or coal suppliers (such as Colombia), could offer to make the necessary boiler modifications, at no up-front cost to the recipient country, in exchange for receiving a long-term fuel supply contract in which their costs incurred in the boiler modification could be recouped.

This is one potential example of how a major energy benefit could be obtained without resort to formal borrowing, and there may well be other alternatives to the conventional approach of forcing capital-strapped countries first to secure a loan for a project. The World Bank and IADB could then conserve their resources for areas where such alternatives are not feasible or fail to attract commercial interest. More innovative commercial arrangements might not develop without more official U.S. government encouragement and attention to such matters as ways to protect investments and contracts. Insistence on open investment opportunities for foreign (i.e., U.S.) direct investment will not be sufficient, however; considerable thought must be given to how public- and private-sector actors can work together, and with outside financial actors, to develop investment and capital formation.

There will still remain a legitimate and indispensable role for technical asssistance programs. The U.S. has considerable technical resources in its national laboratories that could be made available on a cost-free or low-cost basis to countries in the region. While using the labs in this way requires some redefinition in their missions, these resources are too impressive to be left unused.

U.S. technical assistance through AID could also be stepped up. Any major expansion of AID's technical assistance budget is unlikely, however. Despite the Reagan administration's preference for bilateral rather than multilateral programs, a multilateral R&D and training center established within the region—to which the U.S., Canada, Mexico, Venezuela, and other interested countries would contribute—could marshal greater and more diverse resources. The fact that its sponsorship and the thrust of its programs would be regional could both increase its effectiveness and lessen any sensitivities that the center could be used by any one country to promote its own commercial interests in the region. A major, if not the largest, component of the center's program would be training in such areas as program management and planning as well as more technical areas. Such a center ideally would focus its efforts not so much on developing new technologies as on how to better implement what is already available. This regional center could be supported by a regional network of national laboratories with relevant technical and analytical capabilities, which might be established for this purpose.

In contrast to the above area, where more rather than less U.S. policy attention is needed, supply security concerns appear to be less demanding of U.S. initiatives. This is one area where market forces, without additional encouragement from major new policy initiatives, have worked in the U.S.'s favor. The region's two principal oil suppliers have strong economic incentives to maintain or boost output and to be reliable suppliers. The authors believe that the bulk of the arguments weighs against trying to establish "special relationships" or to adopt other measures that would appear to treat the Caribbean as a privileged oil sanctuary for the U.S. Not only is it not clear that either Mexico or Venezuela would find the political implications of such an arrangement acceptable, it should also be recalled that some of the strongest friction in alliance relations has come when the U.S. has been perceived as attempting to decouple its strategic and security circumstances from those of its allies. Rather, diversification of supply can provide security at less diplomatic cost. Use of SPR contracts to maintain close oil relations with Mexico and Venezuela, and perhaps quiet negotiation of emergency supply measures, could complement diversification.

The third set of developments noted in this section—the growing challenge to U.S. influence in the region—is of potentially major importance. As other papers in this study have observed, U.S. ability to influence and unilaterally shape events in the Caribbean Basin is declining, and this is no less true of the energy sector than of the others. Both Mexico and Venezuela have used their positions as the region's chief oil suppliers to extend their diplomatic influence via supply and financial relationships. Oil revenues have provided them a means to employ economic instruments of foreign policy to stake out a role in the region's affairs much as the United States has its economic position. Moreover, Mexican and Venezuelan involvement in various peace initiatives in Central America reflect more activist regional foreign policies that likely could not be financially and diplomatically sustainable in the absence of their role as major oil suppliers. Whether soft oil prices and domestic economic distress will change this picture is not clear as yet. These factors may have the effect of forcing closer Mexican and Venezuelan coordination on oil price and production policies. What is clear, however, is that the energy sector has spawned developments with considerable diplomatic significance.

Acknowledging that influence in the region will be shared, and that other actors with interests that differ from or might be in actual conflict with U.S. interests, does not mean that the United States must accept the current trend. Even though it is not an oil supplier, the U.S. possesses major technical and service resources in the energy field that could be of considerable importance to the countries of the region. These resources could be used to maintain a U.S. presence in energy developments in the region and to use this presence to retain a considerable measure of diplomatic influence. U.S. architect-engineering and construction firms could play a vital role in the energy sectors of these countries, especially where major capital projects are involved. U.S. companies also have specific energy technologies to offer. An expansion of trade in energy technologies and services from the U.S. to the Basin region could offer the U.S. a counterbalance to the oil supply roles of Mexico and Venezuela.

For this trade to occur, however, industry and government must work more closely together to find ways of making such trade more acceptable within the region, and to find means of expanding such trade without simultaneously forcing these countries to borrow heavily to pay for U.S. goods and services. It is unlikely that the "market" will, by itself, magically produce this trade. There is a diplomatic dimension to this area that justifies U.S. government attention and encouragement. Less antipathy toward public-sector involvement on the other side and on throwing open the doors to U.S. investment would be a constructive measure in building a climate more conducive to trade expansion and cooperation.

NOTES

1. Franklin Tugwell, "Caribbean Energy Issues," Atlantic Council Energy Committee Issue Paper, 1981.
2. Inter-American Development Bank, *Economic and Social Progress in Latin America* (Washington, D.C., 1982), Chapter 2. Unless otherwise stated, all data on the economic performance of the region are taken from this report.
3. *Oil and Gas Journal,* January 31, 1983.
4. See "The IMF and Latin America: What Happens to the IMF if a Whole Continent Calls on It?" *The Economist* (December 11, 1982):69–76, and Robert Bond and Marlies Carruth, "Lending to Central America and the Caribbean," issue paper prepared for this study, March 1983.
5. For more on the issue of augmenting IMF resources, see the report of the Atlantic Council's Working Group on International Monetary Affairs, *The International Monetary System: Exchange Rates and International Indebtedness* (Washington, D.C.: The Atlantic Council, 1983).
6. World Bank, *Energy in the Developing Countries* (Washington, D.C., August 1980).
7. U.S. Government, Department of the Treasury, Office of the Assistant Secretary for International Affairs, *An Examination of the World Bank Energy Lending Program* (Washington, D.C., July 28, 1981).
8. Inter-American Development Bank, *Investment and Financing Requirements for Energy and Minerals in Latin America* (Washington, D.C., June 1981).
9. World Bank, *1982 Annual Report* (Washington, D.C., 1982), p. 90.
10. Theodore Moran, "Does the World Bank Belong in the Oil and Gas Business?" *Columbia Journal of International Business* (Spring 1982).
11. See Susan Kaufman Purcell (ed.), *Mexico–United States Relations, Academy of Political Science Proceedings* 34, 1 (1981); Laura Randall, "The Political Economy of Mexican Oil, 1976–1979," in Elihu Bergman et al. (eds.), *U.S.–Mexican Energy Relations* (Lexington, Mass.: Lexington Books, 1981).
12. International Energy Agency, *Constraints on International Trade in Coal* (Paris, 1982), p. 17.
13. Bond and Carruth, "Lending to Central America and the Caribbean."
14. Actually, the supply security theme can be traced back much further to Harold Ickes's idea in World War II of cultivating Saudi Arabia.
15. Richard Neustadt, *Alliance Politics* (New York: Columbia University Press, 1971).
16. Atlantic Council, *The International Monetary System.*

Chapter 8

Options for U.S. Policy in
the Caribbean Basin
in the 1980s

Sidney Weintraub

Prescription in this case is more difficult than analysis, as a result of inconsistencies and discontinuities. For example, poverty and unemployment in Caribbean Basin countries stimulate emigration, but then so does a modest increase in incomes and native skills and in the health and nutritional position of potential migrants. Countries in social turmoil are ripe for government takeovers, but systemic change is less apt to follow grinding poverty in developing countries than it is economic growth and unsatisfied aspirations. There is no substitute for exports of goods and services by small economies in which these exports often constitute upwards of 50 percent of GNP, but new investment necessary to accomplish this is often thwarted by wages that are high and productivity that is low by world standards or by civil war, which dampens the ardor of investors. Increased foreign aid can amplify resources for development, but it cannot always replace the domestic capital that is fleeing the countries. Small markets can be augmented modestly by regional integration with other countries with small markets, but this is often frustrated by unequal benefits from integration and the demands of nationalism, which can be intense. Preferential opening of the U.S. market for regional goods that must now overcome high tariffs or nontariff barriers can make some contribution to employment and foreign exchange availability, but the reality is that the United States is loath to open its market fully for products in which the concession might be significant. National tax holidays attract foreign investment, marginally if other conditions are correct, but the end of the holiday often leads to departure for another place with a new tax holiday.

In other words, glib "solutions" are illusory. One can work at the amelioration of political, social, and economic problems in Caribbean Basin countries, but accomplishment will not be complete and could even be perverse. The underlying objective circumstances are complex and not amenable to treatment by slogans. Even the state of theory is inadequate to permit discussion with full assurance about approaches. Should the emphasis be on absorption in manufacturing of surplus labor, like the Puerto Rican model, in which much labor was not absorbed? Should it be on the development of agriculture, despite its limited potential for employment generation? Should it be on the further development of export markets for countries that often have little to offer other than proximity? Should it be on the elaboration of more tourist facilities, which foster deep social divisions and use female labor more extensively than male? Obviously a combination of these sometimes contradictory approaches is needed and the emphasis will depend on the place.

U.S. actions toward the region must address this ambiguity. This paper is concerned with the options for U.S. policy toward the Caribbean Basin, not in each fundamental area, since these are covered in other chapters in this book, but in terms of overall approaches. The paper seeks first to delineate the objectives of U.S. policy toward the region and to determine whether these objectives coincide with those of the countries of the region and other national actors. It will then focus on policy options to achieve these objectives, or more precisely, to approach achievement. The conclusion will give a personal view on the most desirable policies.

OBJECTIVES OF U.S. POLICY

Reasonable people can differ on the priorities of different U.S. objectives, and the ordering will affect the prescription. If the highest priority is to secure or maintain friendly (or not unfriendly) regimes in power, this can lead to the interventionism that characterizes current U.S. policy in El Salvador, the reluctance to intervene for many years during the Somoza regime in Nicaragua, or the uncertainty that is reflected in U.S. actions toward Guatemala. This priority explains the substantial public financial and moral support given to Edward Seaga's government in Jamaica in order to prevent a return to power of Michael Manley or a reasonable facsimile. In other words, intervention and nonintervention, support for democratically elected governments and for dictatorships, and backing of military and civilian regimes are all consistent with this priority. The exact policy chosen depends on the circumstance and only rhetorically on "abstractions" like democracy, nonintervention, and self-determination. The narrow definition of security can be phrased differently: to deny the region to the Soviet Union for whatever purpose it may have; to keep open sea-lanes, including the Panama Canal; to prevent the spread of "more" Cubas, Nicaraguas, or Grenadas. This is stated crassly in the interest of clarity.

If security is thought of more broadly to encompass not only the existence of friendly regimes, but also many aspects of social justice in the countries of the region, the policy outcome could be quite different. In the case of Guatemala, for example, the narrower definition presumably would call for support of the current regime and the broader—that which equates U.S. security with some concern for social justice—could call for the continued withholding of this support, or for conditioning it on policy changes. (In practice today the United States wavers between the two approaches. We have not made up our mind whether to think broadly or narrowly.) The broad definition presumably would lead to greater financial support for Costa Rica than for El Salvador and more for the Dominican Republic than for Haiti. Whether the definition is broad or narrow, however, the precise U.S. policy is not foreordained but follows from circumstance. Policy under the broader definition also could involve intervention (such as to foster more social justice) or nonintervention, and it could be indifferent to the military or civilian nature of the regime.

It does not necessarily follow that greater social justice is more conducive to political stability than the highly unequal distribution of income and of health, education, and other services. Mexico has been politically stable for half a century despite great inequalities and current instability follows on efforts to increase output and, to some extent, equality. Giving the highest priority to security writ broadly is based primarily on faith, that justice in the long term leads to greater stability than injustice even though short-term turmoil might be increased.

The policy choice is not clarified if the primary objective selected is to curtail the immigration flow to the United States. One need only rehearse the reasons why people emigrate to see this. Civil war leads to emigration, as illustrated by the increased flow of people from El Salvador and elsewhere in Central America. But an end to the fighting would not necessarily lead to an end in the large-scale emigration, since that would depend on which side wins and on whether it effectively seeks to seal the border.

Emigration from Mexico and countries in the Caribbean is brought on by many factors—such as kinship, the establishment of ethnic diasporas from prior immigration, and habits of emigration built up in particular areas—but primarily by the emigrants' desire to earn more money and thereby satisfy their lifetime economic and career aspirations. We are now sowing the seeds of future immigration from Central America as Salvadoran, Nicaraguan, Guatemalan, and other diasporas are being fed by new immigrants. A recurrent phenomenon in these countries is that the majority of immigrants are not the fully unemployed but rather those who already have shown some upward mobility and seek more. The creation of slightly more opportunity in these countries can be expected, for a time at least, to lead to even increased emigration. If the Caribbean Basin Initiative (CBI) becomes law and is successful, the investment stimulated will be largely in assembly plants, creating jobs mostly for women, and this could further stimulate the exodus of men. There is evidence of precisely this outcome from the growth of assembly plants on the U.S.-Mexican border.

This is an example of where the instinctively logical policy, that of creating more job opportunities within the region itself, might have the desired long-term outcome but a contrary short-term result. There may be no short-term U.S. policy to accomplish the objective of curtailed immigration other than an employer-penalty program and/or more stringent border (land and sea) security—and there is no assurance that these policies would succeed.

One of these three objectives (security defined narrowly, security defined broadly, curtailment of immigration), each related in some way to U.S. security, would surely be at the top of the listing of priorities of U.S. officials. Most other objectives are different ways of stating these themes or are instrumental in their attainment. It would, for example, be in the U.S. interest if Caribbean Basin countries were to achieve substantial, sustained economic growth. This would increase opportunities for U.S. exports to the region and might have other desirable effects. As incomes grow, population increases tend to decline, and, over time (generations, not decades), this might reduce the pressure to emigrate to the United States. If one subscribes to the broad definition of U.S. security interests, income growth is a necessary condition for the improvement of social justice. If this income were reasonably equitably distributed, this would be even more desirable.

The United States, in addition to maximizing its exports to the region, wishes to have unimpeded commercial access to the strategic raw materials found in the region, particularly oil, bauxite, and nickel. This access does not necessarily require friendly regimes, but friendship may ease commercial negotiation.

These secondary objectives should not be overstated. They are of some significance in U.S. relations with Mexico, still important but less so for relations with Colombia and Venezuela, and marginal for the rest. The total population of the countries that would benefit directly from the CBI is about 40 million, much of it impoverished and insubstantial as a market. On the other hand, 40 million people with a median age of about sixteen is a substantial source of immigration into the United States.

As the dominant power, the United States has a deep concern about avoiding internal conflict and disputes between regional countries. Conflict stimulates emigration. It also has a contagion effect, some of this undoubtedly stimulated from outside the country, as we have seen in Central America. Nevertheless, it is clear from U.S. behavior that conflict avoidance, as important as it is in the abstract, is subordinate to maintaining friendly regimes. U.S. behavior has amply demonstrated that while we seek stability in the region, we seek regime compatibility even more. Perhaps we should not. This is a legitimate issue for discussion: have we correctly defined our priorities?

The United States, if it were to so choose, could define its security interest in the region as protecting the physical security of the United States and preventing Mexico from falling under the domination of an actively hostile regime. For the rest, one could argue that neutrality is sufficient. The objectives in this case would be for Cuba to refrain from exporting revolution, for Nicaragua to keep its philosophy and its arms at home, for the U.S. to be indifferent to the nature of the Salvadoran government as long as it confines its governing to its own territory, for Grenada to have preached whatever it wished as long as it did so at home, and—this is important—for none of them to provide a base for offensive military action by the Soviet Union. If our objectives were defined in this manner, U.S. policy in the region would be less ideological and probably less interventionist. It is hard to say whether it would be more effective in achieving the basic security interest of the United States. Cuba exports its philosophy not as a reaction to U.S. behavior but out of conviction and, presumably, out of encouragement from the Soviet Union.

Our objective is not defined this way, at least not in practice although it is rhetorically (in fact, U.S. policy toward Cuba was so defined during the Kennedy administration after the Bay of Pigs), and one must ask why. One reason has to do with domestic politics. The "loss" of Cuba has been an issue in presidential campaigns. So has been the fact that Nicaragua was "another" Cuba. Domestic politics have not thus far permitted a benign U.S. approach to the attitudes of other countries in the Caribbean Basin. It is not clear, either, that we could assure that Soviet intrusion into the region would not follow from a more tolerant U.S. attitude toward countries that were pro-Soviet in behavior, or that individual countries would alter their meddlesome behavior.

One should ask three other questions in setting U.S. objectives: What are the domestic constraints to objectives as presently defined? How consistent are these objectives with those of other regional countries? How consistent with those of non–Caribbean Basin countries?

The domestic constraints to achieving current U.S. objectives are formidable. Initially, the tax aspects of the CBI were hardly even considered by the Congress; the preference seemed to be to "forget them quietly." The trade portion of the CBI was not enacted until August 1983 because there was concern about giving duty-free access to less than 15 percent of the imports from the proposed beneficiary countries that were dutiable. Duties are high on these products precisely to protect domestic industry and labor (including, in many cases, industry and labor in Puerto Rico and the U.S. Virgin Islands). Even as proposed by the administration, textiles and apparel were excluded from the one-way free-trade concept (although there was an indication that regional countries would be given larger quotas at the expense of Asian countries). When pressure arose from domestic sugar interests, this took priority over the interests of CBI beneficiary countries. The CBI Congress approved limited the trade benefits of the initiative as was originally proposed. What we have learned, and then tend to relearn every few years, is that trade is the hard option and aid the soft one. There are aid constraints as well, but these did not prevent supplementary appropriations for the CBI, whereas the trade and tax incentives were delayed and watered down.

A similar fate befell immigration legislation in the 97th Congress. The diverse groups that opposed one or another aspect of the proposed legislation kept it from coming to a vote on the floor of the House. Even though we talk of limiting immigration as a first-order objective of the United States, it is not clear how fervently we (those who make decisions for the country) really believe this. The recurrent inability to enact legislation that would seek to curtail illegal entry is evidence of this. Various groups have higher priorities: cheap labor; concern about civil rights of Hispanic Americans; avoidance of complicating Mexico's unemployment/underemployment problem; and others.

The record of U.S. action, now and as far back in the past as one looks, is that the only objective in the Caribbean Basin that can usually override other objectives, particularly domestic ones, is the narrow security consideration. The United States has shown its willingness to act to achieve this objective in the Dominican Republic, Cuba, and now in Central America. By contrast, the United States has been inconsistent in its resolve when it came to achievement of the broader security objective or the curtailment of immigration from the region.

There is both congruence and inconsistency in objectives as viewed from the countries of the Caribbean Basin and from the United States. The United States has an interest in facilitating economic growth in the region, but the objective is subordinate or instrumental for the U.S.; it is primordial for the countries of the region. (Data on the economic performance of the countries in the region are provided in other papers in this project.) This difference in priorities is what one would expect. It is a reflection of the difference between foreign policy, which it is for the United States, and domestic policy, which it is for the regional countries. There is an asymmetry in repercussions from domestic policies. Because of scale, domestic policies in most other regional countries have a minor impact on the United States, whereas U.S. domestic policy has a major effect on them.

Something similar can be said for security. Each country looks to its own security. The real incongruities of the respective security interests are those of scale and responsibility. Other countries of the Caribbean Basin look to the United States for security support. This is true even of Mexico, as witness its relatively low military expenditures. The United States looks to the other regional countries for support only in the sense that it wishes sealanes open and seeks bases in some of them. The threats are quite different. The word "security" is the same, but that is all.

One objective on which there is clear inconsistency is immigration; the United States seeks curtailment and other regional countries would prefer expansion, or more realistically, maintenance of the current situation. (This is true with respect to migration to the United States. Other Caribbean Basin countries find themselves in a position similar to that of the United States when it comes to immigration from Colombia; the Dominican Republic, where immigration from Haiti hovers as a threat; and Mexico, which does not welcome immigration from Central America.) The inconsistency is on the objective and not on the reality of policy, since while the United States debates immigration limitation, it has done nothing substantial to accomplish this (although some legislation, replete with loopholes, is probable in 1984).

For the rest, whether there is consensus or dissonance depends on the circumstances of the situation. Governments of other Caribbean Basin countries seek stability, just as the United States does for them, but large groups in many of the countries do not. The United States seeks friendly governments, and for the most part the other countries also seek friendship with the United States, but on their terms. The difference can sometimes be vitriolic, as in U.S.–Mexican relations, but often not serious. Other Caribbean Basin countries would, in the abstract, prefer nonintervention in their internal affairs by the United States, but there are times, in practice, when intervention is sought. This is true today of the government in El Salvador and was true in 1978 in the Dominican Republic when President Carter spoke up to assure the legitimate transfer of the presidency to Antonio Guzmán after his election.

The CBI is a good example of a case where objectives mesh. They mesh largely because the initiative involves nonreciprocal concessions granted by the United States to promote development, which is the highest priority for the other regional countries, and because the initiative could promote the maintenance in power of friendly governments, which is the highest priority for the United States. The main fly in the CBI ointment is that domestic U.S. considerations overrode many external U.S. priorities in the final shaping of the legislation.

The CBI is also a good illustration of the similarities and differences of objectives of the United States and the middle-income countries of the region. Multilateralism was achieved in the initiative by mutual agreement that Canada, Colombia, Mexico, and Venezuela would pursue their own initiatives in the Caribbean Basin and that the collectivity of actions would be called "multilateralism." Each of these other donor countries would like the area to remain tranquil. Each would benefit from reasonable economic growth in the region. On these points, objectives dovetail. On the other hand, Canada is interested primarily in its trade with the region, especially in the Caribbean; so is the United States, but this has a lower priority. Mexico is interested in economic relations, but also in the avoidance of contamination from instability in the area. This conforms with U.S. objectives. Mexico, however, sees the best chance to avoid instability by maintaining good relations with regimes with which the United States has had bad relations, namely, Cuba, Nicaragua, and even the dissident groups of El Salvador. The objectives of the two countries are similar, but the prescriptions are diverse. This, in part, reflects different internal situations in Mexico and the United States. This has been a source of friction between the two countries, but the similarity of objectives should permit a more friendly discourse than has existed in the past.

The Venezuelan and Colombian positions are, in some respects, similar to that of Mexico in that they share the U.S. objective of tranquility and growth but not necessarily the U.S. anti-Communist ardor or the U.S. conception of the proper diplomacy for dealing with unfriendly regimes. They have not been as vigorous as Mexico in voicing this disagreement, although the intensity of their disagreement with the United States has heightened recently.

The objectives of other actors deserve mention, but they are less significant than those of the regional countries (the United States, the middle-income countries, and the beneficiaries of the CBI) since their interests are less involved. Most West European countries have a modest commercial interest in the region, and probably would prefer tranquility and stability to turbulence, but the issue is of no great consequence to them. They have a tendency to transfer their domestic political contests to the region by furthering socialism or Christian democracy. Their views are shaped more by their own domestic politics than by any responsibility for events in the region. Cuba is far away and they obviously do not share the U.S. obsession with the actions of the Castro government. They tend to be critical of U.S. policy, even if not necessarily of U.S. objectives, but it is mostly the criticism of kibitzers rather than actors.

The non–Caribbean Basin Latin American countries have been minor actors in the region. They care about what happens in the region to the extent that it might affect them (for example, a spread of Castro's influence might eventually affect them and they prefer that this not take place), but they generally assume that they will not be affected. They will support the CBI in general terms—since it is hard to object to aid to sister countries—but may object if and when U.S. trade preferences to Caribbean Basin countries adversely affect their exports (and, indeed, some objections have been forthcoming, for example, with respect to sugar policy in the administration proposal). One should expect some clamor by other Latin American countries for the extension to them of U.S. special trade preferences if preferences to Caribbean Basin beneficiary countries should become meaningful.

Consequently, for purposes of making policy, U.S. objectives must be ordered in importance and assessed on the basis of their realism. They must be analyzed in terms of congruence with the wishes of other regional countries and, to a minor extent, with the wishes of nonregional countries.

The key U.S. regional objective is security. Security is best defined broadly. This definition is consistent with the objectives of other regional countries. The shortcoming with this definition is that it does not always conform to other U.S. priorities. When the security objective broadly conceived cannot be carried out because of domestic constraints, the fallback is to focus on the U.S. security objective more narrowly defined. The CBI aims at the larger vision, but U.S. action in El Salvador, Guatemala, and other places makes clear that U.S. policy simultaneously pursues the narrower objective.

The other major objective, the curtailment of immigration, is consonant with the larger vision of U.S. security over the long term, but less so or hardly at all over the short term. The narrower vision of the U.S. security interest, to maintain friendly regimes almost regardless of other consequences, is unrelated to the immigration objective. When pursuing the security objective leads to internal strife, immigration to the United States tends to increase; when societies are tranquil, the motivations for migration to the United States are the familiarly complex ones of pull-push, kinship, and the aspirations of adventurous human beings.

U.S. POLICY OPTIONS

Certain activities will follow their own pattern with only minor influence coming from the broad U.S. policy approach. Traders will try to maximize their exports or imports within most policy frameworks. Investors will take advantage of whatever comparative advantage a particular place offers, whether this be wages, proximity, or availability of raw materials. The tourist potential of the region is being developed based primarily on natural attractions, such as sun, sand, and clear water. In each of these functional areas, however, policy can have some effect, usually marginal but sometimes absolute, as when the United States imposes a trade embargo. The CBI proposals are intended to enhance trade and U.S. and other foreign investment, just as local tax holidays are designed to attract investment to create employment and exports. A legitimate issue is whether the United States, by its policy measures, should try to influence the natural (market) flow of goods, capital, and services.

One option is for the United States to be nonactivist in its economic policy toward the region. This policy is consistent with providing foreign aid for development and security purposes (although we now tend to overdo the security aid and give less attention to the development aspect), just as such aid is provided elsewhere, but not to seek to prefer the region in trade and tax policy, or to seek direct foreign investment where it would not naturally go without a U.S. government incentive.

The main argument for this policy is that activism is distorting and may be disadvantageous. Any number of examples can be given to support this contention. The Overseas Private Investment Corporation (OPIC) has supported an ultra-luxury hotel in Haiti; the provision of sugar quotas established a syndrome of lobbying venality in the United States and probably delayed economic diversification in regional countries; an assembly plant set up in one island is often at the expense of one in some other nearby place just as important for U.S. interests; the degree of U.S. direct investment has, at times, been so overbearing as to stimulate anti-Americanism, as occurred in various places in Central America, Cuba, and perhaps even in Jamaica under the Manley regime. Trade or investment preferences theoretically prefer the country but in actuality may benefit the U.S. investor or trader even more, leading to local hostility rather than gratitude.

In addition, resentments can be created elsewhere, as in countries whose goods face discrimination in the U.S. market; or in Puerto Rico, which will lose its own preferences to the extent they are shared; or in Asia, which is asked to export less apparel to the United States so that Caribbean Basin countries can export more. The essence of a preference is that it must discriminate, and the more it discriminates, the more valuable it is. Preferences do not normally disappear (although U.S. trade preferences for Cuba and the Philippines did), but become vested; or, as is now happening to Puerto Rico and the Virgin Islands, preferences are diluted by spreading them more widely in a new phase of U.S. activism.

This nonpreferential, nonactivist economic option may (or may not) have validity over the long run, but it is mostly academic for now; the Reagan administration has chosen the path of preferring the Caribbean Basin in its economic policy and has promised to persist in obtaining the necessary legislation. This, then, is a second broad option, which is the current proposed policy, to prefer the region in U.S. economic policy. The administration has made its case for this choice. The proposed policy is based on the belief that preferential trade and tax-induced investment will help create jobs and economic opportunity in beneficiary countries and that this is consistent with the broad definition of U.S. security (that poverty and joblessness breed insurrection)—and that this job creation should help stanch migration from the region to the United States.

What we are now witnessing is a phase in U.S. policy, possibly one that will be durable but (based on past experience) probably will not be, premised on the conviction that peaceful change in the region, under friendly governments, requires economic hope as much as military suppression of dissidence. On a more modest scale, it is the same philosophy that motivated the Alliance for Progress.

The first option listed, nonactivism in the economic sphere, is apt to be associated with a narrowly defined security policy, and the second, preferential economic treatment for the region, with a broader definition of U.S. security policy. This, however, is oversimplification. The United States can be more or less activist in direct security policy under either economic option. The United States can prefer the region economically but otherwise avoid security involvement, or it can be nonactivist economically and activist in a security sense. The latter has been the thrust of U.S. policy until the CBI, to treat the region economically as it treats other regions (or treats the rest of Latin America), but to provide substantial security assistance in Central America and modest security assistance (which is all that is needed at present) in the Caribbean. The CBI adds double activism, in economic as well as security matters, on the thesis that the two are indissoluble.

A third policy option would be to sever the direct security and economic connection in a way different from that chosen by the Reagan administration; this would be a policy of economic preference (that is, the CBI approach), but nonactivism in direct security matters unless there is palpable invasion from an outside source. This policy would be similar to that advocated by and practiced by Mexico, to provide economic assistance and preference to the region, but then allow each government to deal with its dissidents itself, including coalitions when necessary (as in El Salvador). The attraction of this option is that it does not involve the United States in conflicts over which it has no control in any event and, if in Central America, in a region distant enough not to pose a direct threat to the United States. The difficulties of this option are that it is hard to determine how much of any dissidence is home-grown and how much is stimulated and abetted from the outside, and that a U.S. policy of tolerance of nonfriendly regimes could lead to their replication. Dominant powers do not live graciously with unfriendly regimes on their border or nearby. As indicated earlier, this policy option may also be inconsistent with domestic U.S. political reality.

The comparison with Mexican policy is also distorting. Mexico can rely on the United States to maintain a security umbrella—and in this sense can be a free rider—while the reverse is not true.

Under this schema, there are four possible option combinations: security activism and economic activism; security activism and economic nonactivism; security nonactivism and economic activism; and security nonactivism and economic nonactivism. It bears repeating that security nonactivism need not preclude modest military sales or other military assistance, but would not involve the placement of military advisors or the encouragement of a significant military buildup with U.S. security and economic assistance. Similarly, economic nonactivism need not preclude concessionary development assistance, but would not involve preferential trade and tax concessions to beneficiary countries in the Caribbean Basin not generalized to other developing countries. Each of the four policy options can, under certain circumstances, serve the U.S. security objective, and it is a matter of judgment which does it best under specific circumstances. The judgment behind the CBI and actual U.S. behavior in the region is that the combination of security and economic activism is best calculated to meet the broadly defined U.S. security objective in Central America, but that the coupling of security nonactivism and economic activism is preferable in the Caribbean where the local security threat is different. Except for Costa Rica, the Central American republics can fairly be defined as security states, mostly of their own doing but with a contribution from the United States, whereas the Caribbean republics and territories, with exceptions (Haiti in particular), tend to be democracies that expend little of their national output on security.

Within whatever broad framework(s) is (are) chosen, policy must obviously be differentiated by country to reflect local circumstances. The nature of the country differentiation, however, will be greatly influenced by the overall approach. If the Central American approach were made the same as that in the Caribbean (that is, security nonactivism and economic activism), U.S. behavior in El Salvador would be radically different from what it is. Similarly, if the United States had chosen economic nonactivism, there would be no CBI, at least not in its currently proposed form.

Looking at policy as it now seems to be, some of the country consequences are as follows. A military buildup is supported in El Salvador and Honduras, and this is abetted by substantial economic assistance. Because of the conflict in El Salvador, other aspects of economic activism (tax and trade concessions) are unlikely to have any immediate impact, even if instituted. We are moving to a similar position in Guatemala after withholding military assistance for many years on the grounds of human rights. What this signifies, in the framework set up in this paper, is that we are moving in Guatemala from security nonactivism to activism. The primacy of the narrow definition of security in actual U.S. policy has led to a successive curtailment of economic and political relations with Nicaragua. If U.S. policy were instead to favor a broader definition of security encompassing social and economic as well as security and political considerations, this policy could be different, although within limits, depending on how different the Nicaraguan regime would permit it to be. Much the same could be said for Cuba, where there is a tendency to wax hot and cold on the nature of the relationship depending on the fashion in the U.S. administration and on Cuban behavior.

As one looks at Caribbean countries, the differences in broad policy approach has led to distinct U.S. actions. Modest security assistance is granted, such as to facilitate better communications among the islands, or to provide patrol boats for surveillance of coastal areas, but the emphasis is on economic activism. The CBI is really a mishmash in that it permits large-scale economic assistance to Central American countries but with little expectation that most of them will benefit, at present, from the other preferential measures and modest development assistance to most Caribbean islands in the hope that they will benefit from the non-aid economic aspects of the CBI. Jamaica is an exception in the Caribbean; because of the U.S. preoccupation with having friendly regimes nearby, the public economic assistance being granted is substantial and the U.S. government has attempted to activate the private sector to invest heavily (with modest success to date).

Economic activism in relations with unequal countries inevitably involves the granting of nonreciprocal concessions by the United States. The *quid pro quo* is intangible; it is the hope that the concessions will enhance chances for achievement of U.S. objectives, however they are defined. In the U.S. policy process, the granting of economic concessions comes in spurts: the Alliance for Progress, focusing mostly on aid on the U.S. side, and then nothing for more than a decade; the establishment of a Caribbean aid group under World Bank auspices, designed to involve others in the aid process, and then the establishment of a similar but less meaningful aid group for Central America under the aegis of the Inter-American Development Bank; and, now, the CBI. There is little consistency in the conduct of U.S. policy toward the region; it alternates between neglect, security activism, and a search for concessions to grant.

Granting concessions turns out to be excruciatingly difficult because of the variety of needs among countries of the Caribbean Basin (a potpourri of concessions is thus required) and the constraints imposed by domestic considerations in the United States. The domestic constraints are not equal at all times. It is harder to grant a trade or tax concession during a recession than during a period of relatively full employment in the United States. Aid appropriations are particularly difficult to obtain when budget deficits are as large as they are now. In other words, U.S. policymakers must seize their moments, when the external threat seems greatest (which motivated the Marshall Plan, the Alliance for Progress, and the CBI), and when the domestic conditions are most propitious. This process may be inevitable. The United States (and other countries as well) has a tendency to make policy from crisis. When crises were perceived to exist in Central America and the Caribbean which would have repercussions on the United States (that is, there was a concern about U.S. security and a fear of immigrant inflow, a fear aggravated by the high level of domestic unemployment), then U.S. policymakers were galvanized into action. They consulted widely, at home and abroad, and the CBI was the result.

This is a haphazard process that sometimes works and sometimes does not. This process accepts that the official U.S. attention span on the Caribbean Basin will be limited to the perceived crisis of the moment. A proper question to ask, therefore, is whether the policy process could be improved.

One technique that might accomplish this is to establish a continuing framework to include all the countries of the Caribbean Basin, from Canada south to northern South America, under whose auspices policymakers from capitals would meet at established intervals for functional discussions and perhaps once a year for an overall *tour d'horizon* of relations and problems in the Caribbean Basin. This suggestion borrows from other models, such as the structure set up under the Lomé agreement between the European Community and the African–Caribbean–Pacific countries, the Organization for European Economic Cooperation under the Marshall Plan, and the wise men and the country review process under the Alliance for Progress. The continuing interaction could avoid the frenzy that now exists when a new proposal is felt to be necessary, and it permits gradual rather than radical adaptation to changing circumstance. An advantage of such an arrangement is that it can force policy change at all times by lengthening the attention span of U.S. policymakers; they must pay attention for each upcoming meeting. Its disadvantage is precisely the same; it forces periodic attention on the Caribbean Basin when policymakers might prefer to pay attention to some other area.

Another aspect of such an arrangement is that it would bring an organized discussion among the more developed and middle-income countries of the region (Canada, Colombia, Mexico, Venezuela, and the United States), which now takes place mostly bilaterally and sporadically.

It is now conventional wisdom that the United States must pay more attention in its policy process to its own immediate region. It is a wisdom stimulated by crisis and which may not therefore be durable. When a crisis is believed to exist, the instinctive U.S. response is to act, and action takes essentially security or economic form. The action will continue as long as the crisis continues, but usually not much longer. The procedural suggestion made here is designed to force some consistency in U.S. attention to its immediate region. For this reason, I would like to stress this approach as being better suited for the long term than one that seeks to grant economic and military concessions deemed sufficient unto the moment.

CONCLUSIONS

In the preceding section, the various security-economic policy options were presented in what was intended to be (mostly) neutral fashion. This section provides personal opinion.

It is fallacious to provide assurance of outcomes from particular policies. It does not follow that security activism inevitably fails or succeeds. Either outcome is possible, depending on the local circumstances and, to some extent, on the vigor of the U.S. action. It is not clear in the abstract whether U.S. objectives are best achieved by intervention or nonintervention. In the case of U.S. intervention in the Dominican Republic in 1965, for example, partisans of one view or the other can point to subsequent events to justify the conclusion they prefer.

It is not possible to prove that special U.S. economic concessions will accelerate growth in other Caribbean Basin countries, or whether these countries are more likely to prosper when initiatives must come from them. Nor is it possible to demonstrate that economic growth enhances stability over the short run (the evidence is just the opposite for developing countries) and thereby improves the U.S. security position with respect to its neighbors. Examples can be provided of poverty-based stability and growth-based instability, and vice versa.

With respect to immigration, people come from all kinds of countries—democracies, dictatorships, and those in between. People come from deeply impoverished countries (Haiti), middle-income countries (Mexico), and those in between. Immigration expands when conditions in the sending country deteriorate, as is now (1983–1984) taking place in immigration from Mexico, and when sending-country economies are prospering, as occurred during the 1960s and 1970s from Mexico.

Choices, therefore, stem largely from philosophy about the kinds of neighbors we want to have and the type of country we ourselves want to be. I wish here to provide my own outlook.

The problem with the narrowly defined security objective is that it is a short-term objective and when the domestic stability it induces or the dictatorial governments it frequently helps keep in power collapse, the shifts in domestic attitudes toward the United States can be profound. This was the outcome in Cuba and Nicaragua. As a longer-term proposition, therefore, there seems to me to be no substitute for the more broadly based definition of U.S. security that involves U.S. concern for economic growth and social justice in Caribbean Basin countries and a preference for popular participation over authoritarianism. The U.S. influence on accomplishing these results should not be overstated, but neither should the U.S. influence in the Caribbean Basin be denigrated.

One shortcoming with this long-term proposition often is the lack of short-term choice open to the United States. Long-term friendship with the Sandinistas in Nicaragua may turn out to be impossible due to their philosophy and actions. It probably was worth the gamble made by the Carter administration to provide concessional balance-of-payments assistance to the new regime shortly after it assumed power in Nicaragua. That did not work out for various reasons. Castro, once he assumed power, may have had no interest in friendly relations with the United States, but the question of his intent is, at best, murky because of antagonistic U.S. actions. My belief remains, however, that U.S. security interests in the Caribbean Basin are enhanced over time, and occasionally even in the short run, when security is defined broadly—even though I must admit that this policy cannot be followed in all situations.

This implies a U.S. concern with development and U.S. economic policy can be either preferential, as is the intention under the CBI, or not. I confess a sense of deep uncertainty, but I am leery of the preferential approach. It reinforces U.S. dominance in the region (it does what George Washington recommended in his Farewell Address that the young United States should not do in "neither seeking nor granting exclusive favors or preferences"), although this may just recognize reality. It invites complaints from those being discriminated against. It could result, to give just one example, in *maquiladora* moving from Mexico to beneficiary CBI countries to take advantage of U.S. preferences, and this is hardly an outcome to be desired. It is not at all clear how significant the results of trade preferences are likely to be. Econometric analysis is not precise, but it suggests that exports from beneficiary Caribbean Basin countries would increase by about 1 percent over what they otherwise would be without preferences. This conclusion is reinforced by the restrictions the Congress is likely to place on preferential imports (as with the CBI). This is a small benefit for what could turn out to be a wholesale departure from past U.S. trade policy.

The preferences are made necessary in part because of U.S. import restrictions and high tariffs on many products of great export interest to beneficiary Caribbean Basin nations; these barriers exist for textiles, apparel, shoes, certain types of tobacco, rum, certain fruits and vegetables, and other products. This is a trade policy that seeks to grant with one hand what is taken away with the other, and the combination is defined as a concession. Given domestic constraints, this may be the best the United States can do. It may be that the estimates of the trade that would be generated from preferences under the CBI are vastly understated. In other words, there may be no viable alternative to trade preferences to foster development and job creation in Caribbean Basin countries, but I am not convinced that this is the case.

The tax benefits proposed under the CBI are comparable to the trade preferences. They also are designed to induce U.S. investment based on the proposition that this will create jobs, possibly create good will for the United States, and inhibit emigration. The analysis of the tax aspects takes much the same form as that for trade preferences, plus an additional consideration, that it is hard to demonstrate that investors will choose a foreign location in a developing country primarily because of U.S. tax concessions on top of the tax holidays granted directly by the CBI beneficiary countries. (My own view is that all these countries would be better off if none of them gave tax holidays.)

One must also raise questions about the implicit model on which the CBI is based. This is that special trade and tax inducements will lead to the creation of durably viable industries and, eventually, to lower immigration into the United States. The evidence from other preferential schemes, such as those under the Lomé convention and even to Puerto Rico by the United States, is not reassuring. Under Lomé, viable industries were established in those places where it was viable to do so regardless of trade preferences. Puerto Rico must still rely on large-scale emigration and aid (such as food stamps) to sustain the model. The Puerto Rican results, in other words, have been mixed; per capita incomes have been raised (but then U.S. concessions are vastly more extensive than those proposed for CBI beneficiary countries), but the other tensions of the type that the CBI is designed to moderate remain in full force.

My own preference would be for a model that does not rely on preferred economic treatment from the United States for Caribbean Basin countries that would have to continue indefinitely, and regarding which vested interests would become deeply entrenched, because there will come a time when these preferences either will cease or will have to be expanded because they lost whatever earlier vigor they had. My preference, as stated earlier, is for a consultative mechanism that would help sustain U.S. attention on the region over the long term and that would lead to regular, gradual modifications in U.S. policy as opposed to dramatic and usually overblown initiatives.

The aid distribution under the CBI demonstrates the priority for the narrow conception of security (because of the focus on trouble spots in Central America) over the broader definition. Most Caribbean countries will receive modest amounts of aid under the initiative. As with trade policy, this distribution probably reflects the political and budgetary reality in the United States, even though I would prefer more developmental aid in the total.

My own choice of broad policy approach, then, would be for less security activism (less, not none) and less economic activism, that is, eschewing of preferences in favor of nonpreferential trade liberalization (which I recognize may be unrealistic in the current U.S. situation) and an expansion of development assistance, especially during the current rough situation in the world economy. The most significant contribution the United States can make to economic growth in the Caribbean Basin is to run its own economy better, with lower interest rates and higher, more sustained economic growth. Trade preferences pale in importance compared with this.

I do not believe that any of the security-economic options available to the United States will affect immigration over at least the next ten to twenty years. They may inhibit immigration further out in time if development programs help to dampen population growth rates and increase local job opportunities. If one wishes to try to affect immigration over the short term (in the twentieth century), I believe the approach must involve some form of employer penalty program.

In sum, my personal preferences can be stated briefly:

1. Regional security for the United States should be broadly defined, to include economic, political, and social considerations, and not merely the maintenance of friendly regimes in the Caribbean Basin. This will not assure short-term political stability, and might even be perverse; nevertheless, this approach does have more chance over the long-term of securing a stable and friendly region than the alternative of basing policy on a narrow definition of security.

2. There will be times, however, when U.S. policy actions will have to be based on opposition to particular regimes, particularly if they seek to export revolution or when they are incurably oppressive (as in Suriname at present).

3. At times, this suggested overall policy stance may require security activism as defined in this paper, but generally should not. It will require U.S. support for locally generated economic development programs, such as through the provision of development aid and keeping the U.S. market open to goods from the region.

4. I am skeptical (although admittedly uncertain) that trade and tax preferences will achieve the desired objective of substantially increasing employment in beneficiary Caribbean Basin countries because of the inherent limitations of producing in most of them and the U.S. tendency to limit imports or preferences if the countries are successful for a given product. I am even more concerned that much of the investment that does take place in beneficiary

countries will be at the expense of similar production in nonbeneficiary countries, particularly Mexico.

5. Whether or not the proposed preferential system is put into place, it would be useful to set up a continuing consultative mechanism involving all the countries of the Caribbean Basin, from Canada south, to force regular discussion of policy issues, both those of a broad nature and specific functional ones.

6. Finally, none of these measures is likely to have a significant short-term impact on migration. There is thus no substitute for some kind of employer-penalty program for hiring undocumented workers if the United States sincerely wants to try to curtail the inflow of such workers.

Index

Activism, as policy option, 314-317
AFL-CIO, support of trade union movement in Caribbean Basin, 24
Agency for International Development (AID), 32, 47-48, 101, 290, 302
Agriculture: problems of, in Caribbean Basin, 70; recommendations for economic support of, 223
Aircraft, Cuban and Soviet, 150, 157, 160-61, 209-210
Air defense missile systems, Cuban, 160
Alianza Revolucionaria Democratica, 234
Aliens, illegal. *See under* Immigration
Alliance for Progress, 76, 77
American Enterprise Institute, 82
American Institute for Free Labor Development (AIFLD), 24, 82, 118
Amnesty, 46
Angola, Cuban involvement in, 157, 161
Antilles, Lesser, security issues in, 167-168
Arbenz, Jacobo, 205
Arevalo, Juan Jose, 205
Argentina, role of, in Caribbean Basin, 82
Arms limitation, multilateral policy approach to, 179
Arms supplies. *See* Military supplies
Austin, Hudson, 197

Balance-of-payments assistance to Caribbean Basin, 284-285, 300
Banks and banking: international, role in Caribbean Basin, 82, 43-45; multilateral energy lending by, 386-390; U.S. commercial, loans to Caribbean nations, 19
Barbados, 6, 105
Bauxite, 18, 67, 191
Bay of Pigs invasion, 106
Belize, security issues in, 168
Bilateralism, as approach to U.S. foreign policy, 218-219

Bishop, Maurice, 6, 12, 162, 196, 197
Blacks, importation of, to Caribbean Basin, 244
Blanco, Jorge, 79
Borge, Tomas, 235
Brazil, role of, in Caribbean Basin, 82
Broadcasting, 225; recommendations for policy on, 42
Brookhaven National Laboratory, 291
Bulgaria, aid to Nicaragua, 13
Business organizations, U.S., role in Caribbean Basin, 24

Callejas, Alfonso, 234
Canada, interests of, in Caribbean Basin, 20, 82, 89-90, 168-169
Caribbean Basin: border and territorial disputes in, 148; challenges to U.S. security interests in, 141-144, 192-194; class tensions in, 114; common goals of, 85-87; crime in, 115; decline of U.S. influence in, 19-20, 34, 76-77; diversities and common features of, 3, 34, 61-62, 104-105; economic growth rate of, 4-5, 107-108; educational problems of, 69; emigration to U.S. from, 248-251; employment problems in, 109; energy costs in, 280-281, 282; energy resources and requirements of, 109, 277-280; financing of oil imports to, 271-272, 283-285; foreign debt increases in, 29, 110-112; historical development of, 64-67; ideological pluralism in, 79; impact of migration on, 113, 255; impediments to economic development of, 4-5, 67-71; interests of outside nations in, 8, 20, 80-84; intraregional migration in, 244-248; labor market in, 5; major trade routes of, 146; natural resources in, 67-68, 191-192; oil production in, 279-280; oligarchies in,

325

Caribbean Basin: (cont)
69; political diversity of, 115–116;
political instability of, 5–7, 70–74;
political interaction among nations
of, 74–79; population growth in, 114,
246; principal energy issues in,
271–277; radical leftist guerrilla
groups in, 117; resource development
in 274–275, 285, 291–294; role of non-
governmental organizations in,
23–25; role of regional and global institutions in, 90–92; social organization of, 69–70; statistical data for
(by country), 125–137; territory of,
defined, 1; Third World movement in,
8, 83; trade deficits in, 110; U.S. interests and role in, 10–12, 17–19,
62–63, 65–67; U.S. military
assistance to, 76, 100, 180–181,
227–228; U.S. private investment in,
80–81, 190–191
Caribbean Basin Initiative (CBI), 21,
30–31, 45, 80, 102, 104, 174, 221–222,
263–264, 285, 310, 312, 318, 322
Caribbean/Central American Action,
24, 45, 82, 104
Caribbean Community (Caricom), 35
Caribbean Council, 104
Caribbean Development Bank, 30, 45
Caribbean Free Trade Association, 68, 76
Caribbean Group for Cooperation in
Economic Development, 36, 285
Caribbean islands: diversification of
international relations by, 195;
economic problems of, 195; socialist
experimentation by, 195–196. See
also specific names
Carnegie Endowment, 82
Carpio, Salvador Cayetano, 203, 233
Carter, Jimmy, 228
Carter–Torrijos treaties (1977), 153
Casanova, Carlos Eugenio Vides, 204
Castro, Fidel, 7, 13, 68, 79, 199, 208
Catholic church, revised political role
of, in Caribbean Basin, 142
Cayman Islands, as possible site for
U.S. military base, 183
Center for Strategic and International
Studies, 82
Central America: emerging social forces
in, 6; political instability in, 5–7;
security concerns of, 166. See also
names of countries
Central American Bank for Economic
Integration, 30, 45
Central American Common Market, 35,
68, 76
Central American Defense Council
(CONDECA), 169–170
Central American Democratic Commun-
ity, 170
Central planning, 221
Chamorro, Fernando, 234
Chapman, Leonard, Jr., 252

Christian Democratic Party (El Salvador), 201, 202
Churches, U.S., role of, in Caribbean
Basin, 24
Circum-Caribbean: area of, defined, 56;
economic problems in, 60; ethnic,
racial, and linguistic diversity of, 57;
per capita income in, 58–59; political
structures in, 58–60. See also Caribbean Basin
Civil rights. See Human rights
Coal: development of resources in Colombia, 294; energy conversion to, 301
Coast Guard, U.S., role in security assistance programs, 37
Colombia: Cuban involvement in, 7, 209;
foreign policy objectives of, 313;
growth of urban population in, 113;
migration from, 245; radical leftist
guerrilla groups in, 117; resource
development in, 292, 294; security
issues in, 167; U.S. economic interests in, 17
Common markets, failure of, in Caribbean Basin, 68–69
Communication, as important aspect of
Caribbean Basin security, 179
CONDECA. See Central American Defense Council
Confidence building, 179
Conflict, internationalization of, 193–194
Conflict resolution and avoidance, multilateral policy approach to, 178
Contadora Group, 22, 40, 219
"Cooperative socialism," 195
Corporations, multinational, presence of,
in Caribbean Basin, 80–81
Costa Rica: democratic rule in, 6; economic growth of, 283; financing for
energy projects in, 287; labor unions
in, 6; per capita income in, 58; renewed
U.S. presence in, 80; security concerns
of, 166–167; security force in, 181
Council of the Americas, 82
Crime, increase of, in Caribbean Basin,
115
Cuba: economic problems of, 208; influence of, in Nicaragua, 13–14, 198;
intervention of, in Guatemala, 207;
military capabilities of, 158–161;
political structure of, 58; propaganda
broadcasting by, 42; racial composition of, 57; recommendations for U.S.
foreign policy toward, 177, 235–238;
security concerns of, 166; Soviet
economic assistance to, 8; Soviet
military presence in, 83, 189; strategy
for containing influence of, 26; support of guerrilla movements by, 7, 12,
34, 75, 161, 196; threat of, to U.S.
security interests, 11, 142, 147,
150–151, 153–155, 208–210; U.S.
military bases in, 152
Cuban Air Force, 160

Cuban Missile Crisis of 1962, 100
Cuban Navy, 161
Cuban Revolution, 67, 75
Cultural exchange, 40–41

D'Aubuisson, Roberto, 202
Death squads, 15, 203
Debt crisis, 42–43
Democracy: in Central America, 3; clarification of, as goal of foreign policy,
211; as goal of Caribbean nations,
85–86; support of, as goal of foreign
policy, 28, 216–217
Democratic Revolutionary Alliance (Nicaragua), 199
"Democratic socialism," 195
Diplomacy, multilateral, 39
Disaster relief, recommendation for cooperative efforts in, 180
Dominican Republic: democratic rule in,
6; economic growth rate of, 4, 104;
growth of urban population in, 113;
labor unions in, 6; payments for imported oil by, 283; political structure
of, 60; racial composition of, 58;
security issues in, 167
Drug Enforcement Administration
(DEA), 101, 182
Drug traffic. *See* Narcotics
Duarte, Jose Napoleon, 202

Eastern Caribbean Regional Security
System, 168, 178
East Germany, aid to Nicaragua, 13
Ebel, Roland, 69
Economic Commission for Latin America, 90
Economic development: recommendations
for U.S. policy on, 35–36, 44–45,
215–216, 219–225, 314–319; relationship of, to energy use, 274, 297–298
Education: Cuban and Soviet scholarship programs for, 209; exchange programs in, 40; increase in literacy rate
of Caribbean Basin, 113; Soviet versus U.S. scholarship programs for,
225–226
Educational foundations, U.S., role in
policy toward Caribbean Basin, 24
El Salvador: agrarian reform in, 204;
conflict with Honduras, 76; Cuban
support of guerrilla movements in, 7,
208–209; emigration from, 245–246,
250; internationalization of conflicts
in, 194; political upheaval in, 14–15,
201–204; population growth in, 246;
radical leftist guerrilla groups in, 117;
recommendations for U.S. policy
toward, 171, 232–233; renewed U.S.
presence in, 80; role of military in
political evolution of, 200–202; security concerns of, 166; U.S. security
concerns in, 15–16

Emigration. *See* Migration
Employment: of nonresident aliens in
U.S., 46–47; problems of, in Caribbean Basin, 109
Enders, Thomas, 170
Energy lending, multilateral. *See under*
Finance and financing
Energy policy, U.S., principal issue(s)
in Caribbean Basin affecting:
109–110, 271–277, 281–283;
multilateral energy lending as,
286–290; oil import financing as,
283–285; relationship between energy
and economic development as, 274,
297–298; resource development as
47–48, 285, 291–294; specific recommendations for, 298–304; supply
security as, 295–297; technical
assistance as, 290–291
Energy price controls, 298
Energy resources, Caribbean Basin:
development of, 274–275, 285,
291–294; relation of demand to
economic growth, 274, 297–298; supply security of, 275–277
England. *See* Great Britain
European Common Market, 68
Executive Service Corps, 45
Export-Import Bank, 45, 118, 222

Farabundo Marti National Liberation
Front (FMLN), 194, 202, 203, 204, 209
Finance and financing: balance-of-payments assistance, 300–301; multilateral energy lending, 286–290; for
oil imports in Caribbean Basin,
283–285; recommendations for U.S.
policy on, 29–30, 42–45
Fluorspar, 192
Foreign Military Sales (FMS) program,
227
Foreign policy, U.S.: activist and nonactivist options for, 314–319;
bilateral approach to, 173, 219; clari-
fying goals for, 211–212, 214–215;
collaborative option for, 119–120;
domestic constraints on, 20–21, 310;
"drainage limitation" option for,
120–122; East–West versus North–
South approach to, 144–145,
172–173, 213; global versus regional
approach to, 91; hegemonic option
for, 118–119; institutions responsible
for, 101–103; multilateral approach
to, 22–23, 106, 173–175, 219; national
interests and values underlying,
100–104; overall objectives of, 87–89,
215–219, 306–314; political issues in
Caribbean Basin affecting, 115–117;
recommendations for, 92–94,
106–107; social issues in Caribbean
Basin affecting, 112–115; toward
Cuba, 235–238; toward El Salvador,
232–233; toward English Caribbean

Foreign policy, U.S.: (cont)
nations, 231–232; toward Guatemala,
232; toward Nicaragua, 233–235;
unilateral approach to, 171–172. See
also specific policy areas
France, interests of, in Caribbean Basin,
8, 168
Free Trade Area, 45–46
Frente Democratico Nacional, 234
FSLN. See Sandinista National Liberation Front

Gairy, Sir Eric, 196
Galbraith, John Kenneth, 255
Garcia, Benedicto Lucas, 207
Garcia, Romeo Lucas, 16, 206
General Agreement on Trade and Tariffs
(GATT), 30
Gonzalez, Edward, 161
Good Neighbor Policy, 140
Gorshkov, Sergei, 157
Grand Bahamas Island, U.S. military
facilities on, 11, 190
Great Britain: as dominant colonial
power in Caribbean Basin, 64; secur-
ity interests of, 168
Grenada: Cuban and Soviet assistance
to, 12, 83, 196; New Jewel Movement
in, 196; security concerns of, 166; as
threat to U.S. security interests, 12,
162–163, 196
Guatemala: Cuban support of, 7, 207,
209; political insurgency in, 16,
204–208; recommendations for U.S.
foreign policy toward, 232; renewed
U.S. presence in, 80; seasonal migration from, 246; security concerns of,
166; social inequities in, 206
Guerrilla Army of the Poor (Guatemala),
205
Guerrilla movements: arms supply to, 7,
13, 198; Cuban support of, 7, 75,
208–209; in El Salvador, 117, 203; in
Guatemala, 117, 206, 207
Guevara, Che, 141
Guyana: border conflict with Venezuela,
76; racial groups in, 113; security
concerns of, 168; Soviet presence in,
83
Guzman, Antonio, 312

Haig, Alexander, 83, 103
Haiti: emigration from, 246, 249; infant
mortality in, 105; political system in,
58, 116; population growth in, 246;
racial composition of, 57; security
concerns of, 167
Hemispheric Energy Fund, 287
Heritage Foundation, 82
Holland, security interests of, 168
Honduras: breakdown of ruling triad in,
7; conflicts with El Salvador and

Nicaragua, 76; Cuban support of,
209; political system in, 116; possible
site for U.S. military base in, 183;
renewed U.S. presence in, 80; seasonal migration from, 246; security
concerns of, 166
Human rights, 85–86; recommendations
for U.S. policy on, 41–42, 217–218
Human rights organizations, role of, in
Caribbean Basin, 24

"Ideological pluralism," 79
Immigration, U.S.: from Caribbean
Basin, 248–251, 253, 254; control
system for, 262, 264; illegal, 243–244,
250, 252, 253, 262, 263, 264, 265; impact of, 256, 258; public attitude
toward, 257; regional concentrations
of, 253–255. See also Migration
Immigration and National Efficiency
Act (1981), 251
Immigration and Naturalization Service
(INS), 101, 250, 252, 253, 262
Immigration policy, U.S.: curtailment as
objective of, 308, 310; during 1920s
to 1950s, 248–249; during 1960s, 243,
250; issues crucial to formulation of,
258–263; recommendations for,
46–47, 264–267
Income, unequal distribution of, in
Carribean Basin, 6, 58–59, 114
Infant mortality, 105, 114
Information programming, 42; recom-
mendations for policy on, 225–227
Institute for Policy Studies, 82
Intelligence, security, recommenda-
tions for policy on, 38, 39, 182
Inter-American Commission on Human
Rights, 42
Inter-American Defense Board, 82, 140,
178, 181
Inter-American Development Bank
(IADB), 30, 44, 45, 82, 287
Inter-American Defense College, 178, 181
Inter-American Foundation, 118
Inter-American Treaty of Reciprocal As-
sistance (1947), 140
International Development Association,
45
International Institute for Finance, 43
International Labor Organization, 51, 255
International Monetary Fund (IMF), 29,
43, 247, 285
International Peace Academy, 179
International Planned Parenthood Feder-
ation, 118
Investment, economic: international, 45;
U.S., 18, 110, 190–91, 220–221

Jamaica: bauxite production in, 191; economic growth rate of, 104; racial composition of, 58; recommendations for

U.S. foreign policy toward, 231; security issues in, 167; socialist experimentation in, 195
Japan, interests of, in Caribbean Basin, 20, 81, 89–90, 169

Kennedy, Edward, 251
Kirkpatrick, Jeane, 86

Labor force: development of temporary worker program for, 266; impact of migration on, 255–256, 258; migrant, intraregional, 244–247
Labor unions: growth of, 24, 71–72; role of, 6, 41, 51
Language, diversity of, in Circum-Caribbean
Latin American Energy Organization (OLADE), 287
Latin American International Military Education and Training (IMET) program, 227
Lipset, Seymour Martin, 216
Los Alamos National Laboratory, 29

Magaña, Alvaro, 203
Manley, Michael, 9, 195
Mantanza massacre, 200
Market price index, for Caribbean Basin, 111
Marti, Farabundo, 200
Mejia, Oscar Humberto, 16, 208
Mexican National Institute for Nuclear Research, 291
Mexico: economic problems in, 4, 247; emigration from, 152, 248; joint oil financing facility with Venezuela, 284; oil production in, 191, 280, 291–294; per capita income in, 58; role of, in world oil market, 272–274, 283; security concerns of, 165–166; U.S. interests in, 17–18, 32, 149, 190–191
Migration, in Caribbean Basin, 31–32; factors contributing to, 5, 113, 308; impact of, 255–256, 258; intraregional, 244–248; as security concern of U.S., 152, 183; to U.S., 248–251
Mihailov, Mihajlo, 217
Military Assistance Program, 141
Military bases, 11, 152–153, 189–190; recommendations of additional sites for, 183
Military basing, recommendation for U.S. policy toward, 36
Military forces in Caribbean (by country), 156
Military policy, recommendations for, 37, 180–181, 227–231

Military supplies: Soviet, 150, 159–160 162; U.S., 227–229
Missile systems, Cuban, 160
Monge, Luis, 79
Monroe Doctrine, 9, 84
Montes, Melida Anaya, 203
Multilateralism: as approach to U.S. security interests, 22–23, 173–175, 218–219; in Caribbean Basin Initiative, 312
Multinational corporations (MNCs), presence of, in Caribbean Basin, 80–81

Narcotics, control of, as U.S. security interest, 115, 152, 182
National Democratic Front (Nicaragua), 199
National interests, as underlying element in development of foreign policy, 100–101
Nationalism, development of, 33
National laboratories, technical assistance programs by, 291
National Patriotic United Front (Guatemala), 207, 209
National Security Council, 101
NATO alliance, security interests of, 37, 38, 168
Natural resources in Caribbean Basin, importance of, to U.S. security interests, 148–149, 191–192
Netherlands. *See* Holland
New Jewel Movement, 196
Nicaragua: basis for anti-Americanism in, 200; challenges to U.S. security interests in, 147, 161–162, 198–200; conditions under Sandinista government in, 50; conflict with Honduras and Costa Rica, 76; Cuban support of, 7, 13, 161, 198, 209–209; infant mortality in, 114; obstacles to communization of, 13–14, 199; political evolution in, 197–198; recommendations for U.S. foreign policy toward, 39, 233–234; security concerns of, 166; Soviet military supplies to, 162; U.S. security interests in, 12–14; Western European assistance to, 8
Nonactivism, as U.S. policy option, 314–317
Nonintervention, clarification of, as goal of foreign policy, 212
North Korea, aid to Nicaragua, 13

Oil: financing import of, to Caribbean Basin, 271–272, 283–285; importance of, to U.S. interests, 18, 190–192; as natural resource in Caribbean Basin, 67; role of Mexico and Venezuela as major suppliers of, 272–274, 279, 283; supply security of, 275–277, 281, 295–297

Oil crisis, effect of, on Caribbean Basin, 70–71
Oil refineries, 192, 273–274
OLADE. See Latin American Energy Organization
Olney, Richard, 105
Organization for Economic Cooperation and Development, 255
Organization of American States (OAS), 23, 82, 90, 91, 170, 177, 178, 179
Organization of Eastern Caribbean States, 170
Organization of Petroleum Exporting Countries (OPEC), 272, 281
Ortega, Humberto, 50, 189
Overseas Private Investment Corporation (OPIC), 45, 222, 315

Panama: economic growth rate in, 4; financing for energy projects in, 287; per capita income in, 58; political system in, 116; security concerns of, 166–167; U.S. military facilities in, 11, 153, 178, 189
Panama Canal, importance of, to U.S. security interests, 9–10, 149, 283
Panama Canal Treaty, 153
Pan American Health Organization, 90, 120
Partido Revolucionario Institucional (PRI), 166
Pastora, Eden, 199, 234
Peace Corps, 45, 73
Peacekeeping, multilateral policy approach to, 39–40, 178–179
People's Nationalist Party (Jamaica), 195
People's Revolutionary Army (Grenada), 162
Petroleos Mexicanos (Pemex), 292–293
Petroleum. See Oil
Point Salines Airport (Grenada), expansion of, 196–197
Police troops, issue of assistance and training for, 181
Political policy, recommendations for development of, 17, 27–28, 34, 36, 176, 216–217, 218
Political systems, diversity of, in Caribbean Basin, 115–116
Popular Liberation Forces (FPL), 203
Popular Sandinista Army, 198
Population Council, 118
Population growth: in Caribbean Basin, 114; U.S., impact of immigration on, 257, 258, 259
Propaganda, impact of Soviet and Cuban, 193
Public diplomacy programs, importance of, 227
Puerto Rico: migration patterns of, 250; preferred economic treatment of, 322; racial composition of, 57; security concerns of, 167; special relationship of, with U.S., 60–61; U.S. military facilities in, 11, 152, 189

Race, diversity of, in Circum-Caribbean, 57–58
Racial conflict, 58, 113
Radical nationalist regimes, recommendations for policy toward, 38
Radio Liberty, 225
Reagan, Ronald, 286, 295
Recession, impact of, on Caribbean Basin, 33, 272, 273
Refineries, oil, 192, 273–274
Refugees, 259–261; recommendations for U.S. policy on, 265
Regime viability, as goal of Caribbean nations, 85
Religious groups, U.S., role of, in Caribbean Basin, 24
Resource development, 285; in Mexico and Venezuela, 291–294
Rios-Montt, General Efrain, 16, 207
Rio Treaty (1947), 140, 169, 170, 177
Rivera, Brooklyn, 234
Robelo, Alfonso, 234
Roman Catholic Church, role in political reform, 6–7
Roosevelt, Franklin D., 140

Salazar, Jorge, 234
Salazar, Lucia, 234
San Andres Island, as possible site for U.S. military base, 183
Sandinista National Liberation Front (FSLN), 12–13, 14, 27, 161, 194, 197–199, 234
San Jose accord (1980), 284
Scholarship programs. See under Education
Seaga, Edward, 18, 307
Sea lines of communication (SLOCs): Cuban threat to, 161; importance of, to U.S. security interests, 140, 145–146, 151, 155, 188–189; unilateral approach to security of, 171–172
Search and rescue, recommendation for cooperative efforts in, 180
Security assistance: bilateral, 36–37; recommendations for policy on, 227–231
Security interest(s), U.S., 10–16; Cuban threat to, 26, 208–210; East-West versus North-South approach to, 144–145, 172–173, 213; institutions responsible for, 177–178; issues relevant to, 25–32, 145–152, 178–183, 188–192; military threats to, 153–163; overall challenges to, 192–208; policy recommendations concerning, 35–45; regional and

subregional approach to, 169–171; resources important to, 148–149, 191–192; traditional approach to, 139–144; as underlying element in formation of foreign policy, 100–101. *See also* Foreign policy

Sereseres, Cesar, 194

Ships: Cuban, 161; Soviet, 155, 157

Simpson-Mazzoli Immigration Reform and Control Act (1982), 31, 46, 264

Socialism, experimental forms of, in Caribbean Basin, 195–196

Socialist International, 81, 177

Socioeconomic development, as major component of U.S. security policy, 35–36, 215–216

Somoza regime, 12, 14

Sound Surveillance Underwater System (SOSUS), 155

Sovereignty, as goal of Caribbean nations, 85

Soviet Union: aid to Nicaragua by, 13, 162; effect of presence in Caribbean on U.S. security, 10–11, 12, 83, 142, 147, 150–151, 155–158; information programs sponsored by, 42, 225–226; interests in Caribbean Basin, 8–9; recommendations for containing influence of, 25–26, 176–177; role of, in Cuba, 34, 189

Spain: as colonial power in Caribbean Basin, 64–65; interests of, in Caribbean Basin, 8, 81

Stone, Richard, 233

Strategic Petroleum Reserve (SPR), 32, 276, 296, 297

Suriname: political system in, 116; racial groups in, 113; Soviet presence in, 83

Tariff, differential, on oil imports, 296–297

Technical assistance programs, 290–291, 302

Technology transfer, 47, 224, 285

Territorial integrity, as goal of Caribbean nations, 85

Terrorism, 152, 182

"Third Worldism," 8, 83, 92

Tobago, security issues in, 167

Trade, Caribbean Basin: impediments to development of, 68–69; importance of, to U.S. security interests, 148–150, 190; unbalanced growth of, 70, 108, 110; U.S. policy on, 30–31, 45–46, 224–225, 321–322

Trade centers, international, recommended formation of, 224

Trade missions, inter-Caribbean, 77

Trade unions. *See* Labor unions

Transportation, role in breaking down isolation of Caribbean nations, 75

Trinidad, security issues in, 167

United Nations, 90, 91

United States: declining influence of, 19–20, 34, 76–77; as destabilizing force in Caribbean Basin, 73; economic interests of, 17–19, 87, 190–192; foreign policy toward Caribbean Basin, *see* Foreign policy, U.S.; immigration policy of, *see* Immigration policy, U.S.; information programs sponsored by, 225–226; interests and role in Caribbean Basin, 62–63, 65–67; migration from Caribbean Basin to, 248–251; military assistance to Caribbean Basin, 76, 100, 180–181, 227–228; military facilities in Caribbean Basin, 11, 152–153, 189–190; multinational corporations in Caribbean Basin, 80–81; security interests of, *see* Security interests, U.S.; as security threat to Caribbean nations, 165

United States Bureau of the Census, 246

United States Commission on Population Growth and the Future, 257

United States Immigration and Naturalization Service, 46

United States Information and Communication Agency (USICA), 226

United States Information Agency (UAIA), 40

United States Information Service (USIS), 101

Venezuela: border conflict with Guyana, 76; economic problems of, 4; foreign policy objectives of, 313; joint oil financing facility with Mexico, 284; migration of labor to, 247, 248; oil production in, 191; proposal of Hemispheric Energy Fund by, 287; resource development in, 291–294; role of, in world oil market, 272–274, 279, 283; as secure supplier of oil to U.S., 32, 275, 280; security concerns of, 167, 197; trade with U.S., 190; U.S. economic interests in, 17–18

Vermont State Employment Service Division, 256

Voice of America, 42, 225

Western Europe, interests of, in Caribbean Basin, 89–90

West Germany, role of, in Caribbean Basin, 8, 81

Wiarda, Howard J., 5

Wilson Center, 82

World Bank, 30, 43, 44, 45, 82; energy lending affiliate of, 286, 288–290

Zagladin, Vadim, 189